American Anabasis

American Anabasis

Xenophon and the Idea of America
From the Mexican War to Iraq

TIM ROOD

Duckworth Overlook

First published in 2010 by
Duckworth Overlook

LONDON
90-93 Cowcross Street, London EC1M 6BF
Tel: 020 7490 7300
Fax: 020 7490 0080
info@duckworth-publishers.co.uk
www.ducknet.co.uk

NEW YORK
141 Wooster Street
New York, NY 10012
www.overlookpress.com

A catalogue record for this book is available
from the British Library
Cataloging-in-Publication Data is available
from the Library of Congress

ISBN 978-0-7156-3684 8 (UK)
ISBN 978-1-59020-476-4 (US)

Typeset by Ray Davies
Printed and bound in the UK by
the MPG Books Group

Contents

For Andrea and Simon
Companions of my American Anabasis

Preface

This book is a study of the way Xenophon's *Anabasis* – an account of a
Greek march through the Persian empire – has been applied to the story
of American expansion at home and abroad. The Introduction will set out
the book's aims more fully: it is enough here to mention that it focuses on
three specific conflicts (the Mexican, Civil, and Iraq Wars) as well as on
the broader use of the *Anabasis* in accounts of the conquest of the American West. Starting with the remarkable popularity of the ancient Greeks
in contemporary American military culture, it looks back to the great
expansion of the United States during the nineteenth century, arguing
that allusions to Xenophon in this period served to express ideas of
American historical destiny and of a heroic confrontation with the vast
expanses of the American continent. The story of Xenophon in America
demonstrates a shift in the American appropriation of antiquity from
Rome to Greece and from politics to war. While concentrating on how
Xenophon has been used to extol American military achievements, the
book also considers how he has helped to fashion American identity in art
and literature.

American Anabasis does not demand any knowledge of my earlier book
The Sea! The Sea! That book explored how the most famous scene in
Xenophon's work has been evoked in a wide range of sources from different
countries. This book is concerned with nationalistic appropriations of
Xenophon in a single country; it also creates a dialogue between interpretation and reception, running analysis of the *Anabasis* against discussion
of how it has been exploited.

I must also acknowledge here assistance from a number of sources. I am
greatly indebted to Deborah Blake and Ray Davies at Duckworth for their
work on the book. Robin Waterfield kindly granted permission to use his
translation of the *Anabasis* (*Xenophon: The Expedition of Cyrus*, Oxford
World's Classics, 2005); I have sometimes modified it slightly to bring
across particular literary effects. Some arguments in this book have
already appeared in my 'Introduction' and 'Explanatory Notes' to Waterfield's translation (pp. vii-xliii, 196-224), and also in my article
'Panhellenism and Self-Presentation: Xenophon's Speeches', in R. Lane
Fox (ed.), *The Long March: Xenophon and the Ten Thousand* (Yale University Press, 2004), 305-29; I am grateful to the publishers for permission.
Richard Peabody gave permission to quote his poem 'Dubya Anabasis',
from his *Last of the Red Hot Magnetos* (Paycock Press; Arlington, VA,

2004). Bing West and Arlyn Bruccoli graciously replied to email queries. The Principal and Fellows of St Hugh's College, Oxford, granted me sabbatical leave during the academic year 2007-8. I had the great good fortune to be elected for that year to a Fellowship at the Radcliffe Institute for Advanced Study, Harvard University: for helping to make this year so memorable I must thank the director, Judy Vichniac, the staff, and the other Fellows – in particular the other members of my reading group, Andrew Gordon, Frances Kissling, and Catherine Lutz, who commented on the opening section of this book and mutinied when I threatened to write about a different topic; Vivian Gornick, who ran a writing workshop at a very opportune time; and others who read or discussed my work, especially Giorgio Bertellini, Kate Gilhuly, and Emma Teng. I also gained much from working with my Research Partner at Radcliffe, Tavé van Zyl, who expertly commented on early drafts of the first section. While working on the book I have been fortunate in having access to the wonderful library facilities at Oxford and Harvard, including various electronic databases (particularly for nineteenth-century newspapers and periodicals), and I must thank the librarians at both institutions. The Craven Committee also helped finance a further research trip to the Harvard libraries. I received valuable comments from the participants at a workshop arranged by Kate Gilhuly and Nancy Worman at Wellesley College in April 2009, where Chapter 4 was discussed, and the audiences at Radcliffe in May 2008 and at Trinity College, Dublin, in January 2009 who listened to versions of Chapter 1. I have also profited from talking about some of this material with John Ma and with a former student, Tom Phillips, who read the whole book in draft; and in particular from the detailed and extremely helpful comments offered by Nicholas Cole and Alison Rosenblitt. I must again thank my parents Pearce and Beaujolais Rood for their support and interest. My greatest debt, however, is to Andrea Capovilla, who read drafts of every chapter and improved the book at every stage.

T.C.B.R.
August 2009

List of Illustrations

Introduction

The Anabasis Project

American and allied troops were installed in Afghanistan. It was a few
months after the attacks of 11 September 2001. Now preparations were
underway for the invasion of Iraq – and 'Dick Cheney was making another
of his visits to CIA headquarters'. Cheney's visit was part of the 'inside
story' of 'spin, scandal, and the selling of the Iraq War' that was later told
by two journalists, drawing on a range of CIA and government sources.
They gave their book a tragic title, *Hubris*, but their own style strove more
for the sensational as they followed Cheney on his way to the CIA:

> The vice president's limousine sped through downtown Washington and
> headed over the Potomac River on its way to Langley, Virginia. ... Cheney had
> come to Langley to be updated on the latest intelligence on Iraq, including what
> was known about Saddam's unconventional weapons. But another subject
> was on the agenda, a matter of the utmost sensitivity. It was one of the most
> closely held secrets in the U.S. government: the Anabasis project.

Suspense is created as the account breaks off on the grand and unusual
word 'anabasis' (Greek for a march upcountry). Named after one of the
most famous episodes in ancient history, the CIA plan seems here to be
endowed almost with the resonance of myth. But it also draws prestige
from the foundational role of classical antiquity within western culture –
the appeal of Greece and Rome as the source of the west's presumed
cultural and military superiority.[1]

The aim of the Anabasis project was to undermine Saddam Hussein's
rule in Iraq by sabotage, infiltration, and disinformation, and by working
with dissident Kurdish leaders in the north. The CIA officers made some
journeys in Iraq. They also set up a secret training base in the Nevada
desert. Within Iraq, a power pylon was sabotaged and some military and
Baath Party officials were assassinated. But the project was soon over-
taken by the Bush administration's determination to get the war started.

The ancient episode that lent its name to the Anabasis project was also
aimed at regime change. In 401 BC a Persian prince, Cyrus, plotted to
depose his brother Artaxerxes, ruler of the vast expanses of the Persian
empire, by leading an army – including a force of Greek heavy infantry
(hoplites) slightly over ten thousand strong – across modern Turkey and
Syria to a village called Cunaxa, not far from modern Fallujah. Cyrus was
then killed in battle, and his stranded Greek troops – among them Xenophon, the Athenian philosopher and historian who wrote the story of the
march – were left with no option but a long and dangerous retreat through

1

Kurdistan and Armenia to the Black Sea. The Greek army (known since antiquity as the Ten Thousand) did manage to fight its way back to the edges of the Greek world, and it is this retreat to the sea, rather than the march upcountry itself, that has always stood out as the most memorable part of the *Anabasis*. But the army also endured great hardship and losses along the way. No wonder some White House and CIA officials thought that the Anabasis project was misnamed. And even if Cyrus had been successful or the Greeks' retreat easy, a catchy name resonant of 1970s movies (*The Andromeda Strain, The Poseidon Adventure, The Medusa Touch* ...) still seems an inadequate response to the diplomatic complexities of the post-9/11 world.

The CIA's Anabasis project is perhaps the most spectacular use of Xenophon's account by supporters of the attack on Iraq, but the *Anabasis* has also been a point of reference in many other discussions of the 2003 overthrow of Saddam Hussein and the subsequent US-led occupation of Iraq. It has appeared in a wide variety of contexts (poetry and drama, histories and memoirs, travel books and military analysis, newspaper columns and internet blogs) and been used by both opponents and advocates of the Iraq War. It has been taken as a warning against military adventures in the Middle East, but it has also inspired triumphant views of the war and of western military supremacy in general. And in the process, Xenophon's words have been twisted and distorted and the historical events he describes made part of a compelling narrative of empire.

*

Why has Xenophon been invoked so often? Why the *Anabasis*? This book will respond to Xenophon's role in modern America by returning to the appropriation of Xenophon in the American past and by reading the use that has been made of Xenophon against Xenophon's own words. Xenophon, like many other Greek and Roman authors, has been exploited as a foundational text for western culture, with the *Anabasis* itself achieving an extraordinary prominence as the text used for learning Greek in schools: in the United States, as in many other countries, the *Anabasis* was the most widely read classical Greek text from the middle of the nineteenth century. There are fascinating allusions to Xenophon's work in writings by many of the foremost nineteenth-century American writers, including Washington Irving, James Fenimore Cooper, and the Concord transcendentalists, Emerson and Thoreau (see Chapter 3). But it is of course in the military world that most attention has been paid to his war memoir. American soldiers, or orators and writers commenting on American military feats, have made countless isolated allusions to the retreat of the Ten Thousand. But two episodes in nineteenth-century American history stand out for the extent and complexity of Xenophon's involvement: his account of the Greek East helped forge the myth of the American

West during the Mexican War (1846-8), and the ambivalent tale of a grand march upcountry that turned into a heroic retreat shaped contemporary and later responses to the most controversial campaign of the Civil War, Sherman's March to the Sea (1864).

This book will tell the story of the American Xenophon through a double movement: it will move backwards in time before advancing forward again. It will start by exploring in more detail the use of Xenophon in recent discussions of the Iraq War while glancing as well at Xenophontic allusions in other foreign wars waged by the US (Chapter 1). It will then turn to show how the *Anabasis* was exploited in the twentieth century to convey a sense of American control over the expanse of the continent, in fulfilment of what had been seen in the previous century as Manifest Destiny. Xenophon's contribution to this particularly American sense of space and time will be explored mainly through the fiction of Thomas Wolfe, with its emblematic portrayal of the individual American's hunger for physical and spiritual expansion (Chapter 2). We then move further back in time, deepening our analysis of American engagement with the *Anabasis* by exploring in detail the two most important Xenophontic episodes in nineteenth-century America. In Section II, we focus on the Mexican War, examining first the extraordinary range of parallels that were drawn between the retreat of the Ten Thousand and an expedition led by a Missouri volunteer, Alexander Doniphan – another long march through exotic lands involving largely hostile encounters with alien land-scapes and peoples (Chapter 3). Successive chapters will then analyse the deeper ideological underpinning of the cult of Xenophon during the Mexican War: firm ideas of historical progress combined with a deep attachment to models of classical heroism underlay perceptions of the landscapes of the West (Chapter 4), praise of the courage and democratic ethos of the American army (Chapters 5 and 6), and condemnation of the supposed savagery of American Indians (Chapter 7).[2] The Xenophontic exploits of the western explorer John Charles Frémont then bridge the gap between the expansionist war against Mexico and the Civil War that was itself unleashed by the dispute over slavery in the new territories – and that culminated in the other great nineteenth-century American anabasis, the march through Georgia led by William Tecumseh Sherman, one of the most famous and enigmatic generals in American history. Section III then focuses on Sherman, exploring how allusions to Xenophon helped to express shifting responses to his march during the war itself and in years to come. The ambiguous position of the Ten Thousand and of the concept of the anabasis itself becomes fully apparent as we see how parallels with Xenophon were drawn by both the Unionist and the Confederate sides and how the Greek term for a march inland, away from the sea, came to be applied to a march to the sea. The book's themes are drawn together in a Conclusion that ends with a discussion of the place of Xenophon in the drawings and sculpture of Cy Twombly, one of the best-known modern

American artists. This will bring us back to our present and to the continuing ethical and political questions posed by the artistic and literary representation of conflict between the West and its Others. We may by then be in a position to understand why the concept of anabasis has been so rich a symbol for the American journey.

Studying how the terms of the *Anabasis* were transferred to the marches of Doniphan and Sherman will set the exploitation of Xenophon in the Iraq War in the light of two nineteenth-century forerunners – one a long march that led to the conquest of vast new regions in the West, the other a shorter march that is often thought to have played an important role in ending the extraordinarily destructive Civil War. By drawing on the plentiful contemporary sources for both campaigns (letters, diaries, newspaper columns, published narratives) we will be able to get a sense of the controversies and ideological debates that shaped the selective way the war was remembered as well as the extent to which allusions to Xenophon were themselves moulded by the varying demands of public and private contexts. While the CIA Anabasis project shows a deliberate engagement with Xenophon by people involved in planning the run-up to war, when we turn to Doniphan and Sherman we will be concerned more with the perceptions of observers than with conscious allusions by the main agents themselves. For that very reason, however, we will gain a more valuable insight into how widely the allure of the Greeks' military exploits was felt.

Looking at the use of classical paradigms in these two wars will also correct a pronounced bias in the way the story of America's response to antiquity has often been told. The use of classical authors in American political writing in the eighteenth century has been discussed far more than the militarist use of antiquity in the nineteenth century. The Founders have gained in prestige through study of their own readings in classical political philosophy – and the prestige of the classical world has been boosted in return. Rather than celebrating the accumulation of references to Greece and Rome, we will here be focusing on some of the dangers inherent in the spell cast by antiquity. Even if knowledge of Xenophon did not directly contribute to American expansion, the *Anabasis* was still an important part of the culture of American militarism. And its role during and after the war against Mexico exemplifies a key shift in the American interest in classical antiquity. Greek and Roman writings were less likely to be mined for positive or negative political paradigms. It was now the great military exploits of the classical era that assumed most significance in the American imagination.[3]

This book will also respond to the modern use of the *Anabasis* by returning Xenophon's account to history. The march of the Ten Thousand has sometimes been seen as isolated, detached from the main path of Greek history, a mere sideshow in the story of the Persian empire. The French philosopher and historian Hippolyte Taine memorably compared it with the marble temple on the promontory at Cape Sunium in Attica, 'an indivisible whole which detaches itself, simple and shining, from the course of history'. Taine was perhaps hinting that this expedition was an introduction to the essence of Greekness itself: Sunium was chosen by the second-century traveller Pausanias as the starting-point for his guide to Greece. Xenophon's account has also been plundered for its supposedly straightforward picture of quintessential Greek qualities. It seems to offer a unique insight into the character of a Greek army on the march. We see at first hand the soldiers at leisure, holding athletic competitions among themselves. We meet a world marked by the particular forms of Greek religion: vows and sacrifices are frequently made to the gods, seers are constantly consulted, a sneeze is thought to be a favourable omen. This world permeated by the divine is also a world permeated by the particular forms of Greek political life. The propitious sneeze occurs at a meeting where different units gather to debate what steps they should take next. The troops manage to create among themselves a sense of common purpose and a readiness to accept discipline, but that hard-won sense of unity comes to be increasingly threatened by internal tensions as they draw nearer to Greece itself. The life of the Greek cities from which these soldiers came was marked by a similar blend of co-operation and rivalry.[4]

And yet the simplicity of the *Anabasis* is deceptive. Though it can claim to be the first known military memoir, it eludes easy classification. It has no formal prologue setting out its aims. Throughout it seems to explore, through speech and narrative, important ethical and political questions. Parts of it have contact with geography and ethnography. And while much of it is written from Xenophon's perspective, it is not formally a memoir at all: Xenophon uses third-person forms to refer to his own actions during the retreat and may even have published the work under a pseudonym – perhaps to avert suspicions that his account is self-serving. The elusiveness of Xenophon's text has often been ignored owing to the prevailing idealization of the Greek spirit in the modern world. Many characterizations of the *Anabasis* seem bland and one-sided. As we explore Xenophon's portrayal of the Greek army, we need to be sensitive to the highly selective way Xenophon's account has often been read in the past and to ask why modern historians have sometimes been blind to negative elements that Xenophon himself did not shirk from describing. Our focus, then, will not so much be on the day-to-day realities of the Greeks' long march through Asia as on Xenophon's depiction of their experience – the qualities the soldiers displayed, the foreign lands and peoples they passed through. Since the nature and extent of the contemporary fascination with the *Anabasis* makes it important to return to the original text, the treatment will necessarily be selective: I have chosen for discussion a series of revealing scenes that interact directly with the American appropriation of Xenophon in the Mexican War and during Sherman's march and that themselves run as a narrative both parallel to and in tension with the progression of the American anabasis through the nineteenth century.[5]

We will be particularly concerned with the dialogue between the use of the *Anabasis* in American culture and the way the text and the events it describes have been interpreted. It has often been thought that Xenophon wrote his account as a demonstration of Greek superiority or to encourage a Greek attack on Persia, and that the successful retreat itself inspired Alexander of Macedon in his conquest of the Persian empire (334-331 BC). This history of interpretation both reinforces and is reinforced by the sort of appropriation seen in applying Xenophon to the westward expansion of the United States or to the invasion of Iraq. Grasping how the goals of the *Anabasis* have been interpreted in the past is necessary if we are to understand how it has been applied to other events in the past.

To get beyond the imperial exploitation of the *Anabasis* we also need to understand the circumstances in which Xenophon wrote his account. Many aspects of Xenophon's life after his return from his great adventure in Asia in 399 BC are unclear, but we do know that he was exiled from Athens either on his return or a few years later (the date depends on whether he was exiled for serving Athens' former enemy Cyrus or for being present with the Spartans at the battle of Coronea in 394 BC when the Athenians were part of the anti-Spartan coalition). After his exile he was settled by the Spartans at Scillus, not far from Olympia in the Peloponnese, but he was forced to leave after the Spartan defeat at Leuctra in 371 BC, which marked the end of their long-standing superiority on land. And it was probably after his expulsion from Scillus, and at a time when the Spartans were co-operating with the Athenians against the Thebans and the Thebans were actively looking to Persia for help, that Xenophon turned to write up his own experiences in the Persian empire more than thirty years earlier. The circumstances in which he was writing should at least warn us against taking the *Anabasis* as a timeless expression of Greek virtue. Xenophon's account of the expedition may well have been consciously moulded in response to the turbulent condition of Greece at the time he was writing.

The aim of this Anabasis project, then, is twofold: it is to read the story of America through Xenophon and to read Xenophon through the story of America. By creating a continuous dialogue between the *Anabasis* and its American reception, this book aims to explore the grand ideologies of nationhood, the narratives of space and time, that underlie common notions of ancient Greek and modern American destiny, as well as the military triumphs and disasters that have been filtered through those narratives. We begin by returning to the trail laid by the CIA agents and following the fortunes of the *Anabasis* in the years since the American invasion of Iraq.

I

XENOPHON AND AMERICA

1. Xenophon.

1

Dubya Anabasis: Xenophon and the Iraq War

It did not take long for the ultimate goal of the CIA's Anabasis project –
the toppling of Saddam Hussein – to be achieved. The American victory
following the invasion of Iraq in March 2003 was swift. Six months later,
the future of Iraq and the meaning of the American victory were both
looking very uncertain, but books celebrating the American military
achievement were beginning to appear. The Anabasis theme was kept up
in one of the first to be published: *The March Up: Taking Baghdad with
the 1st Marine Division*. Written by two Vietnam veterans, Bing West (an
Assistant Secretary of Defense in the Reagan administration and now
author of several further books on Iraq) and Ray Smith (a famous general
in Marines legend), who both accompanied the Marines on their way to
Baghdad, the book came out in time for acclaim from the *Wall Street
Journal* on the richly symbolic date of 11 September: 'What a brilliantly
fought campaign, and what a wonderful account of it.' Another reviewer
spoke in similar terms of their 'remarkable description of a campaign
conducted by some truly remarkable young Americans': '*The March Up*,
like the *Anabasis*, is destined to be a classic.' The book also received plugs
in high places. It was hailed by a former CIA director as 'the definitive
account about the nature of ground combat as we enter the 21st Century'
and by Senator John McCain (another famous Vietnam vet) as 'the face of
war as only those who have fought it can describe it'.[1]

West and Smith were well aware of the force of their title. They wrote
at the start of the book that *The March Up* was 'inspired by the classic
story of the *Anabasis*', and they went on to suggest deep links between the
ancient hoplites described by Xenophon and the modern Marines they saw
in Iraq. Xenophon's *Anabasis*, they wrote, is 'an account of tough characters bound by an unflinching warrior code': 'When chariots charged them,
Xenophon reminded his hoplites that, unlike horses, they did not require
grass for food, and that their sturdy legs would get them home after the
horses collapsed.' And their own tale was about 'today's hoplites' – 'the
inheritors of Xenophon's code of bravery and camaraderie – men who
would be comfortable with short swords and convex shields, men with
sturdy legs who would eat less grass than a horse'. They did distance the
Marines slightly from the ferocious but costly shoulder-to-shoulder advance of the Greek hoplites, if only by suggesting that they were like 'the

centurions of ancient Rome' instead, soldiers who relied not just on discipline but also on manoeuvre and agility on the battlefield. But West and Smith returned to Xenophon at the end of 'the Marine Corps's longest march from the sea' as they pictured the troops standing on the roof of one of Saddam's palaces, smoking his cigars – tough men who 'chose to serve' and now belong to a 'tribe': 'These men are our defenders, these descendants of Xenophon's hoplites, men with sturdy legs who eat less grass than a horse.'[2]

Like the CIA operatives who gave the name 'Anabasis' to a plan designed as a prelude to invasion, the distinguished army veterans who wrote *The March Up* were using the allure of classical antiquity to give authority to the American imperial project. But anyone who has read the *Anabasis* may well find themselves scratching their heads at some of their words. 'Eat less grass than a horse'? Xenophon does indeed suggest to the Greek soldiers that their lack of cavalry is not as disastrous as they think – though he does not offer this encouragement when chariots are actually charging at them. But he never pats them on the back for eating less grass than a horse. West and Smith in fact invented the quotation to make a quip on the modern hoplites, forced to eat military-issue MREs ('Meals, Ready-to-Eat') while carrying a heavier load than the ancient soldiers. Their referencing is not bound by scholarly standards. Indeed, in an endnote they refer their readers not to the *Anabasis* itself, but to *The Exploits of Xenophon*, a 1955 re-telling of the story for children which its own author, the thriller-writer Geoffrey Household, called 'hack work'. Ancient heroism comes mediated through a modern perspective – and while both the choice of ancient heroes (the Ten Thousand) and the medium (children's book) are telling registers of Xenophon's traditional status and indeed designed to boost that status, the book also threatens the *Anabasis* by coming to stand as a replacement, pandering to the even greater simplification offered by West and Smith.[3]

The contrast West and Smith draw between the Ten Thousand, who 'hacked their way through every army that challenged them', and the more flexible Roman army also suggests a lack of concern for the details of Xenophon's story. Throughout his account of the retreat, Xenophon is in fact keen to show the Ten Thousand adapting to the difficult terrain that confronted them: at one point they organized small mobile units to fill gaps as the line contracted and expanded; on another occasion they formed in columns rather than in a broad line, and spaced the columns out to outflank the enemy and cope with the roughness of the ground.[4]

The shaky grasp of the *Anabasis* displayed by the very writers who claim that their account of the American invasion of Iraq was inspired by Xenophon's work itself reveals the ideology behind the appeal to the Greek hoplites. The lack of concern West and Smith show for what Xenophon actually wrote may be not so much due to ignorance as to an unhappiness with the details of the story. They prefer to reduce the qualities of Xenophon's soldiers – and of the contemporary Marines – to a tough core of manliness. They seem to relish the primitivism of the American troops: each soldier is not just a member of a small 'tribe' of fellow Marines, but also a 'warrior' in 'our American tribe' protecting 'us' from Iraqi men 'from another tribe'. The enemy are dehumanized ('The Marines didn't think of their prey as humans') while the Marines themselves become identified with their weapons: as if to lessen the threat from the impersonal instrument of destruction, a soldier photographed on the roof of Saddam's palace holding his rifle skyward in what could be thought a gesture of triumph is described as 'not aware of the rifle – it is simply part of him, an extension of his body'. At the same time, the two Vietnam veterans themselves enact on the page their idealization of masculinity. When they turn to panegyric and start invoking the ancient Greeks they adopt a tough, manly prose. They repeat phrases ('sturdy legs', 'sturdy legs' ...), pushing their blunt points through in short sentences, hacking their way into the readers' consciousness. As in many celebrations of militarism, the homoerotic glorification of the Ten Thousand verges on the aesthetics of fascism.[5]

The American Marines in Iraq are celebrated in *The March Up* not just as reincarnations of the Ten Thousand, but also by alignment with the most militaristic and undemocratic society in ancient Greece: 'deep inside they hope that those who do not march with them appreciate how much they sacrifice, how Spartan they are.' This language is typical of the extraordinary mania for Sparta in American military culture: several units are known as 'Spartans', among them the 36th Infantry Regiment (motto: 'Deeds not Words'). The cult of Sparta is particularly rampant among the Marines. The 1st Marine Corps is furthering the military education of its commanders by sending them copies of Paul Cartledge's *The Spartans* (2002), a book written to accompany a TV series. A popular 2005 history of the Marines bears the title *American Spartans* – although the only reference to Sparta in the book itself comes in its epigraph, the famous inscription for the 300 Spartans who died resisting the Persians at Thermopylae in 480 BC: 'Go tell the Spartans ...' (also the title of a 1968 Vietnam film). And that inscription also figures as a chapter title in David J. Danelo's *Blood Stripes*, a 2006 Iraq memoir that is dedicated to 'all who follow the Spartan Way' and boasts Kavafis' Thermopylae poem as epigraph as well as further reflections on the Marines' Spartan training. The Sparta of Marines legend can be further reified by contrast with an imaginary 'Athens' – whether that be (as in Danelo's vision) an America where the only values celebrated are 'instant gratification' and 'love of material things' or (for a Rhodes Scholar returning to military service) the romantic city of Oxford.[6]

The appeal of Sparta is brought out particularly well by Nathaniel Fick, a Dartmouth-educated Marines officer who served in both Afghanistan and Iraq. In his memoir *One Bullet Away* Fick explains that, while his classmates signed up as consultants and investment bankers, their six-figure contracts did not appeal to him: 'I wanted to go on a great adventure, to prove myself, to serve my country. I wanted to do something so hard that no one could ever talk shit to me. In Athens or Sparta, my decision would have been easy. I felt as if I had been born too late. There was no longer a place in the world for a young man who wanted to wear armor and slay dragons.' And he chose to become an infantry officer in particular because he 'wanted the purity of a man with a weapon traveling great distances on foot': 'The grunt life was untainted. I sensed a continuity with other infantrymen stretching back to Thermopylae. Weapons and tactics may have changed, but they were only accouterments. The men stayed the same. In a time of satellites and missile strikes, the part of me that felt I'd been born too late was drawn to the infantry, where courage still counts.' Fick here appeals to exactly the same image of ancient heroism that informs the portrayal of the Ten Thousand in *The March Up*.[7]

The model of Sparta also influenced the way Fick was trained as well as the way he tried to inspire his men after he became an officer. He had an army instructor who had pinned up in his classroom a passage from Steven Pressfield's 1998 Thermopylae novel *Gates of Fire* – a book described by another Iraq veteran as 'the unofficial Bible of Marine infantry'. In this passage Pressfield (himself an ex-Marine) describes the spirit of an ideal Spartan hero: 'His was not … the heroism of an Achilles. … He was just a man doing a job … whose primary attribute was self-restraint and self-composure, not for his own sake but for those he led by his example.' The same passage is also cited in the 2007 collection *Leadership Lessons from West Point*, and here readers need to delve into the endnotes to discover that it is taken from a modern American novel rather than an ancient account of the battle. Fick himself took Pressfield's leadership lesson to heart, copying out the passage and later distributing copies of *Gates of Fire* to the soldiers in his command. As with West and Smith's use of a retelling of Xenophon for children rather than the *Anabasis* itself, it is a second-hand image of antiquity that is being fetishized.[8]

The Spartans at Thermopylae and Xenophon's Greek mercenaries appeal so strongly to the American military imagination because they are seen as the spiritual ancestors of the modern Marines – exponents of a pure and authentic style of warfare that presents a true test of manliness and courage. The strong focus on means (the unquestioned patriotic valour of American soldiers) rather than ends (the dubious use to which their valour is put) is a typical strategy in what Susan Jeffords has termed 'the remasculinization of America' in her study of representations of the Vietnam War. Memory of the quagmire of Vietnam is displaced by a decisive march upcountry by Marines who draw on the pristine courage of their Greek forebears. But the claim of spiritual ancestry is a self-serving fiction. Like Nathaniel Fick, the heroes of *The March Up* were born too late. Indeed, all soldiers are born too late: there is no untainted realm of pure warfare; the way soldiers fight, the way they define courage, is always mediated through culture.[9]

1. Dubya Anabasis: Xenophon and the Iraq War

The compulsion to assert a continuity between ancient Greek warfare and the American presence in Iraq reveals some of the tensions in the modern military ethos. The image presented in *The March Up* is driven by the same sort of ideological pressures that the cultural critic Slavoj Žižek identifies in the portrayal of face-to-face battle in Steven Spielberg's World War II film *Saving Private Ryan*. For Žižek, this portrayal is a 'fantasy ... that we construct in order to escape the Real of the depersonalized war turned into an anonymous technological apparatus'. Žižek's analysis perhaps runs the risk of replacing one totalizing fiction with another: all representations of (ancient or modern) war necessarily mediate between the twin poles of impersonal machinery and personal application. Nonetheless, we can still see West and Smith as driven by a desire to prove that the sort of technology lovingly explained in a ten-page glossary has not eliminated the need for soldiers to prove themselves in man-to-man combat. The simplistic image of Greek and American soldiers in *The March Up* draws on a long-standing tradition in American military culture, but seems especially inappropriate in the age of modern TechnoWar.[10]

West and Smith succumb to the same element of fantasy in their very title *The March Up*. That title is reinforced by a jacket image of a line of soldiers on the march, and again by the closing words of the Epilogue: 'those with sturdy legs would stand side by side, regardless of age or rank. This was their march up.' Unlike Xenophon's Ten Thousand, however, the American Marines did very little marching on the way to Baghdad: 'the columns felt like never-ending traffic jams', and one Marine most remembered 'the claustrophobia of being packed inside an Amtrac, day after day'. The conceit in the title of *The March Up* is matched in other recent accounts. The commander of a brigade in the 1st Armored Division writes that the withdrawal of one of his units from Iraq to Kuwait took on 'the characteristics of Xenophon's march with ten thousand Greeks out of Iran [*sic*] and back to their homeland': 'What should have been a sixteen-hour drive turned into a forty-eight-hour odyssey.' Thus a two-day journey in tanks is said to bear comparison with many months of hard walking. The same blindness to technological change appears in a recent history of the Marines which compares 'the dramatic fighting withdrawal of the Marines' at the end of the Chosin campaign in the Korean War with the Ten Thousand's retreat through the mountains of Kurdistan. It is not that there is no similarity: the tactic used by the Greeks was for the rear of the army to support the vanguard when it was blocked by getting higher than the enemy who were causing the block, and for the vanguard to support the rear in the same way when it was harassed from behind; so too the Marines' withdrawal was supported from on high. But in the Marines' case this support came from 'the first appearance of Marine fighter jets in combat'.[11]

Paradoxically these invocations of the Ten Thousand end up involving a denial of history. Xenophon serves in *The March Up* merely as a bookend

– a handy classical allusion buttressing the beginning and end of the gritty story. Within the body of the text itself, the authors look back no further than World War II. They succumb to the myth that each generation in turn has to prove itself in war: 'You put in your turn. This is our turn. This is our war.' And it is when they summon up the ghosts of their own Vietnam generation that they become most emotionally involved: 'we both felt like we could call out a name from our past, and someone there, in that column, would answer.' They also recuperate hostile representations of Vietnam in film: 'This is like *Full Metal Jacket*,' a machine-gunner comments 'approvingly' – and they 'half-expected to see Robert Duvall fly by in a Huey, playing *Flight of the Valkyries*'. What they fail to do is to engage seriously with the history or culture of the land that the Marines are supposedly fighting to liberate. As they cross the Tigris, 'the river of the "cradle of civilization"', they acknowledge that it is 'a historic ride' – though 'the river itself wasn't particularly remarkable, certainly no Mississippi or Ohio'. But they 'couldn't stop to reflect on ancient history' as Major General Mattis, the American Xenophon, was pressing ahead.[12]

The failure to reflect on ancient history is most evident in the closing scene on the roof of Saddam's palace. As he gazes at the triumphant American troops, Bing West presents himself thinking of 'the poem about the ancient king of Babylon, the pedestal of whose statue was discovered in the wind-swept desert made famous by Shelley's poem: "My name is Ozymandias, king of kings: Look on my works, ye Mighty, and despair!"'.' What jars most here is not the howler (Ozymandias was a king of Egypt, not Babylon), but the lack of historical perspective. Shelley's reflections on the transience of power and of monuments of power are applied exclusively to the statue of Saddam, which has fallen victim not to time but to American military power. West's failure to think about the meaning of Shelley's poem for the modern western superpower re-enacts Ozymandias' folly: Ozymandias thinks that mighty onlookers should despair because they have no hope of rivalling his works; the modern reader despairs because time has reduced those works to nothing. Like Shelley's poem, the *Anabasis* too seems to work within *The March Up* in a historical and moral vacuum – a mere word from an antique land, and 'nothing beside remains'.[13]

But we should in fact resist the temptation to dismiss the use of antiquity in *The March Up* as historically and morally vacuous. The very triteness of the book's allusions to the past is itself a sign of the power of the historical narrative that underlies them. West and Smith do project a strong vision of historical destiny. Mesopotamia may have been the cradle of civilization, but civilization has moved on as it has got older. Military power and moral authority first passed on to ancient Greece and Rome. They now sit in modern America.

West and Smith's vision of patterns in time is implicit in their reflections on patterns in space. What is most striking in their attention to geography is not so much the typical American boosterism reflected in their dismissal of the Tigris as the care taken to provide historical ancestry for the American invasion. Like the participants in the British Mesopotamia campaign in the First World War, West and Smith are conscious that they are treading classic ground. They note at the start of *The March Up* that the *Anabasis* chronicles the Greeks' 'march up Mesopotamia – now Iraq' – a suitably vague formulation that obscures the fact that the Ten Thousand approached Mesopotamia from the opposite direction to the Marines. And they note at the end that a task force sent to Tikrit, 'over 900 kilometers from the sea', was following in the footsteps of both Xenophon, 'patron to all true-hearted infantrymen', and Alexander the Great, who won the battle of Gaugamela in 331 BC nearby. This seemingly casual type of geographical allusion is found in many other accounts of the Iraq War: one journalist writes that troops will be at the ancient city of Nimrud (called Larisa by Xenophon), 'though they won't realize it'; another account rather bizarrely reports the Ten Thousand's performance in battle near Fallujah between comments on the city as a haven for prostitutes and smugglers. It is the selectivity in these geographical allusions that points up the underlying ideology: the achievements of Islamic culture are mentioned much less often than ancient Greek heroism and modern Iraqi corruption. And West and Smith themselves make the ideology of their allusions clear when they add that Alexander's victory near Tikrit 'began the long martial ascent of the West over the Middle East and Asia'. The American presence in Iraq is but the latest manifestation of this supposedly uninterrupted western domination.[14]

When West and Smith claim to be inspired by the *Anabasis*, then, they are not just asserting a link between the ancient Greeks and the modern Marines, but also framing their story in terms of a continuous conflict between the (luxurious, weak, despotic) East and the (hardy, strong, democratic) West. This perceived continuity is the dominant strain in current perceptions of Greek history, as is shown by the spell cast in recent years, and especially since 9/11, by the Persian Wars and by Alexander's conquest of the Persian empire, and by the terms in which those events have been represented and discussed. The most popular Persian Wars battle has been Thermopylae, treated not just in Pressfield's *Gates of Fire*, but also in Frank Miller's violent comic-book *300* (1998), which has inspired an equally violent film with the same name (2007) and (in short succession) the parody *Meet the Spartans*. This fascination is also reflected in the production of popular histories: renowned academics write books on Thermopylae and Salamis (also 480 BC) with subtitles that proclaim them as battles that changed the world or saved western civilization, singing the same tune sung by E.S. Creasy's 1851 bestseller *Decisive Battles of the World*, which kicked off with the first Persian Wars encounter, Marathon (490 BC). As for Alexander, among the popular works to cover his conquests are Oliver Stone's ambitious 2004 film *Alexander* and Steven Pressfield's novels *The Virtues of War* (2004) and *The Afghan Campaign* (2006). This extraordinary spotlight on two events from ancient history is accompanied by a mass of reflection in the press and the internet, reading modern portrayals of the ancient conflict with Persia in the light of the war in Iraq.[15]

The opposition between East and West is equally important for under-standing the ideological background of the allusions to the *Anabasis* in *The March Up*. Xenophon's involvement in this opposition has had a long history of its own, stretching far back beyond the recent American fixation. Early in the nineteenth century, at the time of the Greek struggle for independence from Ottoman rule, the Ten Thousand were among the ancient models used to bolster the Greek cause: an 1826 edition of the *Anabasis* called the fighters for Greek freedom 'imitators of the Ten Thousand' in a dedication that was written in classical Greek – and purportedly by Xenophon himself. Xenophon was also used to bolster the western cause three centuries earlier during the Turkish wars of the Holy Roman Emperor Charles V: many of the tropes used in ancient accounts of the superiority of the Greeks and Romans to their 'barbarian' neigh-bours were recycled as both Xenophon and Charles were said to have been victorious through virtue, not numbers; through counsel, not temerity; and through discipline, not rashness. And in the first century BC the Roman general Mark Antony, retreating through Asia hard-pressed by the Parthians, was said to have gasped 'O, the Ten Thousand!' in admiration of their achievements in the same region.[16]

The power of the East/West dichotomy is also reflected in attempts to make the march of the Ten Thousand part of the mainstream of Greek history. Since antiquity, their successful retreat from the heart of the Persian empire has often been regarded as an inspiration for Alexander's conquests: 'the great Alexander would not have been great but for Xeno-phon', the historian Eunapius wrote in the early years of the fifth century AD, expressing a view that was most explicitly stated by Polybius in the second century BC. Some nineteenth-century historians even thought that the march was part of the divinely decreed progress of history, preparing 'the way for the third of the great empires which were to precede the coming of the Saviour of mankind', as prophesied in the Book of Daniel. And even before Alexander's conquests the Athenian orator Isocrates, the main proponent of panhellenism (the call for the Greeks to set aside their differences and unite in an attack on Persia), promoted a united Greek expedition by citing the achievements of the Ten Thousand.[17]

The authors of *The March Up* are heirs to this same panhellenic tradition in the use they make of Xenophon's Greeks. The hoplites' sturdy legs offer support to a historical narrative that is formed through identifi-cation with the ancient Greeks and through opposition to the negative Other – a narrative constructed on the idea that imperial power has been transferred from Greece and Rome to the New World, becoming in the process an Anglo-Saxon racial inheritance. And it is not simply a narrative about the Greeks' legacy of muscular strength and military prowess: it is also strongly shaped by the cultural and political clout of Hellenism.

*

In January 2004 an article on 'Iraq's Future – and Ours' appeared in the leading neoconservative magazine *Commentary*. The article hailed the American invasion of Iraq as 'one of the most miraculous victories in military history', and went on to rebuke those who expected an immediate transformation of Iraq. Along the way the author noted the same parallels with antiquity that appear in *The March Up*. But here the ancient battles appear as foils to the greater achievements of the Americans: 'American troops passed Iraqi palaces [*sic*] with historic and often ominous names: Cunaxa, whence Xenophon's 10,000 began their arduous journey home; Gaugamela, where Alexander devastated the Persian imperial army; and, not far away in south-eastern Turkey, Carrhae, where the Roman triumvir Crassus lost his 45,000-man army and his own head.' The conclusion is that Mesopotamia had 'long been a very dangerous place for Westerners' by the time the Americans invaded.[18]

It is rather surprising to find the battles of Cunaxa (where the Greek hoplites were unbeaten) and Gaugamela (a famous Macedonian victory) used as evidence of the dangers of Mesopotamia. But quite apart from the peculiar choice of examples, the contention that Mesopotamia holds dangers for the West is even more surprising considering the identity of the article's author: the American ancient historian Victor Davis Hanson. Hanson has in the last twenty years been the dominant promoter of the key claim made in *The March Up*, namely that continuity exists not only in the ethos of combat in ancient Greece and modern America but also in western military superiority over the East. And since the 2001 attacks he has also used the cultural prestige of classical antiquity to make his mark in the modern world as a fervent advocate of the wars in Afghanistan and Iraq and as a reputed adviser of the Bush White House.

The lessons Hanson has tried to impart since 9/11 are already strongly inscribed in his earliest writings as a Greek military historian. His first book, *The Western Way of War*, extended the conventional view that the ancient Greeks laid the foundations for western cultural and political values. Inspired by the cultural focus of the leading military historian Sir John Keegan (who has in turn been influenced by Hanson's work), he made the more startling claim that the cultural values inherent in Greek hoplite-warfare laid the foundations for western military supremacy. Hanson went on to propose this message at greater length in his most famous book, *Carnage and Culture*, which was published shortly before the September 11 attacks. The book reviews a series of 'landmark battles' in which 'westerners' have been pitted against 'non-westerners', ranging from Salamis in the fifth century BC to the Tet offensive, and including Gaugamela on the way. Boldly defending the importance of generalization ('so long avoided by academics out of either fear or ignorance') in writing history, Hanson locates in these battles some shared paradigms that have ensured the rise of western power: 'freedom, decisive shock battle, civic militarism, technology, capitalism, individualism, and civilian audit and open dissent.' This consoling message of western military supremacy was reaffirmed in an Afterword to the paperback edition written six months after 9/11. Hanson claimed that his message had been borne out by the immediate American response in Afghanistan, and reaffirmed his belief in the likelihood of western triumph.[19]

Carnage and Culture starts by appealing to the example of Xenophon and the Ten Thousand to explain 'Why the West has Won' (the title of the first chapter). His description of the army is not altogether attractive: he calls them 'enlightened thugs' and claims that many of them were 'murderous renegades and exiles'. But their positive qualities are brought out at the start of the first chapter by a direct quotation of Xenophon's account of a charge by the Greek hoplites – a famous passage that we will explore in Chapter 5.[20]

The qualities that enabled so many of the Ten Thousand to make it out of Asia alive are seen by Hanson as distinctive hallmarks of ancient Greek culture. He calls the army a 'marching democracy' in which 'the soldiers routinely held assemblies in which they voted on the proposals of their elected leaders': 'The ordeal of the Ten Thousand ... brought out the polis that was innate in all Greek soldiers, who then conducted themselves on campaign precisely as civilians in their respective Greek states.' And he sees in these hallmarks of Greek culture the same paradigms responsible for western supremacy in the modern world: 'a sense of personal freedom, superior discipline, matchless weapons, egalitarian camaraderie, individual initiative, constant tactical adaptation and flexibility, preference for shock battle of heavy infantry.' Hanson here adopts many of the terms used five hundred years earlier to bring out the shared superiority of the Ten Thousand and Charles V over their Asiatic opponents. And these are also the terms in which Hanson predicts the continued dominance of the western way of war in the aftermath of the attacks on the World Trade Center.[21]

The grand and ambitious thesis of *Carnage and Culture* sparked controversy when the book was first published – and still more controversy after 9/11. In the Afterword to the paperback edition, Hanson addressed some of his critics. While he took comfort in the praise given by some military historians, he reflected on the 'wrath' the book had aroused in what he termed 'progressive' newspapers and magazines in the United Kingdom, where the book had been given the title *Why the West has Won* – and dismissed as a 'Marathon of misconception'. He derided one critic who saw his work as a '"WASP" apology', pointing out that most of the victories he was celebrating were not achieved by Anglo-Saxons or Protestants. More broadly, he blamed hostility to his work on envy, accusing his critics of being peeved at what they saw as his 'peculiarly American attempt to gloat over the contemporary military superiority of the United States'.[22]

What Hanson did not address was some critics' alarm at the moral bleakness of his vision. By choosing 'moral renegades' like the Ten Thousand as representatives of western values, Hanson was seeking to establish that the western military machine was more lethal than any other – not that it was morally superior. As one American critic astutely noted, Hanson was combining two visions – 'the celebration of the West for its democratic vision of human liberty, and the condemnation of the West for militarism and imperialism' – and arguing that these positions were inseparable rather than incompatible. In his support for the brutal West, Hanson was subscribing to the same tribal view of history presented in West and Smith's account of the Marines' march up to Baghdad.[23]

Hanson also failed to meet his critics' concerns about the sweeping selectivity of his reading of history. This selectivity can be seen in his handling of ancient evidence: he fails to recognize the possibility that depictions of Greek hoplites in action may themselves be ideologically motivated – aimed, that is, at producing precisely the impression of civic equality that Hanson reads as a reflection of reality. Hanson is right to stress the flexibility of Greek hoplite warfare, but he still clings to a vision of the cohesiveness of hoplite battle that many historians regard as inherently implausible.

The crudeness of Hanson's reading of Xenophon is most evident when he illustrates the hoplites' 'disdain' for the Persian cavalry by citing a speech where Xenophon is trying to encourage despondent troops: 'No one ever got bitten or kicked to death in battle by a horse.' But this argument sounds desperately unconvincing at the time (it may even be taken as a sardonic joke). And not long afterwards the Greeks felt their lack of cavalry as they were unable to press on in pursuit of the enemy – while 'even in flight the barbarian horsemen were inflicting wounds, by turning and shooting arrows from the backs of their horses'. In his next speech, Xenophon is forced to acknowledge the truth: 'We urgently need slingers and horsemen.' There was only so much that the hoplites' sturdy legs could do.[24]

The biggest problem with Hanson's use of Xenophon is that he replaces the essentialist view of infantry fighting as a realm where courage and manhood are tested with an equally mythical notion of a cultural continuity underlying western military supremacy. His reading of Greek history is typical of the type of discourse (most famously analysed by Edward Said in his 1978 classic *Orientalism*) that constructs a strong polarity between East and West and elevates the West at the expense of the East. This notion of a continuity in the relations of East and West obscures not only the shifts that have taken place over time in the relations between East and West, but also the complexity of those relations at any one time: 'East' and 'West' are shifting terms, constructed by ideology, not geography.

As we shall see throughout this book, the march of the Ten Thousand is itself a valuable corrective to reading the dynamics of power between European or American and Asian powers in simple binary terms. The Greeks enter Asia as mercenaries serving a powerful Persian prince who has just played a vital role in financing the Spartan victory over Athens in the Peloponnesian War. There were also some non-Greeks among the Ten Thousand (and some Greeks fighting for the Persian king). There was also much cultural exchange between the Greeks and non-Greeks in Asia Minor, and there were Greeks – like Xenophon himself – who were willing to abandon their home cities in the hope of establishing a position with Cyrus. They were drawn to the East because Persia was powerful, not weak and decadent.

*

As the swift American invasion of Iraq has given way to a difficult occupation, Victor Davis Hanson has continued to appeal to ancient Greece to support a hard line on Iraq – but his tone has shifted in the process. It is not just in his 2004 *Commentary* piece that he presents a less glamorous view of Xenophon. In November 2006, he responded in *National Review Online* to what he saw as increasingly defeatist calls for the redeployment (or 'flight') of the American army in Iraq: 'What Middle Eastern illegitimate autocrat,' he asked, 'would want to host a retreating and defeated American army, a sort of modern version of Xenophon's orphaned Ten Thousand?' The fate of the Ten Thousand has become a foil to the superior American skill or even a warning of what the Americans must avoid. The *Anabasis* has also continued to play a role in the way the war has been conceived by many others. But it has become far more common for Xenophon to be invoked by those who had been opposed to the invasion from the start or were dismayed by the ignorance and incompetence displayed by the American forces after the overthrow of Saddam. The use of the *Anabasis* in promoting or celebrating the American attack on Iraq itself creates a space for Xenophon to add his voice to the opposition.[25]

A pre-emptive strike against the imperialist appropriation of the *Anabasis* was in fact made even before Iraq was invaded. In January 2003 Salt Publishing announced plans for an ebook of poems protesting against the forthcoming war. The project was an extraordinary success: within a week a volume was published online; two expanded editions appeared in the next week; and a month later *100 Poets against the War* was published in book form. By the time of the invasion, the ebook had been downloaded onto over a quarter of a million computers, and the poems read out across the world at rallies protesting against the Bush regime's march to war. One of the highlights in the collection was a prose-poem by the American Richard Peabody with the strange title 'Dubya Anabasis'.[26]

Peabody's poem is a wry meditation, in the form of an encyclopaedia entry, on how President Bush will be remembered. Opening with a mock simplicity, the entry wittily traces an unexpected future trajectory for Bush's nickname 'Dubya' – a byword for inarticulate stupidity:

> Dubya Anabasis. Original name, George W[alker] Bush. (1946-?) 43rd President of the United States (2000-?) and the man who started World War III. It's difficult to understand how Dubya became president. His Republican Party (GOP) was famous for rewriting history in the style of evil dictators Stalin and Hitler before them. What we know now, post World War III, is that he was installed into power after a disputed election in which he lost the popular vote but won the electoral vote. A petty criminal, it appears he was a pawn of the corporations who expected to get rich on military excursions into Afghanistan, Iraq, Iran, and North Korea in order to corner the market on the world's oil reserves at a time when natural resources were dwindling. The son of the 41st President (George Herbert Walker Bush) Dubya is thought now to have been a puppet of his father's staff. He disappeared in the fallout following the vaporisation of Washington, D.C. For years it was claimed that he died in a bunker in West Virginia, or was hiding in caves in Texas or Argentina. (*See* Dick Cheney, Chomsky, Gulf War, Heroin Smuggling in Southeast Asia, Iran-Contra, Richard Nixon, Ronald Reagan, Zinn.)

The bland opening statements are defamiliarized by the distant ('post World War III') perspective – and by their very blandness. But as the poem progresses to our future the humour becomes darker, with Bush implicitly aligned with Hitler (the bunker) and Osama Bin Laden (the caves). It finally enters the realm of the fantastic as it reaches its own present, a distant future where the moral and political topography of our own world seems to have been completely overturned:

> Dubya appears briefly as a Taniwha in Keri Waratah's rock opera Whiro, he is presented as a bland and puritanical man of relentless torpor, the 'child is father to the man' who gradually mutates into a mythical demon, as contrasted to the heroic characters like Good Soldier Schweik, or Xing Zi famous for his magical feather cloak.

> Dubya is to this day a curse word passed down by generations of Maori people (*See* also: fuck, merde, scheisskopf, walker, wang ba dan, *et al.*)

The poem ends with no explanation offered for the juxtaposition of the familiar insult 'Dubya' with the strange (surname?) 'Anabasis'. Peabody could be playing on specialist botanical knowledge: Anabasis is the name of a species of small plant – a desert Bush. But the mystery is also part of the way the poet captures an alien future perspective on the past (our

21

present), disrupting the traditional genealogy that derives modern heroism from ancient Greece. This disruption of linear narratives of progress
is strengthened by the allusion to 'heroic characters like Good Soldier
Schweik': in the subversive World War I novel that the Czech writer
Jaroslav Hašek named after his great comic creation, 'Budweiser Anabasis' is the title of an episode where the hero, more at home in the pub
than the army, gets hopelessly lost on his way to report to his unit and is
eventually arrested as a Russian spy. By calling Schweik's trivial local
journey an 'Anabasis', Hašek deflates not just the Austro-Hungarian
empire that tries to control Schweik's movements but also a new Czech
national myth – the famous Anabasis across Siberia by the Czech Legion
stranded in Russia at the end of the war. The term 'anabasis' was also used
by Brecht of the climactic scene in his stage updating of the Schweik story:
it is now the Second World War, and Schweik encounters Hitler on the
German advance into Russia; the play ends with the duo stuck in the snow,
with Schweik mocking Hitler as he desperately tries to advance ('To the
east. To the west. To the north. To the south') but gets nowhere. Like
Hašek and Brecht, Peabody uses 'anabasis' to mock imperial pretensions:
in his imaginary world of the future, Schweik has become a genuine hero
in contrast to the warmongering Dubya Anabasis. The mockery is more
pointed still because the poem's title also gestures towards the great
expedition to the interior of Iraq that Bush was about to launch – and to
the ancient precedent of Xenophon's Cyrus. Even before the invasion itself
began, 'anabasis' is used to signify Iraq and to hint at how the main
perpetrator would himself come to have his Presidency defined by the folly
of that attack.[27]

*

At the same time as poets were penning their anti-war pieces, an Irish
traveller was returning to Baghdad to see friends he had made on an
earlier trip who were now threatened by the coming war. Shane Brennan
had first visited the city in the course of an extraordinary journey on foot
along almost the whole length of Xenophon's march. In the account he
wrote of that earlier trip *In the Tracks of the Ten Thousand*, Brennan
recorded in an Epilogue his return to the Iraqi capital and his thoughts as
he crossed the desert again to leave before the bombing started. His mind
turned again to the soldiers whose steps he had followed, 'Westerners who
had come here 2,500 years ago to overthrow a king'. He did not doubt that
Bush would be more successful than the Ten Thousand – but he did
wonder 'if his army wouldn't have the same problems as the Greeks in
getting home'. Brennan's reflections are picked up and taken further in
the Foreword, where the well-known British travel-writer Tim Macintosh
Smith claims that 'Cyrus' Ten Thousand are now Bush's three hundred
thousand': 'The speed of invasion has accelerated by the same degree, or

more. ... history is served up now in seconds, in pixels. The whole round world is caught in a web spun by all-seeing satellites.' Macintosh Smith opposes the 'clarity' gained by walking – or by reading an account of a long walk – with the dizzying illusions projected by a western superpower in the thralls of its own self-proclaimed technological proficiency. He breaks the direct line connecting the ancient hoplites, marching on foot, and the modern Marines driving along highways in humvees, seeing in the dark through night-vision goggles, enjoying risk-free views of the enemy from unmanned planes, their high-tech gear all efficiently acronymed.[28]

A similar pessimism is apparent in even more recent attempts to bring Xenophon within the orbit of Operation Iraqi Freedom. In an article on 'America's Anabasis', Isaiah Wilson, a West Point professor and veteran of the Iraq War, noted some 'intriguing' parallels with Xenophon's march – 'each began as an unequivocal tactical victory, but each devolved into a strategic quandary' – and anticipated more: 'Xenophon's anabasis lasted close to ten years ... our own *katabasis* (march out of country), many have proposed, may take just as long.' The desire to root the uncertainties of the present in a heroic past leads here to some twisting of the ancient realities. 'An unequivocal tactical victory'? Cyrus may have approached Babylon unchallenged, but he died in his first encounter with his brother's forces. And the Greek hoplites may have defeated the forces opposed to them at the battle of Cunaxa, but then they pressed too far in pursuit and were not on hand to support Cyrus' charge against the King. The battle was not much of a tactical victory. And Xenophon's march was over in two years, not ten. His eastern adventure is already much shorter than America's anabasis. The linking of ancient and modern also twists modern realities: the language of 'tactical victory' is an outmoded way of talking about a conflict such as that in Iraq where the military and civilian realms are blurred and where the final objective is disputed. Indeed, Isaiah Wilson himself questions in his 2007 book *Thinking Beyond War* the continuing applicability of traditional definitions of victory and defeat, with America now embarked on a 'postmodern anabasis'.[29]

An even more striking mark of the changing meaning of anabasis is found in a proposal made in March 2007 by the conservative cultural commentator – and self-proclaimed 'military expert' – William S. Lind. Lind's proposal was that American commanders in Iraq should read Xenophon and make plans of their own for an 'Operation Anabasis' ('a retreat north through Kurdish Iraq to Turkey') in case their lines of communication to the south should be cut. The geographical overlap with Xenophon's route is no longer a curiosity to be noted in passing or a shallow broadening of the historical horizon. In this pessimistic vision the precedent of the Ten Thousand may even offer a route to safety. At the same time, Lind's proposal opens up an ambivalence in the term 'anabasis' itself. Before and during the invasion that term was (correctly) applied to a march upcountry – an expedition away from the coast up to Baghdad.

Lind twists the term so that it is applied to a retreat: the most famous part of Xenophon's account (the Greeks' paradigmatic display of endurance in extricating themselves from Mesopotamia) usurps the name of Cyrus' march upcountry.[30]

The urge to think of Xenophon in connection with the American presence in Iraq is shared by readers of the *New York Times*. Early in 2007, one of the paper's columnists claimed that one thing the invasion of Iraq had achieved was to give a fresh resonance to the themes of time-honoured classics such as *Moby Dick* (the cost of obsession) and Thucydides' account of Athens' invasion of Sicily (imperial avarice and overreach). The columnist then invited his readers to offer their own literary and historical parallels to the situation in Iraq – and one of the examples most commonly cited in the hundreds of responses he received was 'Xenophon's ancient warning ... of how much easier it is to get into a Middle Eastern war than out'. The wheel has come round full circle: the *Anabasis* is now a cautionary tale, not an incentive to conquest.[31]

There is every sign that the compulsion to read events in modern Iraq against Xenophon's narrative will continue. At the same time, all modern readings of the *Anabasis*, popular and scholarly, stand in the shadow of the American military adventure in Iraq. The author of the latest book on the march starts by poignantly reflecting on a former student who had visited Babylon while serving in Iraq – the fabled city that Xenophon's Greeks never got to see – and by hoping that 'someday soon nobody will have to become a warrior to see Babylon'. And as I write, Columbia Pictures, inspired by the success of *300*, have bought the rights to an *Anabasis* screenplay – a project that, if completed, raises the prospect of yet more discussion of the interplay between ancient and modern conflicts.[32]

*

The American military adventure in Iraq has been a tale of two anabasises: an aggressive march up into the country and subsequent anxiety about how to get out of it. Uniting these two anabasises is one common refrain: whether the concept of anabasis is used to promote or attack the American occupation of Iraq, the appeal to Xenophon is drawing on the vocabulary of 'savage' warfare. The Ten Thousand can stand as models for soldiers involved in any form of conflict, but the language of anabasis has had a particular resonance when applied to other American campaigns in Asia against peoples perceived as primitive. The invasion of Vietnam could be described as an 'American anabasis' – and Anabasis Investments is the all too (in)appropriate name of the company that produced the early Rambo movies, the ultimate expression of renewed American masculinization in the aftermath of Vietnam. This imperial logic can work both ways: if Xenophon is used to define Vietnam, then conversely the plot of the *Anabasis* can be compared with a pitch for a Vietnam movie ('*Platoon* meets the *Odyssey*'). Parallels have also been made, as we have seen, between Xenophon's retreat and the Chosin withdrawal in the Korean War, and the tradition of reading forays into hostile terrain in terms of Xenophon also extends to the genre of patriotic war films: the anabasis label was applied to *Objective Burma*, a film made in the last year of World War II featuring a group of paratroopers led by Errol Flynn that is dropped into Burma to find an enemy radar station and then forced to march through the jungle to safety.[33]

A new play staged on Broadway in 2006 with the telling title *Savages* extends the application of Xenophon back to the first major war in which Americans flexed their imperial muscles overseas – the war with Spain that led to the conquest of the Philippines (1899-1902). Written by Anne Nelson, a Columbia professor best known for her post-9/11 work *The Guys*, the play treats an event that took place during the final stages of that war – the court-martial of an American major for ordering prisoners to be shot in an act of reprisal against Philippine insurgency. Nelson portrays the American occupiers facing similar predicaments to their modern-day counterparts in Iraq – and the fact that the American conflict with Spain began in Cuba allows her a brief reference to Guantanamo Bay. Xenophon's presence, by contrast, seems initially to be far removed from present concerns: the officer on trial has carried a copy of the *Anabasis* with him since his schooldays, and as he outlines this piece of 'ancient history' to the ignorant young soldier who is guarding him, Xenophon's heroic retreat ("'The Greeks catch sight of the sea.'" 'He saved them!' (*Long pause.*) 'I read this passage over and over ...') contrasts with the impasse of the American troops in the Philippines, fighting a war against the very people they had come to liberate ('*Fifty-nine* of our boys – die that day. (*Beat. Quietly:*) A few fight their way to the boats. ... (*full of pain and stunned wonder.*) And "the Greeks catch sight of the sea"'). And yet the setting of Xenophon's escape – the Tigris, the 'scorching desert', the 'savage Kurds' – must also look ahead to the Iraq War and its aftermath. Paradoxically references to the *Anabasis* add a contemporary resonance to a historical drama. In the play's opening dialogue, the phrase 'ancient history' had been applied to the Civil War by the northern general who is prosecuting the southern major. By the end, we are left wondering just how 'ancient' Xenophon's story is too.[34]

The idea of anabasis has also been applied to earlier American ventures in foreign lands. In 1805 a small band of American troops ventured across the African desert during the First Barbary War (aimed at stopping pirates attacking American commerce in the Mediterranean). Their 400-mile trek has been termed by historians a 'modern *Anabasis*', with its leader, William Eaton, hailed as 'the American Xenophon' or even 'the blue-eyed Xenophon from Connecticut'. From Tripoli Xenophon accompanied American soldiers to the halls of the Montezumas: as we shall explore in Section II, the invasion of Mexico (1846-8) was marked by countless contemporary allusions to Xenophon – and again particular weight was given to the pacification of 'savages'.[35]

The ultimate source for the image of the Iraq invasion as an anabasis is the bloody conflict between the United States and the native inhabitants of the American continent. Early European settlers found themselves confronted by the prospect of a vast and 'wild' continent with equally 'wild' natives, and haunted in particular by the fear of Indian sexual control over white female captives. Many subsequent American military campaigns have applied to the enemy mental structures derived from this encounter with 'savages': military parlance has credited Vietnam and Iraq with 'Indian country' (wild lands in need of pacification), and General Petraeus, leader of the 'surge' in American troops in 2007, used the Remington cowboy image he kept in his office as a metaphor for his mission in Iraq ('we're just trying to get the cattle to Cheyenne'). The United States used military power to win control of its territory and to extend its influence abroad while sanctioning the use of force by portraying its enemies as primitive and uncivilized.[36]

While interest in Xenophon is at present particularly strong owing to events in Iraq and to the general fascination for ancient Greece in American popular and military culture, the recent use of the *Anabasis* is also part of the continuity in the ideology of American expansion. The American anabasis abroad was prefigured in the conquest of the American continent as Xenophon was made to fit the vision of Manifest Destiny underlying the territorial claims of the United States. It is the trail of this American anabasis that we now follow as we move back in time and from Iraq to America.

Look Homeward: The Idea of America

*A country here, not mine. What has the world given me but this
swaying of grass? ...
To the place called the Place of the Dry Tree:
and the starved lightning allots me these provinces in the West.*
Saint-John Perse, Anabasis

*Fixed to bone only, foreign as we came,
We float leeward till the mind and body lose
The uncertain continent of a name.*
W.S. Merwin, 'Anabasis (II)'[1]

***

In 1893, the historian Frederick Jackson Turner pronounced the closing
of the American frontier in a famous speech in Chicago. The expansion of
US territory across the continent in the 1840s had been followed, particularly after the Civil War, by the steady settlement of the plains as the
Indian tribes were confined to reservations. Turner saw the end of the
frontier as the end of the first phase of American history – a phase which
stretched back to the first European contact with the continent: 'Since the
days when the fleet of Columbus sailed into the waters of the New World,
America has been another name for opportunity.' Turner offers a classic
statement of the view of 'America' as a monolithic entity, a synecdoche for
untrammelled freedom – a view that necessarily obscures the presence of the
continent's earlier inhabitants and blurs the complexity of relations among
the European settlers. For Turner, moreover, 'movement' is the dominant
element in the life of this monolith: 'the people of the United States have
taken their tone from the incessant expansion which has not only been open
but has even been forced upon them. He would be a rash prophet who should
assert that the expansive character of American life has now entirely ceased.'
Turner here foresaw the way in which the notion of the American frontier
would soon be exported elsewhere – to the Philippines and beyond.[2]

   If, as was suggested in Chapter 1, pride in or anxiety over the subsequent exercise of American power abroad has been played out in shifting
and conflicting responses to the *Anabasis*, then a similar complexity can
be found in the story of how Xenophon's text has been applied to US
expansion within the American continent. In the century following
Turner's pronouncement that the frontier was closed, many writers

27

turned to the *Anabasis* to explore the process by which the continent had been explored and settled by Europeans. In 1924, for instance, Louise Phelps Kellogg, a prolific historian of the North-West, used 'Wisconsin Anabasis' as the title of an article describing a journey by the French explorers La Salle and Tonty in the 1670s. More elaborately, the famous expedition to Illinois led by George Rogers Clark in the Revolutionary War was commemorated as *Clark's Anabasis* in a patriotic epic with a style purportedly modelled on Pope, Dryden, Virgil, and Homer: the 'Historic muse!' was invoked to tell of 'The frontier epic of a valiant band / Whose arms won freedom for our native land' – 'A feat which opened up a continent / To pioneer energy and settlement'. Another western writer thought that the 'classic' words 'This is the place' uttered by Brigham Young as he looked down at the Great Salt Lake were 'as enduring as those of the soldiers of Zenophon at the end of the "Anabasis", "The sea, the sea"' – mistakenly comparing the actual end of the Mormon Exodus ('as great an epic of movement as any in the record') with the Greeks' brief euphoria. And others again have invoked that famous Greek shout to bring out the joy felt in the Lewis and Clark expedition when it reached the Pacific.[3]

Implicit in these allusions to Xenophon's journey through Asia is a firm idea of America's moral geography. If the conception of the American invasion of Iraq as an anabasis can be attributed to racial ideologies and topographical coincidences ('western' incursions into Mesopotamia), then applying the idea of anabasis within the American continent is a pointed way of suggesting an exploration or military incursion into an untamed frontier region. The image of anabasis also endows earlier expeditions with the 'classic' status explicitly claimed for Brigham Young's words. It is a figure of nostalgia, evoking a time when the idea of America as opportunity was embodied in the open frontier regions, but also looking homeward towards the foundational role of classical antiquity in American culture. A double nostalgia even operates in Kellogg's account of the 'Wisconsin Anabasis': she begins her article by reflecting that 'the world-famous retreat of the Ten Thousand Greeks ... was once, when Xenophon's account was a universal textbook, the commonplace of every schoolboy' – and by offering her own story 'of as brave and resourceful a party as any Greek ever knew' as 'a footnote to the great *Anabasis*'. Here Xenophon's expedition is to later explorations what Plato is to philosophy – a point of origin that overshadows equally noble successors and yet has itself been overshadowed by the decline of the classical curriculum.[4]

To apply the notion of anabasis to the conquest of the American West is also to cast the story of America as a journey. This image of American history as a journey is inscribed in the very terminology applied to American geography: terms such as 'the Mid-West' or 'back east' (used on the west coast) read the continent from east to west (as if moving 'back east' is going back in time as well as in space). It might be thought that this image would come to seem less fitting following the 'closing' of the American frontier. But in fact the idea of the American journey has become more popular the more distant the pioneer journeys have become. It was precisely with the conclusion to what Frederick Jackson Turner saw as the first phase of American history that the idea of journey needed to be renewed. American history now became a journey in time rather than in space – and the image has remained appealing because it suggests a movement towards a goal. The movement can be paused and resumed, the goal itself can be redefined, but America remains the land of opportunity. It is no accident that the American journey was a leading image in the inaugural address delivered by President Obama as he sought to reaffirm the greatness of the American nation after the grave damage inflicted by the Bush presidency: 'Our journey has never been one of short-cuts or settling for less. It has not been the path for the faint-hearted, for those who prefer leisure over work, or seek only the pleasures of riches and fame. Rather, it has been the risk-takers, the doers, the makers of things ... who have carried us up the long rugged path towards prosperity and freedom.' Obama endowed the American journey with a sense of heroic struggle, using the same terms as a famous fable told by Xenophon – Hercules' choice between instant pleasure and the uphill path of toil that leads to virtue. At the same time, Obama's assertion that America was strengthened by its 'patchwork heritage' gave that journey a strong inclusivity.[5]

If the American anabasis is part of the broader American journey, it has lurking within it a historical consciousness very different from Barack Obama's appeal to inclusivity. The racial undertones present in the Iraq anabasis are also found when anabasis is applied to encounters with the native inhabitants of North America. In the 1930s, for instance, a writer in Oregon published 'a trilogy in the anabasis of the West' – a tract with three sections that set out to celebrate the spirit of the Oregon pioneers while also preserving an Indian war-cry as ethnographic relic, with full musical notation. The same racial element is present in a character's allusion to Xenophon in *The Great Sioux Trail*, a 1918 'romance' about 'the opening of the Great West just after the Civil War': 'Our march often makes me think of Xenophon, whom I studied in the high school. ... What I remember best about the story, they were always marching so many parasangs, so many days' journey to a well of water ... .' The immediate reference here is to Xenophon's famously repetitive account of the start of the Greeks' journey, where each stage is measured in parasangs, a Persian unit of distance. The mere mention of parasangs suggests an engagement with an alien landscape – and here their imaginative transfer to the American plains is made against a backdrop of threat: 'On the plains we've got to think of Indians ... .'[6]

The most shocking American exploitation of the *Anabasis* to assert white supremacy appears in a 1987 tract written by Harold Covington, a neo-Nazi activist from North Carolina. The cover bears the book's Xenophontic title, *The March Up Country*, as well as a swastika by the author's

29

name and an image expressing his idea of America as it is now and as it should be: an outline of the United States with a star of David and a hammer and sickle imposed on it – and a tall muscular man, with rifle thrust upwards and wife and small child clinging to his side, trampling the two symbols underfoot. The aim of the book itself (now widely available in pdf format on neo-Nazi websites) is to boost 'the worldwide White, Aryan resistance movement': Covington first outlines the tools through which he hopes to achieve his goal of a white homeland in the North-West of the United States, then attempts in an Epilogue to inspire his readers to action.[7]

It is in the closing exhortation that the reason for the Xenophontic title finally emerges. The Epilogue begins with a slightly abridged quotation from a speech Xenophon makes in the *Anabasis* after the murder of the Greeks' generals: 'You will know, I am sure, that strength and weapons alone do not always prevail in battle. When an army is stronger in soul, then their enemies cannot withstand them.' There follows a highly inaccurate summary of the Greeks' retreat: Xenophon captures the Great King's baggage train and supplies, feints an attack on Babylon, and decisively defeats Tissaphernes. Though these invented details make the retreat itself more glorious, Covington characterizes the Greek soldiers as 'freebooters', 'ne'er-do-wells looking for a fast buck', 'henpecked husbands', 'drifters', 'violent men who loved combat for its own sake' – and yet 'their kind won us the whole world'. This unattractive portrait seems designed to ground their superiority in an unchanging racial identity that more than makes up for their failings: their 'epic retreat' is 'one of the greatest stories of ... Aryan courage that graces the annals of our mighty race'. Covington's racism is served further by his ignorance about the mythology of race. He writes that the Persians murdered the Greek generals 'with truly Semitic treachery' – though the Persians were Aryan (a word etymologically linked with 'Iran'). And equally fantastic is his claim that the 'disciplined, formidable Greek warriors' partly came from 'the northern plains of Thrace and Macedonia, renowned for breeding the tall, blond soldiers called hoplites, masters of the bow and spear and sword'. Every detail here is incorrect: hoplites did not use bows – and they did not tend to be tall and blond either; and while there were Thracians among the Ten Thousand, they were not hoplites – or even Greek.[8]

It is as Covington recreates the highpoint of this Aryan epic ('The sea! The sea!') that he finally reveals its supposed relevance for modern-day America. He calls on 'my brothers, my sisters' to 'imagine what it must have been like to hear that shout' – and assures them that 'someday, somewhere, that cry will arise from White throats parched with thirst and dry of hope' – 'The sea! The sea!': 'deep down inside, our spears are as sharp and our courage as great as that of the Ten Thousand. We left our Cunaxa in 1945. It will take us longer than it did Xenophon and his men, to be sure – but one day we, too, shall climb the last mountain and see the sea.' Covington here equates the defeat of Nazi Germany with the defeat at

Cunaxa that left the Greek soldiers stranded in the middle of Mesopotamia – a perverse parallel grounded in a longing to make the Greeks'
subsequent march a heroic antecedent rather than a mere metaphor for
courageous struggle. His rhetoric is based on the same logic seen in
historical and fictional accounts that retrospectively applied the idea of
anabasis to the conquest and settling of the American West: he differs in
projecting a Xenophontic march in the future rather than celebrating one
in the past – and in both the extremism of his ideology of white supremacy
and the explicitness with which he celebrates it.[9]

Covington's false image of the Greek soldiers as tall, blond warriors
from the northern plains shows that he was as strongly influenced by
genealogies of race forged in Germany as by the mythology of the American West. His closing appeal to the Ten Thousand can even be paralleled
in German writings after the perceived humiliation of Versailles. *Deutsche
Anabasis 1918*, a short memoir by a German soldier, closes by celebrating
the retreat of a German division through the Balkans at the end of the war
as one wave from an inexhaustible sea of recent military feats from which
the Germans can take heart and prove themselves worthy of the German
name: 'Anabasis means ascent. If German hearts are again strengthened
and raised to Duty, Faith, and Honour, then from the collapse the German
people will have another great Anabasis: Escape, Ascent, Resurrection!'
While this poetic exploitation of the etymology of 'anabasis' does not have
the same spatial focus as Covington's vision of America, the imaginative
geography of the American West did influence the development of the
Nazis' racial ideology: the concept of *Lebensraum* was first articulated by
a geographer, Friedrich Ratzel, who travelled across the United States in
the 1870s; and Hitler was notoriously an admirer of the westerns of Karl
May, and also known on occasion to call the Volga a future German
Mississippi and to dismiss Russians as savage Redskins. Knowingly or
not, Covington's *March Up Country* was drawing on Nazi racial conceptions of ancient Greece and spatial conceptions of modern America.[10]

Germany between the wars also proved receptive to the vision of the
American anabasis offered by the author we will be following for the rest of
this chapter: Thomas Wolfe, creator of some of the most powerful works in
American literature in the inter-war period – including by far the richest use
of Xenophon in conveying and also interrogating the ideology of American
growth. As we shall see, the *Anabasis* is a major source of inspiration for
Wolfe's sprawling first novel, *Look Homeward, Angel* (1929) – and particularly for its recently published first draft, *O Lost*. And it was in Germany that
the novel received its highest praise: it was hailed by Hermann Hesse as the
product of a 'young Siegfried' and by other critics as a 'powerful epic of
America', displaying 'an elemental love for America, the germs of a true
national spirit'. The novel received a more positive response from the non-
Nazi press, but the terms in which it was praised are still a telling sign of
how widely the romantic appeal of America was felt.[11]

2. 'A young Siegfried': Thomas Wolfe in Berlin in the 1930s.

The historical circumstances in which Thomas Wolfe himself grew up will be even more important for us than the context in which his work was received in Germany. Wolfe witnessed in his teenage years the rapid growth in American military might in World War I – the time when the United States was first recognized as a major world power. And the years that followed the war proved to be a boom time not just for the American economy but also for the creation of a distinctively American literary identity. While the first journal devoted solely to criticism of American literature was founded in 1929, lively discussion had already been provoked by the publication of D.H. Lawrence's *Studies in Classic American Literature* in 1923: Lawrence's idiosyncratic account investigated 'the Orestes-like frenzy of restlessness in the Yankee soul' – and even without his sweeping prose his claim that America had a classic literature of its own was striking enough at the time. In the years that followed Thomas

Wolfe – a southerner who shared the Yankee restlessness and even saw himself as an Orestes – was among the writers who journeyed to Europe with the aim of continuing to forge this distinctively American literary tradition.[12]

*

'January 1-10, 1900 – I was conceived. … June-Sept. 1900 – Father drunk. … Oct. 2, 1900 – Eight o'clock at night. Father returns home, enters my mother's room and attacks her. She escapes … Oct. 3, 1900 – Ten o'clock in the morning. I am born.' It was the summer of 1926, and Thomas Wolfe was in Paris with his lover, Aline Bernstein. On an unlined pad of paper he started to jot down a series of loose snippets – the fractured story of his life. He recalled his turbulent upbringing in the mountain town of Asheville, North Carolina, as the youngest of seven children; his parents' unhappy marriage and his mother's decision to leave and set up a boarding house; and the deaths of two of his brothers, including gentle, beloved Ben. He recalled, too, his voracious childhood reading and his privileged formal education – the private schooling denied to his siblings, his undergraduate years at Chapel Hill, and finally his arrival at Harvard ('a deficient enough place'). He broke off before mentioning his failed attempt to establish himself in New York as a playwright and the start of his affair with Aline.[13]

A sensuous, novelistic feeling for atmosphere emerges amidst Wolfe's disjointed jottings: 'The sad rustling of early autumn. Later – thunder in the trees at night – *Ridpath's History* – the Egyptians and Charles the Hammer – *The Golden Treasury* – With Stanley in Africa.' These notes (which he finished in London) were to help with the grand autobiographical novel – 'Dickensian or Meredithian in length' – that he was planning to write. Aline had given him enough money for one year in Europe, but it took Wolfe another year's writing back in New York before the typescript – entitled *O Lost* and almost 300,000 words long – was ready to be sent to the publishers. The novel presented, Wolfe wrote in a note for publishers' readers, 'a strange and deep picture of American life – one that I have never seen elsewhere' – a picture, he later reflected, that was fashioned by the experience of absence: 'I had found out during all these years of wandering that the way to discover one's own country was to leave it … I think I may say that I discovered America during these years abroad out of my very need of her. I found her because I had left her.' Wolfe's picture of American life was rejected by several publishers until his agent approached Scribner's, tempting Maxwell Perkins, renowned editor of Scott Fitzgerald and Hemingway, with a description of the opening scene: 'two little boys standing by the country roadside as a regiment of Confederate infantry marched toward Gettysburg'. Perkins, despite promising that he would read every word of the typescript, lost interest after the opening, and only at the encouragement of Scribner's other readers did he have another look. Wolfe was then summoned to New York and, trimmed and re-titled, his novel was released as *Look Homeward, Angel* in October 1929.[14]

Wolfe's autobiographical outline for the novel included his years at the academy in Asheville run by J.M. Roberts and his wife Margaret. Among other memories, he evoked the text that was for him, as for so many others, the first experience of the Greek language – Xenophon's *Anabasis*: 'Cow bells on a high hill ... The brimming creamy pails ... "O Artemidorus farewell!" ... "From there we proceeded twenty parasangs" – O the sea! The Sea! "The older of these was Cyrus" – The great march to the sea 6000 hoplites – "Merrily, merrily, merrily, merrily, life is but a dream" ... .' 'O Artemidorus farewell!' is a reference to an inscription on a mummy case in the British Museum. When the time came to write the novel, Wolfe invoked that farewell at its emotional highpoint – the death of his brother Ben. He scattered allusions to the *Anabasis*, by contrast, throughout *O Lost*, focusing on the emblematic aspects that he recalled in his outline – the opening sentence ('The older of these ...'), parasangs, and the shout of the sea – and on the term 'anabasis' itself. As we shall see, Wolfe used Xenophon's text as a way of demarcating the personal development of his fictional alter ego, Eugene Gant. And through his portrayal of Eugene Gant Wolfe was attempting to express something grander – nothing less than his discovery of America itself.[15]

'Our senses have been fed by our terrific land; our blood has learned to run to the imperial pulse of America which, leaving, we can never lose and never forget. ... When we ran away from London, we went by little rivers in a land just big enough. And nowhere that we went was far: the earth and the sky were close and near. And the old hunger returned – the terrible and obscure hunger that haunts and hurts Americans ... .' Eugene Gant is at university in North Carolina, reading the Greek tragedians, thinking of 'the lonely earth he dwelt on' – and 'suddenly, it was strange to him that he should read Euripides there in the wilderness'. And equally suddenly another voice is heard in the text – a voice in the future, running away from London, at a time when Eugene himself has never left America; the voice of the 'we' (Thomas and Aline?). And this voice – slightly bombastic, slightly ornate – is a voice that claims to speak for all Americans, speaking of the hunger that 'makes us exiles at home, and strangers wherever we go' – but also of blood that runs to America's 'imperial pulse'; a voice, too, that mimics in its shift to linguistic awkwardness ('... which, leaving, we can never lose') the disruption of leaving this terrific land.[16]

Eugene's loneliness is evoked in a more intimate setting at the end of the university year, as he leaves home for the summer to work in Virginia in support of the American war effort. At night he would ride out by trolley to the beach and listen to the surge of the sea as it 'rolled in from the eternal dark': 'O sea! (he thought) I am the hillborn, the prison-pent, the ghost, the stranger, and I walk here at your side. O sea, I am lonely like you, I am strange and far like you, I am sorrowful like you.' 'O sea ... O sea': here Wolfe echoes his autobiographical jottings on Xenophon ('O the sea! The Sea!'), breaking up the repetition and making the shout more intimate ('You are an immense and fruitful woman ...', he continues). It has become a shout of both isolation ('I am lonely') and identification ('like you'). And within the trajectory of *O Lost* it is also a cry of climax – the fulfilment of a dream.[17]

To see that dream unfold we need to roll back a few years through the dense narrative of *O Lost*. Eugene is at school in Altamont (Wolfe's fictional Asheville), beginning to learn Greek with John Dorsey Leonard – a teacher modelled on the proprietor of the academy Wolfe himself attended. And for Eugene – as for Wolfe and countless others educated in similar establishments – learning Greek means reading Xenophon:

> There were two final years of precious Greek: they read the *Anabasis*.
> 'What's the good of all this stuff?' said Tom Davis argumentatively.
> Mr Leonard was on sure ground here. He understood the value of the classics.
> 'They teach a man to appreciate the Finer Things. They give him the foundations of a liberal education. It trains his mind.'
> 'What good's it going to do him when he goes to work?' said 'Pap' Hildebrand. 'It's not going to teach him how to grow more corn.'
> 'Well – I'm not so sure of that,' said Mr Leonard with a protesting laugh. 'I think it does.'

Mr Leonard seems to protest too much. He is a figure of negation: 'The great wind of Athens had touched him not at all. ... He was simply the mouthpiece of a formula of which he was assured without having a genuine belief.' And then Wolfe inserts two words of Greek into the text – παρασάγγας πεντεκαίδεκα ('fifteen parasangs').[18]

What is the formula that Mr Leonard mouths? Perhaps it is those very parasangs – already evoked, as we have seen, in a western novel, and all too familiar for the beginner struggling through the early stages of the *Anabasis*, where Xenophon charts Cyrus' march towards Mesopotamia:

> From there Cyrus progresses two stages, ten parasangs, to the river Psarus, which was three *plethra* in breadth. From there he progresses one stage, five parasangs, to the river Pyramus, which was a stade in breadth. From there he progresses two stages, fifteen parasangs, to Issi, the last city of Cilicia, settled on the sea, large and prosperous. There they remained three days.

Mr Leonard was not the only pedagogue to be unconvinced by this formula: the editor of one of the standard nineteenth-century school editions of the *Anabasis* was even prepared to ask 'whether, in its absolute lack of interest, a parallel could be found for the above extract in the writings of any other historian, ancient or modern'. Those formulaic parasangs stand in Wolfe's text, however, for more than the mere space traversed by Cyrus and by schoolchildren in his wake. By a bold synecdoche, they represent the very ideals of a humanistic education ("'According to what you say," said Tom Davis, "A man who has studied Greek makes a better plumber than one who hasn't." "Yes, sir," said Mr Leonard, shaking his head smartly, "you know, I believe he does.'"). Wolfe pays homage to – while also satirising – the conviction that studying ancient Greek, parasangs and all, is the best preparation for life.[19]

Wolfe's satire is strengthened by the textual indeterminacy of those parasangs. Who speaks or imagines those words represented on the page in Greek font? Mr Leonard? His bored pupils? In this case deciding about the perspective embedded in those words may not matter that much. But as the scene proceeds the narrative voice becomes more problematic:

'Anabasis' comes from two Greek words meaning to go up. The Greeks went up into Persia. Cyrus the king had two sons, the older of which he called – O the sea! The sea! Θάλασσα θάλασσα ['The sea, the sea']. They went up into an exceeding high mountain. The shades of eve were falling fast Excelsior. From there they proceeded twenty parasangs – ἐντεῦθεν ἐξελαύνει ['From there he progresses'] –

Who speaks here? At the start we seem to hear Mr Leonard as mouthpiece, explaining the meaning of 'anabasis' and why Xenophon's work has that title. There follows a slightly garbled version of the opening sentence of the *Anabasis* – and then a sudden leap. We break out of the dullness of Mr Leonard's class as the text leaves the opening mid-sentence and jumps straight to the ecstatic climax – the scene where the Greeks shout as they catch sight of the Black Sea. This climax is reinforced by the quotation (first in English, then in Greek) of their famous shout and by the biblical lilt of the following sentence (Matthew 4.8-10: 'Again, the devil taketh him up into an exceeding high mountain, and sheweth him all the kingdoms of the world, and the glory of them …'). The biblical tone then gives way to the sentimentality of chivalry, as Wolfe quotes from Longfellow's famous 1841 poem 'Excelsior' – the story of a young man who journeys higher and higher into the mountains. Finally there is a return to reality – or at least to Xenophon's parasangs, and to the Greek words used to mark Cyrus' march through Asia: 'From there he progresses –' – another phrase that exercised a strong hold on those subjected to the *Anabasis* at school, playing a similar role to parasangs in debates over Xenophon's use as a text for beginners.[20]

Wolfe's technique in this passage is strongly influenced by the writings of James Joyce. The particular technique Wolfe was imitating was the breakdown of continuous narrative through the insertion of literary quotations and snatches of colloquial speech. While in London, Wolfe had been briefly introduced to Joyce, and he had another chance meeting with him during a visit to Brussels: 'the idea of Joyce and me being at Waterloo at the same time, and aboard a sight-seeing bus, struck me as insanely funny: I sat on the back seat making idiot noises in my throat ... .' It was his admiration for Joyce that reduced Wolfe to 'crooning': he thought that the best writing in English in his lifetime had been done by Joyce in *Ulysses*, and he was later to describe his own first novel as his *'Ulysses* book'. Joyce had even inserted Xenophon's parasangs in his Dublin: *'En avant, mes enfants!* Fire away number one on the gun. Burke's! Thence they advanced five parasangs. Slattery's mounted foot where's that bleeding awfur?'[21]

So who thinks the sentences of Wolfe's literary re-Joyce-ing? Scholars have debated whether the poetic quotations that are sprinkled liberally throughout Wolfe's novel reflect the perspective of the developing Eugene or the more distant and impersonal viewpoint of the elder narrator. Here, the leap from the opening words of the *Anabasis* to the shout of the sea does seem to express the schoolchild's desire to escape from the dullness of the Greek lesson. More particularly, the leap suggests the hunger that is one of the distinctive hallmarks of the young Eugene/Wolfe – the hunger to seize everything in a moment, to capture all of experience at once. At the same time, Wolfe's perspective is detached. The allusion to St Matthew's gospel is ironized by the biblical context: on that exceeding high mountain, the devil saith unto Jesus, 'All these things will I give thee, if thou wilt fall down and worship me' – and saith Jesus unto him, 'Get thee hence, Satan.' So too with the invocation of 'Excelsior': that poem ends with the chivalrous hero succumbing to an icy death. The irony is increased by the invocation of Xenophon's parasangs. The parasangs formula in Xenophon is always followed by a point of arrival: the name of a town or river, a fixed point of rest. Wolfe undoes this sense of direction. His parasangs are followed by a dash. And then the parasangs themselves drop away, and we are left with the Greek formula for Cyrus' progression, sans parasangs – and then another –. Wolfe strips away the excitement of 'O the sea! The sea!', bringing the reader back to the early stages of Cyrus' march upcountry, closing finally on aimless movement. By the end of the classroom scene, then, this detached perspective hints that Eugene may be just as much a mouthpiece of platitudes as his teacher.[22]

Xenophon's parasangs acquire a direction in the long Greek quotation that opens Chapter 21 of *O Lost*: ἐντεῦθεν ἐξελαύνει σταθμούς τρεῖς παρασάγγας πεντεκαίδεκα ἐπὶ τὸν Εὐφράτην ποταμόν ('From there he progresses three stages, fifteen parasangs, to the river Euphrates'). The start of the sentence picks up the end of the classroom session six chapters earlier: 'From there he progresses –'. But now Cyrus has progressed to the river Euphrates – and Eugene himself has arrived at a figurative river. 'Still prison-pent', he has turned to the inspirational teaching of Mr Leonard's wife Margaret, who 'saw the hunger and the pain' and 'fed him – majestic crime! – on poetry'. 'His thirst was drunken, insatiate': 'it was an age of glorious discovery', as Eugene, now fifteen, comes to know 'almost every major lyric in the language', and some Schiller and Heine on top of that. And part of Eugene's discovery lies in a deeper feeling for Xenophon: 'He committed to memory the entire passage in the *Anabasis*, the mounting and triumphal Greek which described the moment when the starving remnant of the Ten Thousand had come at length to the sea, and sent up their great cry, calling it by name.' 'Starving remnant'? Wolfe here exaggerates, and the force of his romantic distortion is to suggest a parallel with Eugene's spiritual hunger – and to mark a stage in Eugene's own progression to the night scene on the Virginia beach where he greets the sea in 'triumphant loneliness after pain and love and hunger'.[23]

We have seen how Xenophon serves Wolfe's ambition to write a *Künstlerroman* – a novel of the development of the literary artist. But how does Eugene's personal development support Wolfe's vision of a 'terrible and obscure hunger' that 'haunts and hurts Americans'? Before the beach scene in Virginia, Wolfe speaks of 'the hunger for voyages, the hunger that haunts Americans, who are a nomad race'. Wolfe seems to claim on the one hand that Eugene's hunger marks him out as special – as an artist in the making – but on the other that this hunger is quintessentially American. And Eugene's hunger can even be 'half-assuaged' in the 'maelstrom of the war', that is, by his patriotic service in the armaments industry.[24]

To understand this paradox we need to look further at how Xenophon is used to mark Eugene's progression to the twin achievements of artistic creativity and Americanhood. The *Anabasis* makes its next appearance in the section of *O Lost* that is most closely modelled on *Ulysses* – the virtuoso description of the banter between Eugene and some of his classmates as they return home at the end of the schoolday. This chapter is littered with literary fragments culled from canonical authors – Virgil, Shakespeare, Milton, Gray, Coleridge – and from popular fiction (Whitman is juxtaposed with the dime novel, for instance, when the boys spot a hearse: '"Another redskin bit the dust," said George Graves. Come, delicate death, serenely arriving, arriving'). The allusion to Xenophon comes early in the scene, as Eugene's classmates joke that he will one day be a high-ranking lawyer or even governor, and he is 'touched in the moment by the lonely fellowship of men':

> Sounded afar, farfaint, deep in his wooded heart, the lost and dying music of a horn. The memory of great doors, the sacrament of forgotten speechless words ... winged their bright shadows through Eugene's brain with their unspoken sentences of release and restoration.
> The life so short, the craft so long to learn. ... A train, far down a distant valley wailed to the east. Thalatta! Thalatta! He nailed to the wind his heart.

Here we seem to hear in that echo of the Ten Thousand's shout the fruits of Mrs Leonard's encouragement – a personal sense of exultation, Eugene/Wolfe delighting (with a nod to Chaucer) in his own creativity.

That initial impression is, however, complicated by the sound that precedes and ushers in 'Thalatta! Thalatta!' – the wailing of a train.[25]

O Lost is haunted by the sound of train whistles. During the early development of the American railroad, many writers had evoked the sudden sound of a whistle as a symbol of the incursion of the industrial machine into the pristine American garden. Wolfe's whistles arouse altogether different emotions. They tend to be heard in the distance: in the previous chapter, after another of Mr Leonard's *sententiae* ('"The mountains," observed John Dorsey, touched, in a happy moment, by the genius of the place, "have been the traditional seat of liberty"'), Eugene 'turned his face towards the western ranges. He heard, far off, a whistle, a remote thunder on the rails.' They are also often heard at night: after Eugene visits his brother Ben's tomb, for instance, 'in the frosty dark, farfaint, there was the departing wail of a whistle'. Here, the baroque 'farfaint' creates a link with the schoolboys returning home ('Sounded afar, farfaint, deep in his wooded heart ...'), and again with Eugene on the beach in Virginia, where 'a vast aerial music, forever farfaint, like the language of his forgotten world, sounded in his ears'. If, then, one reads the train whistles as a wistful signal of something lost, forgotten, the echo of the Greeks' shout of the sea sounds like an expression more of longing and nostalgia than of triumphant artistic self-celebration.[26]

The profusion of train whistles in *O Lost* stems from one of Thomas Wolfe's deepest private obsessions. He made many jottings about trains and their sounds in his notebooks and spoke of them frequently to his friends. The fascination sprang from a childhood sense of being imprisoned by the mountains that surrounded his home town, Asheville. His editor Maxwell Perkins recalled how it was only when he first travelled to Asheville that he got a sense of how strongly Wolfe's imagination had been shaped by this sense of geographical imprisonment: 'it was this perhaps – and hearing the trains wind out around the labyrinthine mountain walls – that gave him his first great continental vision of America which was always his obsession.' Perkins recalled, too, that once, when Wolfe was meant to be doing some cuts to *O Lost*, he appeared at the Scribner's office with new material instead – a description of one of his sisters hearing train whistles at night; and again how Wolfe spoke of Grand Central Station as the place in New York that he loved best. Wolfe's German publisher confirmed Perkins' observation: Wolfe told him how he had heard at home 'the trains going north in the nighttime', and 'they had always tempted him to go north too, into the darkness of the big cities'; or again how when he was abroad 'an overwhelming stream of nostalgic memories would reveal to him the peculiar characteristics of America – how differently the locomotives whistled there and the trains thundered over the bridges'.[27]

Trains were not just a private obsession for Wolfe. Though the railroad whose whistles he recalled from his childhood was a branch line that

3. 'The Hound of Darkness'?: the transcontinental train as enigmatic image of continental expansion.

reached Asheville in 1880, his focus on trains also builds on the profound significance of the Pacific railroad in perceptions of the American continent in the second half of the nineteenth century. Early promoters of the railroad wrote of it in visionary terms as a way of binding together Europe, America, and Asia: 'Make this road across the American continent, and you will have a millennium of peace on earth.' Later, trains heading from right to left (that is, from east to west) appeared in paintings, realistic or allegorical, of *Across the Continent* and *American Progress*. Wolfe himself gave remarkable expression to this vision in a short story published in *Vogue* in 1938 as 'A Prologue to America'. The story opens with a self-consciously cinematic vision: 'SCENE: A night of dazzling light above America.' The vision 'sweeps the planetary distance of the continent', then 'nears and deepens', scanning the continent. It starts, however, with the same juxtaposition of sea and train found in *O Lost*:

> And now, for the first time, ... a sound is heard. ... it is the sea, that feathers constantly upon the shores of time and darkness – and America. ...
>   The sea –
>   It is the sea – the sea
>   It is the sea – the sea
>   It is the sea – the sea
>   The sea – the sea – the sea
> The vision nears and deepens once again. Faintly, mournfully, infinitely far away, the cry of a great train is heard, as it wails back across America. ... The scene nears and deepens with terrific instancy – the train is now heard plainly: it is the great *Pacific Nine* stroking the night with the pistoned velocity of its full speed ... smashing westward through Nebraska.

Here the (mounting and triumphal?) invocation of the sea and the overt allusion to the transcontinental railroad brings out with a bluster what is intimated in the quieter play on 'Thalatta! Thalatta!' in *O Lost*. And yet there is also a hint of ambiguity in the enigmatic title that Wolfe himself had wanted to give the story – 'The Hound of Darkness', with its hint of Conrad's portrayal of the horror, the horror, at the heart of another continent.[28]

Further echoes of Xenophon – and another train whistle – appear in the scene where the stirrings of this political dimension are heard for the first time in *O Lost*. On a visit with his mother to Washington, DC, for the inauguration of Woodrow Wilson (the President who led the country into the First World War and dominated the post-war peace talks), Eugene is first comforted by seeing the Congressional Library, where 'there is a copy of every book in the world'; and then thrilled at night by the fireworks on Capitol Hill:

> Proud victory, imperial and invincible might, swung through heaven. ... Eugene was touched with the glory of Rome. ... There was the wail of a train in Virginia, and the great dome – absolute, enduring, tranquil, and imperial – brooded above him. He believed in the power, the beauty, and the honor of his country. All that had been told him of her triumphs was true – and more. She could never know defeat. She was chosen of God. He had a moment of pity for people born of other nations, a moment of unreality as he tried to

4. 'At the head of triumphant legions' – like the conquering general in Thomas Cole's vision of imperial greatness.

41

imagine himself as an Englishman, a German, a Dago, a strange dizzy moment when he felt again the mysterious governance of destiny which had singled him out by making him American, which would lead him yet up that proud avenue at the head of triumphant legions. From there they proceeded twenty parasangs.

Here, inspired by the very setting on the Capitol, Wolfe evokes the myth of the United States as heir to republican Rome – while transforming the traditional political narrative through Eugene's militaristic vision of himself leading the triumphant legions like a Roman general. From America as heir to classical antiquity, it is then a short step to America as chosen nation. Wolfe brings out, too, the strong racial component in this American self-image: paradoxically, in the very act of dismissing the English and the Germans, he bolsters the Anglo-Saxon and Teutonic racial identities that underlay the dominant American national consciousness by his dismissive reference to the southern European as a 'Dago'. And then those twenty parasangs ... . The final sentence takes us back to the classroom scene in the previous chapter – and poses again the question of narrative perspective. Those twenty parasangs could be what Eugene thought at the time as he watched the inauguration – or they could reflect the more detached perspective of the narrator. If they are what Eugene thought, he seems again to be mapping the march of American destiny onto the march of Xenophon's Greeks. But those parasangs can also be read as undercutting the myth of American exceptionalism: the narrator satirizes Eugene as he collapses together the triumphant march of the legions with the weary effort required to produce that triumph, inflamed once more by what the poet and critic John Peale Bishop diagnosed as the attempt to endow the immensity of the moment with some sort of transcendental meaning.[29]

A jotting from Wolfe's notebook, March 1927: 'This is my own, my native land. I'd rather write than be president.' Flash forward a decade to Wolfe looking back on his first set of good reviews: 'I felt, like Tamerlane, that it was passing great to be a king, and ride in triumph through Persepolis – and be a famous man.'[30]

*

In November 1926, as he wrote the early chapters of *O Lost*, Thomas Wolfe described in a letter to Aline Bernstein how, when he was ten years old, he had read himself 'blind and dizzy in all romantic legendry' (the *Iliad* and *Odyssey*, the Algers, the Hentys), and how he would imagine himself 'the bronzed young Yank, ... the wonder of the world, adventurously adrift across Europe, Asia, South America – the vanquisher of Dago armies'. Here we see the same sense of racial superiority that Wolfe later attributes to Eugene Gant as he watches the presidential inauguration – and also an attempt to explain that feeling of superiority through the ideological hold of the books Eugene/Wolfe read as a child. Wolfe exposes the same racial hierarchy in the autobiographical notes he wrote in preparation for his novel: 'History – the history we read later – The Liberty Boys of '76 – "The Red Coats" – One American good as 3 Englishmen – 7 Mexicans.' And he carried this theme over to the novel itself, describing Eugene 'deep in the weekly adventures of Young Wild West', 'steeping himself in all the gore of Saxon-Danish warfare', and reading the *Iliad* and *Odyssey* at the same time as 'Diamond Dick' and 'Buffalo Bill' – 'and for the same reason'. He even traces books' potential for racial indoctrination back to an age before he could read: the images within books were potent enough. And it is in elaborating this thesis that he returns to one of the books he mentioned, as we saw earlier, in the early part of his autobiographical jottings – *Ridpath's History* – and with it to the story told by Xenophon in his *Anabasis*.[31]

Ridpath's History of the World was a publishing phenomenon – and a great symbol of American aspiration. It was a splendidly illustrated multi-volume work that was sold by subscription only to allow a broad middle-class to purchase it in instalments. It makes its appearance in *O Lost* when Eugene is portrayed lying 'with well-lined belly before the roasting vitality of the fire, poring insatiably over the great volumes in the bookcase': 'The books he delighted in most were three huge calfskin volumes called *Ridpath's History of the World*. Their numberless pages were illustrated with hundreds of drawings, engravings, woodcuts: he followed the progression of the centuries pictorially before he could read.' And what delighted him most of all were 'the pictures of battle' – the kings of Egypt riding in their chariots, the bearded Assyrian kings, the walls of Babylon. 'His brain swarmed with pictures – Cyrus directing the charge, the spear-forest of the Macedonian phalanx, the splintered oars, the numberless huddle of the ships at Salamis, the feasts of Alexander, the terrific melee of the knights ... the gloomy forests of Gaul, and Caesarean conquests.'[32]

The pictorial aspect of *Ridpath's History* was well represented by the scene from Xenophon that Wolfe isolates – Cyrus' charge at the battle of Cunaxa. The tumult of battle was captured in a close-up picture of some individual struggles in the foreground, while rows of spearmen were seen advancing against each other in the background (Fig. 5). For those who could read, the message of the images was supported by the vivid style: 'In the confused struggle in this part of the field Cyrus discerned at a distance the form of his brother, and shouting out, "TON ANDRA HORO" (I see the man), made a rash plunge in that direction to cut him down.' Here the vividness of Xenophon's own account is reproduced – and, like Xenophon, Ridpath sees the battle through western eyes: the shout that is reproduced is from Xenophon's Greek, not what the Persian Cyrus would actually have said.[33]

Wolfe's perception of the ideological undertones of his childhood immer-

5. 'I see the man!': the battle of Cunaxa in Ridpath's *History*,
the work that enthused the young Thomas Wolfe.

sion in antiquity is strikingly confirmed in an article by Walter Peirce, a
League of Nations official, published in the *Yale Review* in January 1926,
just before Wolfe started to plan *O Lost*. Entitled 'Classics on the Farm',
the article was a memoir of Peirce's childhood on a farm in southern Ohio
in the 1880s. Peirce recalled first how the Zulu war had stimulated him to
play at bush warfare with his brother; Buffalo Bill's Wild West Show then
turned their attention to bows and arrows; and when they reached Caesar,
they 'were already seasoned veterans'. The boys then studied Greek – and
the inevitable *Anabasis*, 'more or less a second edition of the Commentaries [i.e. Caesar's *Gallic War*], but the arms were different'. As the younger
brother, Walter was forced to play the Persians to his brother's Greeks.
They joined, however, in taking from the *Anabasis* a Greek war-cry ('with
total disregard for comparative theology … we whooped Zeus Soter') – and
'the fine drama of Cyrus's shout when he made for his brother in battle,
"Ton andra horo," did not escape us, and in the heat of battle we shrieked
it at each other indiscriminately'. But between the dramatic episodes
there were also the 'weary parasangs' – and 'none of the Ten Thousand
shouted "Thalassa, thalassa" with more enthusiasm than we did when
from a lonely height we descried the end of the fourth book'. Peirce's
light-hearted account is structured by a set of analogies: the British are to
Zulus what cowboys are to Indians, Romans to Gauls, Greeks to Persians.
As in Wolfe, we see how a supposedly humane classical education could be
made subservient to a racist and militarist ideology of western superiority

– and we see, too, the *Anabasis* itself reduced to an opposition of parasangs and sea enlivened by a few picturesque interludes.[34]

Wolfe's account of his childhood forays into the past also brings out a larger point about the orientation of *Ridpath's History* and its like. The western perspective of the account of the battle of Cunaxa was embedded not just in that one scene, but in the very structure of the work. Ridpath's first volume began with Egypt, and then switched to Mesopotamia, tracing 'the natural course of events from the Euphrates to the Tiber – from Babylon to Rome'. Here Ridpath naturalized historical shifts of power through the geographical progression of rivers from east to west: his unstated premise is the westward path of empire – first to Britain, then across the Atlantic to the United States. Wolfe captures Ridpath's historical vision by making the young Eugene drool over depictions of civilizations clashing – the Greek victory in the Persian Wars, Alexander's conquest of the Persian empire. Implicit in his account of the young Eugene's fascination with pictures of battle is the conventional notion of a succession of empires. Indeed, even though Eugene's brain 'swarmed' with pictures in no clear chronological order (Cyrus' charge in 401 BC, then seventy years forward to Alexander, then a century and a half back to Salamis, then Alexander again), he is still said to be able to follow 'the progression of the centuries pictorially'. Nor is this claim absurd: Ridpath did in fact use pictures to anchor his teleological scheme. As his account nears the end of the Persian empire, on three successive double-spreads the whole of one page is devoted to a picture: first, 'The Return of the Ten Thousand under Xenophon' – or, more precisely, the scene where the Greeks catch sight of the sea, with one of the soldiers shown in a gesture of religious awe (Fig. 11); then 'The Victory of Alexander the Great on the Granicus' – after Le Brun's painting in the Louvre; and finally 'Alexander discovers the body of Darius'. This pictorial lavishness, which is unparalleled in the rest of the work, marks and celebrates the decisive shift from Persia to Greece, from Asia to Europe.[35]

*

As Thomas Wolfe neared the completion of *O Lost*, he turned back to the beginning to write a prologue. The prologue (which ran to some 20,000 words) was to help complete what he saw as the 'two essential movements' of his novel – 'one outward and one downward': 'The outward movement describes the effort of a child, a boy, and a youth for release, freedom, and loneliness in new lands. ... The downward movement is represented by a constant excavation into the buried life of a group of people, and describes the cyclic curve of a family's life.' The prologue was to be part of the downward movement – an excavation into the past of Eugene's father. And Xenophon was to be used to propel the downward just as much as the outward movement: Wolfe entitled the whole prologue 'Anabasis'.[36]

The first scene in the prologue is the one that 'excited and delighted' Maxwell Perkins – the account of two boys (Eugene's father Oliver and his brother) watching the ragged rebels tramping past to Gettysburg. The scene is a *tour de force* in its own right, but also important for understanding the development of Eugene Gant's story. The Civil War setting is emblematic of the conflicts of the Gant household: as the Yankee Oliver offers water to the thirsty soldiers, he glimpses in the Confederate line the strange figure of Bacchus Pentland, preacher of the second coming – and uncle of his future wife. The tensions in Wolfe's own upbringing are prefigured through the opposition between North and South. And one of the sources of the tensions in the Gant household is also brought out by that road that leads to Gettysburg: as Eugene's father gazes at 'the scarecrow gallantry of the ragged men', he feels an 'obscure and passionate hunger for voyages' – the same hunger that had led his father from England to the east coast of America, and then 'westward' into Pennsylvania. Oliver is led by this hunger to turn to the South ('not towards a land, but towards a desire'), and then, two marriages later, 'alone and lost again', to resume 'his aimless drift across the continent', turning 'westward towards the great fortress of the hills, ... hoping that he might find in them isolation, a new life, and recovered health'. He travels first by train, then by coach, and as he approaches the mountains that ring the town that is to become his home, 'he could see little dots of men laying the track that would coil across the hill towards Altamont'. Wolfe's 'Anabasis' starts, then, with the march of an army – and then broadens to embrace the hunger that drives the Gants further into the interior, following the course of the railroad. As he maps the westward march of empire in terms of Xenophon's march inland, Wolfe sets that expansion against the catastrophic Civil War while also unearthing the seeds of the hunger that later afflicts Eugene – and all Americans.[37]

The opening scene of Wolfe's 'Anabasis' is itself preceded by a haunting lyric:

> ... a stone, a leaf, an unfound door; of a stone, a leaf, a door. And of all the forgotten faces.
> Naked and alone we come into exile. In her dark womb we did not know our mother's face: from the prison of her flesh have we come into the unspeakable and incommunicable prison of this earth ...
> ... Which of us has not remained forever prison-pent? Which of us is not forever a stranger and alone? ...
> ... Remembering speechlessly we seek the great forgotten language, the lost lane-end into heaven, a stone, a leaf, an unfound door. Where? When?
> O lost, and by the wind grieved, ghost, come back again.

This prelude introduces many of the central images and themes of the novel. Time and again in the course of the novel the themes of exile, escape, solitude, and loss return – and often in language as richly lyrical as the opening lines. The language of loneliness and loss returns, for instance, in one of the key Xenophontic passages – the scene on the beach in Virginia: 'There by the sea of the dark Virginias he thought of the forgotten faces, of all the million patterns of himself, the ghost of his lost flesh. … Why die we so many deaths? How came I here beside the sea? O lost, O far and lonely, where?' It is in this scene, too, that Wolfe resolves the tension in narrative perspective that runs through the earlier parts of the novel: 'O sea! (he thought) I am the hillborn, the prison-pent … .' Here at last Eugene explicitly uses 'the same kind of rhetorical flourish that we have seen the narrator use throughout the book'. He has grown into the man who can write *O Lost*.[38]

After the prologue, Wolfe turned back to the end of his novel. At the outset, he had considered carrying the story much further: 'Should the book end abroad or at home?' In the event, he ended in the town square of Altamont with an extraordinary scene where Eugene converses with his dead brother Ben. Eugene/Wolfe has become the creative artist, able to recover through words images of his dead brother; images of his own past, too, as he stands 'peopling the night with the great lost legion of himself'; and ultimately, too, images of that other legion of the lost, the Confederate army treading to defeat, and of the rest of the cast of *O Lost*. Eugene has also set out on his journey into the interior: 'he stood upon the ramparts of his soul, before the lost land of himself. Heard inland murmurs of lost seas, the far interior music of the horns. The last voyage, the longest, the best.' Wolfe maps Eugene's self-discovery in spatial terms, while at the same time evoking through those 'inland murmurs', through the repeated insistence on loss, the lyrical opening of his 'Anabasis'. The novel closes as Eugene hears 'the whistle wail along the river' and turns his eyes 'upon the distant soaring ranges'. Eugene finds his escape from prison – but it is an escape into loss and darkness.[39]

Like the 'Anabasis' prologue, then, Wolfe's novel as a whole gestures to the great myths of American exceptionalism – the idea of America as chosen nation, innocent and invulnerable, destined to expand and agent of human progress – while hinting at how the expansion of America may be related to a feeling of psychological entrapment. But at the same time it undermines those myths. The door remains unfound, the lane-end lost.

*

Wolfe's subversive and ironic vision aligns him with the use of the An-abasis myth by other modernists. 'The Anabasis' was the title of a 1932 threnody by Allen Tate that ends with the haunting line 'death's long anabasis' (similar to Wolfe's 'the last voyage, the longest'). The motif reappears in *A Mask for Janus* (1952), the first collection of work by W.S. Merwin, one of the most distinguished American poets of the second half of the twentieth century. The book opens with two poems entitled 'Anabasis', both picturing dream-like journeys, boats drifting among islands, approaches to a new country, with hints of New World themes of rejuvenation amidst the plentiful fruit of paradise. There are suggestions, too, that the journey is a tentative poetic manifesto for a new generation: 'We turned from silence and fearfully made / Our small language in the place of night. / ... / We seek a new dimension for the world.' But the possibility of creating a new language seems to slip away as 'Anabasis (II)' ends with mind and body losing 'the uncertain continent of a name'. The very repetition of the title 'Anabasis', applied not to a heroic advance and retreat but to 'voyages with no destination disclosed', underlines the final failure. Like Thomas Wolfe, Merwin uses the idea of anabasis to suggest both a spiritual and a physical journey while at the same time denying the possibility of arrival.[40]

Both Tate and Merwin were influenced by one of the most renowned modernist products – the long 1924 poem *Anabasis* by Saint-John Perse, pseudonym of the Guadeloupe-born diplomat Alexis Saint-Léger Léger, which became well-known in the English-speaking world after a translation by T.S. Eliot was published in 1930. Perse's *Anabasis* is a highly elliptical sequence of ten cantos framed by short lyrics at the beginning and end. It tells the story of a leader who founds a city before embarking on what seems to be an expedition of conquest that moves ever westward over the vast plains of a nameless continent that is generally taken to be Asia (Perse composed the poem while stationed in China). Some readers have thought that the poem's occasionally Whitmanesque rhythms also hint at North America – anticipating the themes of the American epic *Winds* that Perse wrote after he left Vichy France for the United States. And others still have seen the location as Mexico or spoken of the central figure as a 'conquistador'. While attempts to pin down the poem's physical location are futile, Perse is concerned to establish its place within the western cultural tradition – both in its own right, as a repository of erudite allusions, and also as a reflection of western power: to give one example, 'The Place of the Dry Tree' mentioned in the lines cited at the start of this chapter alludes, through Marco Polo, to the supposed site of one of Alexander's victories over the Persian king Darius. Such allusions explain why Perse has often been seen as 'a poet of imperialism', asserting western domination over foreign lands – and so more similar to the crude panegyrists of the American anabasis than to the much more complex use of the motif by Thomas Wolfe and W.S. Merwin. Yet the key point that aligns Perse with Wolfe and Merwin is that his *Anabasis*, too, is a spiritual as well as a geographical voyage – 'a deliberate ambiguity', as he explained in a letter to T.S. Eliot. The journey across the nameless continent to 'the frontiers of the spirit' is an expression of the creativity of the poetic soul – and it ends on a similar note of restlessness (with a hint, too, of a Xenophontic return to the sea): 'Plough land of dream! Who talks of building? – I have seen the earth spread out in vast spaces and my thought is not heedless of the navigator.'[41]

Thomas Wolfe's own modernist 'Anabasis' did not survive the trimming of *O Lost* into *Look Homeward, Angel*. Desperate for publication, Wolfe yielded to Perkins' suggestion that the whole novel be cast through the perspective of the young Eugene. So while they retained the lyrical prelude as an epigraph, they cut almost all of the rest of the material dealing with the history of the Gant family before Eugene's birth. The cuts Perkins suggested removed from *O Lost* some of its encyclopedic ambition – its goal of offering a broad vision of American society. They removed, too, the thematic role played by Xenophon: of the many references to the *Anabasis* in *O Lost*, only half survived the editing – stripped of their power by their isolation, no longer part of the novel's downward and outward movements.[42]

O lost, and by the wind grieved ...

*

'Write the idea of America', Thomas Wolfe had proposed on a trip to Paris in the spring of 1925. Critics have been quick to accuse Wolfe of writing instead the idea of himself: John Peale Bishop, for instance, claimed that 'Wolfe came early on what was for him the one available truth about this continent – that it was contained in himself'. And while part of the blame for that accusation lies with the changes to *O Lost* imposed by Maxwell Perkins, it was also a criticism which Wolfe himself ultimately came to recognize: he came to be critical of his early vision of the artist 'trying to escape' from the world, and thought the hero of his novel had been too coloured by 'romantic aestheticism'. By 1938, after years of exposure to the poverty of the Depression, Wolfe's vision of America – and of himself – was darker and more complex: '– We've got to *loathe* America, as we loathe ourselves; with loathing, horror, shame, and anguish of the soul unspeakable – as well as with love –'.[43]

Underlying Wolfe's self-narrative was his experience of 1930s Germany. As we have seen, Germany was where Wolfe's first novel was most strongly praised. Germany was also the foreign land where Wolfe felt most at home. He was attracted by the manly bonding of the *Oktoberfest*, and was slow to acknowledge the threat posed by Hitler when he visited Berlin in 1935 and again in 1936 for the Olympics: 'The daily spectacle was overwhelming in its beauty and magnificence', making the 'gaudy decorations' of presidential inaugurations seem shoddy by comparison. And this even though he noted the signs of German militarism – 'the liquid smack of ten thousand leather boots as they came together, with the sound of war'. But he soon reacted against Hitler's Germany, describing in his great palinode, 'I Have a Thing to Tell You', an event he had witnessed on a train journey – the arrest of a Jew trying to cross the border with a hidden stash of money. Wolfe was perhaps aware that his appeal in *O Lost* to primitive and destructive energies was similar to the pseudo-Nietzschean ethic of the will to power that found perverted expression in Nazism. His awakened political consciousness was to be displayed in a new novel: 'the whole book might almost be called "You Can't Go Back Home Again" – which means back home to one's family, back home to one's childhood, back home to the father one has lost, back home to romantic love, to a young man's dreams of glory and of fame, back home to exile, to escape to "Europe" and some foreign land, ... back home to the escapes of Time and Memory.'[44]

In 1938 Thomas Wolfe accepted an invitation to lecture at Purdue University in Indiana. After the lecture, he ventured further west to Oregon, bonded over some beers with a couple of journalists, and joined them on a rapid road-trip through the great national parks of the West, capturing the speed in a series of notes written in the same loose style as his earlier jottings for *O Lost* ('– and so goodnight – and 500 miles today – ... and so to bed! And today 467 miles!'). Soon after the trip was over, he was taken ill with what turned out to be tuberculosis. He made his last train journey across the continent to Baltimore, where he died on 15 September, a couple of weeks short of his thirty-eighth birthday.[45]

After his death, a longer version of 'I Have a Thing to Tell You' was incorporated as the penultimate section of *You Can't Go Home Again*. The German episode was followed by a credo written in the form of a farewell to a figure based on Maxwell Perkins: 'I believe that we are lost here in America, but I believe we shall be found. ... I think the true discovery of America is before us. I think the true fulfillment of our spirit, of our people, of our mighty and immortal land, is yet to come. I think the true discovery of our own democracy is still before us.' Wolfe was here trying to fashion a new identity as a more socially conscious novelist, moving beyond his earlier obsession with the vastness of the American landscape and the concomitant rootlessness of the American individual. But he had in fact gone home again to the same myth of American exceptionalism that had driven the soldiers and explorers of the previous century who had conquered on foot and horseback the vast region that Wolfe whizzed through by car, admiring 'the pity, terror, strangeness, and magnificence of it all'.[46]

II

THE MARCH OF DESTINY

6. 'The American Xenophon': Alexander William Doniphan.

The American Xenophon:
Doniphan in Mexico

As the troops moved off majestically over the green prairie, they presented the most martial and animating sight. The long lines stretched over miles of level plain ... while the American eagle seemed to spread his broad pinions, and westward bear the principles of republican government ...

J. Hughes, *Doniphan's Expedition* (1847)

Getting upon some rising ground ... I obtained a fine view of the whole of the Mexican force; and ... as I turned from viewing that dense mass of soldiery to look at our little band as it came slowly but steadily on, my heart felt a little faint. ... But slowly and majestically above our heads sails America's bird, a large bald eagle. 'An omen! an omen!' runs through our ranks, and all eyes glance at him for a moment ...

F. Edwards, *A Campaign in New Mexico with Colonel Doniphan* (1847)[1]

* * *

When Washington Irving revised his *History of New York*, a pseudo-history of the city in its Dutch era published under the name Diedrich Knickerbocker, for a new edition in 1848, the America he was satirizing had undergone remarkable changes in the years since the work had first appeared in 1809. The American eagle had spread his wings towards Mexico, and the process of expansion gave a new topicality to a humorous allusion Irving had made to Xenophon. Irving had mocked the leading American general of the day, James Wilkinson, by inventing as leader of a Dutch expedition in the 1650s an officer named Jacobus Von Poffenburgh with a penchant for Xenophontic self-promotion: 'scarce had he departed for his station than bulletins began to arrive from him, describing his undaunted march through savage deserts, over insurmountable mountains, across impassable rivers and through impenetrable forests, conquering vast tracts of uninhabited country, and encountering more perils than did Xenophon in his far-famed retreat with his ten thousand Grecians.' Already present in the original edition, the analogy with Xenophon now had a stunning new resonance: in 1846 a group of Missouri volunteers under Alexander William Doniphan had led a long march across the American plains into northern Mexico, and their leader had returned the following year to find himself hailed throughout the United States as a new Xenophon. It is the progress of this march that we will now follow as we first explore how the Xenophontic label came to be applied to the Missouri troops, and then read the advance of this republican army through exotic lands in the West against Xenophon's account of the march of the Ten Thousand into Mesopotamia and their subsequent retreat to the Black Sea. The themes of our opening two chapters will come together as we follow an anabasis across the American continent that was also a march of conquest. First, however, we must briefly examine how Xenophon had come to be a powerful symbol in American public discourse even before his role was transformed by the nation's military successes in Mexico.[2]

Washington Irving's satirical reference to the *Anabasis* in 1809 depended upon Xenophon's established position as a classic. Xenophon's status can be seen already in the Revolutionary era. In a letter in 1763 the future President John Adams referred to Xenophon as his 'favourite author' and as an 'ancient and immortal husbandsman' – as if to make him conform to the American agrarian ideal. Adams later proposed that an engraving of Xenophon's famous 'Choice of Hercules' – the allegory whose terms Barack Obama followed in his inaugural address – should be used as the seal of the United States. And while that proposal was unsuccessful, an image of the scene was later adopted as emblem for the prestigious Whig society at Princeton (Fig. 7). The popularity of the Hercules allegory reflected the broader eighteenth-century admiration for Xenophon's philosophical writings, but the retreat of the Ten Thousand was also often invoked: during and after the War of Independence, for instance, it was cited as a parallel to Benedict Arnold's 1775 advance on Quebec through the wilds of Maine and to two of George Washington's celebrated marches – his 1776 retreat from New York to the shores of the icy Delaware and his surprise 1781 attack on Yorktown. These were, however, isolated allusions at a time when antiquity's strongest appeal lay in the civic virtue of Republican Rome.[3]

The analogy between Xenophon and Washington was reaffirmed just before the Mexican War by James Fenimore Cooper. In Cooper's 1843 novel *Wyandotté*, set during the Revolution, an English captain in a remote outpost becomes convinced that America will prevail when he first hears of Washington's retreat: 'Xenophon never did a better thing! The retreat of the ten thousand was boy's play to getting across that water.' Cut off with a small group in an isolated spot, the captain later hopes to emulate these two heroes ('I mean to place old Hugh Willoughby by the side of Xenophon and Washington') – only to die in the attempt. Xenophon's role was repeated in two other Cooper novels published at this time. His retreat had already been named as a source of inspiration for a stranded band in *The Pathfinder* (1840), a Leatherstocking novel set in the Seven Years' War – and here too the allusion was ironic: the soldier who appeals to Xenophon turns out to be a traitor. And in the 1845 novel *Satanstoe*, Xenophon is used to show up a pompous Reverend who claims

SOC: AMER. WHIG ad AMICITIAM LITERAS   MORES que colendas Inst: D. MDCCXIX.

OMNIBUS Litterarum STUDIOSIS

7. Virtue or pleasure? Xenophon supplies the emblem for the
Princeton Whig Society.

that an escape over an icy river matched the retreat of the Ten Thousand:
while admitting that he had not had to retreat 'thirty-four thousand, six
hundred and fifty stadia' (the distance given at the end of our manuscripts
of the *Anabasis*), he argues that 'acts are to be estimated more by quality,
than by quantity'. The satirical force depends on Xenophon's classic status,
as with Washington Irving and other writers who made comic use of
Xenophon. And yet in the first two novels at least the significance of
Cooper's choice of Xenophon goes much further than the superficial irony.
He was writing at a time when the frontiers of settlement were pushing
steadily westward. By setting his stories in the past and by using Xenophon in scenes where characters are trapped in confined spaces and
threatened from outside, he raises the possibility that contemporary
American expansion may be a solution to the terror of captivity – even
though he also views the passing of the old order with some melancholy.
The imperial anabasis to Mexico whose trail we will follow can be seen as
the flip-side of Cooper's vision of anabasis as escape.[4]

Xenophon's irruption into the fiction of James Fenimore Cooper in the
1840s is matched by his growing visibility in American education. It was
in the early 1830s that the *Anabasis* replaced *Graeca Majora* or *Minora*

(collections of short extracts) as the text most widely studied in the opening terms at colleges such as Harvard and Bowdoin, but it had not yet become the text generally read in schools. In 1840 Cornelius Felton, Professor of Greek at Harvard, still saw the need to defend the inclusion of extensive sections from Xenophon when he published a *Greek Reader* aimed at replacing its older rivals: he asserted that Xenophon's works, 'whether considered in relation to their moral tone, or to their literary elegance and transparent simplicity, ought to be studied at an early period by all classical scholars much more than they are'. It was not long, however, before Felton's wishes were realized: the 1840s saw the start of a boom in American school editions of the *Anabasis*, generally based on German models, and in time four books of the *Anabasis* and three books of the *Iliad* became the standard entrance requirement for colleges, maintained in many cases until the 1880s and sometimes longer. The numbers reading the work in Greek were still low: despite a large increase in the number of colleges in the first half of the nineteenth century, only about one per cent of white males aged 15-20 attended college. But the use of the *Anabasis* as a school text did lead to the dissemination of the story in other contexts, and the march of the Ten Thousand also received strong praise in the new breed of American-produced history primers aimed at a wider audience: it was described, for instance, in Emma Willard's 1835 *Universal History* as 'the most memorable retreat on record'. And the successful propagation of its fame in decades to come receives striking illustration in an article on Xenophon in the 1892 issue of the *African Methodist Episcopal Church Review*, where the retreat was called 'the greatest military feat upon the pages of history'.[5]

Xenophon's growing popularity in schools was marked by allusions to him in many American authors besides James Fenimore Cooper. While the school use of the *Anabasis* was inspired by developments in Germany, Cooper's distinctively American spatial awareness is also found in references to Xenophon in two other leading literary figures of the 1840s: Ralph Waldo Emerson and Henry David Thoreau. In Emerson's case, we know that he read the *Anabasis* in 1836 and soon began discussing it in public talks. Particularly notable are his remarks in an 1837 lecture on 'Manners' that were later incorporated in an essay on 'History' published in 1841. The task Emerson set himself was to explain the 'foundation of that interest all men feel in Greek history, letters, art and poetry' by suggesting that 'every man passes personally through a Grecian period'. To illustrate this 'Grecian state' when 'the spiritual nature unfolded in strict unity with the body', Emerson cited 'the picture Xenophon gives of himself and his compatriots in the Retreat of the Ten Thousand': 'After the army had crossed the river Teleboas in Armenia, there fell much snow, and the troops lay miserably on the ground covered with it. But Xenophon arose naked, and taking an axe, began to split wood; whereupon others rose and did the like.' Emerson concludes that we can all sympathize with

Xenophon's soldiers because they are 'a gang of great boys' – and we have all gone through a Greek phase in childhood.[6]

Emerson's remarks on the Greek spirit were influenced by his teacher Edward Everett, who had travelled in Greece and was a strong promoter of the cult of romantic Hellenism both at Harvard and in his later political career. There had been particularly strong interest in Greece in the 1820s during the fight for independence from Ottoman rule. Orators such as Everett and Daniel Webster promoted the Greeks' cause; charitable aid was organized by women sympathetic to their suffering; and while the possibility of sending American military help was rejected in Congress, a number of Americans did cross privately to fight for the Greeks. Philhellenic sentiment was also spread by English poets such as Byron and Shelley as well as by German New Humanism, with its idealization of Greek culture as a whole, embracing its art and architecture as well as the life of the mind. This interest in Greece marked a shift away from the classical republicanism of the previous generation, which had been focused more on Rome and on models of civic virtue rather than on a holistic vision of national spirit. What concerns us most here, however, is not so much how Emerson makes this romantic Hellenism serve his own transcendentalism as his decision to cite a scene where Xenophon cuts wood. While Xenophon emerges from his own account as a model leader, Emerson makes him instead an archetypal figure from the American frontier: wood-chopping was often shown in images of American progress pushing back the wilderness (for instance, the pediment on the Capitol devoted to 'The Progress of Civilization'), and it was also part of the frontier mystique that enveloped politicians such as Abraham Lincoln.[7]

Mention of Xenophon again suggests contact with the wilderness in Henry David Thoreau's account of *A Week on the Concord and Merrimack Rivers* (published in 1849 though written some years earlier). Thoreau digresses at one point to observe that 'a good share of our interest in Xenophon's story of his retreat is in the manoeuvres to get the army safely over the rivers, whether on rafts of logs or fagots, or sheepskins blown up'. Thoreau's comment seems to promote the *Anabasis* as a story of triumph over natural obstacles. And yet the fact that this short digression is so typical of Thoreau's book as a whole – only a tenth is devoted to the journey proper – signals his resistance to the grand narratives of American empire. Famous for refusing to pay his taxes as a protest against the invasion of Mexico, Thoreau here conveys his resistance to expansionism through his concluding reflection on the Ten Thousand: 'where could they better afford to tarry meanwhile than on the banks of a river?' He leaves us with the delightful image of the purported agents of Greek historical destiny pottering about by a river bank.[8]

The possibility of using Xenophon's canonical status to resist the dominant American ideology of spatial conquest was exploited even more powerfully in an abolitionist magazine, *The Anti-Slavery Record*. The front

THE

ANTI-SLAVERY RECORD.

Vol. III. No. VII.   JULY, 1837.   Whole No. 31.

This picture of a poor fugitive is from one of the stereotype cuts manufactured in this city for the southern market, and used on handbills offering rewards for runaway slaves.

8. A runaway slave – more heroic than the
'murderous old Greeks'.

page of an 1837 issue carried an illustration of a woodcut figure of a runaway slave (Fig. 8). The article beneath proceeded to reclaim the image (typically used in recovery notices) as heroic: 'To escape from a powerful enemy, often requires as much courage and generalship as to conquer. One of the most celebrated military exploits on record is the *retreat* of the ten thousand Greeks under Xenophon, for a great distance through an enemy's country. The sympathy of the reader is wonderfully drawn out for these disappointed Greeks … .' Praise for the military exploit has turned silently to praise for Xenophon's account – which then turns to irony as the Greeks are described as 'returning chop-fallen and wofully beset from their unsuccessful attempt to put one Asiatic despot on the throne of another'. This classical paradigm is then trumped by another exploit that is 'far more worthy of being placed upon record' – 'the retreat of the ten thousand native Americans now living safely in Upper Canada, escaping from worse than Asiatic tyranny and having to pass, hungry and hunted, through the wide domains of false freedom'. The dominant racial attitudes at this time can be illustrated by an account the following year of the

3. The American Xenophon: Doniphan in Mexico

'interminable' war against 'savages' in Florida living in a country 'inhabitable only by themselves, and where Xenophon's army could not displace them' (that is, *not even* Xenophon's army ...). In the *Anti-Slavery Record* these paradigms are overturned – and the attack on the conventional status of classical antiquity is further bolstered by moral and religious concerns: 'We trust, too, that in a land of Christians these peaceful fugitives will not receive less sympathy than those murderous old Greeks, in their brazen helmets and bull-hide shields.' Here it is not, as with Washington Irving, the habit of citing the Ten Thousand that is pilloried: the invective is directed at the soldiers themselves. But here too the power of the invective depends on its subverting their conventional status as models of heroic endeavour.[9]

We have seen, then, that Xenophon became even more firmly established as a cultural icon in the years between the publication of the first and final editions of *Knickerbocker's History of New York* – and the rest of this chapter will show how this positive image had become further entrenched during the Mexican War. But while Irving left the possible new allusion to American self-praise in the Mexican War implicit, he did make one alteration to the Xenophon passage – and in doing so he highlighted the key transformation in American culture that made appeals to Xenophon so popular during the Mexican War. His satire of Jacobus Von Poffenburgh had originally been mixed with burlesque: the Dutch general was described 'overturning, discomfiting and making incredible slaughter of certain hostile hosts of grass-hoppers, toads and pismires, which had gathered together to oppose his progress – an achievement unequalled in the pages of history, save by the farfamed retreat of old Xenephon [*sic*] and his ten thousand Grecians'. In later editions the grass-hoppers and toads disappeared, but the Xenophon analogy was made to stem from Von Poffenburgh himself: the general now encountered 'more perils, according to his own account, than did ever the great Xenophon in his far-famed retreat'. That change was perhaps made because James Wilkinson, the model for the invented Dutchman, had in the meantime published his strongly apologetic *Memoirs*, which included an appeal to Xenophon to show that even the best generals had some failures. The 1848 edition then sharpened the satire further by altering the form of the general's boastful account: 'scarce had he departed for his station than bulletins began to arrive from him ... .' By changing a single narrative into a series of bulletins, Irving made Von Poffenburgh indulge in instantaneous self-glorification. As well as helping the humour, however, those bulletins were a reflection on the profound technological changes within America in the 1830s and 1840s. Thanks to the spread of railroads and telegraphic communication, news now spread much faster. Development in printing also led to a vast expansion of the newspaper industry: by the late 1840s there were over 2,500 newspapers in the United States. These technological advances allowed the nationalist feeling inspired by the war against

Mexico to be even more strongly expressed. And nowhere was the new patriotic fervor more apparent than in the cult of celebrity that was created as the heroes of the war returned home.[10]

*

One Friday morning early in July 1847 thousands of the inhabitants of St Louis, Missouri, were gathered in front of the Planter's House Hotel and in the streets that surrounded it. The atmosphere was festive: flags were out and bells were ringing in the churches and fire-stations. The festivities were in honour of Missouri's new heroes – a regiment of volunteers that had just returned from a year's service in the war against Mexico. Since the previous Sunday the volunteers had been arriving by boat from New Orleans; their leader, Alexander Doniphan, had come in on Wednesday. And now, just as Judge James Butler Bowlin, a Democrat member of the House of Representatives, was about to start his welcoming address, another ship, the *Pride of the West*, was seen approaching. On board were more volunteers and some artillery captured back in February at Sacramento. The celebrations were put on hold until the new arrivals had disembarked, and then Judge Bowlin began to speak, praising a 'heroic adventure' that had 'more the character of romance than reality'. His remarks were followed by a procession to the outskirts of the city, along streets lined with cheering onlookers, with women waving handkerchiefs from the windows and balconies above. The stage was now set for the chief orator of the day – Thomas Hart Benton.[11]

Benton was one of the most prominent figures in American political life in the first half of the nineteenth century. Democratic Senator for Missouri since 1820, he was 'the most fervent advocate of America's role in the westward thrust of civilization', driven by utopian fantasies of trade links with Asia. Benton had, however, initially been opposed to the war with Mexico, which had developed from a dispute over Texas. Since the early 1820s the Mexican government had allowed American settlers in Texas, but these settlers soon formed the majority and demanded independence. A successful war with Mexico led to the formation of a Texan republic in 1836, and nine years later, just before the new President James Polk entered office, the annexation of Texas was pushed through – much to the Mexicans' dismay. To add to their anger, the boundary claimed for the new state was the Rio Grande, over a hundred miles south of the traditional border. Opposing armies soon gathered on either side of the border and fought. Benton viewed the US army rather than the Mexicans as the invaders, but nonetheless supported the war when it was under way: he was even proposed by Polk as lieutenant-general of the army in Mexico. And now, with the war still in progress, the great advocate of westward expansion had been chosen to praise the troops who had helped to make that expansion a reality.[12]

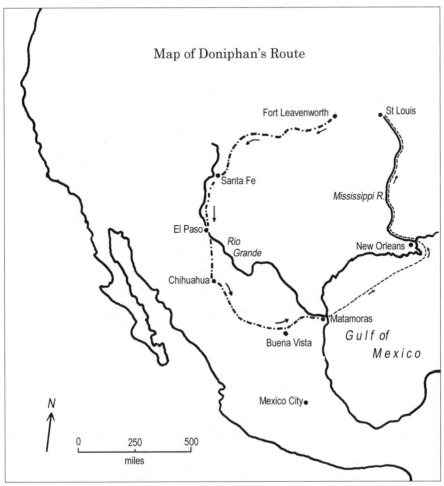

Map of Doniphan's Route

It was a short speech – a little over an hour – and one of Benton's best, in the judgement of a later expansionist President, Theodore Roosevelt. Most of the speech was devoted to an account of the Missourians' 'almost fabulous expedition': they had made 'a circuit equal to the fourth of the circumference of the globe' and returned with 'trophies taken from fields, the names of which were unknown to yourselves and your country, until revealed by your enterprise, illustrated by your valor, and immortalized by your deeds'. He began by telling how the Missouri volunteers had marched a thousand miles for the conquest of New Mexico. 'So lately the ultima thule – the outside boundary of speculation and enterprise', that state had become a new point of departure: the troops forced the 'numerous and savage tribe of the Navaho Indians' to form a peace treaty, and then advanced to the 'beautiful little town' of El Paso del Norte, defeating a Mexican force en route on Christmas day. For all its charms, El Paso had

61

Charge of Capⁿ Reid at Sacramento with the Moⁿ Vols

9. 'One of the military marvels of the age': the Missouri
volunteers' charge at Sacramento.

not been 'a Capua' to the men of Missouri (Benton was implying a contrast
with the degeneration of Hannibal's Carthaginian army when it set up a
base in southern Italy after crossing the Alps and defeating the Romans
at Cannae). The Missourians had next struck on Chihuahua, clearing the
road by the battle of Sacramento, 'one of the military marvels of the age'.
Installed in Chihuahua, they were 'about as far from St Louis as Moscow
is from Paris' – another hint of a contrast with a famous historical
precedent, Napoleon's disastrous invasion of Russia a generation earlier.
Chihuahua, like Santa Fé before it, became the beginning point of a new
journey – this time to join the main American army under Zachary Taylor,
ready to march anywhere, even to 'the "halls of the Montezumas"' if need
be. As it was, the volunteers – 'the rough, the ready, and the ragged' – had
to return home. But home was still more than 2,000 miles away – though
most of that return journey would be accomplished by water.[13]

It was as Benton neared the end of his speech that he suggested a
contrast with another famous march, more successful than either Hannibal's or Napoleon's. The Missourians, Benton claimed, hardly counted the
final stretch by water in their recital of their march – but

62

this is an unjust omission, and against the precedents as well as unjust. 'The ten thousand' counted the voyage on the Black Sea as well as the march from Babylon; and twenty centuries admit the validity of the count. The present age, and posterity, will include in 'the going out and coming in' of the Missouri-Chihuahua volunteers, the water voyage as well as the land march, and then the expedition of the one thousand will exceed that of the ten by some two thousand miles.

Benton then drew to a close, Doniphan responded on behalf of the volunteers, and the citizens of St Louis put on a good feast for their new heroes.[14]

Benton's rhetoric reveals an ambivalence towards antiquity typical of Americans of his time. He appeals to an illustrious example from antiquity, implicitly justifying his claim that the Missourians' march will have the same claim on posterity that the Greeks have on contemporaries. At the same time, however, he trumps antiquity by playing on an equally American obsession: size. What America seemed to lack in history it made up in size: acts were estimated by quantity as well as by quality. This quantitative one-upmanship over classical antiquity was also found in comments on natural features: referring (without quoting it) to Xenophon's modest description of a river in Armenia as 'beautiful but not large', a geographical work published in 1853 alleged that Xenophon had exerted all his powers to render the Teleboas 'immortal' – and yet this river was 'insignificant' when 'compared with the Mississippi and Missouri'. A similar claim can be found in an imaginary dialogue between an American and a European boy published in a school textbook that year: 'as for your great Vesuvius, we have a Niagara that would put it out in half a minute.' So too, Benton implies, the Missouri troops put out the flame of Xenophon's Greeks by virtue of having travelled 2,000 miles further.[15]

Benton bends the historical record to suit his purpose. Did the Ten Thousand count the voyage on the Black Sea as well as their earlier march on land (Benton's figure must in fact include the march *to* – as well as from – Babylon)? We do not know. We only have the story told by one of their number, Xenophon – and while our manuscripts of the *Anabasis* end with a final figure for the length of the journey (11,150 parasangs or 34,255 stades), that passage is a later interpolation in the text, not written by Xenophon himself. What we can at least say on the Greeks' behalf is that the proportion of their travels made on water was far smaller – nearer a tenth rather than a third.

*

For Alexander Doniphan, the lanky commander of the Missouri volunteers, the St Louis reception was merely the start of a season of celebrations. He gave a two-hour oration at Gallatin, and another speech in Independence in front of 5,000 people. On that occasion the local women had prepared a laurel wreath – 'in every age and every clime, the gift of beauty to valor'. Before kneeling to receive the wreath on behalf of the volunteers, Doniphan's heroism was extolled in a speech delivered by one of the women: after evoking the glories of antiquity, and Leonidas at Thermopylae in particular, Mrs Buchanan reflected that 'the mantle of desolation now wraps the mouldering pillars of Athens and of Rome, and fame deserting her ancient haunts, now fills our own fair land with the matchless deeds of her heroic sons'. But again the United States could claim to surpass the ancients: the bloodthirsty soldiers of Sparta, Athens, and Rome had made war their life, while the Missouri volunteers had hurried from 'the quiet labors of the field' to encounter perils 'that would make the cheek of a Roman soldier turn pale'. And now that they were home, 'the triumph which hailed the return of the Caesars, to whose war-chariot was chained the known world, is not ours to give; nor do you need it': the Missourians had 'a prouder triumph than Rome could bestow' in the 'undying fame' of their proud achievements. The 'fairer part of creation' (as the speaker called them) here joined the local men in a display of patriotism that drew in both speech and action (the laying of the wreath on Doniphan's brow) on ancient modes of communal celebration.[16]

Over the coming months the march of the Missouri volunteers would occasionally be compared with other famous marches. Alexander, Hannibal, and Cortes were invoked to boost Doniphan's claim to historical status. But the comparison between Doniphan's Missourians and Xenophon's Greeks was the only one that stuck: the very abruptness of the reference in Thomas Hart Benton's speech at the St Louis reception ('"the ten thousand" counted the voyage ...') is itself a sign that the comparison had already become part of the Missouri legend.[17]

The comparison with the Ten Thousand was spread by the coverage of the Mexican War in the booming American press. It was the *Delta*, a paper in New Orleans, the hub of the press coverage of the war, that made the first known comparison early in May 1847: 'Neither the retreat of the ten thousand Greeks, under Xenophon ... nor any of the various enterprises accomplished by small bodies of men, traversing hostile territory, of which history has any record, exceeded in difficulty, in danger, or in success, the masterly march of Doniphan over vast plains and through the populous valley of New Mexico.' The comparison spread through the widespread habit of reproducing articles directly from other papers: the *Delta* article was prominently reprinted on the front page of a Baltimore paper a few days later.[18]

Comparisons between the Missouri volunteers and the Ten Thousand were often encapsulated in comparisons between the leaders of the two armies. In June 1847, Doniphan was hailed in the Baltimore-based *Niles National Register* as 'the AMERICAN XENOPHON'. Similar sobriquets were splashed about with some abandon in the months and years to come: Doniphan was 'the modern Xenophon', 'the Xenophon of the nineteenth century', 'the Xenophon of the new world', 'the marching Xenophon of the

West', 'the Xenophon of the Mexican War'. It was as if the American nation was filling by flattery its pantheon of heroes: similar classical pseudonyms had been used by political writers in the Revolutionary Era, and Washington himself had typically been cast as the American Cincinnatus (the Roman general who had answered the call to save Rome and then resigned his command again to return to the plough). Now the Americans were cloning famous Greek soldiers as well as paradigms of Roman republican virtue.[19]

The comparison between the ancient and modern generals was spread above all by an article in June 1847 in the *Evening Post*, a New York paper edited by one of the most prominent men in the American literary scene, William Cullen Bryant. The editorial – headed 'Xenophon and Doniphan' – made some surprising slips: Xenophon was said to have lived 'about one hundred years earlier than the Christian era', and his regiment to have been 'about five hundred men'. Such casual mistakes were of course common in newspapers, then and now – and the very form of the mistake could be revealing: Bryant applied to the size of the armies the same sort of numerical one-upmanship that Benton applied to the length of their marches. Indeed, despite the mistakes, Bryant's words were to be reprinted or summarized in dozens of newspapers across the country over the next month – sometimes at one remove, as one newspaper would lift the details from another: the Tallahassee-based *Floridian*, for instance, took its copy from the Charleston *Patriot* – one paper that did in fact manage silently to restore Xenophon's army to its full complement of ten thousand.[20]

Bryant's editorial did draw attention to some differences between the two generals. One of these differences was to the Greeks' advantage: the American march had been made on horseback, the Greeks' on foot and 'at an inclement season of the year'. But the other differences favoured the Americans. Like Benton, Bryant pointed out that the Americans had covered more ground: the length of the entire Greek march was 3,465 English miles, 'as nearly as we can now estimate it', while the Americans had travelled more than 6,000 miles; besides this, 'one was the march of a conqueror, the other was the retreat of an inferior force'. Bryant concluded, however, on a more conciliatory note:

> our object is not so much to draw comparisons between these two expeditions as to notice the circumstances that these two men, whose names are in sound so similar, have each performed the most wonderful in the annals of warfare. If Col. Doniphan will now imitate the example of Col. Xenophon, and give to the world as charming and as perfect a history of his expedition as the latter has done, mankind, two thousand years hence, will admire and honor him.

Bryant's conclusion points to one area where Americans (like the Romans before them) felt some anxiety about their ability to emulate the Greeks: literary and artistic achievement. One of the papers that picked up on

Bryant's words even commented that 'we can hardly hope that Doniphan will write as well as Xenophon' – while claiming 'as a set-off that the American has fought better than the Grecian, and this will make them equal'. More unwittingly, perhaps, Bryant's slippery logic also betrays some of the anxieties behind comparisons with antiquity: how could both Xenophon and Doniphan have led the most wonderful expedition ever?[21]

The same tension appears in other writers who sought to connect Doniphan and Xenophon. John Hughes, the participant who wrote the most detailed account of Doniphan's expedition, commented that 'this most extraordinary march, conducted by Colonel Doniphan, the Xenophon of the age, with great good fortune, meets not with a parallel in the annals of the world'. But a few pages later he wrote that Xenophon's retreat 'forms the only parallel to Doniphan's expedition, recorded in history'. And even within the first sentence there was a bit of a contradiction: Doniphan was only 'the Xenophon of the age', after all, because he had led a similar march.[22]

Bryant's editorial was often the vehicle for the Xenophon comparison in later writings. A participant who dictated his story to his daughter in old age could not remember what Benton had said in his speech of welcome at St Louis, but did recall their receiving 'more than our meed of praise' from Bryant. And already in 1847 the *Evening Post* editorial was reprinted in an encomiastic life of Zachary Taylor, one of the leading American generals in Mexico, and in a lively memoir of Doniphan's expedition written by a young English emigrant, Frank Edwards. Picking up Bryant's closing wish that Doniphan himself should write an account of the march, Edwards explained that he was publishing his own account 'in the absence of such a charming and perfect work from Colonel Doniphan'. He had not allowed Doniphan much time.[23]

The comparison between Xenophon and Doniphan attracted resistance as well as imitation. A correspondent of the *Ohio Statesman* joked that 'the Colonel of our Regiment is supposed to be a descendant of the famous Colonel Xenophon', and went on to allude to the suggested memoir by Doniphan himself: 'the preface of the forthcoming work will not only prove Doniphan's regular lineal and legitimate descent from Xenophon, but that Missouri and Macedonia *are the same* in GREEK!' Why Missouri and Macedonia? Perhaps the writer was confusing Xenophon with Alexander of Macedon, who had (like Doniphan) led a march of conquest. More likely he was alluding to the famous passage in *Henry V* where the Welshman Fluellen compares the play's eponymous hero with Alexander the Great: 'if you look in the maps of the world, I warrant you shall find, in the comparisons between Macedon and Monmouth, that the situations, look you, is both alike. There is a river in Macedon, and there is also moreover a river at Monmouth ... 'tis alike as my fingers is to my fingers, and there is salmons in both.' The Ohio correspondent wittily deflates the Xenophon/Doniphan parallel by giving an American tweak (Missouri for

Monmouth) to Shakespeare's brilliant parody of formal rhetorical modes of comparison.[24]

It was above all in England that exception was taken to aligning Doniphan with Xenophon. While the threat of English designs on California was used by President Polk as an excuse for preemptive action, the memory of past hostility with England was kept alive by claims that the American army in Mexico was reawakening the glory of the War of 1812 and of the Revolutionary War in particular. At the same time, the American republic was sensitive about the reception of its latest heroics in England. The popular novelist George Lippard complained in his *Legends of Mexico* (1847) that the English denied the Mexicans chivalry in order to lessen the Americans' achievements. He could also have complained that the English denied the Americans chivalry: an English traveller who had passed Doniphan's march in New Mexico and was present in St Louis when the volunteers returned commented that 'the brilliant victories achieved by them, which, according to the American newspapers, are unparalleled in the annals of the world's history, have converted these rowdy and vermin-covered veterans into perfect heroes'.[25]

The English took particular exception to the most extreme expression of American bragging – Bryant's editorial in the *New York Evening Post*. A reviewer of Frank Edwards' memoir in the *Athenaeum* commented, on 'the "Macedon and Monmouth" principle', on 'the striking similarity of the names Doniphan and Xenophon' – but added that 'we see little of similitude beyond that which suggested the comparison'. A reviewer of the same book in the *Examiner* also alluded to Shakespeare, commenting that 'since that gallant soldier, Fluellen, discovered the remarkable resemblance that existed between Macedon and Monmouth in the fact of a river running through both, and both rivers having salmon in them, we have had no similar discovery worth mention' – until, that is, William Cullen Bryant had spotted the Xenophon-Doniphan link. 'Nor is there a want of resemblance', the reviewer continued: 'there is a *ph*, an *o*, and two *ns* in the names of both commanders.' But, the reviewer complained, the editor did not always hit the mark. The true similarity was in fact one that subverted the point of the comparison: both marches were 'piratical expeditions'. That is, far from being united in heroic endeavour, the two generals were engaged in illicit predatory raids. The analogy with Doniphan here led to the sort of moral criticism of the Greek mercenaries that we saw earlier in *The Anti-Slavery Record* – but that was notably absent from American panegyric of the Missouri troops. While the abolitionist journal painted a negative picture of the Ten Thousand as a foil to the true nobility of the fugitive slave, American military rhetoric was content to let the Greeks keep their traditional prestige.[26]

The English reviewer went on to undermine American boasting further by attributing their success to superiority in artillery. Sarcastically recommending Edwards' account to the 'romantic reader', he ridiculed a description of 'our heroic Colonel Doniphan ... sitting coolly on his beautiful chestnut charger, with his legs crossed over the saddle, steadily whittling a piece of wood, his eye glancing proudly over the ranks of his little band!!' – 'a picture perhaps worthy of antiquity, though we are not aware of anything like it in the *Anabasis*'. The implicit contrast drawn here with the active participation in battle of ancient generals like Xenophon was boosted in turn by the claim that the Americans 'fought three "battles" as they are called, killing hundreds of Mexicans, taking incalculable plunder, and not losing a single man!!' The reviewer was suggesting that the very imbalance in the losses, however much exaggerated, showed that the Americans (like their descendants in Iraq) had prevailed through technological superiority rather than through innate courage.

The Xenophon tag survived these onslaughts. A year after his return from Mexico, the movements of the modern Xenophon were reported in local newspapers when he started on an East Coast tour. He went first to a Whig convention in Philadelphia, and then to West Point, where, before he spoke, the cadets were reminded that 'we have glowed with enthusiasm on reading the retreat of the ten thousand Greeks' – but 'that wonderful retreat was more than rivalled in the expedition of the Missouri volunteers'. Xenophon then followed Doniphan as he went on to New York and Boston. His life in years to come was to have more than its share of distress (the loss of both his sons in accidents; the early death of his wife). The Xenophon sobriquet proved to be one fixed point: it was still applied in Doniphan's old age, when he would make trips to the West for the sake of his health, and it continues to be used by modern historians.[27]

*

The repeated comparison between Xenophon and Doniphan is a sign of American euphoria over Doniphan's achievements and of the high status that was attached to Xenophon's own exploits: the fact that the Missouri regiment's march had been 'likened to, and even excelled the deeds of the Greek Xenophon' was glossed by one newspaper as 'the highest praise that could be bestowed'. Doniphan, admittedly, was not the only general to receive such high praise during the Mexican War: Xenophon was also invoked to glorify Winfield Scott's decisive push inland to Mexico City and John E. Wool's 900-mile trek from San Antonio to Saltillo. But no other general apart from Doniphan had a cult of Xenophon built around him.[28]

It was not just because the two names were thought to sound similar that the analogy between Xenophon and Doniphan flourished. What made Doniphan's march stand out from the marches of other US generals in Mexico was its length: it was – and still is – the longest in American military history. It was also, as William Cullen Bryant noted in his *Evening Post* editorial, Xenophon's use in schools that made his name familiar to many Americans. In return the modern Xenophon could now be exploited to boost school use of the *Anabasis*. A fortnight after Doniphan's return to St Louis, a new school edition of Xenophon was promoted with claims that 'the expedition of the Greeks under Xenophon, the great achievement of antiquity, has been, in our own time and history, greatly surpassed in romance, peril and self-sacrifice, by the glorious exploits of the Missouri volunteers' – and so the young student 'will have a new stimulus to turn over the pages of the Greek General, and compare his adventures with those of our own countrymen'. The publishers here pandered to American pride even though it meant demoting the exploits narrated in the Greek text itself.[29]

The analogy between the ancient and modern generals was made even easier by the habit of extracting Xenophon from his historical context. This was not how all American analogies with antiquity were applied: when a writer in the *Southern Quarterly Review* in January 1848 made an extensive comparison between the Mexican War and the Roman war against the Numidian ruler Jugurtha, disturbing political implications were foregrounded – especially the use of military leadership as a path to political power (a theme that had been suggestively analysed by Sallust, the historian of the Jugurthine War). Comparison with the war against the 'modern Jugurtha', the Mexican dictator Santa Anna, suggested the danger that the American republic could follow the destructive trajectory of the Roman. Xenophon, by contrast, tended to be treated as a timeless paradigm of patriotic valour.[30]

The famous retreat of the Ten Thousand was even more useful for comparative purposes because it could also be seen as inferior to Doniphan's march. It was not just that Doniphan's march was supposedly longer: the Greek trek could be used to affirm American superiority precisely because it was a retreat rather than an advance into unconquered territory. William Cullen Bryant, as we have seen, contrasted 'the retreat of an inferior force' with 'the march of a conqueror'. The same difference was noted during Doniphan's visit to West Point ('his was not a retreat ...; his progress was onward'), and again when Xenophon's march was compared with other marches in the Mexican War: according to John E. Wool's biographer, 'the Greeks were retreating, flying from danger: the Americans advancing to meet it'; and Winfield Scott's 'advance' was also opposed to Xenophon's 'retreat'. The retreating Xenophon could even be used for sarcasm: one newspaper wrote that a withdrawal by Santa Anna rivalled the glories of Xenophon. Underlying the opposition between a noble retreat and an advance was the American faith in progress; it is this pride in the onward march of American civilization that explains why Thomas Hart Benton's speech at St Louis plotted Doniphan's expedition as a series of possible endings (Santa Fé, Chihuahua) that became new beginnings. In time the opposition of retreat and progress was even to be enshrined in the most famous American military anthem, Julia Ward Howe's 'Battle Hymn of the Republic'

(1862): 'He has sounded forth the trumpet that shall never call retreat; / ... / Our God is marching on.'[31]

To understand fully the appeal of Xenophon, however, we need to look beyond the facade erected by the rhetoric of newspapers and public orations. I have said that the invocation of Xenophon in these contexts is dehistoricized – but that is true in only a superficial sense. Underlying the array of tropes through which the *Anabasis* was used to shed lustre on the achievements of the Missouri volunteers was a deeply ideological construction of American identity and space.

The ideological sub-current beneath the development of the American cult of Xenophon during the war against Mexico can be illustrated from some remarks in an article on the *Anabasis* written by the French philosopher Hippolyte Taine in 1856. Taine started by expressing the pleasure, after months of serious reading, of pulling military memoirs down from the shelves – and in particular ancient classics like the *Anabasis*, which he had just re-read 'with such pleasure'. The ancients, Taine explained, had 'the best subjects': 'Nothing more curious than this Greek army, a travelling republic that deliberates and acts, that fights and votes, a sort of Athens wandering in the middle of Asia.' Taine here expressed a view of the Ten Thousand similar in many ways to Victor Davis Hanson's recent image of the Greek army as a 'marching democracy' – a view that suggests another reason why Xenophon was seen as an appropriate parallel for Doniphan. The Americans gloried in the fact that Doniphan had led a regiment of equals: Thomas Hart Benton closed his St Louis speech by stressing that the Missouri troops had shown 'what citizen volunteers can do'.[32]

Taine's essay on the *Anabasis* also suggested another reason why the ancients had the best topics: 'Asia was worth America, and Artaxerxes was more than worth Montezuma'; and Xenophon's Greeks were 'like the first navigators into the new world'. This reading of the Greeks' march upcountry into Asia in terms of the European discovery of the Americas was influenced by the contemporary literary vogue for the Spanish conquest of Mexico, inspired above all by W.H. Prescott's epic history, published in 1843. It was also a time of French political interest in Mexico: within a few years the French were to make a bloody intervention in the Mexican civil war. At the time when he was writing, however, Taine's thoughts must have been more directly swayed by the American victories against Mexico. He was not in fact alone in this perception: as we shall see in the next chapter, many American writers characterized the terrain of Mexico and the American West in terms of the exotic East. For the Americans in the era of Manifest Destiny, confident in their right to expand across the continent, this orientalized landscape was a stage for the demonstration of American superiority – just as effete Asia was thought to have succumbed to virile Greece.[33]

It is dangerous, however, to be trapped within a closed system of thought in which the analogies drawn between the republican armies of ancient and modern times and between the exotic spaces of Asia and the American West are allowed to reinforce each other. Within this system of thought, Xenophon's *Anabasis* stands as a comfortable demonstration of the superiority of western values. Precisely because they have been so useful for western interests in the last two centuries, the terms through which Hippolyte Taine characterized the *Anabasis* need to be interrogated more closely. This process of questioning will be the task of the next four chapters as we follow Doniphan's Missouri volunteers and Xenophon's Greeks on their long marches and see how they confront foreign lands and peoples while also facing up to their own isolation hundreds of miles from home.

East and West: Promised Lands

We were in the biblical city of Ur, and I remember being impressed with that. It was still very early in the war.

The place was a slum, though. Bedouins herded goats past us, paying no more attention to us than we did them. Mud-brick houses broke up the skyline. Donkey carts and starving people milled about, rummaging through the belongings of the dead. It was a sight one would expect to find after stepping out of a time machine. Aside from the very occasional beat-up taxi-cab, it was like looking at a portrait from five thousand years ago ...
John Crawford, *The Last True Story I'll Ever Tell* (2005)

I'm having the time of my life. ... I feel like I'm in one big Bible story. When I was four years old ... my recently adoptive father would read me these illustrated Bible stories. Add AK-47s and shabby cars to those stories, and you have Iraq 2004. ... This place is so harsh and backward and perpetually stuck in the fucking Stone Age in most ways, but you have to love it because of that. ... there's something genuine about these people and their life that I can't help but admire. I wish to god I spoke Arabic, because I have a thousand questions I want to ask them ...
Jason Christopher Hartley, *Just Another Soldier* (2005)[1]

* * *

'In the summer of 1846, the wild and lonely banks of the Upper Arkansas beheld for the first time the passage of an army.' So the young Bostonian adventurer Francis Parkman observed in his classic account of *The Oregon Trail*, along which he was travelling that same summer. Even though the army passed by slightly too soon for Parkman himself to see it, he does evoke, with some awe, a sense that the army's appearance on the Arkansas' banks marked an exciting step in American history. That sense was shared by most of the volunteers serving with the Army of the West. Few of these men had experienced life on the march before, and the sense of the unusual was increased by the wild and lonely terrain through which they were passing. Many of them were being exposed for the first time to the vast expanses west of the Mississippi, and in their letters, journals, and memoirs they responded with enthusiasm to the new scenes. John Hughes, the most detailed chronicler of Doniphan's expedition, wrote to the Liberty *Tribune* that 'there is a novelty in this *anabasis* or invasion of Cols. Kearny and Doniphan': 'For the first time since the creation, the starred and striped banner of a free people is being borne over almost one thousand miles of trackless waste.' Others were struck by 'scenery as varied and magnificent as can be found'. And though there were difficulties and disappointments to surmount, the expansive scenery lifted the soldiers' mood: it seemed at times 'more like a pleasure jaunt than a serious march', even though all that the soldiers knew was that they were going to Santa Fé, 'and where to beyond that point no one knew or cared'.[2]

This chapter will read the accounts that Doniphan's troops gave of the American West and the provinces of Mexico against Xenophon's description of the Persian empire in the work lightly evoked in John Hughes' description of Doniphan's 'anabasis'. As we explore the representation of space in the American accounts and in the *Anabasis* itself, we will come to understand better the ideological underpinning of the American myth-making that saw Doniphan and his Missouri volunteers elevated into modern equivalents of Xenophon and the Ten Thousand. As the American soldiers entered and explored unfamiliar regions that seemed to be marked by decay and atrophy and yet also rich with promise for the future, they drew on many long-standing images of landscape. But none was more striking or persistent than the sense that the regions of Mexico and the West were somehow oriental, similar to the lands traversed by the Ten Thousand in their trek through Asia. Mexican landscapes seemed to offer a repertoire of biblical scenes, with under-exploited farmland and degraded villages clinging to an outmoded way of life.

The accounts of the regions Doniphan's army crossed in its long march evoked Xenophon not just by creating a sense of the American West as an oriental landscape, but also in their very form. The military memoirs produced by the American soldiers often resembled the popular genre of travel narrative: they could be praised as charming precisely for their descriptions of the country. In their blend of travel and war, they resembled the *Anabasis*, which was similarly read in the nineteenth century as 'combin[ing] with the character of a military history, that of a book of travels likewise'.[3]

For modern readers, the tendency to align military memoirs with travel books may well seem rather disturbing. The problem is not just that it seeks to dilute the militariness of the war memoir by association with the aesthetic pleasures of foreign travel. It is also that travel literature has itself been subjected to searching ideological critiques. Many critics in the last few decades, particularly in the wake of Edward Said's *Orientalism* (1978), have argued that traditional travel-writing has been intimately bound up with the discourse of western imperialism. Travel-writing, in one view, is 'a double-pronged quest for domination, not only of actual experience (foreign lands and foreigners) but also of literary experience (prior travel texts and their authors)'; or again, another writer has argued, it has always been 'predicated on privilege', reflecting 'the movement of world history as seen from the perspective of the centre'. These critiques suggest that descriptions of space always draw on previous travel accounts and on fixed cultural preconceptions, and they highlight the commentary on time – the evocation of national narratives of progress – that is often implicit in descriptions of space. These will be important issues in exploring the texts produced by the expeditions of Xenophon and Doniphan. The most fundamental question for the accounts of these expeditions, however, has to do with domination pure and simple: how do their descriptions of space relate to the participants' actual imperial ambitions, whether those ambitions lie in the past or the future? What vision of historical destiny shaped the stories that were told of the lands crossed by the two marches?[4]

Let us revisit the wild and lonely banks of the Arkansas twenty-eight years after they first beheld an army. Richard S. Elliott, a volunteer in Doniphan's company, and since then a journalist, is travelling by train across the ground he rode over with the Army of the West. What a difference he finds – and not just in the speed of his movements: 'It is so charming to visit a country which you have conquered in earlier days, when it had no people in it, and find happy homes and increasing population.' He even declares himself 'touched with melancholy' when he thinks of the fate of Julius Caesar, 'poor fellow', who 'never enjoyed the felicity of returning to Gaul after 28 years' absence to find broad regions full of people, where all was desolation when he conquered the country'. Elliott here strips ancient Gaul of its inhabitants with the same disregard for reality with which he imagines the great plains of North America as an empty space, devoid of people and homes.[5]

Xenophon, as far as we know, never enjoyed the felicity of returning to Cappadocia or Cilicia, to Syria or Mesopotamia. What would he have seen had he had the chance to return a generation later to the route of his long march? Not that much difference, perhaps. But another generation on, and he would have seen the aftermath of a geopolitical earthquake. The countries that lay along the route of his march had now been conquered by Alexander of Macedon. His route stretched towards areas further east that were now populated with settlements in which Alexander's mercenaries lorded it over the native populations. A century more, and there were even more cities founded by the early kings of the Seleucid dynasty, heirs to most of the Asiatic part of Alexander's empire. And these were cities that lay on or near the route of Xenophon's march. In Asia Minor, there was Laodicea, not far from Colossae, one of Cyrus' early stopping-points; nearby Apamea had been refounded from Celaenae, where the final contingents arrived for Cyrus' push upcountry; and the coins of Tarsus now bore the name Antioch-on-the-Cydnus. Further east the great new capital of Antioch lay not far from the spot where Xenophon had passed through the Syrian Gates, and Thapsacus, where Cyrus, like Alexander after him, crossed the Euphrates, was now Greek Zeugma ('Bridge'). And a site Xenophon passed in the uncertain days following Cyrus' death was now a new regional capital, Seleucia-on-Tigris.

Beacons of Hellenism was how some Greeks chose to see these new settlements in the East. Modern historians tend rather to see them as complex communities with varying patterns of exchange and power-relations between their Greek and indigenous populations. Whatever the case, all this lay in the future for Xenophon himself – and in a future rather more distant than the wave of emigration to the West lay for Doniphan and his men. Near or distant, however, our knowledge of the future unleashed by the passages of these armies must be set aside as we turn to explore the accounts of Doniphan's troops and of Xenophon himself. We must restore the perspective of the participants as they set out on journeys into terrain that would in both cases be figured as strange and oriental.

*

John Hughes' memoir of Doniphan's expedition offers a vivid snapshot of the army as it sets out to cross the great prairie, with the same solicitude felt for the army's safety as 'at the departure of a fleet for some distant land'. It was, he writes, 'a scene of the most intense and thrilling interest', 'worthy the pencil of the ablest artist, or the most graphic pen of the historian': there were 'boundless plains, lying in ridges of wavy green not unlike the ocean', with files of cavalry winding their way across them, banners fluttering, and canvas-covered wagons 'glistening like banks of snow in the distance'. The march in the days and weeks ahead provided other striking sights. The gushing Diamond Springs possessed 'charms' greater than 'the most enchanting spots ever depicted by the pen of the eastern romancer'. There were plains with grasshoppers 'as numerous as were the locusts sent by the afflicting hand of Providence in swarms upon the land of Egypt'. After an eighteen-mile march, there was plunging and splashing in the River Arkansas, 'one of the finest streams in the world for bathing purposes', 'no less beautiful than the golden sands of the fabled Pactolus' – the Lydian river in which Midas washed off his touch of gold. There were struggles through the hot desert, 'the great American Sahara', encountering opposition from the elements as serious as that suffered by 'the Roman army under Metellus, on its march through the deserts of Africa'; and one final push of twenty miles to the banks of the River Purgatoire, a 'lovely, clear, cool, rippling mountain stream', 'not less grateful to our army, after four days' unparalleled marching on the desert, than was that stream to the Israelitish army, which gushed from the rock when struck by the rod of the prophet'.[6]

Hughes was not alone in framing the terrain through which Doniphan's expedition passed in terms of the geography and history of the Old World. Another of Doniphan's troops wrote in his journal as he looked back at the army from a vantage point that 'we had a column like the picture in the journey of the Israelites' – perhaps Francis Danby's *Passage of the Red Sea* (1825), widely reproduced in engravings. And when the army had crossed into Mexican territory proper, Richard S. Elliott noted that the palace at

Santa Fé was built of raw brick, 'as were those of Nineveh', while the humbler folk lived in houses 'with flat roofs, as in Bible times', where they would sleep on fold-up beds, again in the biblical style.[7]

It was more particularly the lands of the Ottoman Empire (including the deserts of North Africa) that provided the frame for Doniphan's men as they responded to their new experiences. Together the resonances of the bible, Greek myth (the Pactolus), and Roman history (Metellus' march, described in Sallust's *Jugurtha*) calibrate a sense of the American West as a return to the East. This perception was already captured by Thomas Hart Benton when he spoke at the reception for Doniphan's men on their return to St Louis: the country through which the volunteers had passed, Benton noted, was a region of 'strange features', 'more Asiatic than American'. East may be East and West West, but in the region crossed by the men of Missouri the twain did meet.[8]

Benton's words suggest that the tendency to draw on the distant East to evoke the distinctive feel of the American West was well established. Indeed, Benton's son-in-law John Charles Frémont, the most famous western explorer of the 1840s, had already commented on the 'strange and grotesque appearance' of his cavalcade marching through a landscape of desert and mountain 'in a sort of procession, looking more like we belonged to Asia than to the United States of America'. In the same vein another traveller in the West compared trains of wagons stretching in the distance with the caravans 'described in the Bible and other Eastern books', and found that the camp at night summoned up 'many a memory of oriental reading'. And other American troops also found that Mexico brought reminders of the East as they fought their way to the halls of the Montezumas. For many, one of their first encounters of Mexico was a 'miserable village' at the mouth of the Rio Grande that they called Bagdad – though it had been 'somewhat improved and Americanized' by the following year; and just beyond that lay the 'almost oriental city' of Matamoras, marked by its 'strange Moorish architecture'. This image of Mexico as an oriental space had been fostered by a work that many soldiers read – Prescott's three-volume *History of the Conquest of Mexico* (1843). Writing in a self-consciously romantic mode, Prescott presented the 'fair city of Mexico' as an 'Indian empress with her coronal of pearls' or a 'city of enchantment', looking to Cortes and his men 'like a thing of fairy creation' or 'like the spectacle which greeted the eyes of Moses from the summit of Pisgah' when he first saw the promised land. Here the city of Mexico is orientalized by being portrayed as a luxurious feminine object that is subjected to the lofty gaze of the European invader, master of all he surveys.[9]

The orientalizing of the American West and the interior of Mexico had deep ideological implications. It was in part, as one scholar of American geography has noted, because 'the republic lacked a shaping sense of a dense anterior history' that 'national self-definition – the feeling of nationhood itself – required the illumination of geographical comparison'. As we have seen, American nature surpassed European nature, particularly in its rivers. And Old World cultural models were also matched or trumped by American nature: strange rock formations in the West were often compared with castles, while the domes of Yosemite even surpassed European cathedrals.[10]

More than American boosterism was at issue in the transfer of the orient to the American West. For Thomas Hart Benton, the Asiatic appearance of the West chimed well with his aspirations for the region: through the West lay his dreams of the passage to India that, he hoped, would make the United States the world's dominant trading nation. Benton's dream had long historical roots in Columbus' belief that the land he found across the Atlantic was the Indies: in 1849 Benton even proposed carving an image of Columbus on a peak in the Rockies, looking still further west, as if to make up for the great discoverer's unfortunate mistake. Perhaps, then, the West was like the East because it led there, completing the circuit of the transfer of civilization from East to West, with the West now poised to rejuvenate the decayed East.[11]

Above all, the oriental comparison made Mexico and the West suitable for domination. The language of orientalism was often used to suggest that the East was weak, decadent, and despotic, but it could also imply that the East was still a haven of aristocracy, a more suitable and authentic site for the display of chivalry and masculinity than the increasingly urbanized and industrialized lands of Europe. This perception of the orient was most strongly fostered by art and popular literature during the heyday of European imperial ambitions, but it was also readily adopted by Americans: a round-the-world traveller in the 1860s wrote that 'the word ['orient'] implies something gorgeous, dazzling, beautiful, – bright colors, crimson and gold, fragrant flowers ... luxury, ease, comfort'. And the same view of the East as 'a beautiful dreamland' was expressed by the orientalizing language that contemporary Americans adopted during the Mexican War. The events of the war resembled 'the fictions of romance and chivalry', with Doniphan's expedition taking its place as 'one of those military adventures which convert the realities of history into the brilliant and enticing scenes of romance'. The air of romance was the greater because the theatre of war reawakened thoughts of Cortes and the Spanish conquerors in the early sixteenth century, recently subjected to Prescott's lavish and dramatic treatment. The effect of this image of Mexico was to suggest that the journey to the west and south was a journey to the past and to oppose the modern and progressive Americans to the stagnant and idle Mexicans. In much the same way modern American soldiers have scorned (or in rare cases been intrigued by) the supposedly primitive and biblical scenes that have met their eyes in Iraq.[12]

The sense of the West as a land ripe for domination was strengthened by comparisons with the Israelites. Ever since the first beleaguered puritans arrived in the New World, they had looked on America as a new

Israel. Now the hopes for a promised land were being transferred to the West. This language was particularly important for the Mormons, but by no means confined to them: one early emigrant to California had his family painted looking down from a height on the *Promised Land*, and the obvious religious overtones of the image were also found in descriptions of California as 'the modern Canaan, a land "flowing with milk and honey"'. In this vision, the orient was not stigmatized as a land of the past, but rather a source of positive associations that could be transferred to a new setting in the American West. Indeed, the American army that was carrying out the work of Providence by conquering this region could even transfer divine aid from east to west: at one point in Doniphan's march through the Mexican desert 'the God who made the fountain leap from the rock to quench the thirst of the Israelitish army in the desert' sent rain to help the trains struggling in the rear. The same idea of divine destiny underlies a parallel drawn in a 1885 address to a reunion of Oregon Pioneers: the story of the pioneers' '2,500 mile march through hostile country, over unexplored desert and mountain' was held to exceed the distance covered during the long wandering of 'the host led by Moses and Aaron'.[13]

Marking the West as oriental also legitimated its conquest by aligning the Americans with the Greeks and Romans – the ancient foes of Persia and Parthia, and inventors of many of the stereotypes used to disparage the Mexicans. Hughes, as we have seen, compared Doniphan's men crossing the desert with the hardy Roman troops of Metellus fighting in North Africa; and he took this racial stereotyping further by repeatedly praising the 'Roman fortitude' of American soldiers while aligning Mexicans with Rome's one-time enemy, Carthage. The orientalizing of the army's route was equally suitable, however, for the main parallel that was used to elevate Doniphan's feats – the march of the Ten Thousand.[14]

One reason why the vision of the American West as an oriental space made comparisons with Xenophon easy was that the march of the Ten Thousand was itself sometimes compared with the Israelites' return to their promised land. An American diplomat in the Ottoman empire wrote that the joy of Xenophon and his men as they looked down on the Black Sea from the summit of Mount Theches was 'greater than that of Moses and his Israelites when they beheld the Promised Land'. The same comparison was implicit in the illustration of Xenophon's scene in the world history by John Clark Ridpath that enthused the young Thomas Wolfe: the Greeks on the mountain top stare towards the left of the picture (i.e. towards the west) with the same joyous gesture as emigrants pictured greeting the promised lands of the West (Fig. 10, 11). This vision of the Greeks' retreat as a return to a promised land makes it easy to understand why a nineteenth-century American biblical scholar could compare the leadership of Xenophon with that of Moses, or again why the speaker at the 1885 Oregon reunion could boast that the length of the pioneers' march

10. 'The plains! The plains!' Westward the course of empire ...

11. 'The sea! The sea!' Westward the gaze of the Ten Thousand ...

exceeded not just the Israelites' wanderings but also the distance covered in Xenophon's retreat from the Euphrates.[15]

The same boast was also, as we have seen, repeatedly made in the comparisons between the marches led by Xenophon and Doniphan that gripped the American public in the 1840s. Here too, however, the similarities went far beyond a mere catalogue of miles. We have already noted that the war with Mexico inspired the comparison Hippolyte Taine drew in 1856 between the Asia confronted by Xenophon's Greeks and the America conquered by the Spanish. Later in the century, the comparison was updated when John Clark Ridpath was invited to give a Memorial Day speech. Taking 'The Citizen Soldier' as his theme, Ridpath provided the gathered crowd with a sketch of the role of the volunteer soldier in American history. When he came to the Mexican War, he bemoaned the cause for which the conflict had been fought, while praising the valour of the American troops. But he also paused to dwell on the setting where the battles had been fought: 'There lay the Rio Grande, the great international river, dividing the two warlike republics. Its appearance to the men of the North was like the Euphrates to the eyes of the Greeks of Xenophon.' His words suggest that the American troops in Mexico resembled the Ten Thousand not just in the distances they travelled, but in the terrain they covered: the North/South axis within the American continent is made to mirror the conventional West/East division in the European imagination.[16]

Like all geographical analogies, Ridpath's configuration of space is open to question. The Rio Grande was the river that the United States claimed as its border with Mexico following the annexation of Texas, and it was this claim that provoked the war with Mexico in the first place. Ridpath retrojects the boundary established by the American victory in the war onto the geographical imagination of the American soldiers in the 1840s. Ridpath's choice of the Euphrates also demands scrutiny. The Euphrates was later the border between the Roman empire and its main enemy in the East, the Parthians. Its historical resonance was strongly felt by nineteenth-century travellers: one German traveller, standing one night above the river, pictured in his mind 'Cyrus and Alexander, Xenophon, Caesar and Julian' crossing it by moonlight. The historical grandeur of this romantic vision may well raise suspicions that the later emblematic significance of the Euphrates is being pressed back to Xenophon's own time. Just as Doniphan's men had marched across a vast stretch of desert before they reached the Rio Grande, so too the Ten Thousand had come a long way through the satrapies of the Persian empire before they first saw the Euphrates.[17]

The teleology inscribed within Ridpath's perception of space is confirmed by the terms in which he imagines the space beyond the Rio Grande. It was a land with 'the strangest of aspects', 'so far away as to excite the imagination' and 'picturesque in the last degree'. The invasion had culminated in the American troops looking down from the mountain heights upon 'the far-off shining city of an ancient race', and the troops had brought back victory and fame from 'the land of the ancient Aztecs'. For all his moral critique of the American presence in Mexico, Ridpath offers his audience a historical perspective that seems to naturalize and justify the American conquests. The modern inhabitants of Mexico are removed from view by the focus on the Aztecs and by the aestheticization of the land as picturesque. At the same time, the progressive Americans are elevated through the heroic paradigm of the Ten Thousand.[18]

There is a disturbing gap in Ridpath's comparison between the Americans and Xenophon's Greeks. Ridpath offers a snapshot of Mexico, but he does not explain how the Euphrates and the land beyond it appeared to the Greeks. This lacuna should not make us dismiss Ridpath's comparison as empty rhetoric: his very casualness is a revealing sign of the ideological pull and rhetorical force of classical antiquity. Rather than dismissing the comparison out of hand, we can try to fill in the space that Ridpath leaves blank – precisely in order to question his romantic geography as it constructs a historical trajectory that sees the Ten Thousand as precursors of the mid-nineteenth-century American soldiers on their way to Mexico. And we can start to fill in that blank space by following the American and Greek soldiers as they cross the unfamiliar expanses that lay west of the Mississippi and east of the Euphrates.

*

Morning on the prairie. A band of 400 buffalo suddenly emerges from the Arkansas and comes streaming through the camp with their clumsy lope, like 'the motion of a ship in a heavy sea, first bows up, then stern'. It is a scene of 'beautiful confusion' as the soldiers charge on the buffalo with their guns and drawn sabres, relishing the prospects of the chase – riding after the thick mass of beasts over the open expanse, picking their target and drawing alongside it, then the deadly aim between the shoulders: 'nothing except a charge upon the Mexicans could have animated the men more, or produced more thrilling sensations.' The soldiers return by evening, and there is meat for all to go round. It is a democratic feast amidst the aristocracy of nature: 'In this delightful country,' one of Doniphan's soldiers wrote, 'nature has done more than art has or can accomplish to furnish large rural parks more elegant than royalty ever luxuriated in.' With characteristic confidence in the superiority of the American continent, this soldier rates the prairies above the traditional hunting grounds of European royalty – and of Persian princes like Cyrus, for that matter, accustomed to hunting in the groomed environment of the 'paradise'.[19]

The ship-like motion of the buffalo offers a hint at another key element in the American experience of the prairie – the sense that crossing this vast flat space was like a voyage across an ocean. This image was familiar from earlier accounts of the American plains: already in the sixteenth-century the Spanish explorer Coronado had spoken of 'plains, with no more landmarks than as if we had been swallowed up in the sea'. The same comparison was made in the most widely-read account of the Santa Fé trail, Gregg's *Commerce of the Prairies* ('the grand "prairie ocean"', with 'not a single landmark' and all 'as level as the sea'), and also by other contemporary adventurers such as Francis Parkman and Washington Irving. The chroniclers of Doniphan's expedition subjected the image to numerous further elaborations: we have already seen John Hughes likening the departure of Doniphan's men to a fleet setting sail and describing the wavy green ridges of the plain; for others, the occasional mounds in the plain were islands and the murderers of a trader 'land pirates'.[20]

Gunpowder aside, accounts of Doniphan's soldiers hunting in the ocean-like prairie could almost be describing Xenophon's Greeks in the Arabian desert. There the Greeks hunted a 'wide variety of animals' – ostrich, bustard, gazelle, and, most numerous of all, the wild ass – with the same alacrity with which the Americans pursued the buffalo – though with more varied success. Owing to its speed, the wild ass was 'impossible to catch, unless riders took up positions at intervals and then chased them in succession' – but 'bustards can be caught if one puts them up quickly, because they fly only a short way, like partridges, and soon give up' (the same didactic tone appeared in some American accounts). But one creature eluded capture altogether: 'No one managed to catch an ostrich, and any horseman who set off after one soon stopped; the bird would pull a long way ahead by using not only its feet, to run away, but also its wings, which it would raise and use as a sail.'[21]

Xenophon's image of the ostrich wing as a sail follows beautifully from the start of his account of the Arabian desert: 'All the land in this place was flat and as completely uniform as the sea, except that it was covered with wormwood.' This pithy sentence is the ultimate ancestor of the image of the American prairies as an ocean – as some nineteenth-century readers recognized. One of the classic accounts of the American plains, Captain Basil Hall's *Travels in North America* (1829), went beyond the straight sea-prairie resemblance by comparing the isolated trees that rose above the horizon with 'strange sails heaving in sight', and a reviewer thought it probable that Hall here had in mind 'Xenophon's picturesque description of the Arabian Desert'.[22]

The comparison of the prairie or desert with the sea may seem natural: both desert and sea are flat and expansive – and when they are not flat, they can be seen as similar in their waviness. Yet the comparison and its elaborate developments are also ways of controlling experience, rendering the desert familiar yet keeping a hint of the unfamiliar, as well as playful ploys in a quest for literary domination (or at least novelty). More potently, the image of the plain as a sea draws on some of the symbolic force of the sea itself. Since antiquity, the sea has often been perceived as a realm of

12. Among the Buffalo.

danger and adventure, a perilous region to be overcome by heroic wanderers in the mold of Odysseus and the Argonauts. For the American soldiers as much as for the Greeks, hunting on this sea-like expanse could be viewed as a test of manhood and skill – the stuff of romance but also (as Xenophon himself theorized in another work) good preparation for war. The same view of hunting is implied by many nineteenth-century descriptions of hunting in the British colonies: as one British imperial historian has written, hunting was 'a mark of the fitness of the dominant race, a route to health, strength, and wealth, an emblem of imperial rule, and an allegory of human affairs'. These words seem equally applicable to the hunting episodes in accounts of Doniphan's expedition and in the *Anabasis* – or at least, in Xenophon's case, they suggest how easily his account fits later models of imperial hunting; and many travellers in the Middle East in the nineteenth century did indeed have his account in mind as they pursued the 'highly picturesque' wild ass.[23]

For the Americans, the comparison between desert and sea carried a further significance. The great inland sea foreshadowed the ultimate goal of American expansion, the Pacific Ocean itself, the fulfilment of the Manifest Destiny that was spreading the American republic from sea to shining sea – and leading to the inevitable demise of the buffalo. This spirit was expressed in expansionist newspapers like the *New York Herald*, which spoke of 'the pioneers of Anglo-Saxon civilization and Anglo-Saxon free institutions' seeking 'distant territories, stretching even to the shores of the Pacific', and 'the arms of the republic' embracing 'the whole hemisphere, from the icy wilderness of the North to the most prolific regions of the smiling and prolific South'. These pretensions were at the same time mercilessly parodied in the British press: in one piece in the London *Athenaeum*, an imaginary Kentuckian defined his country's boundaries as bounded 'on the east ... by the rising sun – on the north by the aurora borealis – on the west by the precession of the equinoxes – and on the south by the day of judgment!' Within this grand continental vision, the ocean-like prairie could be viewed as a new centre rather than as a danger to be overcome. One of the most eloquent advocates of the prairie's potential was an officer in the Army of the West, William Gilpin, who argued that Mexico and the United States would be united within a century, with a shared capital positioned in the great plains.[24]

The American vision of Manifest Destiny breaks down Ridpath's seductive symmetry between the expeditions of Doniphan and Xenophon. The sea-like desert held no promise for the Greeks: it was merely the way to the heart of Persian power. Nor did the Greeks hunt in the conviction that they were forces of progress: their inability to catch the ostrich leads Xenophon to a pragmatic reflection on their own limitations, their inability to impose their will on the desert.

And yet Xenophon does provide a clear foreshadowing of the Americans' transcontinental vision. Just as the Americans imagined their power spreading from the poles to the tropics, Xenophon too speaks of an empire that 'extends south to a region where men cannot live because of the heat and north to a region where they cannot live because of the cold'. But it is the Persian empire he is defining – and the definition itself is offered in a speech delivered by Cyrus. For the Greeks, this type of language reflected the Persians' dangerous tendency towards excess: Herodotus presented Xerxes promising to 'make Persian territory end only at the sky, the domain of Zeus, so that the sun will not shine on any land beyond our borders'. Or this language seemed offensive to some Greeks at least. Cyrus was in fact picking his words well: the officers in the Greek army are attracted by his vision of the Persian empire. Cyrus tells them that, if victorious, he will put his friends in charge of the territories of the empire – and one by one the Greek generals make their way to his tent to ask what will be in it for them; to seek a promise, perhaps, of a position of power somewhere in the immense expanse that lies between the icy North and the sultry South.[25]

*

As the American army advanced from the great plains into Mexican territory, the soldiers began to observe ranches in decay, villages that had been deserted, mines that were abandoned. Some of the ruins were recent – Mexican settlements that had been abandoned owing to Indian incursions. Others were more ancient and exotic, and in particular the old Aztec ruins at Pecos, where an immense church was all that survived of the old town, said to have been built by 'a race of giants fifteen feet in height' – 'but these dying off, they were succeeded by dwarfs with red heads, who, being in their turn exterminated, were followed by the Aztecs'. The soldiers even saw a thigh bone dug from the floor of the church that 'could never have belonged to a man less than ten feet high'.[26]

The picture of decline was counterbalanced by the delights of the old Mexican provinces. Criticism of the failings of human culture went hand in hand with admiration for what were seen as the country's abundant natural gifts – gifts now ready to be exploited by the Americans. This perceived abundance of nature created a sense of Mexico as an exotic and desirable space, a distant land of marvels, that served the interests of Anglo-Saxon imperialism as readily as criticisms of Mexican failings.

Particularly expressive of this imperialist vision is the way the local women tended to be included in the natural marvels of Mexico. Accounts of Doniphan's expedition are full of admiration for their beauty: some American troops even stayed behind to get married. The focus on Mexican women was a way of casting Mexico itself as feminine and ripe for conquest: during the war one US paper dismissed arguments over annexing Mexico with the pragmatic advice that the Americans should 'go to work and annex her daughters', while another opined that 'like the Sabine virgins, she [Mexico] will soon learn to love her ravisher'. The same pattern of thought reappears in a later American military engagement in Central America: the filibusters who briefly seized power in Nicaragua in the 1850s also praised the beauty of the local women, and again some of them found wives and stayed there – 'like the Lotus-Eaters', one of their companions wrote. This arch allusion to the story of how some of Odysseus' crew lost their chance of a home-coming by eating the fruit of the lotus casts the women of Nicaragua as a similarly enticing natural product of a remote and wonderful land.[27]

An image of spatial remoteness was also fostered by comments on the extraordinary fertility of parts of Mexico. The American troops enjoyed the local produce as much as the local women. After their tough march to El Paso, they spent their time in the town 'pleasantly in feasting upon a variety of the best viands and finest fruits', both fresh and dried, including grapes far excelling the raisin, and the richest wines. One of Doniphan's soldiers was struck by 'the largest onions I ever saw': 'I measured one to-day that was 20 inches in circumference.' And in some parts the lushness of the vegetation led them to descriptions of Mexico as a 'paradise' or the 'Eden of America'. This gilded picture was the counterpart to the vision of Mexico as a land of ruins; so too eighteenth-century writers described the inhabitants of the New World as either noble savages or primitive barbarians depending on their philosophical whim.[28]

The duality of the American image of Mexico was intriguingly mocked in a journal written by William Richardson, a volunteer in Doniphan's army. 'In this lovely and fertile valley,' he wrote, 'we are enjoying all the *blessings* of life. We are charmed by the surpassing beauty of the Spanish ladies, and living in so much *harmony* with each other, that we almost imagine the "Garden of Eden" to have been again raised for our enjoyment.' The journal continued, however, in a tone similar to Dickens' debunking of the myth of the American Eden in *Martin Chuzzlewit*: 'and then, Oh heavens, what a luxury, amid these joys, to feel the delightful sensations produced by the gentle and graceful movements of a Spanish *louse*, as he journeys over one's body.' These words were in fact written not by Richardson himself but by 'some wag' in his absence – though he confessed that his own hyperbolic praise had been waggish itself. The passage as a whole points to a deep scepticism towards the conventionality of the dual image of the West at the same time as it highlights the difficulty of escaping it.[29]

The same blend of decay and splendour that runs through nineteenth-century accounts of Mexico appears in Xenophon's description of Mesopotamia. In their march across the Arabian desert, the Ten Thousand came to 'a large, deserted city called Corsote', and, after Cyrus' death, as they followed the course of the Tigris north, they stopped at 'a large deserted city', named Larisa and previously inhabited by the Medes, and then, a stage further on, 'a large deserted fortification' near Mespila, another city that had previously been inhabited by the Medes. By the banks of the Tigris the Ten Thousand had in fact stumbled without knowing it on Nimrud and Nineveh – the former a capital built by the Assyrian king Assurnasirpal II in the first half of the ninth century BC, the latter the site of a palace built by another Assyrian king, Sennacherib, towards the start of the seventh.[30]

Xenophon gives some sense of the dimensions and appearance of these imposing ruins. The walls of Larisa were twenty-five feet in breath and a hundred in height, with a perimeter of two parasangs; and they were 'built of bricks made of clay, and underneath there was a stone base of twenty feet'. Mespila was even grander, with walls the same height but foundations of fifty feet and a perimeter of six parasangs. His descriptions read like small-scale versions of Herodotus' accounts of the monuments of Egypt and the grand Asian cities like Babylon that he claims to have seen; and, like Herodotus', they may be read as portrayals of the marvels (*thaumata*) of the East.

Xenophon presents the Persian empire as splendid in its produce as well as in its buildings. When the men come to the Tigris, they camp near a 'great and populous' city next to a 'paradise' which was 'large, beautiful, and thickly wooded with a variety of trees'. It is at this point, too, that Xenophon notes how Mesopotamian agriculture was boosted by an elaborate system of canals: 'from the canals ditches were cut to extend over the country, big ones at first and then smaller ones, until in the end they were little channels like the ones in Greece for the millet fields.' Xenophon also uses a similar analogy to bring out the imposing size of the fruit: 'the sort of dates which are to be seen in Greece were set aside for the servants, while the ones reserved for the masters were choice fruit, marvellous in their size and beauty.' Unlike in his account of Larisa and Mespila, Xenophon here openly uses the language of the marvel (*thauma*), conventional in descriptions of distant lands. And this sense of eastern wonders is reinforced when the men eat the cabbage of the palm for the first time and marvel (another *thauma* word) at its appearance. Xenophon is even alert to the patterns of exchange by which fertile Mesopotamia could feed less fortunate regions: in an area of the Arabian desert bereft of grass and trees, the inhabitants quarry millstones and sell them at Babylon in return for grain. There is a hint here of Herodotus' utopian accounts of balanced eastern systems of exchange (the Babylonian marriage auctions, for instance, where the money paid by rich men for beautiful brides is redistributed to poor men who receive ugly brides).[31]

The combination of ruins and marvels seems paradoxical. Ruins are often seen as a sign of decay and viewed with the romantic sensibility typical of nineteenth-century travellers in the Middle East. The ruins of a deserted village could be seen as 'discordant' to European taste, a 'memento of human ruthlessness', because the sight of misery was particularized: 'in the ruins of a poor little village, we see nothing but poverty robbed of its pittance.' Grand ruins such as those of Nineveh and Nimrud, by contrast, were more likely to induce 'that pleasing melancholy with which we are in general affected on visiting the wrecks of ancient magnificence'. But the site of ruins could also spark energetic thoughts that were more at home with a vision of the marvels of a distant land: when Austen Henry Layard, excavator at Nineveh and Nimrud in the 1840s, watched from a mound 'the grass-covered heaps marking the site of ancient habitations', he reflected that 'the great tide of civilisation had long since ebbed, leaving these scattered wrecks on the solitary shore': 'Are those waters to flow again, bearing back the seeds of knowledge and of wealth that have wafted to the West?' It is a classic scene: the world-renowned archaeologist looking down from a height on the site of his own glory, seeing through the eyes of the western colonialist, tinged with a faint sense of human weakness before the tides of history. A somewhat similar response was offered by an Austrian woman who accompanied the ill-fated British attempt to navigate the Euphrates in the 1830s. As she reflected that 'a few wretched nomad tents, and long-eared goats, grazing here and there' were the only traces of life in a country where 'at every step you meet with evidence of a former flourishing state of civilisation', she looked, like Layard, to a different future: 'on the shores of the fructifying Euphrates, civilisation will flourish anew. ... This rich country is too near over-peopled Europe ... for it long to remain closed against European civilisation.'[32]

The Americans in Mexico viewed the sight of ruins with the same progressive eyes. By describing deserted settlements, they suggested that the region was habitable, but also that it currently held no 'settled, civilized communities to prevent the arrival of enterprising Anglos'. And they also viewed the Mexican landscape as ripe for further exploitation even when it was not disfigured by ruins. It was from the fertile valley of El Paso that Hughes sent the Secretary of War a dispatch in which he argued that 'an energetic American population' would yield ten times as much. The same strongly racialized definition of land use appears in a memorandum on northern Mexico by another participant in Doniphan's expedition which Thomas Hart Benton had printed and distributed by the Senate. Proper American industry could even compensate for the ruins of Asia: in the lavishly produced 1870s series *Picturesque America*, the borders of the Mississippi were described as 'a long succession of smiling fields and cheerful habitations' where the energetic Americans 'have built up great cities, destined to be in the future what Nineveh and Babylon were to Asia'.[33]

How did Xenophon view the deserted cities of Asia? The stories he tells about how Larisa and Mespila were captured could be taken as a hint that he shared the upbeat vision of the enterprising Yankees. He claims that Larisa was besieged by the Persian king 'at the time when the Persians seized the empire from the Medes', and taken only when 'a cloud covered up the sun and hid it from sight until the inhabitants left'; and that Mespila was also besieged by the Persian king and captured when 'Zeus dumbfounded the inhabitants by a thunderstorm'. It has been suggested that these stories testify to Persian weakness, since the Persians conquered the cities 'only owing to chance acts of nature'. But at Mespila the 'chance act of nature' is explicitly attributed to Zeus. Perhaps, then, it is the stress on a transfer from Median to Persian power that raises the prospect that Persian power may in turn diminish. But if Xenophon wanted to hint at the idea of a succession of empires, it is curious that he ignores altogether the fact that Nimrud and Nineveh were originally Assyrian cities. The sequence Assyria-Media-Persia (like the succession of giants, dwarves, and Aztecs at Pecos) would have produced a stronger sense of transience.[34]

Xenophon's account of Larisa and Mespila remains enigmatic. The neglect of the Assyrian background is hard to explain, especially as Xenophon portrays the Assyrians in his *Cyropaedia* as enemies of the Medes and Persians. We can at least say that the very fact that Xenophon describes the sites shows his openness to the allure of ruins: as one modern scholar observes with regret, he nowhere tells us what an inhabited Mesopotamian city looked like (the only other structure he describes in the same way is the long defensive 'Median wall'). So in this respect at least Xenophon does create the sense that Mesopotamia is a land of the past. But those ruins carry no hint that Greeks could create a better future.[35]

Nor does Xenophon's account of marvels of Mesopotamia suggest that Greeks could exploit them better than the Persians. In locating marvels in remote Asia, Xenophon was following a tradition in which, as Stephen Greenblatt observes, marvels served 'as one of the principal signs of otherness and hence functioned not only as a source of fascination but also of authentication'. The dates of Mesopotamia, however, are not only an authenticating mark of the genuine East. They also put the Greeks in their place: Xenophon's claim that the dates Greeks eat at home are like the ones servants eat in Persia wittily overturns the conventional Greek picture that in Persia everyone but the king was a slave.[36]

Or does Xenophon encourage his readers to change places with the Persian masters? The would-be western conqueror should, after all, long to be in their position of power and privilege, reversing the terms of the analogy – rather as Cortes did when he told one of Montezuma's vassals that 'he served a monarch who had princes for his vassals as powerful as the Aztec monarch himself'. The seductive marvels of Mesopotamia seem ripe for possession.[37]

But it also emerges that the splendours of Mesopotamia are dangerous. The magnificent dates, when dried, were 'a tasty accompaniment to wine'. But, Xenophon adds, they 'gave one a headache' – as did the cabbage of the palm. The linearity of the text reproduces the soldiers' responses: first enchantment, then disillusion. What seems attractive at first proves to have a sting in the tail. This is a pattern found in many accounts of the enchantments of the New World – think of the satire on Eden in William Richardson's journal. In Xenophon's account, it returns in an even more spectacular form when the Greeks approach the Black Sea coast. They camped in some well-stocked villages where 'there was nothing for them to marvel at' (again marvels, *thaumata*, are the criterion for inclusion) except for numerous swarms of bees. Some of the soldiers ate their honey and went out of their minds, suffering vomiting and diarrhoea and lying on the ground like drunkards: 'it looked like the aftermath of a defeat.' The marvels of Asia prove to be a more potent threat than its warriors.[38]

*

When Richard S. Elliott returned to the American West in 1874 to admire the region's development since he had crossed it with Doniphan's army twenty-eight years earlier, he was savouring a pleasure that many of the troops had felt during the expedition itself in anticipation of the changes that their conquests would bring. 'What a cheering reflection,' John Hughes exclaimed, 'that these beautiful ridges and outstretched plains will ere long be dotted with the cities, villages, and habitations of civilized life!' Another soldier wrote that the sight of the prairies would often cause 'Bryant's beautiful lines' to rise to his lips, and he would fancy, with the poet (and author of the classic comparison between Xenophon and Doniphan), 'The sound of that advancing multitude / Which soon shall fill these deserts.' The memoirs of Doniphan's expedition even included specific recommendations for settlement, including the area around the old Indian meeting-place known as Council Grove.[39]

Doniphan's troops felt many other pleasures during their march: the thrill of the plain stretching out to the horizon like a sea; earthly paradises full of wonderful food and wine; the sight of ruins – a melancholy hint of decay, but an incentive to their own Anglo-Saxon enterprise. Some of those pleasures were shared by Xenophon's men too. And as we have followed the trail of the two marches, we have gained a better sense of why the march of the Ten Thousand was so tempting a parallel for the Army of the West. The troops under Alexander Doniphan, 'the modern Xenophon', were not merely matching – or surpassing – their ancient Greek counterparts step for step; they were crossing landscapes similar in many way to the eastern lands experienced by Xenophon and viewing them, whether they knew it or not, with a perspective that was shaped in part by the way Xenophon's Greeks saw the world. Many readers of Xenophon, however, have implied an even closer link between the two armies. They have approached the *Anabasis* as if they were reading it through the eyes of Doniphan's men as they relentlessly pushed the borders of the United States further west, and claimed that Xenophon too was holding out the exhilarating prospect of new settlements in dimly known lands.

Is it necessarily wrong to read the *Anabasis* as supporting Greek colonization in the East? The possibility of a settlement in Mesopotamia is in fact hinted at twice in Xenophon's account of the tense days of negotiation that follow Cyrus' death. First, Xenophon claims that the Persians are afraid that the Greeks may stay where they are 'with the Tigris and the canal to either side as their defences, and with supplies available from the extensive, fertile land (which even had people already living there who could cultivate it)'. Later, after the murder of the Greek generals, Xenophon bolsters the army's morale in a speech in which he raises the same possibility. Alluding to the existence of autonomous people within Persian territory, some even with many 'prosperous and great cities', he argues that the army should make it look 'as if we were going to settle here'. He then raises the prospect of their living 'a life of ease and luxury, enjoying the company of these fine great women, the wives and daughters of the Medes and Persians', and ends by claiming that the Greeks back home 'might see people who have a wretched life in their own countries grow rich by coming out here'. Like the Americans in Mexico, Xenophon here figures conquest in terms of sexual control over women.[40]

Xenophon's speech to the dejected troops is the passage most commonly cited in readings of the *Anabasis* as a panhellenic tract. Such readings make it sound as if the extracts I have quoted reflect the tenor of the whole speech. But Xenophon's words need to be read in their rhetorical context. He wants to make it seem that the Greeks will stay in Mesopotamia as a ruse to make the king help them on their way: 'I think that it is right and reasonable for us to make it our first endeavour to reach our own folk in Greece and to demonstrate to the Greeks that their poverty is of their own choosing.' He also warns the Greeks that if they once got used to the luxuries of Mesopotamia – including the glamorous women – they might be 'like the Lotus-Eaters' and forget their road home. The rhetoric, eloquent of the Greeks' perception that they were on a new Odyssey, foreshadows the American 'Lotus-Eaters' in Nicaragua (the filibusters who married local women). The key difference, however, is that Xenophon invokes the Lotus-Eaters as a threat: this famous episode had already been allegorized by Plato as a warning against desires focused solely on the pleasures of the present. Xenophon, then, raises the possibility of their staying in Mesopotamia only to reinforce the importance of their returning home – and he knows that none of his comrades wants to stay anyway. At the same time, he suggests that the very practicality of a Greek settlement in the luxurious East is another reason for returning home. To show that Greeks can resist the dangerous allure of eastern luxuries is to suggest that Greeks are glad to be poor. Xenophon is not promoting a settlement in the East, but giving two reasons why the Greeks should go home.[41]

It is not only in the *Anabasis* that Xenophon warns of the dangers of eastern luxuries. Those dangers are also one of the leading themes of his *Cyropaedia*, probably written soon after the *Anabasis*. Xenophon there describes how Cyrus the Great wrests imperial control away from the Medes, only to begin adopting himself the forms of Median ceremonial. A biting epilogue brings out how the Persian empire begins to decline after Cyrus' death. In warning of these dangers, Xenophon was following the lead of Herodotus, whose vast history concludes with an anecdote in which Cyrus reflects that 'soft lands tend to breed soft men', for 'it is impossible for one and the same country to produce remarkable crops and good fighting men'. In these works it is the Persians, originally tough and poor, who are threatened by luxury – but the warning is felt to apply to Greeks too. The *Cyropaedia* has even been read as a warning against Greek ambitions in the East.[42]

Once we are alert to the undertones of the *Anabasis*, the attractive parallels with Doniphan's expedition begin to break down. Doniphan's soldiers viewed themselves as agents of Manifest Destiny. The American West was theirs to appropriate. The frontier offered a vast reserve of land that offered a cure to problems within the eastern cities. Xenophon's text makes similar gestures. But it draws back, darkens the picture. It does not promote colonization in Mesopotamia: no Greek before the time of Alexander seriously advocated that. Even the arch advocate of panhellenic expansion, Isocrates, was focused much more on the idea of settlement as a cure to problems within Greece than on the practical realities of colonizing Asia. When Isocrates is specific he thinks in terms of Greeks settling along the shoreline of Asia Minor – and, as we shall see, it is when the Greeks return to the Black Sea that the idea of founding a new city is raised as a possible solution to the mercenaries' problems.[43]

If the myth of the American West has at some level distorted the way Xenophon has been read, it has not been a one-way exchange. The vast

American gains in the Mexican War were themselves understood by some critics at the time to carry some of the dangers that Xenophon had analysed. 'The United States will conquer Mexico', Ralph Waldo Emerson reflected in his notebook in 1846, 'but it will be as the man swallows the arsenic, which brings him down in turn. Mexico will poison us.' Emerson here expressed the fears of the Whig anti-imperialists who opposed the war with Mexico. These fears were based in part on the prospect of racial intermingling with the Mexicans, and in part, too, on the slavery issue: the Whigs realized that the question of whether the new territories would be slave-holding could threaten the Union – as indeed happened. But behind those fears there lay anxieties over the dangers of luxury and of imperial overstretch that received classic expression in Greek and Roman political thought – anxieties that the conquest of new territories would pose a threat to the manhood of the republic itself. Those anxieties underlie W.H. Prescott's presentation of the 'Asiatic pomp and luxury' of the Aztec rulers, with courts like 'the voluptuous precincts of an Eastern harem' where they received the 'Oriental adulation' of their slavish subjects: the soft land of Mexico had bred soft people. The Spanish conquerors in turn had been softened by their environment. Would the Americans go the same way?[44]

Spartan Courage: The Culture of Militarism

Siek doesn't like our grab-ass, and he yells at us to resume the game, but we do not listen. He must know what terrible treat will soon be played out for the colonel and the reporters. ... Combs pulls Kuehn from the bottom of the pile and yells, 'Field-Fuck!' Fowler starts the fun, thrusting his hips against Kuehn's ass ... I stand back from a turn with Kuehn. I feel frightened and exhilarated by the scene. The exhilaration isn't sexual, it's communal – a pure surge of passion and violence and shared anger, a pure distillation of our confusion and hope and shared fear. We aren't field-fucking Kuehn: ... we're fucking the sand and the loneliness and the boredom ...

I believed I'd enlisted in the Marine Corps in order to claim my place in the military history of my family ... . By joining the Marine Corps and excelling within the severely disciplined enlisted ranks, I would prove both my manhood and the masculinity of my line ...

Anthony Swofford, Jarhead (2003)[1]

* * *

Christmas afternoon, 1846. Colonel Alexander Doniphan is playing a game of three-trick loo with some officers at Brazito, a 'little arm' of the Rio Grande. The day had dawned bright, and the Missouri volunteers had celebrated with songs of Yankee Doodle and Hail Columbia, before setting off for a march of eighteen miles. Now some of the men have scattered, searching for wood and water or for grass for the animals, while other soldiers are still arriving from the rear. Suddenly a cloud of dust, 'as if the whole of Mexico was coming down' on them, was seen towards the south, and the call came: 'To arms! To arms!' Colonel Doniphan sprang at once to his feet: 'Boys, I held an invincible hand, but I'll be d-mned if I don't have to play it out in steel now.'[2]

Doniphan's response to imminent danger was a calculated display of *sang froid*. His composed understatement was a way of quietly emphasizing what was at stake in the shift from the game of cards to the game of war. His invincible hand would now be replicated in steel – and the disciplined display by the troops under his command would be a powerful assertion of American manhood against a larger but feebler army. This image of toughness would be promoted not just by pithy one-liners but also by extensive comparisons with the Greek hoplites who had battled through Asia more than two thousand years earlier. Nor were Xenophon's troops the only ancient model used to convey the strength of Doniphan's troops: like the modern Marines in Iraq, the soldiers in Mexico also looked back to the renowned military prowess of the Spartans.

Sparta was frequently invoked to celebrate the achievements of American troops during the Mexican War. The Spartans had not been strongly favoured by the Founding Fathers: they were seen as 'military monks' (Jefferson) living in what was 'little better than a well regulated camp' (Hamilton). Now, by contrast, their militarism was more acceptable. More than one American army was hailed in the enthusiastic press at home as a 'Spartan band'. The leading general in Mexico, Zachary Taylor, was 'a Spartan' or even likened to 'the great Spartan' Agesilaus (the subject of an encomium by Xenophon). Many individual acts of heroism by American troops 'would have immortalized a Spartan'. And mothers and children at home were given the same label: a woman who told her son to follow his dead brother to defend his country was 'a Spartan mother', a boy who was confident that his father would rejoin the army despite losing his sword arm was 'a young Spartan'.[3]

In this chapter we will explore a series of key confrontations in which Doniphan's army in Mexico was seen as displaying a Spartan courage in opposition to the dangerously oriental Mexicans. At the same time, we will see that the appeal to Spartan models of valour and discipline forms a further link with Xenophon's portrayal of the Greek mercenaries in Asia – a link that says as much about the power of myth-making involved in all appeals to Spartan militarism as it does about the realities of warfare, ancient or modern. We start, however, by returning to the laconic Doniphan as he prepares to play out his hand in steel near the banks of the Rio Grande.

*

There were only 500 American troops present for the battle itself. They did not know the number of Mexicans facing them. As the troops watched the Mexicans advance from afar, they heard Doniphan appeal to the memory of their forefathers and in particular to a Missouri defeat against the Florida Seminoles on the same date nine years earlier. They also had a good chance to gaze at the 'most gallant and imposing appearance' of the Mexican troops. First they saw the Mexicans' 'red coats shining' as they approached with what one soldier regarded as 'a great deal of pomp and show' ('as they generally do', he added). Then the Mexicans drew up 'in good order', and the Americans had a better look: 'gay enough they looked', another soldier noted, 'their cavalry in bright scarlet coats with bell buttons, and snow-white belts, carrying polished sabres and carbines and long lances, with red and green pennons'. The Mexicans' 'bright lances and swords glittered in the sheen of the sun' as both sides waited for the battle to begin.[4]

The American soldiers gazed at this Mexican finery with a fascination mixed with strong distaste. They carried the same ambivalence beyond the battlefield too. On the road and in towns and cities they were frequently struck by the juxtaposition of ostentation and poverty. They deplored in particular the gaudiness of the grand and costly cathedrals, often framing their aesthetic aversion in overtly anti-Catholic terms. They also abhorred the luxury of the upper ranks of the Mexican military, but here they drew on a different set of associations: the idea that their journey through Mexico was like a journey to the lavish orient (see Chapter 4). Mexico was seen as oriental not just in its biblical architecture and in its landscape, but also in the splendour of its inhabitants' clothing. Strongly moulded by Prescott's portrayal of the Aztec rulers, this perception is memorably expressed in a scene in George Lippard's novel *Legends of Mexico* (1847) where readers are invited to place themselves inside the tent of a Mexican general: 'Within the tent, seated on a luxuriously cushioned chair, near a voluptuous bed, glistening with the trappings of oriental taste, you behold a man of warrior presence, his gay uniform thrown open across the breast, while he holds the goblet of iced champagne to his lips.' The rich language – 'luxuriously', 'voluptuous', 'glistening' – mimics the rich interior, appealing strongly, like most oriental fantasies, to the visual: Lippard makes you want to behold the scene, the blend of manly presence and ornate softness caught in suspension like the champagne frozen on its way to the general's lips.[5]

Condemnation of the Mexican upper-classes as luxury-loving orientals was reinforced by contrasts with the rugged demeanour of the American troops. In *Legends of Mexico*, the tent scene is followed by a visit to the 'rude' camp beds and 'plain apparel' of the American general Zachary Taylor, fondly known as 'Old Rough and Ready'. Among the Missouri volunteers, Doniphan displayed the same scorn for finery as Taylor, wearing the same clothes as his men and even joking that his men were 'rough, ragged, and ready, having one more of the R's than General Taylor himself'. Some onlookers described the 'vermin-covered' volunteers less favourably: when they took control of Chihuahua the Americans residents in the city were supposedly 'so thunderstruck by the savage exterior' of the troops 'that they ran back to their houses to ascertain first to what tribe or nation they belonged'. The difference between Mexican and American attire was grounded in a telling political contrast: one contemporary history claimed that the 'simplicity' of General Taylor was 'significant of pure republican institutions', while the 'semi-barbaric splendor' of his Mexican opponent, surrounded by officers in 'rich dresses' ever ready to pay 'the most abject respect to their chief', accorded with 'the despotism of the Mexican government'. Here Prescott's conception of the Aztecs is transferred more or less unchanged to modern Mexico.[6]

The American response to Mexican luxury mirrors a key theme in Greek depictions of Persian extravagance. When the Ten Thousand captured the tent of the Persian governor of Armenia, Xenophon takes care to

13. Mexican lancer in full finery.

mention the silver-footed couches and goblets that were in it, as well as 'some men who claimed to be the governor's bakers and cup-bearers'. His account reads like a small-scale repetition of a famous scene in Herodotus' account of the battle of Plataea (479 BC): after their victory the Greeks took control of the Persian camp, and found within it 'pavilions hung with gold and silver decorations, couches overlaid with gold and silver, various kinds of golden vessels, including bowls and cups'. The scene in Herodotus is famous because of what happens next: the Spartan regent Pausanias has Persian and Spartan meals prepared side-by-side in the tent of the Persian general Mardonius, amidst the luxurious trappings left by Xerxes. The Spartans' diet was famously simple (their black broth was particularly notorious). By exposing the contrast between the feasts enjoyed by the Persian leaders and the Greeks' meagre provisions, Pausanias was pointing up a moral: why did the wealthy Persians bother invading impoverished Greece? While Pausanias' question convicts the Persians of folly, it also poses a problem for the Americans in Mexico. If the opposition between lavish Persians and hardy Greeks is repeated in the opposition

96

14. 'Simplicity of Old Zack's Habits.'

between Mexicans and Americans, then that only points up a key difference: it was the plain Americans who were invading luxurious Mexico, not
the other way round. American moral criticism of Mexican luxury deflects
attention from the material rewards reaped by the invading army.[7]

It is not that Greeks always resisted the attractions of oriental trappings. Herodotus' scene in the Persian tent at Plataea is laden with irony:
the Spartan Pausanias was later to adopt oriental dress and diet as ruler
of Byzantium; he was even thought to have plotted to subjugate Greece to
the Persian king. Another Greek who seems to have delighted in fine
trappings is Xenophon himself. He describes how, before exhorting the
dejected mercenaries the morning after their generals had been killed, he
'put on his most splendid war-gear' because, no matter whether he was to
meet victory or death, both 'deserved the finest display'. The same fond-
ness for decoration appears in Xenophon's account of a parade of Cyrus'
army early in the march upcountry performed in front of Epyaxa, queen
of Cilicia, a region that lay further east on Cyrus' route. The queen admires
the 'brilliance' of Cyrus' army, and Xenophon illustrates that brilliance by

focusing on the bronze helmets and the dark red or purple cloaks worn by the Greek troops.[8]

Red cloaks were particularly associated in the Greek world with the Spartans, and Greek attempts to explain why the Spartans chose that colour offer an intriguing glimpse into the ambiguities of luxury in the Greek world. Xenophon himself wrote in his *Constitution of the Spartans* that red cloaks bore least resemblance to women's clothing and were most suited for war. Other theories were that red was terrifying to the enemy, made the Spartans used to the colour of blood, and disguised their wounds. These explanations are, however, as the classicist James Davidson observes, 'rather defensive in tone, the self-conscious forging of a myth': red cloaks could in fact look rather luxurious to the Athenian eye. The explanations are offered to preserve the illusion of Greek moderation. And in Xenophon's parade the fact that it is a foreign queen who admires the splendour of the red cloaks is another way of defusing the threat posed by luxury to the Greek self-image.[9]

Cyrus himself may not have meant the red cloaks of his Greek mercenaries to evoke Sparta at all. Red, as the military historian John Lee observes, was also used by Persian royalty: Xenophon describes in two rich passages in his *Cyropaedia* how the elder Cyrus' army 'flowered with red' and how Cyrus led from his new palace at Babylon a procession resplendent with purple and red cloaks. If the younger Cyrus' mercenaries were all in the same colours, then that must be because Cyrus himself had equipped them. Perhaps he put his hoplites in red not to make them look Spartan but to evoke Persian royal fashions. Or is Xenophon suggesting a fusion of Spartan and Persian, as in the *Cyropaedia*, where the originally egalitarian Persian society is painted in faintly Spartan colours? In either case it is the Greek hoplites who show the sort of pomp that American soldiers associated with the Mexicans.[10]

Contemporary Americans grasped that the example of Persia lay behind their denigration of the Mexicans' oriental pomp and luxury. In Lippard's *Legends of Mexico*, the Mexican army before the battle of Buena Vista is described as looking 'like the army of a Persian despot': 'so gaily flutter its innumerable red flags, from their flag-staffs of sharpened steel, so far, so wide it grows into space, so triumphantly it looks down, upon the little army, arrayed upon these northern ridges.' As in the descriptions of the Mexican advance at the battle of Brazito, the picture Lippard offers of the Mexican army with its gaily fluttering red flags implies by contrast the prowess and manhood of the American troops that oppose them: the position of the Americans on the 'northern ridges' may even hint at the common opposition between the balanced climate of the North and the soft and tropical South. And if Persia connoted luxury and weakness, then Greece could be shorthand for a hardy masculine physique: in a comparison that drew on the idealization of Greek sculpture promoted since the eighteenth century by the homoerotically-tinged writings of Winckelmann, another 1847 novel about the Mexican War described the hero (an American volunteer) as having 'limbs that developed muscle and strength which would in the days of Grecian splendor, have made him a favorite model for the sculptor's eye'.[11]

It is not just Greek masculinity and Persian luxury that were in play in the alignment of Greek with American and of Persian with Mexican. Lippard's description of the Mexican army also dwells on its size: the 'innumerable' flags of the Mexican army growing 'so far, so wide' into space contrast with the Americans' 'little army'. This opposition hints at the Greeks' greatly exaggerated estimates of the size of Persian armies: Herodotus makes the size of Xerxes' invading force two and a half million (and double that if you include the camp followers); even Xenophon, a participant, credits the Persian king with an army of 900,000 at Cunaxa. The same rhetoric of numbers was also used in the stories told about Doniphan's troops as they watched the Mexican line at Brazito – and found themselves confronted by a choice also faced by their Greek counterparts in Mesopotamia more than two thousand years earlier: to surrender or to fight.[12]

*

A man on horseback suddenly emerges from the glittering Mexican ranks. As he approaches 'with the speed of lightning', the American troops see that he is carrying a black flag with 'a skull and cross bones worked upon it'. Sixty yards from the American line, the messenger stops and waves his flag. Doniphan sends out an interpreter to see what is up. The Mexicans are basking in their superior numbers. The Americans discover that they are demanding 'the surrender of our entire force': 'by submitting, ... our lives would be spared; if we did not, every man would be put to death.' The American interpreter replies at once: 'If your general wants to see our commander, let him come here.' The Mexican retorts: 'We shall break your ranks, then, and take him there.' It is the American who has the last word: 'Come and take him.'[13]

Now for the scene in the Mesopotamian desert the morning after the battle of Cunaxa. The Greeks have learnt that Cyrus is dead. Some envoys arrive from the Persian king and from the satrap Tissaphernes, among them a Greek, Phalinus, a self-proclaimed military expert who has a position of honour in Tissaphernes' court. The envoys report Artaxerxes' terms: as the king is the victor, the Greeks must hand over their weapons and come to the king's doors (a common Greek phrase for the Persian court). The Spartan Clearchus, who has assumed the position of leader after Cyrus' death, replies that the Greeks are the victors and winners do not normally hand their weapons over. He then leaves the floor to others. Some urge humility: perhaps they should offer to help the king subdue a rebellion in Egypt. Phalinus himself warns the Greeks that the king 'is in a position to bring so many men up against you that you wouldn't be able to kill them all even if he made it easy for you'. A young Athenian, Theopompus, retorts that 'we have nothing going for us except our weapons and our courage' – and so 'if we keep our weapons, we think we can make use of our courage'. Phalinus laughs: 'You sound like a philosopher.' It is the Spartan Clearchus who has the last word: 'if we must become friends with the king, we would be more valuable friends if we have our arms than if we hand them over to someone else; and if we must fight, we would fight better if we have our arms than if we hand them over to someone else.'[14]

The Greeks' refusal to hand over their weapons after Cyrus' death was also described by the first-century BC Sicilian historian Diodorus. In Diodorus' account (probably derived from the fourth-century BC historian Ephorus), the Greek generals listen to Artaxerxes' demand, and then each of them 'made a reply much like that which Leonidas made when he was guarding the pass of Thermopylae, and Xerxes sent messengers asking him to lay down his arms'. Diodorus then explains the allusion: 'Leonidas at that time instructed the messengers to report to the king: "We believe that if we become friends of Xerxes, we shall be better allies if we keep our arms, and if we are forced to wage war against him, we shall fight the better if we keep them."' Diodorus attributes to all the Greek generals the final response given by Clearchus in Xenophon's account, and he points out that that response was modelled on the heroic resistance at Thermopylae. By refusing to surrender despite the odds against them, the Ten Thousand were showing the same spirit as the 300 Spartans.[15]

The Americans at Brazito also showed the Thermopylae spirit. The interpreter's response to the demand that Doniphan appear before the Mexican commander – 'Come and take him' – echoed the most common – and laconic – version of Leonidas' reply at Thermopylae. This ancient parallel was not lost on at least some of the soldiers: their interpreter, one of them wrote the next day, was 'unwittingly using the phrase of the Spartan at Thermopylae'.[16]

This primal Thermopylae scene was reprised later in Doniphan's march. A dozen soldiers – among them John Hughes – were dispatched across Mexico to gain instructions from the main American army. One morning, as they broke for coffee at the base of a high mountain, they were surrounded by seventy-five armed Mexicans. There was, Hughes reported, 'but one sentiment in our little band, and that was to fight until the last man expired'. They at once formed into line of battle and gave 'the Spartan reply': *Here we are, if you want us come and take us!*[17]

These episodes suggest that, like the modern Marines, the soldiers in Doniphan's army looked back with particularly warm feelings on the Spartans, renowned in antiquity for their militarism. One of the officers, William Gilpin, was later to exhort an audience to confront danger 'with Spartan, with American, will' – as if the two were the same. Another soldier imagined in his journal a parting scene in which the weeping father tells his son to have 'a Spartan's courage'. More pathetic are the words written in a mother's letter to her son, found in his belongings after his death: she wrote that she felt 'like the Spartan mother who presented a shield to her boy as he was going to battle, and said: "Return with it or return upon it – with it or on it".' The hackneyed saying still had the power to move – especially as the son died, like so many others, not in battle but of fever.[18]

The soldiers felt an especially strong attachment to the heroic defence of Thermopylae. Just before the start of the war, a newspaper that criticized Polk's war policy for endangering the American troops near the Mexican frontier was nonetheless sure that the men would not shame themselves: 'they will consecrate their camp as an American Thermopylae.' Soon afterwards the 300 defenders of an isolated fort opposite Matamoras were hailed as a 'Spartan band' in Lippard's *Legends of Mexico*. And in the same novel, immediately after comparing the Mexican force at Buena Vista with the army of a Persian despot, Lippard again evokes Thermopylae as he celebrates the Americans' response to a Mexican demand that they surrender. A sole Kentucky cavalryman is led into the presence of the Mexican general Santa Anna: 'But Taylor ... What does he mean to do? Surrounded by twenty thousand men, he must surrender?' At those words the young Kentuckian, 'born of the land of Boone', utters 'the phrase, which has already been linked with the "*Come and take me!*" of ancient story: "GENERAL TAYLOR NEVER SURRENDERS!"'. As Lippard's flamboyant account shows, Leonidas' words could be applied to any refusal to surrender to larger numbers. At Buena Vista, moreover, the Thermopylae parallel was boosted by geography: the Americans, 'like the Spartans of old, were defending another Thermopylae' – the pass of Angostura.[19]

The American Spartans springing up all over Mexico were reviving the spirit of an event that had already become legendary – the defence of the Alamo (1836). Comparisons with Thermopylae were made soon after the defenders had died to a man against the Mexican onslaught: they were described as a 'Spartan band' or as 'American Spartans', and the Alamo itself was 'the Thermopylae of Texas' or a 'new Thermopylae'. The comparison was spread above all by the catchphrase 'Thermopylae had her messenger of defeat; the Alamo had none'. These words, first uttered in a speech at the Alamo in 1842 and then inscribed on a monument in Austin, Texas, the following year, neatly convey the Americans' sense of superiority: even in heroic defeat, the Americans outdid the Greeks. (They did not add that the sole survivor from the 300 Spartans felt such shame that he deliberately courted and met a heroic death the following year at the battle of Plataea.)[20]

So strong was the cult of Thermopylae at the time of the Mexican War that it could even be used to elevate the global role of the American republic. The year before the war broke out, a *New York Herald* editorial spoke of America as refuge for the 'down-trodden masses of the whole European world', 'a pillar of cloud by day and a pillar of fire by night to the followers of liberty throughout the civilized world': 'This is, indeed, the world's Thermopylae.' This extraordinary fusion of classical and biblical (the pillars evoke the Jewish exodus from Egypt to the promised land) points to the underlying ideological appeal of the Thermopylae allusions that were scattered with such abandon on the battlefields of Mexico. At the same time, to cast America as 'the world's Thermopylae' was also, knowingly or not, to appropriate a phrase applied to Britain during the Napoleonic Wars.[21]

Americans could also blur the Thermopylae paradigm with the experience of the Ten Thousand – just as the Greek generals themselves seem to have done the morning after Cunaxa when they echoed Leonidas' dismissive reply to Xerxes. These were the two ancient episodes used in an 1848 newspaper satire on the Democrat presidential candidate Lewis Cass. The article purported to present an overheard conversation in which a supporter of Cass appealed to his heroic generalship in the War of 1812: 'Talk of your Leonidas and your Xenophen [*sic*], your defence of Thermopylae, and your retreat of the ten thousand, will you? Open your heads if you dare about the heroes of Monterey, Buena Vista and Cerro Gordo; what are all these trifling affairs to the acts of the renowned hero of Duck Creek ...?' And what had happened at Duck Creek? Cass, 'at the head of only two hundred and fifty men', had attacked a log bridge 'garrisoned by a strong garrison of Canadians and Indians, fifteen in number' – 'and with his tremendous disparity of numbers, he actually succeeded in putting the enemy to flight'. Despite the playful inversion, the anecdote's stress on a disparity of numbers does still hint at the link between the self-image of the American troops in Mexico and the experiences of both the Ten Thousand in Mesopotamia and the Spartans at Thermopylae. The same link appears in a more serious form in a funeral oration for the Kentucky soldiers who fell at Buena Vista delivered by John C. Breckenridge (later a leading Confederate). Breckenridge praised the American army as a 'Spartan band' (Thermopylae language), and then developed a longer comparison with Xenophon's Greeks: 'Far from their country, their communications cut off, encompassed by overwhelming numbers, and in the presence of a relentless foe, our little army stood like the ten thousand Greeks in the midst of the Persian Empire, the history of whose retreat is classic story.' While he went on to degrade the Greeks with characteristic American one-upmanship ('That was retreat – this was victory'), Breckenridge's focus on the Americans as 'encompassed by overwhelming numbers' explains why they could be seen as similar to the Greeks in Mesopotamia and the Spartans at Thermopylae, exploiting the same rhetoric mockingly twisted in the Cass anecdote.[22]

'One American good as 3 Englishmen – 7 Mexicans': Thomas Wolfe's vision of American manhood battling against the odds hits on a longstanding element of US victory culture, nourished in the twentieth century by war films and westerns and before that by history schoolbooks. Thomas Wolfe perhaps exaggerated when he pitted one American against seven Mexicans – but not by much. Three against one are the odds which Zachary Taylor, head of the US army in the war against Mexico, banked on when informed that the Mexican general Santa Anna was advancing with thirty thousand men: 'In that event, I shall want ten thousand.' And one of Doniphan's own soldiers joked that the Mexican commanders 'knew nothing of arithmetic, but tried to stand against the Missourians with five men to one' – which merely meant that 'there were *five* chances for a Mexican to be killed against *one* for a Missourian'.[23]

The American scorn for mere numerical superiority also appears in Xenophon. The American economist Alvin Johnson, who thought of the 'blithe and gallant and resourceful' Xenophon as 'the first American', cited a speech where Xenophon 'assured the Greeks they had nothing to fear from the million soldiers Artaxerxes had brought against them': 'Doesn't that sound like a Yankee?' The same attitude is revealed in a speech Cyrus delivers to the Greek generals in the run-up to Cunaxa. Cyrus explains that he did not seek their help 'for lack of barbarian troops', but because he thought that they were 'better and stronger than many barbarians'. And the opposition he draws between barbarian *anthropoi* (literally 'humans') and Greek *andres* (literally 'men' – i.e. real men) hints at the source of this sense of superiority. The ability of Greek courage to overcome greatly superior Persian numbers was a standard element in eulogies of the Persian Wars, but it is most memorably encapsulated in Herodotus' description of the Persian charge at Thermopylae: the Persians' failure to break through showed that they had 'many *anthropoi*, but few *andres*'.[24]

The appeal to the bravery of the Spartans outnumbered at Thermopylae creates a problem for both the American troops in Mexico and Xenophon's Greeks in Asia. The parallel involves an inversion of invaders and invaded. The Spartans at Thermopylae were defending Greece against the Persians. The Americans and the Ten Thousand, by contrast, were both in foreign lands. For invading troops, whether Greek or American, to invoke Thermopylae is to claim that, no matter where they are, they are defending the cause of freedom and upholding the cause of the West in the long clash of civilizations. The inversion is slightly less of a problem for the Greeks, who had followed their employer Cyrus to Mesopotamia and had not set out to conquer the land for themselves. But Xenophon brings out all too clearly the awkwardness of their moral position: at a critical point after the murder of the Greek generals, he warns the Greeks that Artaxerxes will do everything 'to make us suffer in agony' in return for trying to dethrone him. The Americans had even less excuse to be in Mexico – and they occasionally let the Thermopylae cat out of the bag: instead of the Americans being the defenders, as at Buena Vista, it was sometimes the Mexicans who failed to defend a Thermopylae-like pass, or else an American general who stormed 'the Thermopylae of the country'. The force of the classical allusion is turned around: the Americans are now aligned not with the heroic Greeks, but with the Persian despot.[25]

The allusions to Thermopylae are problematic for another reason. Both the Greek generals after Cunaxa and the American interpreter at Brazito have been thought to echo Leonidas' reply to Xerxes' demand that the Spartans hand over their weapons. But that reply is not mentioned in Herodotus, our most important source for Thermopylae. Nor is Xerxes' demand, for that matter. The American 'Come and get him' response does at least echo the most famous version of the Thermopylae legend (the source is Plutarch's *Spartan Sayings*). But the reply given by Xenophon's Clearchus to the Persian demand that the Ten Thousand hand over their weapons echoes the words used by Leonidas only as they are reported by Diodorus. It is possible that Diodorus' source Ephorus borrowed the reply from Xenophon, whose account formed the basis for Ephorus' own narrative of Cyrus' expedition. Rather than Clearchus consciously making a Thermopylae gesture, Ephorus could have been incorporating Xenophon's scene in the Thermopylae legend – and in that case all we have is evidence that this key scene of the *Anabasis* could be read as a revival of the Persian Wars spirit.[26]

A further problem lurks in our Brazito cameo. The scene between the Mexican messenger and the American interpreter appears in all the memoirs of Doniphan's expedition, but it is told in notably different ways. Most accounts present the Mexican message not as a demand for surrender but as an invitation to talk. And while some of these accounts do report the response as 'Come and take him', in the journal that speaks of a demand for surrender the American interpreter cuts short the Mexican 'harangue' by telling him to 'go to hell and bring on his forces'. It is as likely that Thermopylae influenced the way the story was told as that the interpreter himself echoed Leonidas.[27]

The main paradox in appealing to Thermopylae is that that battle was a defeat. 'Come and get me': the Persians did just that, eventually; and Xerxes even had Leonidas' body mutilated. It was Greek myth-making that made that defeat something greater than a victory, by stressing that the Spartans were undefeated until the Persians were informed of a side path. Thanks to that myth-making, Thermopylae can be invoked as readily to celebrate victories over superior numbers as to cast an aura of heroism on defeats (it was later to be used in accounts of Custer's last stand and in a chilling order to the German troops abandoned at Stalingrad). In the case of the Ten Thousand, the hints of Thermopylae prepare for a contrast: the Greeks do manage to get away. How would the Americans, outnumbered three to one, fare at Brazito?[28]

*

The messenger with the black flag has retired, and the stage is now set for the Mexican charge. Doniphan and his officers are 'as calm and collected as when on drill'. At three or four hundred feet the Mexicans start firing, but Doniphan tells his men to lie on their faces and withhold fire until the Mexicans are within sixty paces. Closer and closer the Mexicans come, 'pouring in volley after volley', but still the Americans do not respond. Finally, as the Mexicans advance to the American line with exultant cries of '*bueno, bueno*', the Missouri troops stand up and fire. The Mexicans fall back before the blast and the Americans charge them off the field. The battle has lasted half an hour. Losses for the Americans are seven or eight wounded, and none dead; estimates for the Mexican dead range from three to sixty-three.[29]

Many of the American soldiers regarded their first taste of battle as nothing more than a 'Christmas frolic'. Nonetheless, Brazito was hailed in the press at home as a 'Glorious Victory!', and the soldiers were the pride of Missouri: William Gilpin, one of their officers, claimed in a speech a month after their return that he found 'at all times the most admirable discipline, the most prompt and spontaneous obedience; at all times a modest, unassuming bravery'; another soldier wrote that they behaved like 'veterans', exhibiting 'a coolness and obedience to orders worthy of any troops'. The overall lesson of the battle was spelt out by a German doctor who accompanied the troops in the later stages of their march: 'this first successful skirmish taught them their own strength and the weakness of the enemy, and imbued them with the daring, invincible spirit that marked their long, conquering march through Mexico.' Similarly the retreat of the Ten Thousand was thought in antiquity to have exposed the weakness of the Persian empire, teaching a lesson that was understood by Alexander of Macedon seventy years later.[30]

Not everyone was forthcoming in praise of the Missouri volunteers. One of the traders scoffed that at Brazito 'the companies were formed in as good order as undisciplined troops could be by officers entirely unacquainted with military tactics' – that is, they drew up 'in a straight line'. This was perhaps unfair: when the volunteers gathered at Fort Leavenworth they spent twenty days drilling twice a day on a stretch of prairie they named 'Campus Martis'. But Francis Parkman thought that, while the volunteers had known how 'to keep their ranks and act as one man', they were 'worthless indeed' if 'discipline and subordination' were the criterion of merit. The difference in spirit between the volunteers and the regular army is well conveyed by two episodes. First, an exchange between Doniphan and General Kearny, who was in charge of Doniphan's contingent as far as Santa Fé: when Kearny told Doniphan that he needed to adopt 'more strict and soldier like discipline', Doniphan replied that 'more strict discipline would break down the men & horses', but that 'when the time comes for efficient action, you will find these men unflinching'. Next, a moment of insubordination after a march of over twenty-five miles across the desert: Doniphan's deputy (a West Point graduate) ordered a battalion that was some miles ahead to drill in the hot sun, in a breeze 'as withering as the breath of the Sahara', and the ensuing uproar, in John Hughes' understated words, 'came near resulting in a total disregard of the order'. The officer was subsequently subjected to underhand persecution by his men until he resigned to rejoin the regular army.[31]

Charges of indiscipline on the march only reinforced pride in the way victory was won. The troops themselves agreed on the hallmarks of their invincible spirit: the cohesion and restraint they showed in holding fire, the ability to 'whip any number of the enemy' brought against them, the belief that American ruggedness was better than Mexican pomp. This spirit was born of a strong sense of racial supremacy, but it was grounded, too, in a perceived continuity between Doniphan's troops and the fighting qualities of the Ten Thousand and the Spartans. And the repeated praise of the volunteers' obedience in battle, their ability to keep rank and act as one man, suggests that there was more to the widespread cult of the military virtues of Greece than admiration for the Greeks' toughness and for their ability to beat larger armies. Discipline and unity in battle were also Greek – and especially Spartan – ideals: as Herodotus makes the exiled Spartan king Demaratus tell Xerxes, the Spartans are 'as good as anyone in the world when it comes to fighting one on one, but they're the best when it comes to fighting in groups'.[32]

*

The ability of Cyrus' Greek mercenaries to act as one man, to stay together like Spartans, is asserted near the start of the *Anabasis* in the scene where the Greek troops parade in their red cloaks before Cyrus and the Cilician queen Epyaxa. The parade seems unimportant in itself, but in Xenophon's hands the scene becomes a minor literary classic:

> Cyrus inspected the Greeks, all of whom wore bronze helmets, red cloaks, and greaves, and had their shields uncovered, by driving his chariot past them, while the Cilician queen rode in a carriage. When Cyrus had driven past them all, he halted his chariot in front of the middle of the phalanx, and sent his translator, Pigres, to convey to the Greek generals his request that they should have the entire phalanx move forward with levelled weapons. The generals passed these orders on to their men, and when the trumpet sounded they advanced with their weapons levelled. Soon they were moving faster and faster, until with a shout the soldiers spontaneously broke into a run and charged towards the camp. This terrified the barbarians; the Cilician queen fled in her carriage and the merchants in the market abandoned their wares and ran away, while the Greeks, hugely amused, dispersed to their tents. But the Cilician queen was very impressed by the brilliance and the discipline of the army, and Cyrus was delighted to see how frightened the barbarians were by the Greeks.[33]

Xenophon's splendid set-piece has inspired some later accounts of disciplined troops at drill. Rider Haggard may have had it in mind when he penned the charge of the Kukuanas in his 1885 classic *King Solomon's Mines* ('It was a splendid sight to see them, each company about three hundred strong, charging swiftly up the slope, with flashing spears and waving plumes, and taking their appointed place ...'), though his fictional Africans are more closely modelled on the Zulus, the 'Black Spartans'. Even closer to Xenophon's scene is the vivid conclusion to Rudyard Kipling's *Jungle Book* story 'Her Majesty's Servants' (1894) – a parade put on before the Viceroy of India and the Amir of Afghanistan. The line of British Army soldiers grows into 'one solid wall of men, horses, and guns', and as it comes on straight towards the dignitaries the effect is so frightening that the Amir starts glancing behind him, as if he is about to slash his way out. But, unlike the Ten Thousand, the British army stops dead and salutes. Kipling's story closes with an old Central Asian chief hearing how it was done: 'there was an order, and they obeyed.' The chief wishes it were so in Afghanistan – 'for there we obey only our own wills'. And that is why, a native officer informs him, 'your Amir whom you do not obey must come here and take orders from our Viceroy'. The obedient troops in British colours contrast with the wild and wilful Afghans.[34]

Xenophon's account of the Greeks' parade-ground charge has been read as a decisive demonstration of the superiority of the western way of war – an imperial spectacle similar to the parade in Kipling's story. It was quoted in full by Hippolyte Taine in his 1856 article on the *Anabasis*: this, Taine suggested, was 'how the Peruvians feared the Spaniards' (he went on to speak more broadly of the expeditions of Cortes and Pizarro as similar to those of Xenophon and Agesilaus, the Spartan king who invaded Asia Minor not long after the return of the Ten Thousand). And the drill is also cited by Victor Davis Hanson as the epigraph for the opening chapter ('Why the West has Won') of *Carnage and Culture*, the book whose unrelenting message of western military supremacy provoked controversy at the time of the 9/11 attacks (see Chapter 1). Hanson (who also, like Taine, compares the Ten Thousand with Cortes' small band in Mexico) implies that the drill of the Ten Thousand encapsulates the western way of war: discipline, unity, a display of brute power – a good laugh for the Greek soldiers but a fearsome sight for the barbarians who behold it; and above all, a taste for shock battle face-to-face with the enemy.[35]

A problem with the way Taine and Hanson read Xenophon is that they take his account at face value. Throughout his essay on the *Anabasis* Taine expresses his admiration for Xenophon's artlessness: Xenophon's account is 'the pure image of events ... he announces nothing in advance, he does not intervene in the narration ... there is nothing between us and the facts'. The same faith in Xenophon's narrative is implicit in Hanson's readiness to take the description of the parade as an unproblematic representation of Greek military superiority. But Xenophon's description of the drill is far from artless. The scene gains prominence by its position near the start of the narrative, by the level of detail allotted to the event in an otherwise fairly swift-moving section, and by the non-Greek perspectives (Cyrus, Epyaxa) embedded within it. Xenophon's account also draws on an established literary tradition to create its effect. The term used to describe the Cilician queen's response to the hoplites' performance (*thaumazein*) has connotations of the marvellous – the stock material of Greek geographical descriptions of distant lands (we saw in Chapter 4 that Xenophon uses the same term for the sweet dates of Mesopotamia). But Xenophon inverts the usual direction of the movement: instead of Greek men marvelling at the exotic Other, a foreign woman marvels at the world of Greeks. But what is admired in the world of the Greeks is not vast buildings or the extraordinary richness of the natural world (India's massive gold-gathering ants, Arabia's aromatic spices), as in Herodotus' depiction of foreign lands, but military discipline. The verb used to describe Cyrus' delight (*hedesthai*) at the sight of the troops also draws on conventional characterizations of oriental despots. The delight felt by foreign kings is an expression of power (they are pleased at the services offered them), but it is also often tinged with foreboding. Here, not for the only time, Cyrus is prematurely adopting a regal gaze.[36]

Xenophon's literary artistry is also reflected in another point that Taine and Hanson fail to acknowledge – the fact that depictions of scenes such as the hoplites' charge are themselves parts of narratives. Xenophon's account of the charge stands where it does for a purpose: its effect is modified and complicated by the progression of the story. The note of irony in Cyrus' response to the parade is strengthened when Xenophon describes the Greek hoplites in operation during the battle of Cunaxa. Connecting his account with the parade scene by verbal and thematic repetition, Xenophon describes how Cyrus is 'pleased' (*hedomenos*) when he sees that the Greeks have defeated the Persian unit opposite them and set out in pursuit. Some of his entourage even start 'doing homage to him as king' (that is, they perform the gesture known as *proskunesis*, which the Greeks represent as falling to one's knees in oriental slavishness). As in the earlier scene, Cyrus' pleasure is derived from the sight of Greek troops in action and associated with his own royal pretensions. But the Greek charge was not the one that Cyrus had initially wanted. He positioned the Greek hoplites on the right of the battle line, next to the River Euphrates and well away from the Persian king, who was in the centre of the royal army, outflanking the left wing of Cyrus' army. He then ordered the Greek general Clearchus to lead the Greeks across the battlefield directly against the king. But Clearchus refused, afraid that the Greeks would be encircled. Xenophon suggests that Cyrus was basing his strategy for the battle on the same shock effect of Greek hoplites that was seen in the charge that frightened the Cilician queen. The Greeks do carry out a charge with the ruthless precision seen in their earlier drill – but it is only against the troops stationed opposite them. They are not at hand to support Cyrus in the heat of battle as he makes the impulsive charge against his brother that has stuck in the minds of Thomas Wolfe and other schoolboy readers of the *Anabasis* ('*Ton andra horo*' – 'I see the man!').[37]

The narrative irony at Cyrus' expense need not detract from admiration for the hoplites. The Greeks still claim that they were victorious against the Persian contingents that opposed them. Their performance in the battle was cited by the Athenian orator Isocrates half a century later in a letter written to encourage Alexander of Macedon's father, Philip II, to launch an attack on Persia: the Greeks who took the field with Cyrus, Isocrates claimed, 'won as complete a victory in battle over all the forces of the king as if they had come to blows with their womenfolk' – an overt condemnation of the effeminacy of the Persian forces. And yet the fact that Clearchus' refusal to follow Cyrus' battle plan was prompted by the fear that they would be encircled by the superior numbers of the Persians undermines Cyrus' earlier dismissal of mere numbers. The heavily-armoured Greek troops may be able to push through the lighter Persian lines, but Cyrus would have had more of a chance with rather more than ten thousand of them.[38]

To isolate the hoplites' parade-ground charge as a sign of a continuity in western military efficiency and discipline is to be taken in by the cunning of Xenophon's narrative. The *Anabasis* as a whole shows that much more was needed for a military adventure in Asia than the qualities displayed by the hoplites on the parade ground – cavalry and slingers for a start. The hoplites' charge took place on a flat plain – ideal hoplite terrain. Not long afterwards, Cyrus sent some of the hoplites through more mountainous terrain, and two companies (100 men) were lost altogether. And after Cyrus' death the hoplites had few enough chances to charge on the sort of level ground on which they performed for Cyrus. It required extraordinary versatility and strong leadership for the Ten Thousand to overcome the obstacles that faced them in the mountains of Asia. But hoplites could not have done it by themselves.[39]

It is not only our view of the Greek hoplites that is modified by the progression of Xenophon's narrative. He also makes us reassess our perception of the non-Greek troops. When Xenophon presents Cyrus disparaging the king's army before the battle of Cunaxa by saying that 'they attack with a lot of shouting', he draws on a conventional view of noise as characteristic of unruly barbarian troops. Cyrus' remarks are then explicitly overturned in the account of the battle itself. The royal army actually advances 'as silently as they could, calmly, in a slow, steady march' – rather like the Spartans in Thucydides' account of the battle of Mantinea. They are in fact less noisy than the Greek hoplites, who utter a shout on the parade-ground as they start to charge towards the tents.[40]

The parade scene is itself soon followed by a scene where it is Persians rather than Greeks who put on a display of discipline – a scene that also points to the power of a rather different value-system from the individualism and civic militarism that Hanson sees as constants of the western tradition. The Persian display comes when the army has come upon a muddy stretch of ground which was hard going for the wagons (a problem that often faced travellers on the American prairie). Cyrus first asks the barbarian troops to shift the wagons, and then, when things seem to be going slowly, he tells the Persian nobles to lend a hand:

> It then became possible to witness a fine bit of discipline. They let their outer robes of purple drop to the ground without caring where they stood and sprinted, as if they were competing in a race, down a very steep hillside in their expensive tunics and colourful trousers, with some of them even wearing torques around their necks and bracelets on their arms. As soon as they got there, they leapt into the mud in all their finery and lifted the carts free of the mud more quickly than one would have thought possible.

This memorable scene picks up some of the terms of the Greeks' earlier display. But now it is implicitly the Greeks who are watching a display of Persian running and discipline. The effect is stronger for the visual brilliance of the scene. Xenophon's stress on the fact that the Persians were wearing jewellery and fancy clothes (Greeks did not wear trousers) could easily be taken as a condemnation of oriental decadence and effeminacy. But his message here is that these luxurious garments did not impede the efficient extraction of the carts. One nineteenth-century traveller in Persia found this scene alone proof that the Persians had for some time at least survived their alleged corruption by Babylonian decadence. Another traveller was reminded of it when a new carriage was presented to the Shah, and the Chief Executioner and other persons of rank, 'all in their court dresses', fastened themselves to it and dragged the king 'backwards and forwards to his great delight'. Persian nobility, past and present, could, it seems, respond with the same vigour shown by early American pioneers.[41]

Some scholars have resisted Xenophon's apparent readiness to admire the energy of the Persian nobles. One of the most sensitive modern critics of Xenophon suggests that there is 'more than a little humor in the scene of these begrimed dandies sloshing in the mud, while Cyrus remains apart, ever the Persian prince' (he contrasts the personal involvement of Greek generals like Clearchus and Xenophon). Yet in a similar scene in Xenophon's *Oeconomicus* it is Cyrus himself whose energy and industry are admired. The Spartan Lysander, given a tour of the 'paradise' at Sardis by Cyrus, first marvels (the verb *thaumazein* is used) at the beauty of the trees and the way they were planted, and, as he gazes at Cyrus, 'seeing the beauty of the robes that he wore, and smelling his perfume, and seeing the beauty of his necklaces and anklets and other ornaments that he wore', is astonished to discover that Cyrus arranged the whole plantation and even planted some of the trees himself. Once again the expected link between ornate decoration and softness is overthrown.[42]

5. Spartan Courage: The Culture of Militarism

Xenophon brings out the value system underlying this Persian luxury after Cyrus is struck down during the battle of Cunaxa. He notes that the 'most loyal' of Cyrus' staff-bearers leapt off his horse and threw himself over Cyrus' body – and, according to one report, killed himself there: 'For he carried a golden dagger, and also wore all the usual accoutrements that noble Persians wear, such as a torque and armlets, which had been given to him by Cyrus as rewards for his loyalty and reliability.' Xenophon is here asserting the fundamental role played by gift-giving in Persian royal ideology. The wearing of jewellery in the Persian court was honorific, with a calibrated system of honour determining the king's gifts of clothes and jewellery. Xenophon describes elsewhere how Cyrus rewards the ruler of Cilicia with 'gifts which are regarded as tokens of honour at the king's court', including a golden torque and armlets – as nineteenth-century observers noted, 'precisely the presents which a sovereign of Persia would consider at the present day as most suitable to his dignity as marks of his royal favour and esteem'. From this perspective, it is, paradoxically, Persian luxury that ensures courage: those who are honoured by Cyrus honour him in return. Cyrus did not need to get his hands dirty. This system of ethics (analysed in more detail by Xenophon in his *Cyropaedia*) is grounded in inter-personal relations, not in the abstract (and to some extent incompatible) concepts such as individualism and civic militarism on which Victor Davis Hanson bases his theory of western supremacy. To borrow a concept from David Cannadine's analysis of the British empire, it is not so much orientalism as 'ornamentalism' – 'hierarchy made visible, immanent and actual'.[43]

The high value Xenophon seems to attach to this Persian practice of gift-exchange seems at odds with his apparent warnings that the luxuries of the East pose a threat to the Greeks (see Chapter 4). His warnings are, however, against the dangers posed by luxuries that promise pleasure only in the present. What he seems to value is the cultural use of wealth to construct an orderly system of values that transcends the present.

The political implications of Xenophon's apparent admiration for a system grounded in the top-down largess of a monarch have also met with resistance. Hippolyte Taine contrasted the 'overzealousness' of the Persian nobles dragging carts from the mud with the Greek soldiers' 'independence' and 'republican habits'. This contrast could also be read back into the parade scene. It is the non-Greek troops who stick most closely to orders: the admiration Epyaxa feels for the discipline of Cyrus' army presumably includes them as well. The Greeks go beyond orders by running right up to the tents. They obey their own wills, acting spontaneously (the Greek is *apo tou automatou* – they run on automatic). Xenophon could be suggesting that the spontaneous Greeks combine discipline when it counts with a certain amount of freedom and relaxed camaraderie at other times. If so, his presentation of the Greeks would be strikingly similar to the twin image of the Missouri volunteers as undisciplined on the march but acting as one when facing the enemy. It would fit, too, the terms in which Victor Davis Hanson defines the roots of western supremacy.[44]

But could Xenophon also be suggesting that the Greeks' republican independence posed a threat to their own safety? In the parade scene, their spontaneity is on display in a risk-free setting. It does not threaten the army's overall order. But there are times in the army's long march when the army's equilibrium comes to be tested severely – when the cohesion between such potentially conflicting values as discipline and individualism breaks down. Similarly the profits reaped by American discipline in battle come to be threatened by American indiscipline outside battle. Perceptions of the lands and troops confronted by Xenophon's Greeks and the Missouri volunteers may have been shaped by negative ideas of oriental despotism, but as we follow the Greek and American armies further through alien lands we will find them struggling to offer positive political visions of their own.

6

A Wandering Democracy:
Freedom on the March

Burke surveyed the platoon, hands clasped behind his back.
He yelled, addressing us all. 'I am your mommy and your daddy! I am
your nightmare and your wet dream! I am your morning and your night! ...
Do you understand me, recruits?'
    'Sir, yes, sir!'
    'If your daddy is a doctor or if you come from the projects in East St Louis
or a reservation in Arizona, it no longer matters. Black. White. Mexican.
Vietnamese. Navajo. The Marine Corps does not care!'
                            Anthony Swofford, *Jarhead* (2003)[1]

Anthony Swofford's account of Marines training suggests that more than
individual manhood is at stake in American military culture. Armies are
not just vehicles for expressing masculinity: they are complex political
bodies in their own right. Often taken as representative of the nation they
defend, they also supply or usurp the place of family; often seen as
promoters of freedom, they are strongly marked by hierarchy, oscillating
between rigid codes of discipline and resistance to the image of the soldier
as a mere machine. In the last chapter, we saw how the military prowess
of the US army during the war against Mexico was stressed through the
sort of appropriation of ancient exemplars that had previously been
more common in the political realm. Instead of seeking inspiration in
the balanced constitution of republican Rome, Americans now derived
glory from matching the achievements of Greek armies. And yet the
earlier political engagement with antiquity did continue: as we shall
see in this chapter, Greek paradigms were also used to define and
debate the political basis of the American army and to suggest connec-
tions between military power and political freedom. At the same time,
the ideal of the citizen soldier that was regarded as the supreme
expression of political freedom also points up a paradox in the widespread comparisons between the Missouri army in Mexico and the Ten
Thousand in Asia: Doniphan's soldiers were volunteers, Xenophon's
were mercenaries – representatives of a class despised in the American
republican tradition (the British army had made heavy use of mercenaries against American troops in the War of Independence). In this
chapter, as we once more examine how the two armies are portrayed
confronting similar problems, we will probe this apparent paradox by

setting the ideals of the democratic army against the realities of life on the march in both ancient Asia and modern Mexico.

The first reality the Missouri volunteers faced as they gathered at Fort Leavenworth in June 1846 was the need for military hierarchy. While they were to march in the first place with the regular army under General Stephen Kearny, the ten companies still had to have officers of their own – and they were to be allowed to choose them themselves. It was already known that Alexander Doniphan was to stand. Doniphan had been one of two men called on by the Governor of Missouri to recruit volunteers, and when the volunteer companies were making their way to Fort Leavenworth they received especially good treatment in Doniphan's home town, Liberty – a ploy, some suspected, to boost Doniphan's candidacy for the colonelship. In the event Doniphan faced competition only from John W. Price, who had served as Lieutenant Colonel in the Florida War a decade earlier, but without much success ('it would have been better to keep that fact a secret', someone in the crowd interjected during the hustings). Doniphan, one of the older volunteers, was elected Colonel 'without serious opposition' (or at least by a 'respectable majority'), and further elections were then held for the posts of Lieutenant Colonel and Major. There were also elections within individual companies for the posts of Captain and Lieutenant.[2]

The Missouri volunteers were following the American tradition by electing their own officers. Elections had been used to select officers for the Lewis and Clark exploratory expedition across the continent in 1804-6, and traders travelling together along the trails across the prairie would also adopt military procedures for their own safety, electing one overall commander. The strength of feeling about this democratic procedure is shown by the response of Doniphan's infantry company when it was prevented from holding elections: a few men 'who aspired to the command and who regarded more their own interest than that of the company' realized that they could not succeed and 'so poisoned the mind of the general that he revoked the order' – 'to the great mortification of our company, who expected to have a field officer of their own choosing'. Later, when President Polk designated Sterling Price as commander of some Missouri reinforcements who were to follow in Doniphan's steps, the troops nonetheless 'thought he ought to be chosen by their free suffrages, or some other man in his stead', and so held an election – which Price won.[3]

The spirit of freedom shown in the conviction that the troops had the right to choose their own leaders was viewed as the hallmark of the American volunteers. As Francis Parkman travelled on the Oregon Trail in 1846, he described an Indian encampment he encountered as a 'wandering democracy' – but he could equally have applied that phrase to the Missouri volunteers: Doniphan's regiment, he noted, 'marched through New Mexico more like a band of free companions than like the paid soldiers of a modern government'. Their lack of hierarchy was reflected in

15. 'A band of free companions': the Missouri volunteer.

Doniphan's preferred leadership style: he did not wear military dress, he had no bodyguard, and he shared the same conditions as the other soldiers, often preparing his own meals. He was also admired for his approachability: soldiers could talk to him 'with the greatest freedom' even at night. The spirit of freedom that was thought to prevail in the ranks of the volunteers made them seem representative of the United States as a whole. John Hughes went so far as to claim that 'there was a national feeling in the army of the west': 'Every soldier felt that he was a freeman; that he was a citizen of the MODEL REPUBLIC.' The volunteers were also seen as representative in class terms: 'every calling and profession contributed its share' – 'the lawyer, the doctor, the professor, the student, the legislator, the farmer, the mechanic, and artisans of every description, all united as a band of brothers to defend the rights and honor of their country'. Doniphan's army was the United States on the move.[4]

The widespread praise of the volunteers' democratic spirit did meet with some opposition. Their elections were not always regarded in a rosy light: carpers noted that whisky was distributed as a bribe and that many were moved by political ambition to stand for office and, if elected, adopted extremely populist measures. A former British officer who encountered Doniphan's army on a journey through Mexico thought the system was 'palpably bad': the volunteers have 'privileges and rights, such as electing their own officers, &c., which they consider to be more consonant to their ideas of liberty and equality', and as a result 'discipline exists but in name'. He even claimed that sentries were 'voted unnecessary' even though the army was in enemy country. This negative view was shared in the upper ranks of the regular US army. One officer complained that 'the volunteers will scarcely work': 'daily labor was not embraced in their conceptions of war; it goes some way to prove that democracy and discipline – of the military sort – are not entirely congenial'. General Kearny felt the same and even made some attempts to impose on Doniphan's men the type of discipline found in the regular troops under his command. But John Hughes was critical of him for even trying: 'the former are bred to freedom, the latter trained to obedience … . In battle, feeling, principle, honor, fire the one, science, experience, discipline, guide the other. They are equally brave.'[5]

It was more common to allege that volunteers were even braver than regular soldiers. As we have seen, this was the message that Thomas Hart Benton imparted when he greeted the Missouri volunteers on their return to St Louis: 'you were all citizens – all volunteers – not a regular bred officer among you: and if there had been, with power to control you, you could never have done what you did.' Benton was following the strong trend of giving the regular army less praise than the volunteers – a legacy of the suspicion of standing armies within the republican tradition as well as a reflection of their different make-ups (the regular army contained many German and Irish immigrants and more troops from the cities of the North-East, while the volunteers were from more rural areas in the West and South). Soldiers in the regular army were also disparaged for serving for money – even though volunteers were paid too.[6]

It was precisely their spirit of freedom that was thought to give volunteers the military edge. In his popular 1847 novel *Legends of Mexico*, George Lippard imagined how the 'tyrants of the old world' had been struck with awe the previous year at the 'transformation of a plain working people, into a formidable, yes, an unconquered army': 'The Man who sits upon the Russian throne, worshipped as a God, and yet never for one moment secure from the assassin's steel, beheld the wondrous sight, and reviewed his armies of slaves, with new anxiety, asking from his satraps an explanation of that magic word – "THE PEOPLE!".' Here the Russian despot with his army of slaves is aligned with the Persian king (note those 'satraps') and opposed to democratic America. Some readers may even have sensed an echo of one of the most famous Greek depictions of Persian despotism: in Aeschylus' *Persians* (472 BC), a play celebrating the Athenian victory at Salamis, the Persian queen, anxiously waiting news of Xerxes' campaign, questions the chorus about the location and military strength of Athens:

QUEEN: Who leads them and is sole commander of the army?
CHORUS: They are called neither the slaves nor subjects of any single man.
QUEEN: So how then can they withstand hostile invaders?
CHORUS: Well enough to have destroyed Darius' large and excellent army.

The connection between freedom and military strength intimated by the tragedian Aeschylus was later made explicit by the historian Herodotus. The fact that the Athenians grew in strength once they were free from tyranny shows, Herodotus claimed, that 'freedom of speech is to be taken seriously', given that while they were under tyrants 'they fought below their best because they were working for a master, whereas as free men each individual wanted to achieve something for himself'.[7]

The belief in the military power of freedom that shaped contemporary responses to the Mexican War was also supported by explicit appeals to antiquity. Especially revealing is an article in the *New York Herald* in October 1847 headed 'The Military Spirit of the American People – The Progress of Republicanism'. The article bemoaned the fact that Yankees had had a poor military reputation in Europe until recently, as they were thought to be wholly absorbed in the pursuit of money. The present war in Mexico had opened European eyes to the truth: 'since the heroic times of ancient Greece and Rome, there has not been seen in the world a people so decidedly martial, or eminently qualified for military achievements, so soldierlike and spirited, in and for battle, as the American people.' This military superiority was grounded in American political institutions: 'The European soldier is a slave – the American a free man. The European is a machine – the American is spirit and life'; for 'a democratic people ... must rule and prevail and shine and succeed above all other people', and 'there have been no democracies in the world since the days of Leonidas and the Thermopylae until now with us in America'. Here the mania for Sparta within American military ideology sits uneasily with historical reality: the egalitarian militarism of the Spartan elite has sometimes been reclaimed for democracy (the Spartan Association was the name of a powerful working-class political group in 1840s New York), but the Spartan system had little of the political freedom associated with democratic Athens.[8]

Democratic Athens was also invoked to promote a sense of the values underlying American military might. At an army reunion after the Civil War, a speaker cited the achievement of the 'volunteer and disciplined citizens of Athens' at the battle of Marathon as the citizen soldier's first contribution in 'the struggle of man for liberty'. In similar vein the Whig politician Daniel Webster, the most famous orator of his day, quoted extensively in an 1852 speech from what has often been regarded as the supreme expression of the spirit of Athenian democracy – Thucydides'

117

version of Pericles' oration for the Athenian soldiers who died in the first year of the Peloponnesian War. Webster included in his extract Pericles' famous description of the Athenian political system: 'It has been called by the name of DEMOCRACY, as being the government not of the few but of the majority' (he would have caught the Greek better had he spoken of 'government *for* the majority'). Despite his own opposition to aggressive American expansionism, Webster also picked up some of Pericles' strongly militaristic statements – including the boast that the Athenians have 'forced every sea and every land to be accessible to our enterprise' and have 'everywhere planted, together with our settlements, eternal monuments of injuries and of benefits'. As in his translation of Pericles' definition of democracy, Webster's translation again exposes American concerns: 'together with our settlements' makes literal what is only a metaphor in the Greek. The mistranslation helps pave the way for Webster, after closing on Pericles' call to the Athenians to place 'your happiness in liberty, and your liberty in courage', and to 'shun no warlike dangers in defence of your country', to ask: 'Is it Athens or America? Is Athens or America the theme of these immortal strains? Was Pericles speaking of his own country, as he saw it and knew it, or was he gazing upon a bright vision then two thousand years before him, which we see in reality, and as he saw in prospect?' Though himself opposed to the Mexican War, Webster here subscribed to the model of democratic courage, hinting to his metropolitan audience that the ancient Greeks expressed in words what the modern Americans have realized in deeds. He even went on to claim that the contests of ancient Greece are outweighed by those of modern times: more than Periclean eloquence would be needed to do justice to 'the heroes and the martyrs of the American revolution'.[9]

The ethos of the citizen soldier could further suggest that the superiority of American soldiers to their ancient counterparts had to be reflected in the superiority of their democratic credentials. So while John Logan, a leading general in the Union army during the Civil War, did concede that 'the American volunteer, so far as mere physical strength, strong endurance, and iron courage are concerned, may not be a better "Greek" than he who fought the battles of Sparta and Athens twenty-five centuries ago', he insisted that the US volunteer is 'the most invincible of soldiers' owing to his 'Americanism': 'He is a citizen of the freest government that the world has yet seen.' In some mysterious way American freedom gives the US volunteer an edge over the Greek even though they are equals in strength and courage. Logan's slippery logic may have sprung from a private grievance (himself a volunteer, he had seen an officer trained at West Point promoted over him during the war), but he was still expressing a widely-felt message. The mysterious edge given by American freedom even enabled another American general to proclaim at a reunion of Mexican War veterans that 'Troy would have been conquered by an American army in six months'.[10]

*

The army of Greek mercenaries is in the desert. Six months into his campaign, Cyrus is finally expecting to face his brother in battle. He decides to address his Greek generals and captains – leaders of the troops he hopes will conquer Persia for him. He starts by telling them that he is confident that Greek soldiers are 'braver and better than hordes of barbarians'. He then stirs them further for the coming battle: 'Endeavour, then, to prove yourselves worthy of the freedom you possess. I envy you this freedom. Why? I assure you that I would choose freedom over all my wealth, even if I was far better off than I am now.' Cyrus – or at least Xenophon's Cyrus – here modifies a commonplace of Greek oratory. In Greek historical narratives, commanders often call on their troops to be worthy of their country or of the past deeds of their countrymen. In his speech, Cyrus makes freedom stand for Greece. But in doing so Cyrus does implicitly evoke the past deeds which secured the Greeks their freedom – their victories in the Persian Wars. Freedom was the rallying cry of the Greeks as they fought against the Persian invaders: the messenger in Aeschylus' *Persians* reports how the Greeks on board their ships at Salamis shout to each other to 'free your fatherland, free your children, your wives, the shrines of your ancestral gods and the graves of your forefathers'. Cyrus also addresses the Greeks' pride in their internal freedom – the freedom they enjoyed within their cities as well as their freedom from foreign masters. By showing their superiority to the unfree barbarians, Cyrus claims, the Greeks will prove themselves worthy of their freedom – and it is their freedom that will make them superior.[11]

Cyrus' words have been grist to the mill of many proponents of the superiority of the Greeks' political culture. They are cited by Victor Davis Hanson in *Carnage and Culture*, his 2001 survey of landmark battles in the history of western military supremacy, in support of the thesis that the battle of Salamis exemplifies the value of Greek (and by extension western) freedom: Cyrus, Hanson claims, 'acknowledges that the priceless freedom he alone enjoys by virtue of being an autocrat in Persia is extended on the other side of the Aegean Sea to the common man'. Hanson in fact misreads Cyrus' rhetoric: in keeping with the common Greek view that everyone in Persia was a slave except for the king, Xenophon makes Cyrus, the king's brother, deny even his own freedom. Read properly, Cyrus' words seem to offer even more support for Hanson's thesis – or at least for the view that Xenophon is advocating Greek superiority. And this is how Cyrus' speech has been interpreted by many other scholars: through Cyrus' words, Xenophon is said to transform the expedition into 'a crusade against the barbarian' and even to make Cyrus 'a champion of democracy'; and the attribution to a non-Greek of a perception of Greek superiority is thought to give that perception even more authority.[12]

119

The supposedly democratic freedom Cyrus attributes to the Greek mercenaries has been regarded as the dominant characteristic of their march. The army has been variously described as 'a democracy of ten thousand citizens equipped as soldiers'; 'a hopelessly undisciplined body of troops' that 'resolved itself from time to time into a parliamentary body, debated the issues of its march, and voted sanely what course to take' ('few things in Greek history are more instructive'); or again as a 'a parliament of 10,000 members' who 'marched and voted themselves over many miles of the most difficult country in the world' ('it sounds like a dream of Gilbert and Sullivan' – but 'nothing is more characteristically Greek'). The army, like Daniel Webster's America, has also been seen as Athens transplanted: Hippolyte Taine, as we have seen, described it as 'a sort of Athens wandering in the middle of Asia', and this memorable formulation is echoed in the American popular historian Edith Hamilton's claim that 'what brought the Greeks safely back from Asia was precisely what made Athens great'.[13]

Cyrus' appeal to Greek freedom can only be taken as a serious expression of Persian inferiority if one ignores the strongly jarring notes in his speech. Cyrus may proclaim that he envies the Greeks their freedom, but he ends (as we saw in Chapter 4) with what is in effect a call to exchange freedom for wealth: 'If you show yourselves men and if my fortunes turn out well, I shall see to it that those of you who want to return home will be envied by their friends when they get there, though I think I shall make many of you prefer what they will get from me here to what they will have at home.' Cyrus is then challenged by a certain 'Gaulites, a Samian exile' to prove that he will be able to fulfil his promises. He responds by making a further speech in which he stresses the vastness of the Persian empire: 'All the territories between these two extremes are satrapies of my brother's friends, but if I'm victorious, I am bound to put *my* friends in charge of them.' Cyrus may be appealing to the ambition of the Greek commanders, but the very fact that he is challenged to defend his first speech seems another hint of the value of Greek freedom. Cyrus' Greek audience does not meekly follow his word: they make him prove his point by further argument. Yet the value of free debate among the Greeks is at the same time undermined by Xenophon's description of the Samian exile who makes the challenge as 'a trusted adviser of Cyrus'. We are left to infer that this Samian was put up by Cyrus himself. And following Cyrus' second speech the generals and some others flock to Cyrus for private meetings to find out what will be in it for them if he wins. Far from being a resounding proclamation of the glory of Greek democracy, Cyrus' lofty talk about liberty is followed by a seedy picture of Greek generals on the make, scrambling for their share of the booty that never came.[14]

*

6. A Wandering Democracy: Freedom on the March

Two days after their glorious victory at Brazito on Christmas day 1846, Doniphan's troops occupied El Paso del Norte, a city of some 10,000 inhabitants. There was at first much to enjoy in the new setting, above all the excellent food and wine. But slowly the troops' stay in the city was prolonged while they waited for more artillery to arrive, and they became more and more rowdy. In his speech at St Louis, Thomas Hart Benton claimed that El Paso was not a 'Capua' to the Missouri volunteers – implying that they were not corrupted by its luxuries. But if not quite a Capua for the soldiers, their behaviour at El Paso certainly posed problems for the army's leader: Doniphan was reduced to pleading with the Mexicans not to sell alcohol to the troops, and gambling in the streets was so rampant that he banned it. Besides this, three men from one company were court-martialled for rape, and some Mexicans arriving from Chihuahua who refused to reveal information about the Mexican forces were strung up in a bar and let down when barely still alive. Such incidents made the time at El Paso 'very disagreeable' for one soldier: the army, he explained in a journal not intended for publication, was 'composed of men of a restless and roving disposition, and the little discipline which prevailed was totally insufficient to prevent rioting and dissipation, which endangered the health of the troops as well as their efficiency'. Similar troubles had made the army's stay at Santa Fé equally disagreeable: one soldier was dismissed for refusing an order to serve as officer of the guard; another for threatening a regular officer with a drawn sabre; and a company captain shot a private who tried to knife him. The behaviour among the volunteers in other parts of Mexico was even worse: there were twenty murders by Americans in Matamoras in the first month of the American occupation, and some Texan volunteers went on a two-hour killing spree in Mexico City after one of their number was killed. No wonder John Hughes claimed that the Missouri volunteers were better on the march than at garrison duty, for 'it is more agreeable to be actively employed in marching, than confined in camps and placed on continual guards and watchings'.[15]

The problems caused by the troops' behaviour at El Paso were increased by the weakness of their position. Their orders from General Kearny had been to make for Chihuahua (the next large town to the south) and meet the army of General Wool there, but as weeks passed with no sign of the artillery and no word from Wool himself more and more of the soldiers began to be worried by their position. In a single day's fighting at Brazito they had shown their resolve against superior numbers: it was another thing to occupy a city for a long period of time, with the threat of insurgency from the Mexican inhabitants. One soldier, Marcellus Edwards, noted early in February 1847 that their situation was 'rather critical – leaving an enemy in our rear, marching into the heart of their country, expecting to meet a powerful one in front'; another, Jacob Robinson, wrote even more gloomily that 'there seems to be considerable dispute in camp whether we can safely march against Chihuahua', and that 'if a vote of the regiment was taken we would go no farther'. Newspapers in the US expressed the same worries: claims that Chihuahua would be an 'easy conquest' were 'delusions' to 'entrap' Doniphan and 'lead him far off into the interior where he might be entirely cut off'.[16]

The army's difficulties were compounded by uncertainty over General Wool's position. There had been rumours about Wool in the past that had turned out to be unreliable: at the end of October, when they were still at Santa Fé, there had even been a report that Wool had 'taken Chihuahua with 6000 men & no fight'. When the troops left Santa Fé in December, they still thought that Wool was going to Chihuahua, although there were already some fears for him. But now, as the army's stay in El Paso grew longer, firmer news seemed to have arrived. An American who escaped from Chihuahua was said to have told Doniphan that Wool had abandoned his march. Whether they had heard that story or not, most of the troops were sure that Wool was no longer coming to Chihuahua or at least that he had not yet arrived there. The choice was now simple: advance or retreat. The gloomy Jacob Robinson would have preferred retreat – 'but our commanders have said onward – and onward we must go'.[17]

Most descriptions of Doniphan's army as it began to leave El Paso disregard the fears expressed by Marcellus Edwards and Jacob Robinson. The German doctor Frederick Wislizenus viewed the army's resolution in strongly heroic terms: 'surrounded in the rear and front by enemies – thrown in the middle of a hostile country – cut off from all communication and support of their own country, they took the only resolution that could avail in such emergency; they marched on, to conquer or die.' A similar picture is presented in John Hughes' vivid recreation of the army's 'buoyant hopes':

> With an army less than one thousand strong, he was on his march leading through inhospitable, sandy wastes, against a powerful city, which had been deemed of so much importance, by the government, that Gen. Wool, with three thousand five hundred men and a heavy park of artillery, had been directed thither to effect its subjugation. What then must have been the feelings of Col. Doniphan and his men, when they saw the states of Chihuahua and Durango in arms to receive them, not the remotest prospect of succor from Gen. Wool, and rocks and unpeopled deserts intervening, precluding the possibility of successful retreat? 'Victory or death' were the two alternatives. Yet there was no faltering, – no pale faces, – no dismayed hearts. At this crisis, had Col. Doniphan inquired of his men what was to be done, the response would have been unanimously given, LEAD us ON. But he needed not to make the inquiry, for he saw depicted in every countenance, the fixed resolve 'To DO or DIE.'

Whereas Jacob Robinson thought that the soldiers would vote against advancing further, Hughes portrays an army so strong in its republican feelings that the leader did not even need to hold a vote to confirm the men's determination to press on. Paradoxically the lack of a vote makes the army seem even more exemplary as a wandering democracy, representing the model republic of the United States.[18]

It is all the more strange, then, that the editor of a later edition of Hughes' memoir added a note at this point claiming that 'the question of continuing the march towards Chihuahua was put to a vote of the troops, and there were but two or three dissenting votes' – even though the main text clearly implies that no vote was taken. The mistake is perhaps to be explained by an episode a few days after the departure from El Paso – an episode which also complicates slightly Hughes' picture of the army's firm resolution. A mail delivery caught up with Doniphan's army bringing letters from home as well as newspapers that carried further news on the movements of General Wool. The soldiers disagree on what the news actually was: according to Marcellus Edwards, it was that Wool had divided his force, sending half to join General Taylor and half to Chihuahua; Frank Edwards, by contrast, alleges that it was now that they discovered that Wool was no longer making for Chihuahua. Both these accounts disagree with other reports which suggest that the army already knew of Wool's change of plan before it left El Paso. The main problem, however, is raised by Frank Edwards' account of what happened next: 'In this situation, a council was held; and the question agitated, whether we were to go on to Chihuahua, or turn back to Santa Fe? It was decided to proceed.' Here we do have an image of the army engaging in open debate to resolve a difficulty – the sort of debate that was not, according to Hughes and Robinson, held earlier at El Paso (though Edwards presumably means a council of the elected officers rather than one of the whole army). If this council (which is not attested in any other source) explains why Hughes' editor alleged that a vote had taken place at El Paso, it also raises a question about Hughes' own account. If the army's spirit as it left El Paso was as Hughes describes it, why was a council needed a few days later?[19]

One common strand underlies the conflicting accounts of the departure from El Paso. Despite the confusion about who knew what when about the plans of General Wool and about how the decision to advance on Chihuahua was made, the soldiers serving under Doniphan are all prepared to think of the army as a free, republican unit. Speculating about what would have happened had a vote been taken may underline that a vote was not in fact taken – but it also suggests that deciding by vote was regarded as a possibility, an ideal, perhaps, but one that was not altogether unrealistic. The image of the democratic army is notably more prominent, however, in the published narratives that achieved wide distribution (like John Hughes' or Frederick Wislizenus', which Thomas Hart Benton had distributed by the Senate) than in journals that were unpublished (like Marcellus Edwards') or published in small editions that received little attention (like Jacob Robinson's). The accounts aimed at a large public were much more likely to make the army's behaviour fit pre-existing perceptions of volunteer units as emblematic of the American republican spirit. The positive image projected by these popular accounts also counteracts the threat that the army could be defined by the scenes of disorder and indiscipline at El Paso. Indeed, John Hughes' published narrative is much less forthcoming about specific misdemeanours than his diary: it would not do to let these individual crimes diminish the collective glory of the model republic. And yet these hints of the army's democratic potential are themselves subservient to the stress on the forward movement of Doniphan's army: no matter whether Doniphan read the resolution in the faces of his men or debated the army's position with his fellow officers, the army would march on, deeper and deeper into Mexican territory. It was too late to turn back.

*

There was trouble at Tarsus even before Cyrus arrived. The inhabitants fled before his arrival, only the shopkeepers staying in the hope of a profit. A small detachment sent by a shorter mountain route got there first, losing 100 men en route, and the survivors 'were so angry about the deaths of their comrades that they looted not only the city, but the palace too'. And then, Xenophon writes, 'Cyrus and the army stayed at Tarsus for twenty days ...'. It is by the slightest of touches that Xenophon signals further trouble to come. When he describes earlier stops in the march, he writes that 'they' – that is, Cyrus and the army together – 'stayed' at Colossae or Peltae or Iconium for three, seven, however many days. Now Cyrus is separated from his army – for 'the soldiers refused to carry on'.[20]

The dispute at Tarsus arises from the mercenaries' growing suspicion that the task they had been hired for – an attack on the Pisidians – had been a ruse to gather a large army for an altogether more dangerous undertaking. Now that they have left the mountains of Pisidia behind them, the troops suspect that Cyrus wants to lead them against the Persian king. Not all of the Greeks, however, are keen on stopping at Tarsus. The Spartan Clearchus, leader of one of the Greek contingents, tries to force the troops he has himself hired for Cyrus to go on, but narrowly escapes being stoned. Foiled in his attempt to impose his will by force, he calls his troops together – and Xenophon conjures up a key Greek democratic institution as he speaks of the meeting as an 'assembly' (*ekklesia*).

Clearchus' assembly gets off to a surprising start. To the troops' astonishment, he stands weeping before he says a word. After some time he starts to speak, recalling how Cyrus had given him money which he had used not on himself but on the troops – and for the cause of Greece. While acknowledging Cyrus' help, he proclaims his loyalty to the Greek soldiers: 'It will never be said of me that I led the Greeks into barbarian lands and then betrayed those Greeks by preferring the friendship of the barbarians

... . I think of you as my fatherland, my friends, and my allies.' The language Xenophon makes Clearchus use seems to ignore the actual composition of his contingent: of the 2,000 troops he had hired, 800 were Thracians – the very people he had used Cyrus' money to fight against. Xenophon makes Clearchus speak as if to a purely Greek audience. And the appeal to a shared Greek identity is reinforced by an allusion to a famous scene in Homer: the meeting between Hector and his wife Andromache in the city of Troy where Andromache reminds Hector of the misfortunes that overtook her home city, telling him 'you are father and honoured mother and brother to me'. Clearchus skilfully panders to his audience by alluding to a key Greek cultural text. He also takes on the weak, feminine position, suggesting that the soldiers are his protectors. But he removes Andromache's family terms and replaces them with the language of masculine comradeship (fatherland, friends, allies). His suggestion that his small unit is a surrogate Greece proves to be popular: 2,000 soldiers who were not originally in his contingent now join him. Clearchus draws on Greek political and cultural institutions to create a larger unit that is seemingly a microcosm of Greece.[21]

For the nineteenth-century historian George Grote, a champion of democracy ancient and modern, the 'remarkable scene' at Tarsus illustrated the qualities of 'the Greek citizen-soldier'. Grote praised 'the combination of the reflecting obedience of citizens with the mechanical regularity of soldiers' shown by the Ten Thousand throughout their march, but here he stressed in particular the appeal made to the soldiers' 'reason and judgment' – 'the habit, established more or less throughout so large a portion of the Grecian world, and attaining its maximum at Athens, of hearing both sides and deciding afterwards'. This view seems to be supported by the way Xenophon builds his account around the opposition in Greek thought between force (*bia*) and persuasion (*peitho*): Clearchus as leader tried to force his troops to move on, but is then forced himself to turn to persuasion. Indignant as the soldiers were at the fraud practised on them, they did not act impulsively.[22]

And yet Clearchus' rhetoric is not all that it seems. He first speaks of his dealings with Cyrus in terms of reciprocity: Cyrus gave him money; he is paying Cyrus back by helping him. He then appeals to the feelings of his Greek audience by claiming that he will put their interests even above his reciprocal attachment with Cyrus. But his definition of his relationship with Cyrus in terms of the Greek ethic of reciprocity obscures the imbalance in the relationship: Cyrus' gift to Clearchus was made specifically with the expedition in mind, and not as a free gift which Clearchus is returning. The attack on the Thracians was a screen allowed by Cyrus to buy time and remove suspicion. Clearchus makes it seem more impressive that he is putting the Greeks first.

Xenophon brings out in what follows that Clearchus has been manipulating his audience to make them stay with Cyrus (just as we have seen

Cyrus manipulate them by putting up the Samian exile Gaulites to query his ability to fulfil his promises). Finding himself in an impasse, Cyrus summons Clearchus, but Clearchus refuses to visit him – while secretly sending a message to reassure him. Clearchus then calls together his soldiers along with anyone who 'wanted' to hear (Xenophon's phrase echoes a common formula used for the democratic ideal of voluntary civic participation). In a new speech, he begins to speak of the possible threat from Cyrus: whether they stay or go, the army has to look to its own safety. After this, some speakers put up by Clearchus claim that there is no way for the army to stay or leave without Cyrus' permission; one speaker even proposes that they should elect new generals and ask Cyrus either for ships or for a guide to take them back home. This proposal, Xenophon hints, was made precisely to allow the next speaker to point up its folly. After this 'it was decided' (and again Xenophon's language has overtones of civic decisions) to send a delegation to Cyrus to find out more about his aims. Cyrus spins a new lie (he tells them he is marching against a rebel on the Euphrates) and promises a pay rise, and the troops are willing to leave. Xenophon's language suggests that Clearchus has once more used the forms of Greek democracy to get his way with the troops.

Clearchus' canny creation of a feeling of unity among the various Greek contingents at Tarsus is itself part of a battle for leadership. When Cyrus paraded the Greek hoplites before the Cilician queen Epyaxa, it was another general, Meno, who had the right wing – the most honoured position. Soon after the mutiny at Tarsus, two generals whose troops had left to join Clearchus desert. When the army reaches the Euphrates, Cyrus finally reveals that he is leading the army against the king – and Meno tries to regain Cyrus' favour by leading his own contingent across the river first, knowing full well that he could always lead them back again if the other soldiers refused to cross. Not long afterwards, as the army crosses the desert, there is a fight between soldiers from the contingents of Clearchus and Meno, and Clearchus is nearly stoned. It is only at the battle of Cunaxa that Clearchus emerges as the most powerful general: he is on the right wing at the battle and after Cyrus' death he takes up unopposed the leading position among the Greek generals. Finally, after Clearchus' death, Xenophon reveals that he was the only general who knew from the start that Cyrus was planning to march against the Persian king: in other words, he had had all along the special standing hinted at by his secret message to Cyrus at the very moment when he was bringing together the Greek soldiers with the slogans of panhellenism. The democratic character of the Greek citizen-soldier first revealed at Tarsus was created by an exile from undemocratic Sparta in cahoots with a rebellious Persian prince.

*

16. 'Latest from the Army' – thanks to letters sent to family and papers.

Doniphan's force of a thousand Missouri volunteers is at Chihuahua, capital of a large province of northern Mexico. They had marched into the town a few days after a spectacular success against well-defended Mexican lines at Sacramento, where they had captured the black flag that had been displayed at Brazito. But what they were to do once they were established at Chihuahua was a tricky question. And their own behaviour made a long stay in the town unattractive to their leaders: one soldier complained in his diary that 'drunkenness, licentiousness, profanity, the needless destruction of property, and uncalled for abuse practiced upon innocent natives are engaged in with impunity'. Doniphan himself wrote in a letter that the troops were 'wholly unfit to garrison a town or city' and 'will soon be wholly ruined by improper indulgences'. What was the army to do now? Soon after their arrival, Doniphan had sent a dispatch to the US Government: 'We were ordered to report to General Wool at this place. On my arrival I found, from Mexico reports, that he was at Saltillo surrounded by General Santa Anna. Should he be defeated or driven back, I fear an immediate retreat will become necessary. We have been in the service nine months without receiving one dollar of pay.' In another letter he explained that their position would be 'ticklish' if Santa Anna should compel Taylor and Wool to fall back: 'We are out of the reach of help, and it is as unsafe to go backward as forward.'[23]

The problems in Chihuahua seemed to confirm some soldiers' doubts about the decision to move on from El Paso. Richard S. Elliott, who served in the army as far as Santa Fé but stayed there to run a newspaper, wrote a letter in March expressing his reservations. He was not sure whether

Doniphan heard of Wool's change of direction before he left El Paso or soon after, but thought that 'if he did, he ought not to have left that point, or if he had left, he ought to have returned'. He accused Doniphan of a lack of 'prudence and foresight'; while the 'many gallant men' with him 'would have received with galled feelings any retrograding order', the commander should not have consulted 'that unbridled enthusiasm whose objects were bold adventure and personal distinction': 'I am inclined to suspect, too, that others look upon the Colonel's unprofitable march much in the same light as I do, but do not care to say so. I regret that his bravery ... should have been so uselessly expended.' Elliott was rash to express his doubts so openly: the Missouri newspaper of which he was a regular correspondent ran his comments with the note that 'the disposition to criticise will meet but little encouragement amid the encomiums, the admiration, and the applause which a whole country will shower upon the victors'.[24]

Doniphan again favoured a resolute response to his army's difficulties: 'High spirits and a bold front, is perhaps the best and safest policy.' But splits within the army were growing. Jacob Robinson offers a typically downbeat assessment in his journal: 'Our officers as well as privates are very much divided in opinion. Some are for remaining in Chihuahua until relieved or our time expires; others for leaving immediately.' Frank Edwards suggests that a bigger range of options was aired at a 'Council of War': 'there was danger at all points! A few of the officers proposed staying in Chihuahua, others were for trying to join General Taylor, and some suggested a retrograde march to Santa Fé; most, however, were in favor of pressing home by way of Monterey.' Edwards goes on to report another council held a few days later in which most of the officers were for remaining in quarters, but Doniphan won the day by banging his fist on the table while uttering the phrase that came to encapsulate the Missourians' longing to return to their families: 'I'm for going home to Sarah and the children.' What was less clear was how they would get home. Soon afterwards, on 5 April, the artillery and one battalion did leave Chihuahua in the direction of Parral, where the state government was said to have fled. On the third day, however, the expedition suddenly returned to the town – 'the first retrograde movement we have made', and a move that was not to the liking of 'the chivalric sons of Missouri', who soon found that the Mexicans were 'laughing us to scorn; and even the women throw it at us, forgetting the example set by their own troops'. There were conflicting stories as to why the army had retreated: some said Doniphan had heard that the state government had now fled to Mexico City; others that news came that a Mexican army was advancing and, in the words of a disgruntled trader, 'our Gallant Col ... toddled back in double quick time frightened out of his wits'. That Mexican army at any rate never appeared, and the soldiers became 'convinced at last that it was but a hoax' invented to keep the troops in Chihuahua as long as possible.[25]

Or was the Parral expedition a cover for a more ambitious scheme?

According to a biography of one of the army's officers, William Gilpin, published forty years later, some of the younger soldiers wanted to push further into Mexico, and Gilpin took the lead in forcing Doniphan to put the question to a vote. Doniphan then tried to pack the council with soldiers who would favour caution, but to no avail: when the question was put, 'it was decided to push on to the city of Mexico'. Here we do have a vote taken by a section of the army – and an extraordinarily ambitious scheme results: stranded and outnumbered in the province of Chihuahua, the small troop of Missouri volunteers resolves to march to the halls of the Montezumas themselves, seeking to grab in advance the glory that would be won by General Winfield Scott the following year.[26]

This vision of democratic energy is subjected by Doniphan's modern biographer to a less democratic sequel. He reconciles the story of a march on Mexico with the other sources by explaining that Doniphan 'kept the larger purpose of the march envisioned by Gilpin secret from anyone outside the confines of the regiment's senior leadership'. And while he accepts that the swift retreat to Chihuahua was occasioned by a report of hostile bands in the vicinity, he speculates that Doniphan knew that the report was exaggerated, but exploited it anyway to undermine a plan he had never favoured.[27]

If this modern reconstruction is right, then Doniphan overrode the officers' vote with the cunning of a Clearchus. But we should hesitate to make Doniphan too duplicitous – or too democratic. Both views rest on the dramatic vote to march on Mexico City – but this story is hard to accept. For one thing, Gilpin's biographer gives no source. For another, all other accounts agree that Doniphan resolved his impasse not by following the majority view of his troops but by sending an express of twelve men to receive orders from General Taylor, commander of the regular US army in Mexico. And while two contemporary accounts suggest that this express was sent only after the retrograde movement to Chihuahua, it was in fact dispatched on 20 March, over a fortnight before the army made its brief move south. It is extremely unlikely that the Missouri army would have embarked on such an extravagant plan as a march on Mexico just after sending for orders. Indeed, when William Gilpin made a speech a month after the Missouri volunteers returned, he reviewed the campaign without mentioning any proposal on his part to make for Mexico (though he did argue – wrongly, as it turned out – that 'one great result' proved by Doniphan's campaign was that 'it is by the route of the plains and the table-lands of Mexico only that the Mexican nation can be conquered and held in subjection by the Americans').[28]

The stories told about the fortunes of the Missouri army in Chihuahua expose a tension in panegyrics of Doniphan's force of volunteers as a model republican unit that displayed the military advantages of democratic freedom. Elevating the achievement of the troops in political terms seems paradoxical when it was precisely when the army was isolated in a city for three months that its internal harmony was most threatened. It was at Chihuahua that the troops' misdemeanours were at their worst and that disagreements over the army's aims and ambitions were at their greatest. The ideology of the citizen-soldier obscured the very real problems of indiscipline: the almost universal praise of the volunteers in public contexts reflects one extreme in the negotiation necessary in the armies of all democracies between the assertion of military discipline and hierarchy and the claims of political equality and comradeship. On the ground, the predicament of the Missouri volunteers stranded at Chihuahua thanks to bungled orders from higher authorities was resolved in the end not by a vote but by appealing to the leader of the regular army. Cyrus' Greek soldiers stranded in Mesopotamia had no such happy alternative.

*

It is related of Xenophon, how, when the principal officers of the Greek 'Ten Thousand' were slain by the treachery of the Persians, that he, a mere volunteer, was elected a general, and conducted them, through that consummate retreat, back to their native country. At the close of our war, doubtless there were scores – perhaps hundreds – who would have proved equal to as great an emergency ...
Capt. George W. Burnell, 10th Vermont Infantry (1891)[29]

The crisis that has been hanging over the Greek army ever since the death of Cyrus has finally arrived. There have been days of tense negotiations – a few small marches away from the battlefield, and all the time an uneasy awareness of the Persian army, always somewhere close to them but never quite in sight. But now the Greek leader Clearchus together with four other generals and twenty captains has gone to meet the Persian satrap Tissaphernes in person. Clearchus wants to clear up their mutual suspicions. Instead the Greeks' worst fears of Persian treachery are realized: Tissaphernes has the leaders seized or killed.

In a passage famous for its emotional intensity, Xenophon recreates the mood in the Greek camp as news of the disaster arrives:

> The Greeks reflected on their desperate predicament. They were close to the king's headquarters; they were surrounded on all sides by countless hostile tribes and cities; there was no longer anyone who would sell them provisions; they were at least 10,000 stades from Greece; there was no guide to show them the way; there were uncrossable rivers blocking their route home; even the barbarians who had made the journey upcountry with Cyrus had betrayed them; and they had been left all alone, without a single horseman in their army ... . Weighed down by these depressing thoughts, few of them managed to eat anything that evening and few lit fires; a lot of them spent the night not in their quarters, close to where the weapons were stacked, but wherever they happened to find themselves. But sleep was banished by

distress and by longing for homes, parents, wives, and children, whom they
no longer expected ever to see again. And so they all passed a restless night.

The accumulation of short clauses vividly conveys the accumulation of the
Greeks' troubles. They are leaderless and stranded far from home. It is as
if their long march up from the Aegean has led them to a realm of
darkness.[30]

Xenophon's scene gains in resonance by echoing two accounts of how his
fellow-countrymen, the Athenians, responded to earlier disasters. The
first disaster is the collapse of the Athenian armada to Sicily in 413 BC, the
emotional highpoint of Thucydides' history of the Peloponnesian War.
After describing the surrender of the surviving Athenians in Sicily, Thucydides turns to the response in Athens to the news that the fleet is lost:
'Everything grieved them on every side, and after what had occurred,
terror and the most extreme consternation came over them ... they also
saw neither enough ships in the shipyards nor money in the treasury nor
staffing for the ships, they were without hope of survival in the present
situation.' Just like Xenophon's Greeks, the Athenians are encircled by
dangers with no apparent means of escape. The second disaster is described by Xenophon himself in his *Hellenica* – the Athenian defeat at
Aegospotami in 405 BC: it was night when the news arrived and groans
began to be heard, first in the Piraeus, then up the long walls to the city;
and, like the mercenaries cut off in Mesopotamia, the Athenians were
unable to sleep through grief, mourning the dead and their own fate too.[31]

Xenophon's account picks up these earlier Athenian disasters at the
very moment when the mercenaries are about to be saved by an Athenian –
himself: 'There was in the army a man called Xenophon, an Athenian ... .'
Xenophon – and Xenophon alone – is stirred to action by the army's
despair. He starts by gathering and addressing Proxenus' remaining
company commanders, then all the surviving officers, and finally, as a new
day starts to dawn, a meeting of the whole army. The Athenian turns the
despondent army into a new Athens.

The transformation of the army starts with an act of exclusion. When
Xenophon gathers together the surviving officers in Proxenus' contingent,
a man named Apollonides, who speaks in the Boeotian dialect, insists that
they must try to win the favour of the king. When Xenophon breaks in and
calls him 'an embarrassment not just to his homeland but to the whole of
Greece', he is told that this man 'doesn't belong in Boeotia or anywhere in
Greece', since 'he has both ears pierced, Lydian-style' – and 'this was true'.
Apollonides is then driven away from the meeting – a scapegoat who
unifies the remaining officers and defines the masculinity of the Greeks
by contrast with the supposedly effeminate Lydians.[32]

The representative Greekness of the army is further strengthened in
Xenophon's address to the army as a whole. Xenophon encourages the
soldiers by appealing to the precedent of the Greek resistance in the

Persian Wars, citing as evidence of the courage of their forefathers the trophies that were set up to commemorate the Greek victories – even though the number of Greek cities that actually took part in the Persian Wars was very small (one city that notoriously took the Persians' side was Thebes, home of Proxenus, the friend who summoned Xenophon himself to serve with Cyrus). Xenophon goes on to appeal to a shared freedom to unite the troops: the greatest evidence of their ancestors' military might, he tells them, is 'the freedom of the cities where you were born and raised' – 'for you pay homage to no mortal master, but only to the gods'. As with the scapegoating of Apollonides, Hellenic identity is forged by contrast with an excluded other – in this case, the Persians, who were renowned for paying homage to their kings (Xenophon alludes to the ritual of *proskunesis*).[33]

The freedom that unites the Greek mercenaries cut off in Mesopotamia is asserted through democratic measures. They elect new officers to replace the ones who have been seized by Tissaphernes – a measure likened by the nineteenth-century geographer James Rennell to the election of officers on the recent Lewis and Clark expedition across North America (Rennell also thought that the mercenaries exemplified the democratic spirit of Pericles' funeral oration – the text that Daniel Webster thought described modern America). In his speech to the army, Xenophon ends by proposing that they cut back on unnecessary luggage and allow officers to punish any soldiers who disobey orders, and then insisting that these proposals be put to the vote. He also appeals to the same spirit of participation lauded in Pericles' funeral oration when he invites the ordinary soldiers to try to think of better proposals. While Xenophon's proposals smack of democratic Athens, it is a Spartan general, Chirisophus, who at once takes the lead in inviting the soldiers to vote ('everyone raised their hands'). Xenophon then makes further proposals about the formation the army should adopt on the march, and these too are agreed by a unanimous show of hands. And when he suggests further modifications (including the creation of a cavalry unit) near the start of the march, he writes that the following day 'about fifty horses and horsemen passed muster' – using a verb cognate with *dokimasia*, the term used at Athens for the examination of magistrates before they entered office.[34]

The democratic momentum displayed by the army in Mesopotamia is increased by the comparisons and contrasts Xenophon implies with the mutiny in Tarsus. In both passages the Greeks are described as being in a state of *aporia* ('impasse'), and this echo is reinforced by multiple other parallels. At Tarsus Clearchus expressed a fear of going in person to Cyrus: now the Greeks are in despair because Clearchus did go in person to Tissaphernes. There Clearchus told the Greeks it was no time to sleep: now Xenophon tells himself it is no time to sleep. Clearchus also brought out how difficult it would be for the Greeks to return home without a guide: here the lack of a guide is again one of the Greeks' problems. There a common soldier suggested they should elect new leaders: here they do elect new leaders. The contrast between the two scenes underscores the scale of the Greeks' difficulties. The worst that was feared at Tarsus has now been fulfilled. History has repeated itself, the first time as farce, the second as tragedy – until Xenophon saves the day. And Xenophon leads the Greeks to salvation by adopting the form of democratic debate that had been perversely manipulated by Clearchus when the Greeks were all in the pay of a Persian employer.[35]

Later historians have glorified the spirit shown by the soldiers en masse in the assembly after the arrest of the generals. Contrasting the later misfortunes of the Roman emperor Jovian in Mesopotamia, Edward Gibbon was among the first to focus on the Greeks' resilience as an exemplary display of their character: 'Instead of tamely resigning themselves to the secret deliberations and private views of a single person, the united councils of the Greeks were inspired by the generous enthusiasm of a popular assembly: where the mind of each citizen is filled with the love of glory, the pride of freedom, and the contempt of death.' While Gibbon follows the high value placed on republican virtue in neo-classical political theory, it was again George Grote who first saw distinctively democratic values at work in the assembly: 'Xenophon insists on the universal suffrage of the whole body, as the legitimate sovereign authority for the guidance of every individual will ... . The complete success of his speech proves that he knew how to touch the right chord of Grecian feeling.' It is this assembly more than any other passage that has contributed to the praise of the Ten Thousand as a city on the march.[36]

And yet some aspects of this assembly of Greeks held near the banks of the Tigris may strike us as rather odder than we might expect from the conventional idealization of the army as a democratic unit subscribing to the same notions of freedom and voluntary participation that have fired up later armies such as Doniphan's troop of Missourians as they ventured across the great plains. For a start, the Greek soldiers raise their hands first not to vote on a proposal about their military and political structure but in response to a sneeze: as Xenophon starts to talk about their hope of survival, someone sneezes – and Xenophon instantly breaks off to propose that they vow to offer a sacrifice to Zeus the Saviour as soon as they reach friendly territory ("If you agree with this motion, raise your hand." Everyone raised their hands.'). Secondly, freedom is far from being the only source of inspiration in Xenophon's speech: his final appeal (placed after the thought of seeing their families again) is to the troops' desire for wealth ('if you want to grow rich, do your best to conquer, because victors not only keep their own belongings, but also take what belongs to the losers'). As in Cyrus' speech of encouragement to the officers, so too in Xenophon's speech to the whole army, the language of Greek liberty is heard, but this idealism is tarnished by a realistic appeal to self-interest.[37]

Our reading of Xenophon's speech to the gathered army is in any case conditioned by the speeches he has given earlier to the surviving officers.

133

In addressing the generals, Xenophon, far from using democratic language, draws on traditional notions of heroism: 'In peace-time you had more money and standing than them; in a time of war like this you should insist on being better than the rank and file, to plan for them, and, if the need arises, to work for them.' This is not far from the heroic ethos expressed by Sarpedon in the *Iliad*. And it is after this stirring appeal to privilege that the officers elect new generals to replace those who have been captured; unlike the Missouri volunteers, the common soldiers were not given the chance to elect their generals. Xenophon seems in fact to be subscribing to a top-down model of leadership. The army's survival does not spring from an upsurge of democratic feeling within the ranks, but from the inspiration provided by one man – Xenophon himself: as he tells the officers: 'without leaders ... nothing ever comes out right or good in any sphere, and certainly not in warfare, where ... discipline makes for survival.'[38]

*

The Missouri volunteers have returned to St Louis and the vast crowds assembled at the edge of the city have listened to the eloquent words of Thomas Hart Benton. Now it is time for the volunteers' leader to speak. The tall, lanky figure of Alexander William Doniphan stands up to address the crowd. He begins with some remarks suitably flattering to the first speaker: 'The minute description given by the orator of scenes through which we have passed has excited our wonder. Indeed, so correct and minute are his details, that they resemble history, and I might almost say that they have become a part of history.' He goes on to speak of the extraordinary reception the men have received, first in New Orleans, then all along the course of the Mississippi, and now in the Missouri capital: 'It has been said of Republics, which have existed heretofore, that they have been ungrateful' – but 'it is not true of our own'. And before standing down to tremendous applause, he offers a final vision of the future awaiting his fellow-citizens: 'May your destiny be onward, and as rapid as the great stream that washes the border of your great city.' The country's destiny would rival the grandeur of its natural resources – and in particular the river that was one of the glories of the Americas, far surpassing puny Old World competitors like the Nile and Euphrates.[39]

Doniphan's response to Benton was not all panegyric. A darker note appeared in the middle of his address as he recalled his disgust at receiving in the heart of Mexico some newspapers carrying reports of opposition to the war at home. He was especially critical of Thomas Corwin, the Whig senator from Ohio who had, Doniphan recalled, denounced those engaged in the war as 'little better than a band of robbers'. Corwin's most famous speech against the war had been made in the Senate in February 1847 when he was opposing extreme financial measures proposed by President Polk to support the war effort in Mexico.

6. A Wandering Democracy: Freedom on the March

Corwin had likened his countrymen in their greed for space to robber-chiefs like Tamerlane and Alexander, and, like modern liberals alarmed at the erosion of civil liberties in the name of a 'war on terror', he had turned on the powers being usurped by President Polk: 'what is the difference between your American democracy and the most odious, most hateful despotism ...? You may call this free government, but it is such freedom, and no other, as of old was established at Babylon, at Susa, at Bactriana, or Persepolis.' The model American democracy was, Whigs like Corwin feared, wandering into tyranny. Lurking behind these fears was the precedent of the ancient Roman republic, which was generally regarded as having been corrupted by its successes abroad. Now a campaign in the vast regions of the West that had been figured as oriental both in their landscape and in their political subjection was suspected of promoting oriental despotism at home.[40]

Doniphan would have none of Corwin's carping. Far from being in the service of peace, speeches opposing the war had merely prolonged it. And as for the American republic, it had not only shown an unprecedented gratitude to military victors. The very victories won by the American troops had been proof of its excellence: 'We have shown, to the astonishment of the world, that volunteer troops can be depended upon – that private citizens can be transformed into good soldiers by a proper discipline.' And while officers of the regular army would seek to climb the 'ladder of fame' by their 'deeds of chivalry', the volunteers who had served their country in her emergency would now peacefully mingle once more with their friends. Succumbing to emotion, Doniphan confessed that the soldiers in his command had become 'endeared' to him through the sufferings they had endured together during their long and arduous march. Now he would never see many of them again.

At the core of Doniphan's emotional farewell to his band of volunteers was the ethos of the citizen-soldier – the same ethos that has led Xenophon's Greek soldiers to be called in modern times an Athens on the march. The modern military ideology to which Doniphan appealed was born of the suspicion of standing armies and professional soldiers within the republican political tradition: it is strange to find it imposed on soldiers who marched to Mesopotamia as mercenaries serving a foreign prince. This image of the Greek army was certainly fostered by Xenophon's habit of applying Athenian political labels to aspects of the army's decision-making that bore some relation to what was familiar to him from Athens: other sources would doubtless have told stories about the soldiers' meetings as diverse as those found in the journals and memoirs of the men who followed Doniphan into Mexico. This image relies in any case on a very selective reading of Xenophon's memoir – above all, a willingness to accept at face value some of the Greek boosterism found in the speeches attributed to Cyrus and to Xenophon himself. Idealized claims made in the speeches in the *Anabasis* are all too often contradicted by the surrounding narrative or even within the speeches themselves.

The modern image of the army as an Athens on the march is further belied by Xenophon's account of their progress towards the sea. Modern eulogists claim that they marched and voted over the toughest terrain in the world: Xenophon mentions only the marching. It is only after the army has arrived at the Black Sea that it begins to hold meetings again – and, as we shall see, Xenophon himself views these meetings with suspicion: they are a mark first of foolish optimism, as the troops neglect practical steps to secure their return home, and later of the dangerous instability spread by the troops' desire to secure a profit before they return to the Greek mainland. The wandering democracy even briefly wanders into autocracy as it elects one man to rule it in the hope that this will bring in more profit. Democracy on the march would have taken up too many busy afternoons of looting and fighting.

To label Xenophon's Greek soldiers timeless paradigms of democratic freedom is to neglect both the changes that took place within the army as it crossed Asia and the changes in political thought that have taken place in the centuries since their long march. It is to neglect, too, the necessary partiality of any such appropriation of ancient precedent for modern times. As our anabasis trail has led us from St Louis to Chihuahua, from the coast of the Mediterranean to the heart of Mesopotamia, we have seen this partiality in action. Xenophon has been used to elevate the achievements of the Missouri volunteers as they filled out America's destiny in space and time: in space by the vast distances they traversed and won for the United States, in time by their contribution to the creation of an idealized American self-image as both a revival of ancient virtue and an exceptional and unprecedented paradigm of republican excellence. We now turn to an even deeper illustration of the ideology of Hellenism and of the American exploitation of Hellenic ideology – the two armies' encounters with barbarism in the shape of the ancestors of the Kurds and the native inhabitants of the American continent.

7

The Savage State: Kurds and Indians

I then called my brother to tell him the news and he told me, 'Well, have fun playing cowboys and Indians out there' ...
Colby Buzzell, *My War: Killing Time in Iraq* (2005)

Despite all the high-tech bullshit we carry, personal defence is still the most primal act. Every time we leave our FOB, we lock and load. In the Old West, gunslingers went everywhere strapped, because they never knew when they'd be in their next gunfight. There is nothing different about being in Iraq. It's an oddly exhilarating way to live ...
Jason Christopher Hartley, *Just Another Soldier* (2005)[1]

* * *

In the course of their long marches, Xenophon's Greeks and Doniphan's Missouri volunteers confronted powerful nations that now seemed softened by luxury and burdened by too much history. But the invading armies also had to face enemies of a different sort from the Persians and Mexicans. Though they prided themselves on their tough and republican spirit, they found themselves opposed by people who had a wild freedom of their own – people who seemed to have too little rather than too much history. For the Greeks, these opponents were the Carduchians in the mountains of Kurdistan and the other tribesmen who blocked their way to the Black Sea. For the Americans, they were the indigenous inhabitants of the American West, including the Navajos and Apaches, peoples known by the generic name Indians. Carduchians and Indians alike appeared to be locked in a state of savageness, and yet also able to pose the invaders uncomfortable questions about the fragility of their own civilization.[2]

This chapter will explore the racial ideology underlying American appeals to classical paradigms. We will see how American Indians and Xenophon's Carduchians, together with their supposed modern descendants, the Kurds, could be linked in the imperial imagination by an ideology of space and time that was expressed in a historical narrative built upon Enlightenment ideas of progress. These racial stereotypes were propagated in a wide variety of genres – including both visual media and written accounts such as military and travel memoirs. As well as exploring a range of nineteenth-century evidence, we will continue to read the modern use of Xenophon against Xenophon's own account and analyse the pressures that mould all readings of encounters between 'civilization' and 'savagery'.

It was the burden of conquest that forced Colonel Doniphan's Missouri volunteers to confront the Navajos. Doniphan had been left in control of Santa Fé by Stephen Kearny, overall commander of the Army of the West, when he pressed on towards California. Kearny soon began receiving complaints from the local inhabitants about Navajo raids. He left it to Doniphan, now in effect governor of the territory of New Mexico, to sort out what had suddenly become an American rather than a Mexican problem. The troops, still unpaid and without adequate clothing, were understandably more keen to press south towards Mexico than to pursue the Navajos. Separate parties nonetheless ventured into the mountains and gathered at Bear Spring for a grand rendezvous. Speaking through an interpreter, Doniphan threatened war on the Navajos unless they agreed to a treaty. The Navajo leaders expressed their bafflement that they were being rebuked for fighting the Mexicans – when that was precisely what the Americans were doing themselves. They agreed to a treaty all the same – but few supposed that it would last long.[3]

Doniphan's troops came to blows with a different Indian tribe in their march from Chihuahua to join the main American army in Mexico. Some Apache raiders made off with a considerable number of the army's live-stock, and Doniphan sent in pursuit a small force under Captain John Reid. As he followed the Apache trail, Reid met a local ranch-owner who had had eighteen women and children as well as much livestock taken by the raiders. Reinforced by Mexicans, Reid's patrol caught up with the Apaches and, luring them into the open with a decoy, killed seventeen of them in a firefight. The Indians then withdrew, abandoning their captives and several hundred head of cattle.[4]

Like Doniphan's troops, Xenophon's Greeks were at first reluctant to venture into the mountains. But as they retreated north along the Tigris after Cyrus' death, they soon found themselves with no choice. There were towering mountains on one side, a deep river on the other, and the Persians were burning villages behind them. After returning to some villages not damaged by fire, the Greeks quizzed some prisoners who told them that 'the way north, through the mountains, would take them to the Carduchians' – 'a belligerent, mountain-dwelling people who had never submitted to the king; in fact, they said, the mountains were so harsh that the king had once sent an invading force of 120,000 men against the Carduchians and not one of these men came back'. The timeless story of the utter destruction of a Persian army emphasizes the dangers that lay to the north. Despite this warning, the Greeks felt the way through the mountains was their only hope of safety.[5]

Xenophon further stresses the threat posed by the Carduchians once the Greeks have fought their way through the mountains. He pauses his account to offer the troops' own reflections on 'the hardship they had

17. 'Indian atrocities': an image of savagery boosting the
US claim to be defenders of civilization.

endured' during their seven days marching through Carduchian territory:
'there were battles every single day, and they suffered more losses than on
all the occasions they had clashed with the king and Tissaphernes put
together.' These reflections give some shape to Xenophon's sketchy account of the actual fighting: the Carduchians had constantly charged and
retreated, at times blocking the way in front, at times attacking the rear,
while the Greeks had responded by taking to the heights to threaten the
enemy from above. A series of clashes on narrow mountain passes, it
emerges, had been more terrifying than a pitched battle in the desert
against the might of the king's army, scythe-bearing chariots and all. Nor
were the Carduchians the end of the Greeks' dangers. More tough opponents lay in their path to the sea and beyond – the Taochians in their
mountain strongholds; the Chalybians, 'most valiant' of all the peoples
through whose land they passed; the Mossynoecians and Paphlagonians
along the Black Sea coast; and finally, across the Hellespont, the highland
villagers of Thrace whom the Greeks were ordered to subdue when in the
pay of the Thracian despot Seuthes.[6]

139

The Ten Thousand's encounters with these highlanders have often been described with the terms applied to American fights against Indians. The Carduchians and their neighbours tend to be cast as savages, far more alien from Xenophon's Greeks than the Persians whom they initially had to confront. So too the alleged brutality of the indigenous inhabitants whom Doniphan's troops encounter along the way makes the Americans seem much more akin to the Mexicans, their professed opponents. Americans could even claim to be defending rather than attacking the Mexicans. One leading account of Doniphan's expedition claimed that the treaty with the Navajos entitled Doniphan to the olive as well as the laurel: 'he has justly earned the distinguished titles of VICTOR and PACIFICATOR.' Doniphan was given the stature of a Roman general triumphing over the wild tribesmen of Spain or Gaul.[7]

The image of Americans as protectors of the weak explains the attention paid to Doniphan's Indian engagements. Captain Reid's rescue of the Mexican prisoners was rapturously praised in newspapers: the Americans had become 'friends and protectors' of the Mexicans, 'rescuing their wives and children out of the hands of the pitiless savage'; and this action was 'a better example of the indomitable spirit and gallant heroism of the Missouri troops' than their earlier victories at Brazito and Sacramento. It was also this 'sudden and romantic episode' that received most attention in Thomas Hart Benton's speech welcoming Doniphan back to St Louis. Benton hailed an event of 'a novel, extraordinary, and romantic kind' – 'Americans chastising savages for plundering people who they themselves came to conquer'. To stress the Americans' role as bearers of peace, he even read out a letter of gratitude from the Mexicans – 'a trophy of a new kind in war'. The conquering Americans had won the gratitude of the very men they had conquered.[8]

Celebrations of Reid's exploits against the Apache raiders implicitly drew on the enduring significance of the captivity narrative in colonial American history. Colonial aggression was diluted by emphasis on the Indians' savage treatment of white captives (and especially women). Now the Americans were extending the same protection to non-Anglo-Saxons. At the same time, Reid's violent encounter looks ahead to the sort of combat that would be typical of the Plains Wars in the coming decades, as more and more of the West was 'opened up', and beyond that to the continuing role of the captive in the mythology of the frontier.[9]

The terms in which Reid's fight was celebrated help us understand further the drive towards identifying ancient Greek and modern American. Xenophon and Doniphan were not simply employing the might of republican armies to assert control over oriental and despotic lands. The fact that a skirmish with Apaches could be hailed as more significant than victory in battle over Mexicans suggests that opposition to savagery was an even more powerful force in American ideology. Central to the American anabasis was the brutal assertion of progress by violent attacks on tribes that were themselves dismissed as brutal and violent.

7. The Savage State: Kurds and Indians

The power of the racial hierarchy implicit in invocations of Xenophon emerges from American responses to the modern inhabitants of the mountains of Kurdistan. In the nineteenth century Kurds were generally thought to be direct descendants of Xenophon's Carduchians, even though they lived then (as they do now) across a much broader area. Some of the Americans who visited the region were also prepared to draw a distinctly American parallel. They thought that Kurds resembled not only the ancient Carduchians as Xenophon had portrayed them, but also the Indians encountered in modern-day America. 'The wild simplicity of the Kurds' reminded one American missionary in the 1830s of 'the aborigines of America', and another missionary in the 1890s found that the Kurds 'closely resemble our American Indians' in their 'generally untamed appearance' and also in their habitations. Missionaries were the main American presence in the area at this time, but they were not alone in their attitude to the Kurds. Indeed, an American diplomat in the 1890s could even write that the Kurd 'gives to the government and to diplomacy more trouble than our aborigines give to the Federal Government'. He was making a sly compliment to the policy of establishing reservations for American Indians whose land had been taken by white settlers.[10]

The comparison between Kurd and Indian remained potent at the end of the First World War. An American report drawn up during the Paris Peace Conference claimed that 'in some respects the Koords remind one of the North American Indians', elaborating the comparison by dwelling on their physical features ('tawny skin, high cheek bones, broad mouth, and black straight hair') as well as their mien ('rather quiet, morose, dull'), and temperament ('passionate, resentful, revengeful, intriguing, and treacherous'). These racial stereotypes necessarily coloured American policy on whether the modern Kurds deserved the right to self-determination. Even more chillingly, a Turkish foreign minister in the 1920s could express the hope that the Kurds would suffer the fate of the 'Red Hindus' (i.e. the Red Indians) – that is, extinction or confinement to reservations. Conversely, a sense of affinity for the oppressed Kurds ('Iraq's Indians') explains why there has been at least some support among American Indians for action against Saddam Hussein – as well as resentment when army commanders have persisted in terming untamed parts of Iraq 'Indian country'.[11]

*

The chief was of such magnificent physique that one of our party, Doctor Wislizenus, desired to secure his skull for a specimen; so he chopped off his head with a hatchet, removing the flesh by boiling it each day in a large kettle. While we were traveling, this kettle with its gruesome contents hung on the wagon pole, and that was the last I ever saw of the mighty chief ...
William Clark Kennerly, *Persimmon Hill*[12]

Nineteenth-century theories of race are crucial to understanding the appeal of the comparison drawn between the Ten Thousand's march across Asia and Doniphan's expedition across North America. It was the pseudo-science of race that led a German doctor accompanying Doniphan's march to decapitate the Indian chief killed by Captain Reid's party – and later to send the skull to America's leading craniologist. Unlike Dr Wislizenus, Xenophon and his comrades did not measure any skulls as they trekked through eastern Anatolia. It was not so much the Greeks' actions that were of concern to racial theorists as Xenophon's description of the peoples he encountered. The *Anabasis* enabled reputable writers to assert similarities between Xenophon's Carduchians, the modern Kurds, and American Indians, and these similarities could be taken up and propagated even in privileged contexts such as school editions of Xenophon. It is against this widespread doctrine of racial hierarchies that the triumphant celebrations of American military achievements that greeted Doniphan's return must be read.[13]

One reason Americans found it easy to apply similar racial stereotypes to Kurds and Indians is that Kurds have been interpreted through ideas inspired by early encounters with American Indians. The inhabitants of the New World provoked great intellectual uncertainty in Europe. Who were they? Where had they come from? The questions posed by American Indians were to shape new ideas about human development. Inspired by reports about native American life, French and Scottish theorists in the eighteenth century posited that human societies across the globe went through similar stages of development. According to this 'stadial theory', societies progressed from 'savagery' (when people lived by hunting) first to a pastoral stage ('barbarism'), then to a civilized agricultural stage, before finally entering a mercantile economy marked by manufacturing and corruption.[14]

The influence of the Indian on these theories of development was tacitly recognized by the American artist Thomas Cole in his grand series *The Course of Empire* (1834-6). Cole depicted the same valley in five different stages of development: first, *The Savage State*, a wilderness inhabited by hunters; then *The Pastoral State*, an Arcadian fantasy with agriculture and a Greek temple; next, two images of a quasi-Rome – *The Consummation of Empire* (Fig. 4) and *The Destruction of Empire*; finally, an uninhabited scene of *Desolation*. While the series as a whole was a pointed warning of the transience of empire, one striking feature of the first painting was that the hunters, though European in appearance, inhabited the tepee-shaped huts of American Indians. Cole was suggesting that the glories of Greece and Rome had emerged from states of savageness like those that confronted colonists in America – who were themselves forging anew the all too transient glories of Greece and Rome.[15]

The universalizing tenets of stadial theory explain why it was so easy to draw comparisons between the inhabitants of different parts of the globe. American Indians invited comparison not just with modern Kurds, but also with Scottish highlanders: one account of Doniphan's expedition found that the Navajos, thanks to their 'bold and fearless character' and to 'the magnificent mountain scenery of the country which they inhabit', awakened in the mind 'reflections not unlike those which anyone is apt to entertain of the Highlanders and Highlands of Scotland, from reading the Scottish bards'. The avowedly literary nature of this romantic construction is here made doubly plain: American Indians are read through a poetic image of Highlanders. The same comparison was made by the writer who did most to spread the cult of the Highlander, Sir Walter Scott: he noted that his character Rob Roy (a famous Highland outlaw early in the eighteenth century) blended the 'wild virtues' and 'unrestrained license' of an American Indian.[16]

The logic that enabled stadial theorists to align American Indians with Kurdish and Scottish highlanders also made it possible to align Kurds and Scots. William Elliot, a British traveller who died young in Mesopotamia in the 1830s, noted that the Kurds were 'probably the descendants of those that flourished in the days of Cyrus and Xenophon', and went on to reflect on 'the similarity between these Koords, as they *are*, and the Highland clans as they *were*, not many centuries ago': 'They are as devotedly attached to their mountains as the Scotch or Swiss … . They are proud, haughty, and overbearing exactly in proportion to their ignorance, and, like our own clans of old, despise, more or less, all arts but those of war and plunder, and all professions but that of arms.' Elliot here introduces to the comparison between peoples another key part of stadial theory – time. Theories of human progress were concerned not just with mapping the supposed primitivism of highlanders, but also with developments through time: Adam Ferguson, for instance, wrote in his *Essay on the History of Civil Society*, one of the key texts of the Scottish Enlightenment, that 'the inhabitants of Britain, at the time of the first Roman invasions, resembled, in many things, the present natives of North America' (he alluded specifically to a lack of agriculture, to painting the body, and to the use of animal-skins as clothing). Elliot maps time through space in a similar way. To travel in Kurdistan now was to journey to the Scottish past – before the Highlands had been subjected to pressures of modernization. His account of the Kurds is coloured by the allure of the pre-modern – the same desire for a retreat from the present that led him to adopt native dress and a native name as he travelled in the East.[17]

Xenophon's description of the Carduchians proved to be a fascinating test-case for modern theories of human development. It offered the chance to compare past and present: one nineteenth-century English geographer even wrote that he knew of 'no tribe of people more interesting to the historian of the human race than the Curds'. As they ventured to Kurdistan, travellers sought traces of the customs Xenophon had described. Their discoveries strengthened the perceived genealogical link between the ancient and modern inhabitants of Kurdistan by positing a continuity in customs. Together with their Armenian neighbours, also described by Xenophon, the Kurds were seen as a living museum, suspended in time, preserving their language and manners from antiquity. Travellers could observe with a patronising fascination how oriental customs had not changed since Xenophon's day.[18]

The sense of a stagnant orient is particularly strong in a travelogue written by John Macdonald Kinneir, a Scottish traveller early in the nineteenth century. Kinneir noted that the habit of holding a black cloth before the eyes against the glare of the snow was 'still practised in Armenia and Koordistan'; that the villages in Armenia are 'still built in exactly the same manner'; that cattle, men, women, and children 'all live in the same apartment in this country at the present day'; and that wheat and barley are 'still cultivated'. All these indications of continuity could be found described on a single page of Kinneir's book. Only one thing had changed: Kinneir was struck by Xenophon's description of barley wine, but he 'could never discover any liquor of this kind whilst in Armenia'. An easy explanation was at least at hand for the lack of liquor in neighbouring Kurdistan: the formidable Isabella Bishop Bird, who travelled through Persia and Kurdistan later in the century, found that the only way the Kurds had changed since Xenophon's time was that they had become 'Moslems and teetotallers'.[19]

While the modern Kurds were marked as primitive by association with the ancient Carduchians, the wild people Xenophon encountered could themselves be tarred by comparison with the savage ancestors of the British. A reviewer in 1830 was struck by Xenophon's description of how the Taochians, inhabitants of the Pontic mountains, resisted a Greek attack by rolling stones down from a fortress. He argued that this account could help explain 'the masses of stones not unfrequently found in our ancient hill-forts': like the Taochians, the ancient Britons had gathered heavy stones 'for the purpose of overwhelming assailants'. Implicit in this analogy was a confident belief in how far the British had progressed since Xenophon's time. Their Asiatic counterparts, by contrast, had remained stuck in the past, in the same state as the wild natives of America.[20]

The association of Kurds and Indians with the past involved a striking double standard. On the one hand, both peoples retained a savageness that had once been universal. But they could also be seen as relics of a noble past. When one of Doniphan's Missourians compared the Apaches killed in Captain Reid's attack with 'bronze statues', he was drawing on the common analogy between the sturdy physique of American Indians and classical sculptures such as the torso of Hercules and the Belvedere Apollo. The same hint of nobility appears in other remarks on the physical appearance of Indians: Frederick Wislizenus, the German doctor who followed Doniphan's expedition, remarked on the 'Roman bend' found in the nose of certain Indians, while the painter George Catlin thought that

7. The Savage State: Kurds and Indians

18. *The Dying Tecumseh* (1856): the doomed Indian warrior as classical hero.

their 'daily feats, with their naked limbs, must vie with the Grecian youths'. Classical paradigms were also invoked to describe Indian costumes: the curve of a bear-skin cap could recall 'the crest of an old Greek helmet', while the mounted Indians of the plains were dressed 'in the classic style of the ancient Roman and Grecian cavalry'. Indian customs also recalled ancient precedents: Indians could be compared equally with the Greeks in their councils, with the early Romans in their warlike disposition and their hostility to philosophy, and with later Roman orators like Cicero in their eloquence. These descriptions were all superficially flattering – but really designed to cast the Indians as relics. By contrast, Anglo-Americans whose achievements merited comparison with antiquity were heirs to the glory of antiquity rather than noble survivors.[21]

The notion that the Kurds shared with the American Indians a savage state that had once been universal was another self-serving fiction. Travellers came to Kurdistan with the notion of the stagnant orient already in mind. They were fascinated by observable signs of continuity and blind to tensions and shifts within Kurdish society. So strong was the grip of the past that one English army officer even described how he imagined he saw in the midst of his researches Xenophon and his soldiers 'living in body and soul' before his eyes. It was as if the geographical remoteness of Kurdistan could somehow reverse the passage of time and restore antiquity, intact and visible.[22]

The immutability of Kurdish customs since Xenophon's day was easily explained by the harsh environment in which Kurds lived. Like American Indians, the Kurds were seen as unchanging in their wildness because they lived in a wilderness. Just as the American historian Francis Parkman could claim that 'the Indian is hewn out of rock', so too the nineteenth-century traveller Robert Ker Porter could call the Kurds 'as unchangeable as their rocks'. Porter explained that he found the Kurdish mountaineers just as they were in the time of Xenophon: 'unsubdued,

145

untameable, fierce, and inhospitable as their own slippery rocks on the verge of a precipice.' It was their rocks that made them wild.[23]

The same physical environment that held Kurds and Indians in a state of savagery offered exciting challenges to European and American explorers. Robert Ker Porter went on to exploit the notion of continuity to highlight the dangers that he faced himself: 'the natives of certain defiles we had to pass through' were 'reported to be equally barbarous with those of the age of Herodotus or Xenophon'. The ancient citation affirms his prowess in surviving the threats posed by the modern barbarians. Accounts of Doniphan's forays into the mountains of New Mexico were similarly lavish with attributions of heroism. Doniphan's men were said to have 'surmounted difficulties of the most appalling nature' – 'craggy mountains of stupendous height' and narrow passages between 'precipices and yawning chasms, fearful to behold'. One account even claimed that their 'march over the grander and loftier summits of the Cordilleras' excelled 'the passage of the Carthaginian general over the Apennines' and 'the march of Bonaparte ... over the snow-capt peak of the Alps'.[24]

These grandiose celebrations of European and American manhood unwittingly expose another racial double standard. By advancing in winter into the mountains of the Navajos, Doniphan's troops could be said to show that 'the energy of the Anglo-Saxons knows no bounds' and that '*men*, at least AMERICANS, can accomplish whatever is within the scope of possibility'. And yet the Missouri volunteers were being praised for venturing into realms that were everyday setting for the Indians – and tainted by association with primitiveness.[25]

The primitivism of the Kurds and American Indians was further implied by their subjection to a shared aesthetic – the picturesque. The language of the picturesque informed the perceptions of one of the Missouri volunteers, Frank Edwards, as he described his experiences accompanying Doniphan in the march across the plains. Edwards (whose account was itself praised for 'picturesqueness') recalled observing 'a beautiful and noble-looking Indian woman' swinging a child who was hung from the roof by a thong of deer's hide: 'The whole scene, cabin, woman and papoose staring at us with its large eyes, realized one of Cooper's life-like Indian sketches.' Later an Indian woman with a basket of grapes on her head and three or four naked children at her side 'made a picturesque object'. This type of language was ubiquitous in accounts of American Indians, Kurds, and other 'savages'. Kurdistan and its inhabitants, for instance, received particular stress in the preface to Robert Ker Porter's account of his travels in the Middle East, where they were described as 'a picturesque country and people, hardly explored, and ... rendered particularly interesting by tracing the march of Xenophon'.[26]

The apparently favourable language of the picturesque was laden with dark associations. A modern scholar has called the word 'that most gentle of the era's codes for "alien"' – but it was not always that gentle a term.

7. The Savage State: Kurds and Indians

Initially common in the eighteenth century as a way of describing gently varied landscapes sculpted to resemble the paintings of Claude, the picturesque came in time to be applied to landscapes marked by ruins and to peoples and lands regarded as backward. Picturesque people preserved local variety and resisted the unifying trends of modernity. They were to be found in villages and, with the growth of the cities, in ghettoes. The bitter undertones are brought out forcefully by an American traveller's response to the sight of some English soldiers in Canada: 'how picturesque appear, amid the motley throng, these red-coated soldiers.' But he then breaks off: 'Picturesque! I like them not – they indicate a subjugated people.' His comment openly exposes the confusion of codes involved in applying to British soldiers terminology that was thought appropriate to the degraded inhabitants of mountains, impoverished villages, and urban slums.[27]

*

Nineteenth-century perceptions of 'savages' like the Kurds and American Indians made comparisons between the achievements of Xenophon and Doniphan easier because they also informed the way the *Anabasis* itself was read. Xenophon's account began to be aligned with picturesque travel books. We have already seen that Xenophon's description of the Arabian desert could be found 'picturesque'. That same quality was also found in the work as a whole: a reviewer in 1830 called it 'a series of historical pictures, excellently painted'; the previous year, another reviewer wrote that some of the military campaigns described in one of Sir Walter Scott's works were as 'picturesque' and 'animated' as Xenophon's expedition. Implicit in this comparison was a pointed alignment of the lands traversed by Xenophon's Greeks with the highland and medieval scenes favoured by Scott: it was not least for their attention to the vagaries of local landscape and dialects that Scott's novels were admired.[28]

The comparison between Xenophon and Sir Walter Scott was appealing. The author of a 1824 translation of the *Anabasis* found 'the picture' towards the end of the *Anabasis* of a Thracian feast, complete with drinking, dancing, and the exchange of gifts, 'the most perfect on record': 'the whole scene wears the air of barbarism and ferocity, and nearly corresponds with many of the pictures of the Scotch clans, drawn by the author of Waverly (*sic*).' The picturesque Xenophon is here being admired for his vivid narration and his ability to catch distinct local customs. But the language of 'barbarism' also castigates the attractive scene as primitive.[29]

The tendency to read Xenophon's account through nineteenth-century perceptions of the picturesque savage is most strikingly shown by a painting exhibited at the Paris Salon of 1843: Adrien Guignet's *Episode in the Retreat of the Ten Thousand* (Fig. 19: now in the Louvre). The foreground of the painting shows a cavalry charge by loosely-clad tribesmen.

19. Adrien Guignet, *Episode in the Retreat of the Ten Thousand* (1843).

Left, right, and centre, they are converging on a group of soldiers slowly retreating in the middle. More tribesmen stand on rocks nearby, firing arrows or throwing stones at the soldiers. They look like archetypal American Indians – but the salon catalogue explains that they are Carduchians.[30]

A loner fond of roaming amidst the gorges of the old royal hunting park at Fontainebleau, Guignet was directly inspired by contemporary French representations of North Africa and the Middle East: his other works include images of Greeks and Turks fighting in narrow defiles. But his painting of the ancient Carduchians seems to owe as much to images of American Indians as to the vogue for the Orient. The French had a long-standing interest in Indians stemming from their own colonial adventures in North America, and this fascination had been fed more recently by the novels of James Fenimore Cooper, which were very popular in France (though Cooper described the Indians of the eastern forests rather than the horse-rearing Indians of the plains beyond the Mississippi). Two years after Guignet's painting was exhibited this interest was further enforced when George Catlin's gallery of American Indians was exhibited in Paris. And even if it cannot be proved that Guignet himself drew on images of America for inspiration, his painting of Kurdistan can still strike modern viewers as a powerful foreshadowing of cinematic scenes from the American West – a still from a John Ford western, a forlorn hope with Custer in Greek armour desperately battling for survival against the odds.[31]

Whether intentionally or not, Guignet was able to make the Carduchians resemble Plains Indians only by blatantly departing from the *Anabasis*. Guignet makes the Carduchians cavalrymen, even though Xenophon describes them living in villages perched on the sides of mountains – not horse-rearing terrain. Guignet is right at least that the Carduchians were archers, but Xenophon describes them using bows 'between four and five feet long' which they would rest against their feet as they drew – not the smaller bows that Guignet's figures fire from horseback.[32]

Guignet's mistaken depiction of the Carduchians stems from some dubious antiquarianism. His salon description reveals that he had learnt from the Greek geographer Strabo that the Carduchians had the same customs and the same manner of fighting as their descendants, the Parthians. A link with Rome's famous eastern enemy adds historical grandeur to the picture – but the alleged kinship is highly implausible, and the text of Strabo is now generally emended to remove the Parthian connection.[33]

The false link with the Parthians offers a further reason for the American aura in Guignet's painting. Early French accounts of some American tribes had drawn comparisons with the Parthians and the other famous nomads of antiquity, the Scythians; there was even speculation that

American Indians were descended from these tribes. This identification lived on at the time of Doniphan's expedition: an officer in the Army of the West wrote of the Indians as 'savage Scythians' and 'Parthian Apaches'. School editions of Xenophon also drew comparisons between the tactics favoured by American Indians and Parthians, tracing them back to the Persian cavalrymen faced by the Ten Thousand in Mesopotamia.[34]

The description of Guignet's painting in the salon catalogue describes the Ten Thousand in the same sort of heroic terms that were applied to Doniphan's troops in the mountains of New Mexico. Contrasting the Greeks' success with the army of 120,000 Persians that had been totally lost in the mountains, the catalogue spoke of the 'superior tactics' and 'intrepidity' through which they endured 'unbelievable toils'. This description picked up on a key feature of the painting's composition: Guignet emphasizes the Greeks' intrepidity by placing them right in the centre, holding fast against the barbarians who rush at them like a force of nature. The energy and violence of the Carduchian horsemen seems to call for the imposition of imperial control and to make stronger our admiration for the unflappable figures who resist them.

The thrilling movement of Guignet's painting seems also to invite a romantic identification with the Carduchians themselves. Salon critics spoke admiringly of the painting's sense of movement and animation – its 'fury full of dash' rendering 'the terrible pêle-mêle of a battle'. What creates this effect is the fact that the Carduchians are shown from behind: the viewer is in the position of their rear and caught up in the torrent of their charge. Guignet invites us to place ourselves imaginatively in the Carduchians' position and to enjoy their exhilarating freedom. There is a creative tension between the points of view expressed by the catalogue and by the picture itself: the catalogue praises staunch Greek heroism and views the natives through an ethnographic lens, as ancestors of the famous Parthians; the painting encourages us to view the Ten Thousand, with their suspiciously Roman-looking pikes, as the embattled authority of those who seek to impose themselves on others. From this perspective, the Carduchians are the true heroes – symbols of freedom, standing for resistance to discipline and orthodoxy. The charge of the men on horseback presents the storming of exemplary neo-classical virtue by the forces of romanticism.[35]

*

The popular image of Xenophon's picturesqueness and Guignet's painting of the Carduchians reflect the same tension found in perceptions of Kurds and American Indians. Kurds and Indians were denigrated as savages, and yet contempt was mingled with a lingering regret at their imminent loss of their wild freedom. Reacting against the cosmopolitanism and universal values of Enlightenment philosophy, many were attracted to the image of the lawless life led by outlaws and bandits inhabiting wild mountainous areas. This fascination was reflected in the enthusiasm for the seventeenth-century Italian painter Salvator Rosa, whose scenes of bandits and battles were thought to have inspired Adrien Guignet (Guignet himself painted the legendary scene of Rosa living amongst bandits). The full romantic pull of the primitive was perhaps best expressed by the poet Baudelaire in his comments on a painting of North African chieftains displayed in 1859: he claimed that the figures of the chieftains, with their 'patrician dandyism', recalled 'those savages of North America, brought here by the painter Catlin, who even in their state of decadence made us dream of the art of Phidias and the grandeurs of Homer'. Baudelaire drew together in one sweeping sentence images from the epic and classical periods of Greece, from the Anglo-Saxon encounter with the American Indian, and from the French imperial ventures into Africa. He expressed the allure of the primitive with an escapist relish. But, with a bravura dismissiveness, he also elided all distinctions between Indian and African as he locked them in a classical past.[36]

It may have been easier to construct from afar an image of barbaric chivalry, but even writers within America could respond with an ambivalent admiration to the nobility of the savage. The prolific adventure writer H.W. Herbert paused in a panegyrical essay on Xenophon to reflect on an episode in the later stages of the Greeks' march to the sea. When the Greeks came to the land of the Taochians, they fell short of provisions since the locals had stored their supplies in precipitous mountain strongholds. The Greeks attacked and took one of the strongholds, and, Xenophon reports, 'what followed was terrible to behold': 'Women threw their children off the cliff and then hurled themselves off afterwards, and the men did the same.' As he recounted this incident, Herbert was drawn to a parallel with a famous event during the Greek War of Independence: when some inhabitants of a fortress in Suli (a mountainous region of North-West Greece) found it impossible to resist the Ottoman forces, their women threw themselves and their children down a precipice. The desperate action of the Suliote women was widely celebrated: romantic writers described Suli as a place 'where Grecian freedom linger'd still', and its inhabitants were said to have raised themselves 'in the eyes of the world from bandits into heroes' and given their country 'a name equal to that of an ancient republic of Greece'. The romantic cult of the Suliotes makes the comparison with the Taochians particularly striking: 'a wild people of the Pontus' was being directly compared with people who preserved the character of the ancient Greeks. The comparison Herbert was suggesting was in fact remarkably similar to a jotting Charles Darwin made while travelling in South America in the 1830s: seeing an escaped slave throw herself off a cliff to avoid recapture, he wrote that 'in a Roman matron, this would have been called the noble love of freedom' – but 'in a poor negress it is mere brutal obstinancy'. While Darwin exposes the hypocrisy of current racial attitudes, Herbert was prepared to glorify the distant Taochians – as long as he did not have to dwell on the fact that Xenophon's heroic Greek soldiers were the oppressors forcing them to their brave but gloomy expedient.[37]

Even the idealized picture of primitive heroism contained within it traces of the alterity of the savage. Kurds and American Indians could as easily be subjected to contempt as to the romantic gaze of the disenchanted western aristocrat: nostalgic admiration for the noble savage was itself based on an imperial construction of space and time – on a vision of the primitive living the life of the past in a wilderness whose spatial distance diminished year by year. Whether an object of scorn or longing, the Kurd and the Indian together reinforced by opposition the myth of progress enshrined in the Army of the West as it advanced across the Great Plains, treading figuratively in the steps of Xenophon's anabasis through the tough mountains of Asia.

Transferring the trajectory of Xenophon's *Anabasis* to North America was made easier by the fact that Xenophon's own account of the tribes encountered during the retreat employs some of the same rhetoric found in descriptions of the American Indian. Patterns of inversion, for instance, are found in Xenophon's portrayal of the Mossynoecians, a people who lived along the Black Sea coast: 'The soldiers who took part in this expedition agreed that, of all those whose lands they passed through, the Mossynoecians were the most alien and the most remote from Greeks in their customs.' The soldiers had been shown 'soft and extremely pale' boys who had been 'fattened up on a diet of boiled nuts'. What was most alien about the Mossynoecians, however, was that they 'wanted to have sex in the open with the kept women whom the Greeks had brought, because that was their custom there': 'They used to do in public what others did when no one was looking, and when they were alone they did the kind of things that others did in company.' Sex in public was in both ancient and modern colonial times a regular marker of the savage. Xenophon self-consciously makes this alleged habit part of a regular pattern of inversions. Despite the peculiarity of Mossynoecian customs, however, they are in at least one respect very similar to Greeks: the Ten Thousand find them engaged in a civil war and exploit their internal differences by uniting with one faction against the other. It is the Mossynoecians' all too Greek lack of cohesion that makes it easier for the Greek soldiers to press onwards.[38]

Xenophon also adopts the rhetoric of empire when he implies that the Carduchians and their neighbours live in the past. A sense of temporal distance is suggested firstly by the fact that the Carduchians live scattered in villages – in what was seen by Greeks as an old mode of life. Xenophon further evokes Greek images of primitive life in his comment that the nearest village beyond the Centrites (the river that marked the boundary between the Carduchians and the Armenians) was at a distance of 'not less than five parasangs: for there were no villages near the river because of the wars against the Carduchians'. This passage was cited by the American geographer Ellen Churchill Semple as evidence for 'primitive waste boundaries', alongside examples from Roman accounts of the Germans – and more recent practice in American Indian lands. Xenophon himself was inviting comparison with Thucydides' analysis of the spatial distribution of villages in the unsettled conditions of early Greece: just as Thucydides thought that the early Greeks settled at a distance from the sea owing to piracy, so too Xenophon asserts that the threat of the Carduchians meant that there were no Armenian settlements near the river that marked their border.[39]

Xenophon again evokes Greek accounts of human development when he describes the army's arrival at some villages in Armenia. The Greeks found that goats, sheep, cattle and poultry all 'lived with their young inside the houses and were fed indoors'. That is, they had arrived at a place where distinctions between humans and animals had not fully developed. These Armenian villages evoke the lack of differentiation between humans and animals typical in Greek accounts of primitive societies.[40]

It has sometimes been argued that Xenophon's account of the seemingly primitive conditions of Kurdistan and Armenia justifies their future subjection. But we need not assume that these lands are treated by Xenophon with an imperialist contempt. He brings out with some amusement how the Greek soldiers adapt to local customs. In the villages of Armenia, for instance, there were jars of barley wine with barleycorns floating on top, and 'unjointed reeds of various lengths had been placed on the jars; one drank by picking up a reed, putting it in one's mouth, and sucking'. As for the wine itself, it was 'very strong, unless it was diluted with water, but it made a very pleasant drink when one got used to it'. Drinking undiluted wine was commonly seen as a mark of savagery – but Xenophon suggests that the Greeks soon got to like it. Even more strikingly, he goes on to describe how he drank from jars 'where he had to bend over and slurp the wine down as if he were an ox'. Here the comparison with bestial conditions is made overt. Like the American Indians, the Armenians seem to live close to nature.[41]

Xenophon's consciousness of how environment shapes customs is best illustrated by an episode in the Ten Thousand's winter in Thrace. He explains that it was so cold that their water and wine froze and many of the soldiers got frostbite – and 'this made them understand why the Thracians wear fox-skin hats which protect their ears as well as their heads'. While Greeks often cast peoples who wore animal skins as primitive, Xenophon here offers a rational explanation of the practice. He shows the same awareness of environment when he comments that the Mossynoecians used dolphin blubber 'for the same purposes that the Greeks use olive oil'. This remark is as much a way of aligning as of separating the Greeks and Mossynoecians. Though the Mossynoecians seemed alien to the Greek soldiers, Xenophon reveals a structural similarity in their customs.[42]

Xenophon extends his argument about spatial determinism to the military sphere. At one point he presents himself arguing why a detachment must fight with a ravine behind it rather than in front: 'crossing a difficult ravine and putting it behind us is actually an unmissable opportunity ... we should let the terrain teach us that our only chance of safety lies in victory.' Xenophon's words can be taken as emblematic: the military lesson of the *Anabasis* as a whole is that terrain is a teacher.[43]

One reader who understood Xenophon's lesson was James Wolfe, the British general who fought against the French in Canada in the Seven Years' War. The story has often been told that, as he was demonstrating his soldiers' skill at attacking and retreating on hills, Wolfe asked an onlooker his views of the manoeuvre: 'I think, said he, I see something here of the History of the Carduchi, who harassed Xenophon, and hung upon his rear in his retreat over the mountains. You are right, said Wolfe; I had it from thence; and I see you are a man of reading ... .' What is most striking about this anecdote is the fact that Wolfe learns the lesson from the savage Carduchians. So, too, many accounts of Indian-fighting stress the need to fight like Indians to beat them.[44]

Xenophon is conscious that the Greeks too must become savage to survive. Early in the retreat they mutilate Persian bodies to frighten the enemy – behaviour one scholar finds 'startlingly un-Greek'. And when the troops approach the Black Sea coast and find one more tribe opposing them, Xenophon bluntly tells them to 'find a way to eat them alive' – an appeal in words to behaviour seen as the hallmark of savages. How far the troops have moved from usual Greek customs is further brought out in the athletic games they hold after reaching the coast. A tough Spartan is chosen to lay out a wrestling-ground. When the soldiers ask how they will be able 'to wrestle on hard, shrub-covered ground like this', they receive a suitably laconic reply: 'It'll be a bit more painful for the one who is thrown.'[45]

At the start of their retreat, Xenophon's Greeks, like the Americans in New Mexico, had tried to forge an image of themselves as defenders against troublesome tribesmen. Cyrus had initially told the Greeks that he was hiring them to fight the Pisidians, the inhabitants of a mountainous area of Anatolia uniformly described as warlike in ancient sources. After Cyrus' death, the Greeks suggested that they could help the Persians against the 'troublesome' Pisidians and 'stop them constantly bothering you and spoiling your contentment'. The Persians did not take up the offer: they preferred to leave the Greeks to deal with the Carduchians – or the Carduchians to deal with the Greeks.[46]

By the end of the retreat, Xenophon has cast doubt on any claim the Greeks have to being defenders. In describing how the Carduchians 'abandon' their villages when confronted by the sudden onset of a large army, Xenophon uses a word commonly applied to the Athenian decision to abandon Athens in the face of the Persian invasion in 480 BC. The

154

Carduchians take to the mountains in the same way that the Athenians took to their ships before the battle of Salamis. The Greek mercenaries are again figured as Persians when they are advancing along a narrow path and find the way ahead blocked by the Carduchians. The Carduchians are in the position of the Spartans defending Thermopylae, and the Greeks are like Xerxes, forced to try to find another way round. The guides with the Spartan general Chirisophus, who is leading the front of the Greek army, tell him that there is no other road – but then Xenophon produces two prisoners to quiz. When the first of them denied knowing any other road, 'he was slaughtered' in front of the other prisoner (Xenophon's sinister shift to the passive obscures precisely who gave the order). 'The remaining man then said that the first man had denied knowledge of an alternative route because he had a married daughter living there, but that he would show them a route which even the yoke-animals could manage.' The Greeks have worse moral luck than the Persians, who were told of another route by a Greek traitor.[47]

If Xenophon suggests that the soldiers veer dangerously close to barbarism during the march to the sea, then we can read their response to the alien Mossynoecians as a reassertion of Hellenism after their arrival at Trapezus, a Greek city on the Black Sea coast. At the same time, Xenophon's account of how they had escaped from the horror of the interior seems to reassert by opposition the norms of Hellenism even as the Greeks adapt to the demands of native customs and rough terrain. The structuring of Xenophon's account seems to anticipate the rhetoric of empire deployed in celebrations of the winning of the American West. And yet, as we shall see in Section III, as the Greeks advance along the coast their victory comes to be endangered further by the bestial spirit that remains within them as well as by threats from outside. Their victory over the savage state is precarious.

*

In his account of Doniphan's expedition, John Hughes recounts a story that he had heard from a trader who had travelled on the Santa Fé trail early in the spring of 1846. The trader's party had observed, just after a storm, and shortly before sunset, 'a perfectly distinct image of the "bird of liberty", the American eagle on the disc of the sun' – and they had 'simultaneously, and almost involuntarily exclaimed that in less than twelve months the eagle of liberty would spread his broad pinions over the plains of the West, and that the flag of our country would wave over the cities of New Mexico and Chihuahua'. Doniphan's expedition had realized the portent – as Hughes himself suggested through the metaphor he applied to the army as it advanced over the plains: 'the American eagle seemed to spread his broad pinions … .' And their success had even been sealed by the sight of an eagle flying overhead before their first battle

20. The American eagle bearing westward 'the principles of republican government'.

against the Mexicans: "'An omen! an omen!" runs through our ranks ... .' This was destiny at its most manifest.[48]

The Missouri army whose tracks we have been following for the last five chapters was not simply an embodiment of the American eagle. For Hughes, the expedition was itself part of what he termed 'the westward march of civilization'. Hughes was adopting one of the key metaphors of the westward expansion of the United States: the growth of the republic was most commonly envisioned either in terms of the movement of water, as a tide or a series of waves, or through the military image of the march. Countless orators and writers spoke of the ('onward', 'westward', 'advancing') march of 'liberty' or 'progress' or 'the Anglo-Saxon race'. The metaphor was used with particular force by John O'Sullivan, the editor who popularized the notion of America's 'manifest destiny': in an essay on 'The Great Nation of Futurity', he spoke of 'the vigorous national heart of America, propelling the onward march of the multitude' and asked 'who will, what can, set limits to our onward march?'[49]

The phrase Hughes himself used had been employed by Thomas Jefferson in a letter written in 1824. Jefferson imagined a 'philosophic observer' journeying 'from the savages of the Rocky Mountains, eastwardly towards our seacoast', noting the successive stages of development plotted by stadial theory – savages living in a state of nature, 'covering themselves with the flesh and skins of wild beasts'; Indians in a pastoral state on the frontier; then 'our own semi-barbarous citizens, the pioneers of the advance of civilization'; and so on until reaching man in 'his, as yet, most improved state in our seaport towns'. For Jefferson, this imaginary journey, 'equivalent to a survey, in time, of the progress of man from the infancy of creation to the present day', could be summed up as 'the march of civilization'. John Hughes' own experience crossing the plains beyond the Mississippi did not suggest quite so neat a match between spatial and temporal distance, but he did subscribe to the same opposition between barbarism and civilization. Indeed, by writing an account of how the Missouri volunteers had subdued effete Mexicans and wild Indians during their long trek, he was making the military metaphor of the march of civilization concrete. Doniphan's expedition was (fulfilling) the march of destiny.[50]

Xenophon too had a vision of how the Greeks' long march could be integrated into a narrative of national expansion. He records how, as the army made its way along the shore of the Black Sea, he pondered its size and proficiency and the strange circumstances that had brought it to the Black Sea coast, 'where it would have taken a great deal of money to organize such a large army': 'As a result of these reflections, it occurred to him that it would be a fine achievement to found a city and acquire extra land and resources for Greece.' But while Xenophon himself was tempted to expand the colonial presence of the Greeks in the Black Sea, his plan was deeply unpopular. Most of the soldiers, he explains, longed to return home. And another officer directed the troops' attention instead to the availability of 'fertile and prosperous land' in the Chersonese (by the Hellespont). Xenophon's account of his brief fantasy of a new colony is tinged with irony: he describes his ambitions using a verb ('to acquire extra') associated in earlier historians with the doomed imperial ambitions of eastern kings and the Athenian democracy. He also sets his thoughts of a new city immediately before a speech where he lambasts the soldiers for their increasing indiscipline, including unprovoked attacks on Greek and non-Greek traders and officials – 'the behaviour of wild animals rather than of human beings'.[51]

The *Anabasis* supports a remark made by Frederick Jackson Turner in his 1893 lecture on 'The Significance of the Frontier in American History'. Turner drew to a close with an analogy drawn from antiquity: 'What the Mediterranean Sea was to the Greeks, breaking the bond of custom, offering new experiences, calling out new institutions and activities, that, and more, the ever retreating frontier has been to the United States directly, and to the nations of Europe more remotely.' As Turner intimates, Greek eyes in Xenophon's time were focused on the Mediterranean and its annexe, the Black Sea, not on Mesopotamia or the highlands of eastern Anatolia. The Ten Thousand's long march led them through distant lands, some of which seemed too soft, others too hard – and none of them seemed ripe for settlement. Their retreat was not a trek through a frontier region, but a journey out of difficulties. It was only when they had to confront further difficulties on the fringes of the Greek world that the prospect of settlement arose.[52]

It was Alexander of Macedon's conquest of the Persian empire that changed the Greeks' mental map of the world, expanding their sense of frontier. Ancient authors, as we have seen, naturally sought to link Alexander with the Ten Thousand: Arrian, a second-century historian of Alexander, even entitled his work *Anabasis* after Xenophon. The similarity in the accounts went beyond the title: Arrian portrayed Alexander, like Xenophon, surmounting one difficulty after another. But whereas Xenophon found his way out of impasses that were forced on him, Alexander actively sought out difficulties. Xenophon's Greeks felt a 'longing' to return home: Alexander's 'longing' was to attempt the impossible – to venture into the Hindu Kush and beyond, to capture mountain strongholds that had been impassable even to the fabled Hercules. Arrian's account of Alexander's mastery of space is suffused with the same rhetoric found in Xenophon. But that language has now become part of the genuine rhetoric of empire – heralding conquests that, like the American expansion in the West, were foreshadowed by eagles that appeared near the start of Alexander's march and during the decisive battle of Gaugamela.[53]

It would have been more apt for American celebrations of Alexander Doniphan's expedition to link him with his Macedonian namesake than with Xenophon. It is not that Alexander's imperial feats were totally neglected in celebrations of Doniphan's march: one participant looked back on the volunteers from St Louis as 'three hundred Alexanders in uniform, each ready to conquer a world if he could only get the right kind of chance'; and a contemporary newspaper noted that 'the march of Alexander the Great to the Indus was as long, in point of distance', before adding that 'the time consumed in it was much greater'. Just like Xenophon, Alexander could be evoked and trumped in the same sentence. But political ideology prevented widespread use of Alexander. As a king, Alexander stood in a very different relation to his troops from Xenophon or Doniphan, both of whom could be seen as in a sense first among equals, leaders of armies that were also political units. Alexander was also tainted by his use in anti-war arguments. Thomas Corwin, a Whig from Ohio, drew on him in a famous speech in the Senate in February 1847, a report of which angered Doniphan in Mexico: 'the mighty "Macedonian madman"', Corwin had argued, after wandering to the plains of India 'in quest of some California there', had 'died drunk in Babylon' – and the descendants of his Greeks are 'now governed by a descendant of Attila!'.[54]

The dubious reputation of the Macedonian conqueror in republican America led Alexander William Doniphan to be twinned with Xenophon, hero of an earlier march through the savage mountains of Asia. It was not just that 'Colonel Doniphan and Colonel Xenophon' had a pleasing ring to it or that Xenophon was preferred to Arrian as a school-text. Xenophon was cultivated because he was the acceptable face of Alexander: Americans now gave more priority than before to the military achievements of antiquity, but they did not forget the political vision of the republic's founders. To cite Xenophon was also to appeal to the widespread view that the anabasis of the Ten Thousand had itself been a march of destiny, exposing the weakness of the Persian empire and preparing the way for Alexander. But the philosophical Xenophon was free from the stigma that could be attached to the outrages perpetrated by the Macedonian monarch. Xenophon had also led a retreat, not a dubiously provoked attack. Xenophon was an Alexander without blemishes. It was a role he would be made to play time and time again in years to come as writers and adventurers grappled in reality and in imagination with the conquest of the American wilderness.

Intermezzo

Xenophon and Frémont

The United States emerged from the war against Mexico a profoundly changed country. The change was most obviously physical: the Treaty of Guadalupe Hidalgo, signed in February 1848, confirmed the United States in its possession of Texas (with the Rio Grande set as border) and added a further half-million square miles to its territory (including all of the land that now forms the states of California, Nevada, and Utah, and also most of New Mexico). Thanks also to the 1846 agreement with Great Britain over Oregon, the country now spread from the Atlantic to the Pacific, fulfilling in remarkably quick time the Manifest Destiny that was thought to underlie its claim to the breadth of the American continent.

The physical changes to the United States brought deep political disquiet in their wake. The dispute over the extension of slavery led to bitter guerilla fighting in Kansas, and the old Whig party split over the issue. The Republican Party was formed in 1854 specifically to prevent the extension of slavery to the new territories acquired in the recent expansion of the United States: unlike today, it was a party that had its strongest support in the North, while the pro-slavery Democrats were dominant in the southern states.

The war against Mexico also marked a change of spirit, with a strong renewal of militarism and patriotism: even the anti-war Whigs put up the hero of the war, General Zachary Taylor, as their presidential candidate in 1848. The soldiers in Mexico were widely thought to have revived the spirit of the Revolution and the 1812 war against Britain. Examples from classical antiquity were still cited to exalt the American achievements, but these achievements were now more likely to be military than political. Inspired by the romantic philhellenism of the 1820s, orators and writers were also much more keen to turn to the Greeks rather than the Romans for precedents. And celebration of military feats spread more quickly through the land thanks to the growth of the popular press, with newspapers often carrying letters directly sent by soldiers at the front. At the same time, the growth of the American railway network was crucial in helping the swift transfer of information. People in remoter areas would often read in their local newspapers the exploits of the troops celebrated in the same articles that had earlier appeared in the urban centres. It was in Missouri that Colonel Doniphan was most fervently celebrated as an American Xenophon, but the comparison was also disseminated in panegyric spreading

159

out from New York, bolstered by the authority of William Cullen Bryant's *Evening Post*.

The appeal of Xenophon came from a range of deep and complementary impulses. The expanse of the American West could be read in terms of the Asiatic wastes. Soft Mexicans and hard Indians were viewed in terms similar to the Persians and the mountain tribes of antiquity. American manhood was defined in terms of supposedly Greek ideals, and American freedom, if not seen as exceptional and unprecedented, veered between Rome and Greece. The Americans were able to imagine themselves as something old and something new. They had joined the race for imperial glory.

The political turmoil caused by America's conquests led to shifts in Xenophon's use. Memory of the earlier Missouri anabasis to Mexico may have resurfaced in the winter of 1855 when a Boston paper ridiculed a brief invasion of Kansas by some pro-slavery 'border ruffians' from Missouri as an 'anabasis' that it would 'certainly not need the pen of a Xenophon to describe'. Xenophon was now moving further away from a purely military role in defining America's place in the world. And as the political parties prepared uncertainly for the 1856 election, with the future of Kansas still remaining to the fore, he even entered the American political arena at the highest level. Once more Greek conceptions of space were used to bolster the American sense of mission, but now the march of American destiny was quickening its step towards civil war.[1]

*

'Cambridge was alive last night', the *Boston Daily Atlas* proclaimed one morning in July 1856 – as if that were a rare event. The event that had brought the Massachusetts town to life was a political meeting that had been called to ratify the nomination of John Charles Frémont as the first Presidential candidate for the Republican Party. Since the early 1840s, Frémont had cultivated a heroic persona as leader of several expeditions mapping and exploring routes into the American West: he was now one of the most famous men in the land, popularly pictured hunting grizzly bears or raising the Stars and Stripes on the highest peaks of the Rockies, and hailed as the conqueror of California thanks to his role in the war against Mexico. Illegitimate son of a French immigrant, his French-sounding name gave rise to abuse, particularly from supporters of the strongly anti-Catholic and anti-immigrant third party, the 'Know-Nothings'. Though he had little political experience, Frémont had been chosen by the Republicans as a candidate whose strong opposition to slavery could unite the new party. And so that July night the streets of Cambridge were packed with 'the friends of Free Speech, Free Kansas and Fremont' (his supporters often dropped the accent).[2]

Presiding in the packed Lyceum Hall was a distinguished scholar,

21. John Charles Frémont; 22. A ribbon from the 1856 campaign.

Cornelius Conway Felton, Professor of Greek (and later President) at Harvard. Later that year, as he looked back on his involvement in the election, Felton told an old friend that he would 'laugh doubtless at the thought of my speaking unto the people on political subjects' – 'but I have done so'. The political role was indeed something of a departure from Felton's usual run of lectures on Greece, ancient and modern, but he carried it out in assured fashion, to judge from the report in the *Daily Atlas*. As he rose to give the key address of the evening, he noted how fitting it was that the meeting was being held under the shadow of old Harvard, 'the nursing mother of patriots – near the Old Elm, where Washington drew his sword to lead the hosts of freedom'. The ghosts of revolutionary Cambridge were being stirred up in support of Frémont, the new defender of American freedom. Felton went on to lament the recent troubles in the country at large, reading from an English newspaper's condemnation of the 'Brooks outrage' (the violent beating in the Senate chamber of the anti-slavery Massachusetts senator, Charles Sumner). Felton then turned to the Republican candidate himself. He praised Frémont as 'one of the *few* noble, scientific men of the country' –

161

'and now, just for the fun of the thing, let us have a scientific man for President'.[3]

During his speech Professor Felton also took the opportunity to make a few classical allusions. The *Daily Atlas* only reported one of these, 'in regard to the Anabasis'. But the paper did add that it had been greeted with 'laughter and applause': Frémont, Felton had said, 'had wrote an Anabasis – California!'

What did Cornelius Felton mean by this quip? Why did he joke of Frémont writing an Anabasis? To understand Felton's humour we need first to look at Frémont's exploits in California in some more detail. His adventures in the West had their origins in a romantic entanglement. Fifteen years earlier he had married the daughter of one of the leading advocates of western expansion, Thomas Hart Benton, the Missouri senator who welcomed Doniphan's hardy army of volunteers back to St Louis. Frémont had already gained experience as a surveyor in his native state, Georgia, and the surrounding mountains, and also in the plains between the upper Mississippi and the Missouri. It was Benton's support that saw Frémont put in charge of expeditions of his own further west.

Frémont led first a four-month expedition exploring routes between the Missouri river and the Rocky Mountains, and then a round journey through Oregon and California that took more than a year. The Rocky Mountains were again the aim of his third expedition in 1845, but as war with Mexico loomed his remit was secretly broadened. With sixty men Frémont arrived in California early in 1846 and at once aroused the suspicions of the Mexican government. Told to leave California, Frémont responded by picking a defensive position in the mountains and raising the American flag, while rejecting help from the American settlers in California. He did soon withdraw to Oregon, and it was there that a secret message from President Polk reached him in May 1846, just as the Mexican War was starting. Frémont at once returned to California and fomented the Bear Flag Revolt of the American settlers. With the arrival off Monterey of a US fleet led by Commodore Robert Stockton, Frémont abandoned the cause of the independent republic and was appointed commander of the US troops occupying California.

Frémont's California expedition had a bitter end when he was caught in a power struggle between Stockton and the leader of the Army of the West, Stephen Kearny. Kearny, who had led Doniphan's Missouri force as far as Santa Fé, arrived in California late in 1846. Even though Kearny was his army superior, Frémont backed Stockton. He was then forced to return to Washington and found guilty in a court-martial. Although he was at once reinstated in the army by President Polk, he resigned in anger.

In making a classical joke out of Frémont's involvement in California, then, Cornelius Felton was giving a positive spin to the most disputed of Frémont's earlier actions and brushing aside any hint of controversy. Indeed, already at the time of the American capture of California the name of Xenophon was invoked to defend Frémont's controversial behaviour. In November 1846, Thomas Hart Benton enclosed Frémont's report on his actions in a letter to the President. He added his own authority to Frémont's self-justification:

> To my mind, this entrenching on the mountain, and raising the national flag, was entirely justifiable under the circumstances of the case; and the noble resolution which they took (refusing the aid of their countrymen) to die if attacked under the flag of their country, four thousand miles distant from their homes, was an act of the highest heroism, worthy to be recorded by Xenophon and reflecting equal honor upon the brave young officer who commanded and the heroic sixty-two by whom he was supported.

Although Benton was summoning up the memory of the writer rather than the warrior Xenophon, it is the stirring exploits and distant setting of the *Anabasis* that explain his choice of Xenophon rather than, say, Thucydides: in particular, Benton's lavish attention to the 'brief, heroic note, written in pencil' in which Frémont responded to the warning from the Mexican governor evokes the resolution of Xenophon's Greeks cut off in Mesopotamia.[4]

Benton's bold appeal to Xenophon invited opposition at a time when Frémont's actions in California were disputed and his motives nebulous. The following summer, when there was a petition to make Frémont Governor of California, an American in San Francisco wrote to *The Californian* under the pen-name 'Justice' saying that he 'look[ed] in vain for one brave act of his while in this country'. He claimed that the leaders of the Bear Flag Revolt made all the plans themselves and that Frémont had hesitated when asked to help. Frémont had 'done all in his power ... to cause the hatred of the Californians and the disgust of his fellow countrymen': 'does it require "the pen of a Xenophon" to record such deeds?' 'Justice' was here either slightly misquoting Benton or alluding to another defence of Frémont. Whatever the case, his charge shows the danger inherent in the appeal to antiquity. Xenophon could as readily be turned against Frémont as used to support him.[5]

A decade later, with Frémont now running for President, Cornelius Felton must have been sure of a favourable reception at the ratification meeting in Cambridge when he joked of a California Anabasis. He was picking up on what lay at the heart of Frémont's appeal as a Presidential candidate: his life of adventure. At the Republican convention earlier in the year, his supporters had self-consciously enacted life in the wilds of the West, sealing his nomination with 'three times three perfect Davy Crockett war-whoops, with a touch of the buffalo bull and wild cat'. They also lavished praise on his complexion, 'sun-burnt and frost-blistered in his adventurous journeyings', while claiming that his opponents' attacks passed 'as harmlessly by him as did the arrows of the Indians in the gorge of the mountains'. Frémont was the man to overcome all difficulties in his

163

path: 'no mountain was so high that he did not scale it, no snow so deep that he did not wade through it, and no savage so fierce that he did not either soothe or subdue him.' He was hailed in verse as 'a braver Ulysses', and even rumours of cannibalism during his ill-fated winter crossing of the Rockies in 1848-9 were turned to good account: 'Swear,' a poet made him address his weary followers, 'that no more ye will pollute earth's sod / With anthropophagy; and so help you God.'[6]

It was above all Frémont's contribution to America's imperial destiny that was celebrated. He was '"the conqueror of California"; the founder of our Pacific empire; the hero of Science'. It was 'his indomitable bravery and heroism' that 'gave to his country a FREE empire upon the shores of the Pacific', and he was often hailed specifically as 'the pathfinder of empire': 'To his hands was committed the magnificent task of opening the golden gates of our Pacific empire.' Parallels were drawn between Frémont and Columbus, discoverer of America, and Washington, the leader of the Revolution: it was as if the path Frémont was said to have found through the Rockies was on a level with Columbus' sighting of the New World, as if Frémont's political stance on slavery would bring in a new dawn of freedom equivalent to the birth of the Republic in 1776. As he addressed his rapt audience of Cambridge supporters that July night in 1856, Cornelius Felton was suggesting that Frémont was also a new Xenophon.[7]

To call Frémont a new Xenophon was to draw on the general cultural cachet of Xenophon in mid-nineteenth-century America. Felton himself, as we saw in Chapter 3, had promoted Xenophon's claims in the popular *Greek Reader* he edited for schools. Introducing a selection from Xenophon's writings, he praised the 'illustrious writer' for his military exploits: surmounting 'innumerable' difficulties 'from the hostility of the natives, the want of provisions, and the occasional severity of the weather', Xenophon had led a retreat that 'has justly been considered one of the most memorable recorded in the annals of war', and then written the *Anabasis*, 'one of the finest specimens of military history'. Frémont, Felton was implying, had conquered similar difficulties in his famed trips seeking routes across the Rocky Mountains, when his group had several times been attacked by Indians and on occasions trapped by snow and near starvation.[8]

Felton's audience in July 1856 would have caught a more specific allusion to the surprising role that Xenophon's use in the schoolroom was playing in the Presidential campaign. Six years earlier, Dr John Robertson, a schoolteacher in Charleston, had published an interstitial translation of the first two books of the *Anabasis*. In the preface Robertson recalled (without naming him) his 'once beloved and favorite pupil'. He had assumed at first that the boy was meant for the Church – but when he 'contemplated his bold, fearless disposition, his powerful inventive genius, his admiration of warlike exploits, and his love of heroic and adventurous deeds', Robertson 'did not think it likely he would be a minister of the

164

Gospel'. Robertson went on to spell out the boy's subsequent career – 'one of heroic adventure, of hair-breadth escapes by flood and field, and of scientific explorations, which have made him world-wide renowned'. That boy, as his readers were left to work out, was John Charles Frémont.[9]

Robertson's account of the schoolboy Frémont was cited extensively during the Presidential campaign both in biographies of Frémont himself and in countless newspaper articles. Imparting as it did an aura of heroism to Frémont, it brought out into the open the (generally suppressed) ideological underpinnings of the educational role of classical literature: 'When the Greek class read the account that Herodotus gives of the battle of Marathon, the bravery of Miltiades and his ten thousand Greeks raised his patriotic feelings to enthusiasm.' What made the account particularly relevant, however, was that it contained a startling prediction. That boy, Robertson noted, was 'now a senator' – and he 'may yet rise to be at the head of this great and growing Republic'. Similar predictions, Frémont's supporters were quick to note, had been made about the young Washington – who was also the same age as Frémont then was when he became President.[10]

If Frémont's one-time teacher was exposing the nationalistic justification for the role of Classics in the modern classroom, he also laid bare some of the contradictions in this role. Robertson closed his account of his gifted pupil with a sentence that some of Frémont's backers decided to omit – a prayer 'that he may ever be opposed to war, injustice, and oppression of every kind, a blessing to his country and an example of every noble virtue to the whole world'. It was better to exalt Frémont as a patriotic adventurer stirred by the Athenian prowess displayed at Marathon.

As well as evoking the surprising prominence of Dr Robertson's school edition, Cornelius Felton's *Anabasis* joke was following the widespread habit of glorifying the conquest of the West by alluding to Xenophon as a parallel. Frémont's explorations, Felton's words implied, had been doing the same work as the expedition of that other modern Xenophon, Alexander Doniphan, when he led an army of Missouri volunteers across the prairie to Santa Fé and on to El Paso and Chihuahua. The comparison was perhaps hard to avoid at a time when, by a neat inversion, Xenophon himself was often read as a sort of Greek version of Frémont. Xenophon was described as the leader of 'a vast exploring expedition which penetrated to the very heart of Persia'. And the Ten Thousand, though their march in the pay of a pretender to the Persian throne was seemingly far removed from the highway of Greek history, were seen as pathfinders for Alexander's conquests seventy years later. This imperial reading of Xenophon in classical scholarship was complemented by the imperial appropriation of Xenophon in public discourse.[11]

But why describe California as a *written* Anabasis? Modern postcolonial scholars often conceive of writing about foreign lands or peoples as ancillary to the act of conquest; by collapsing together the act of writing with the territory conquered, Felton seems instead to conceive of conquest as a mode of writing. Felton's trope of imagining space as a book is found in other nineteenth-century descriptions of the American continent. Frederick Jackson Turner wrote that the United States 'lies like a huge page in the history of society': 'Line by line as we read this continental page from West to East we find the record of social evolution.' The conceit was applied to Frémont himself by his great promoter, Thomas Hart Benton, in his 1856 memoirs: 'All that vast region, more than seven hundred miles square – equal to a great kingdom in Europe – was an unknown land – a sealed book, which he longed to open, and to read.' And Frémont's gloomy topographer Charles Preuss, moaning about his preference for 'eternal prairie and grass', wrote that it was 'as if someone would prefer a book with blank pages to a good story'. This use of language hints at writing itself as an activity, a gesture of dominance: writing was often used to figure the superiority of the white Anglo-Saxon to the unlettered Indian, whose presence is suppressed in the image of the prairie as a blank page. Cornelius Felton's *Anabasis* joke also makes the American continent a blank page – on which Frémont has now written a good story.[12]

Cornelius Felton had a further reason to speak of Frémont writing an *Anabasis*. It was precisely through Frémont's published accounts of his expeditions that he had achieved his great fame. These reports were a family affair, written up from Frémont's notes by his wife Jessie and then, thanks to the influence of his father-in-law Thomas Hart Benton, published and circulated by the Senate. It was the account of the first exploration Frémont led that introduced the figure of the guide Kit Carson to an eager public, and the *Report of the Exploring Expedition to Oregon and California* published in 1845 played in turn a major role in stimulating emigration to the West. The romance of the Frémont product is best caught by his account of his first sight of the Great Salt Lake: 'as we looked eagerly over the lake in the first emotions of excited pleasure, I am doubtful if the followers of Balboa felt more enthusiasm when, from the heights of the Andes, they saw for the first time the great Western Ocean. … to travellers so long shut up among mountain ranges a sudden view over the expanse of silent waters had in it something sublime.' At moments such as these it was easy for Frémont's readers to forget that most of the trails he was surveying were long familiar to trackers, not to mention the native Americans. Frémont certainly displayed physical courage and endurance, but it was above all a helpful political alliance and the power of the written word in the age of print that made a Xenophon of him.[13]

Frémont's writings became particularly important after the discovery of gold in California. A new edition of his account of Oregon and California began with a self-advertisement (dated January 1849) that explicitly addressed the reader 'commencing his pilgrimage' to the 'golden bosom' of 'this rich and rare land', promising a fund of information about routes and an account of the land's 'transcendent loveliness'. Frémont's readers were tempted by the promise of an account of an 'El Dorado' where 'the "set time" for the Golden age, the advent of which has been looked for and longed for during many centuries of iron wrongs and hardships, has fully come'. His writings played a key role in the construction of the American desert as an oriental space crossed by long trails heading for the promised land beyond the mountains (see Chapter 4).[14]

Cornelius Felton was not the first to align Frémont the writer with the author of the *Anabasis*. Already a reviewer in 1846, distancing Frémont from 'fashionable tourists', exclaimed that it was 'delightful to see a gentleman uniting, like Xenophon, the scholar to the soldier'. Though writing for a Catholic periodical, this reviewer was appealing to the same sort of feeling as Felton when he called California a written *Anabasis* rather than a military conquest and said that it would be fun to have 'a scientific man' for President. Felton's speech was successful because he found a way of appeasing the instincts of his Cambridge audience – listeners who were likely to have been hostile to the war with Mexico and to be afraid of the effects of western expansion. Felton's invocation of the *Anabasis* was a neat way of avoiding the paradox that it was precisely the conquests of Frémont and others that had opened up the issue of slavery in the conquered territories. He succeeded in evoking the way in which the great military heroes of the Mexican War (Scott, Doniphan) had been praised and in drawing on all the romantic and heroic associations of Hellenism. But he displaced the potentially negative connotations of military conquest by a literary turn, enacting or at least mimicking by his own pleasantry Frémont's own adroitness in constructing himself as a man of science while making a sublime spectacle of the workings of imperial power.[15]

*

John Charles Frémont's nomination, the Boston *Daily Atlas* reported, was duly ratified by the 'ancient and famous seat of learning' across the Charles river. Felton's strong stance was praised: 'it was gratifying ... to see one whose duty it was to study conservatism ... take such a stand.' And the meeting broke up as 2,000 supporters arrived from Boston with beautiful transparencies illustrating scenes in the life of Frémont.

The election took place later in the year. Frémont carried most of the states in the North, but he lost overall to the Democrat James Buchanan. Cornelius Felton consoled himself for Frémont's defeat at the time with the thought that 'we shall elect him next time'. Four years later, a different Republican candidate was elected, and a new and bloody page in the story of the American anabasis was about to be written.[16]

THE WAR BETWEEN THE STATES

23. William Tecumseh Sherman.

Advance and Retreat: Sherman in Georgia

How did the century envisage its own movement, its trajectory? As a re-ascent towards the source, an arduous construction of novelty, an exiled experience of beginning. These meanings, together with a few others, are conjoined in a Greek work: 'anabasis' ...

Alain Badiou, *The Century* (2005)

Gladly would I talk of Greece and Rome (but I fear they are gone by) ...
William Tecumseh Sherman (speech in St Louis, July 1865)[1]

* * *

May 1865. It was an 'extremely beautiful' morning in Washington, DC, and 'the streets were filled with people to see the pageant, armed with bouquets of flowers for their favorite regiments or heroes'. After four years of civil war, with more than half a million dead, people had flocked to the nation's capital to watch the two armies that had preserved the Union. The Army of the Potomac, which had fought a long campaign in nearby Virginia, had paraded through the streets the previous day. Now the crowds were to see an army with which they were not familiar. Over the course of the previous year Sherman's army of westerners – the Armies of the Tennessee, the Ohio, and the Cumberland – had fought its way from Chattanooga to Atlanta, and then from Atlanta to Savannah, cutting a path through Georgia in what had already come to be known as Sherman's March to the Sea. Their final push north through the Carolinas had hastened the end of the war, forcing the Confederate army in Virginia to surrender before it was trapped.

Sherman's march had already established itself as the most controversial of the war. The damage inflicted on private property in Georgia and the Carolinas was deeply resented in the South. But it was not just the material harm Sherman had inflicted that gave rise to disquiet. In the course of the long march there had also been great uncertainty over the strategy that was being pursued. As Sherman advanced towards Atlanta, apparently dependent on a fragile railroad for his supplies, was he being drawn into a trap by his wily adversary, Joe Johnston? And when he later burnt and abandoned Atlanta and cut loose through Georgia with sixty thousand men, was he in retreat? As his moves were eagerly traced in both the North and the South, both sides turned to Xenophon to interpret his moves. His march was called an 'anabasis', but the exemplary status of

24. 'The sight was simply magnificent': the Grand Review.

'anabasis' was now in tatters: in the South the term was used to denigrate Sherman, in the North to praise him. During the war against Mexico, Xenophon had been used to glorify the foreign conquests of the armies of the United States. In the fractured world of the American Civil War the meanings of the great classical paradigms had changed.

But now Sherman's army was gathering for its last march. The previous evening, after the Army of the Potomac's disciplined march through the streets of Washington, Sherman had called on his commanders to tell the troops to 'brush up'. Now at nine o'clock the general and his staff began to ride slowly down Pennsylvania Avenue, with the Fifteenth Corps following closely behind. As he reached the Treasury Building, Sherman looked back. He described what he saw towards the close of his *Memoirs*, which provoked controversy when first published in 1875 but are now widely celebrated as a classic of military autobiography: 'The sight was simply magnificent. The column was compact, and the glittering muskets looked like a solid mass of steel, moving with the regularity of a pendulum.' Sherman then rode on between the packed stands erected on both sides of the street, saluting the President with his sword as he passed the platform set up in the grounds of the White House. Turning into the presidential grounds, he approached on foot and shook hands with Johnson, Grant, and other members of the cabinet. And there he stood for the next six and a half hours, watching 'the most magnificent army in existence' pass by, 'sixty-five thousand men, in splendid *physique*, who had just completed a march of nearly two thousand miles in a hostile country'; 'an army in the proper sense, well organized, well commanded and disciplined' – 'and there was no wonder that it had swept through the South like a tornado'.[2]

Sherman's description of the review conveys his pride in the efficiency he had instilled in the army – 'a mobile machine', as he described it in his *Memoirs*, 'willing and able to start at a moment's notice and to subsist on the scantiest of food'. Sherman's pride reflected his dedication to efficiency and his liking for organizations where efficiency could be imposed without the bickering and jealousy of the political world: he had written to his brother four months earlier, straight after his capture of Savannah, that he 'would rather be an engineer of a railroad, than President of the United States'.[3]

Sherman's admiration for the western troops was shared by the crowds that lined the streets. 'Bronzed and scarred veterans' with 'battle-rent flags', they seemed 'ragged' and 'dirty' by comparison with the army that had marched the day before. But they made up for it in toughness, in the length of their stride, in their attractive informality. As they 'chatted, laughed and cheered, just as they pleased', they seemed 'not half so stiff'. Some corps even had freed slaves walking behind them as well as wagons filled with chickens and other food. It was a triumphant restaging of their life on the march through Georgia – a fitting climax to the grand review designed as a proud affirmation of the struggle for the preservation of the United States. As it marked the separate identities of the armies of the East and the West that had together fought for the Union, the grand review staged many central tensions in American ideology: tensions over race, over local and national identities, over the balance between discipline and freedom in the civic and military realms. But the review was also a way of integrating the two armies and subjecting them to a newly strengthened ideology of centralized nationhood. The armies in the Mexican War had been welcomed home in state ceremonies, not made to march in a splendid national spectacle.[4]

The triumphal parade through the streets of Washington, past the Capitol, past rows of Senators, necessarily drew on the long-standing identification of the American Republic with Rome. But what was now performed was a Roman identity forged by force of arms rather than by political aspirations. And yet this military identity did have a dark political underside. The generous peace terms Sherman had offered his opposing general in North Carolina led to a fierce dispute in a country still deeply unsettled by the assassination of Lincoln. Some feared that Sherman was aiming to exploit his popularity to further his own power – but his defenders would later insist that he was no Caesar. At the same time, debates over national identity and historical destiny were staged through the conflicting use of Greek models too. Greece and Rome were both gone by, as Sherman wryly pointed out on his return to St Louis, his army's headquarters. But it was still worth making a point of his own failure to make a classical allusion in an after-dinner speech. And during the civil war itself and in the difficult years of reconstruction and reconciliation to come there were still many who were glad to interpret their present in terms of Xenophon's past.[5]

*

Got late rebel papers they call on the people and soldiers to rally and crush out Sherman. A second Anabasis. Crossed the little Ogeechee River and camped at Station 4 ½ …

A.M. Geer, diary, 5 December 1864[6]

As he left Atlanta Sherman looked back on a sight very different from the gleaming rows of troops he saw marching along Pennsylvania Avenue six months later. It was early on the morning of 15 November 1864 that the Union army moved out of the city. Sherman himself stayed another day to supervise the destruction of the public buildings. The next morning, as he reached the first hill outside the city, he 'paused to look back upon the scenes of our past battles': 'Behind us lay Atlanta, smouldering and in ruins, the black smoke rising high in the air, and hanging like a pall over the ruined city.' In the distance could be seen 'gun-barrels glistening in the sun'; closer at hand, the Fourteenth Corps marching 'with a cheery look and swinging pace', catching up the strain of 'John Brown's soul goes marching on' from a passing band. And then 'we turned our horses' heads to the east; Atlanta was soon lost behind the screen of trees, and became a thing of the past. Around it clings many a thought of desperate battle, of hope and fear, that now seem like the memory of a dream; and I have never seen the place since.' Here Sherman added to the *Memoirs* he wrote ten years later a rare touch of lyricism. He hints at some nostalgia for the great expedition that won him world-wide fame.[7]

Few in the army and few outside it knew what was in store as Sherman left Atlanta. Following his progress from afar, a staff officer on the Union side wrote early in December that 'Sherman has disappeared in Georgia' – 'and nobody knows what awful strategy he contemplates'. Another officer involved in the campaign itself thought at the outset there was 'something romantic' in its conception: 'I am really charmed with it. Nothing in military history compares with it except the invasion of Mexico by Cortez' – for Cortez had burned his ships and told his army that 'they must conquer or die', and 'so with Sherman'.[8]

How was the march seen in the South? In Augusta, 150 miles from Atlanta, the daily *Constitutionalist* made its view clear three days after Sherman's departure: 'SHERMAN ON HIS RETREAT THROUGH GEORGIA! His Hour has Come if Georgia Acts Promptly and Bravely! THE MODERN ANABASIS!' The line taken by the paper was that Sherman, finding his way to the north blocked, was making a bold retreat to the rear: 'it is the Anabasis of Sherman. It is plain his only object can be the making

25. 'A second Anabasis': Sherman's troops on the march.

of a certain and secure base. He must move fast and obtain his object speedily, or he is lost. ... He is retreating – simply retreating.' The paper went on to make even more explicit what was meant by the appeal to the memory of Xenophon: 'This movement is the modern Anabasis, and like the Greek of old, he has only one object at heart, and that is, to reach the sea; and as Xenophon's weary and long suffering ten thousand sent up shout after shout, "Thalatta! Thalatta!", so Sherman will gladly cry, The sea! The sea!' The heroic and imperialistic vision of the *Anabasis* exploited by American writers during the war against Mexico has been displaced. In the earlier war, it had sometimes been noted that the *Anabasis* described a retreat, not an advance, but writers had still clung to a view of the retreat as a triumphant demonstration of Greek superiority. Now, the *Augusta Constitutionalist* was building up instead an image of Xenophon's troops as an exhausted body of soldiers engaged in a desperate retreat through Asia. It was trying to encourage the people of Georgia to do far more to stop Sherman than the Persians had done to stop Xenophon.[9]

The *Augusta Constitutionalist* may have been among the rebel papers that fell into the hands of Allen Morgan Geer, a soldier in the 20th Illinois Regiment, three weeks after the departure from Atlanta. By then Sherman's army was nearing the coast. Before noting what was presumably the main event of the day – the crossing of the little Ogeechee River – Geer picked out for his journal just one phrase from all the rebel papers he had seen: 'A second Anabasis.' It is not quite certain that Geer saw the *Constitutionalist* itself, for by this time the article had probably been

175

printed elsewhere and its terms adopted by other southern papers. Whichever papers Geer saw, his jotting seems to express a certain puzzlement: 'A second Anabasis'? Why are they calling our march that? Equally it could be a sign of scorn, even of pride: little do you know what an Anabasis is … . Confronted by Geer's laconic diary, we can only speculate about the precise tenor of his response to the term that he found was being used to brand the Georgia campaign.

We can get a clearer idea of how the southern coverage of Sherman's march was read in the North. The rebel newspapers Geer encountered in Georgia were also being scanned in the North for clues to Sherman's progress – and ridiculed for their dismissal of Sherman. One northern paper alluded explicitly to the *Augusta Constitutionalist* early in December: 'his march is compared to the famous retreat of Xenophon's ten thousand; it is "the modern Anabasis".' It then undercut the comparison by speculating that the editor had now 'perhaps packed up his traps and got out of the way of the "retreat"'. This was partly bluster at a time when many in the North were still uncertain about Sherman's prospects. But the lack of opposition in Georgia was becoming clear both in the North and abroad. A fortnight later, the article in the *Constitutionalist* was picked up in Britain in the *Daily News*, and this paper too felt confident enough to contradict the reading of the march as an 'anabasis': 'How Sherman must chuckle over these scoldings if he reads them.'[10]

Xenophon was used in other British papers to articulate the uncertainty that continued to be felt about Sherman's aims. Taken aback by Sherman's boldness, journalists had recourse to stark alternatives. Particularly striking were the polarities proposed by the *London Herald*:

> General Sherman's movement will result in either the most tremendous disaster that ever befell an armed host, or it will be written upon the page of history as the very consummation of the success of sublime audacity. The name of the captor of Atlanta, if he fails now, will become the scoff of mankind, and the humiliation of the United States for all time. If he succeeds, it will be written upon the tablet of fame side by side with that of Napoleon and Hannibal. He will either be a Xerxes or a Xenophon.

The alliterative coupling of Xerxes and Xenophon was much quoted in other newspapers both in Britain and in the United States, and it was remembered for decades to come: it was cited, for instance, in an address delivered to veterans by one of Sherman's sons in 1908. Like other journalists at the time, the writer was resorting to a brilliant epigram to mask his bewilderment. His words were memorable, however, not just for this delightful antithesis: more pointed was the historical vision underlying the choice of examples.[11]

The choice of Napoleon and Hannibal as parallels should Sherman be successful was surprising. The *Herald* was pointedly choosing two foreign generals who were renowned for strategic genius; it was picking up, too, the long-standing equation between Napoleon and Hannibal that had been fostered by Napoleon himself. Yet both the French emperor and the Carthaginian general had ultimately been unsuccessful. Indeed, the example of Napoleon was precisely what the Confederates were hoping Sherman would follow: in a speech in September 1864, the Confederate President Jefferson Davis predicted that Sherman could not keep up his long line of communication: 'retreat, sooner or later, he must' – 'and when that day comes, the fate that befell the army of the French Empire in its retreat from Moscow will be reacted'.[12]

The opposition of Xerxes and Xenophon gave the precedents chosen by the *Herald* a marked racial component: if Sherman failed, he was a Persian; if he won, a Greek. The sleek military contrast between the failure of Xerxes' invasion of Greece and Xenophon's successful retreat from Persia drew on a deep-seated ideological opposition between Persian despotism and Greek freedom.

No such uncertainty appeared in the pages of the leading British newspaper of the day, the London *Times*. The paper, a strong supporter of the cotton-producing South, displayed a consistent hostility to Sherman. Early in the Atlanta campaign, it spoke of Sherman's advance as 'mysterious', opining that he would have 'no option but to retreat by the same line as he advanced'. When Sherman was in control of Atlanta, it still thought that he was suffering a reversal: 'From the besieger he had become the besieged.' Here the *Times* was exploiting the rhetorical stock of ancient historians: the same phrase had been applied by Thucydides to the Athenian invasion of Sicily and copied by Roman imitators. Finally, as Sherman marched through Georgia 'to extricate his army from an untenable position', the paper adopted a more explicit comparison with antiquity:

> The 'ten thousand' Greeks were led by XENOPHON from the plains of the Euphrates to the shore of the Black Sea, but the enterprise was undertaken by the wreck of an army. The retreat itself is celebrated in history, but it told the world that the invasion of Persia was a ruinous failure. It is possible that SHERMAN may save as much of his army as he can march to the shore of the Atlantic; but not the less will the invasion of Georgia have been signally defeated.

The London *Times* was at one with the Georgia newspapers in its use of the *Anabasis* to convey its depreciation of 'the wild and desperate effort of an outmanoeuvred General'. And it was made to remember its mistake: the Xenophon editorial was quoted with suitably sarcastic comment at the end of the war in gloating Union publications with titles such as *Rebel Brag and British Bluster* and *The Glory and Shame of England*.[13]

Xenophon could be used to take away the shine of Sherman's achievement even after his arrival at the coast. An Irish newspaper wrote on 26 December that Sherman had 'at last reached the neighbourhood of the sea after a march only less arduous than that of which Xenophon was the leader and the historian'. As in the *Times* editorial, the tone here was negative: the Xenophon analogy is applied to Sherman's whole march in order to stress its arduousness. The paper went on to argue that there was little chance of his capturing Savannah. It had no way of knowing that the Confederate force had withdrawn from the city several days earlier. But it took at least a conscious effort to tarnish Xenophon by treating his retreat as nothing more than a dull slog.[14]

There was a trend, then, for newspapers in both the southern states and Great Britain to denigrate Sherman's march by likening it to the retreat of the Ten Thousand. This negative reading of the Greek retreat contrasts with the praise generally bestowed on it. It was an attempt to fashion through discourse a world where the fortunes of war were reversed – as if by overthrowing the powerful position held by Xenophon's glorious retreat in public discourse they could eliminate the threat posed by the physical unleashing of Sherman's army on the Georgia countryside.

Xenophon's stake in the controversy over Sherman's march increased when the news of the fall of Savannah reached the North. Two days after Sherman offered Lincoln the city as a 'Christmas-gift', a positive image of Xenophon was promoted in an editorial in the *Chicago Tribune*. Previously critical of Sherman's generalship, the paper now compared Sherman's march with 'the Anabasis and the best efforts of Marlborough, Napoleon, and Wellington'. The fact that the paper chose to speak of 'the Anabasis' rather than adding Xenophon to the list of modern generals suggests that it was responding to the negative southern use of the term. It made the Greek anabasis a glorious march again rather than a term of abuse.[15]

'Anabasis' was used in a similar way to put the anti-Sherman rantings of the British press in their place. As the year closed with news of Sherman's arrival at the sea, the weekly *Spectator* railed against the *Times*' misrepresentations in an editorial that was much reprinted on both sides of the Atlantic: 'General Sherman's great anabasis, which the *Times* has at last ceased to call a retreat, ended in his gaining the sea coast of Georgia. ... Thus the "escape" of General Sherman from Atlanta will probably, as the *Times* remarked, be "the turning-point" of the war. But this "turning-point" will consist in providing the North with a double instead of a single military lever for cracking that hard nut the Richmond army of General Lee.' By speaking of Sherman's 'great anabasis', the journal was implicitly distancing itself from the *Times*' hostile use of the Xenophon paradigm. At the same time, 'anabasis' has here undergone a further extension of meaning. The term was often used of expeditions upcountry like that of Cyrus, marches away from the sea. Alternatively, the fame of the Ten Thousand meant that 'anabasis' could also be applied to retreats towards the sea. Yet the *Spectator* uses 'anabasis' for a march towards the sea that is expressly contrasted with a 'retreat'. The editorial was right about Sherman's achievement – but premature in other ways:

even after Sherman's capture of Savannah was known, the partisan *Times* did continue to call his march a 'retreat'.[16]

Xenophon was used to add the lustre of classical antiquity to Sherman's march in other contexts at this time and in years to come – but above all in the columns of newspapers and in orations that were subsequently published as pamphlets or in journals. The negative image of Xenophon's march as a retreat did persist, but it was now a foil to a positive assessment of Sherman's strategy. In January 1865, a new army journal, the *United States Service Magazine*, celebrating Sherman's march as 'the boldest movement of its kind known in history', rejected comparisons with Napoleon's doomed march on Moscow in favour of 'the famous Anabasis'. But it went on to note that 'the Greeks were fleeing homeward': 'Their glad shout, "The sea! the sea!" when they beheld the sunlit waves of the distant Euxine, was a cry of thanksgiving for their safety. Sherman reverses all this; he seeks the sea indeed, but with a triumphant advance; and although his glorious veterans will hail it as eagerly as did the ten thousand, it is because it is the sign not only of perils over, but of new conquests.' The whole section was headed 'THE ANABASIS REVERSED'. As in some of the eulogies for the march of Doniphan's volunteers from Missouri to Mexico, American self-assertion and belief in progress was made manifest in the preference for a 'triumphant advance' over a retreat, however glorious.[17]

The rhetorical tropes used to glorify Doniphan's Mexican adventure were also replayed in claims that Sherman's march excelled Xenophon's. A striking example of this boast appeared in *The Great Rebellion*, a popular musical allegory put on by J.M. Hager. This was a theatrical piece devoted to the Civil War that toured the American cities, starring some of the key states as characters and requiring a cast of several hundred young women gathered afresh in each new location. The play recreated important events in the run-up to the war and in the war itself, culminating in Lincoln's assassination and in a vast final tableau of peace, including a sample of Sherman's foragers (the famous 'bummers'). Sherman himself was celebrated (by 'Massachusetts') as a man who 'knocks apart the rebel arch / By history's longest and most daring march', and this claim was supported by an allusion to two familiar antecedents (with a sanitized memory of the French retreat from Moscow): 'He who can dwarf Napoleon's Russian fame, / And over Xenophon's write Sherman's name!' The steady progression of Hager's extravaganza from city to city offered a slow-motion imitation of the quick-fire dissemination of the Xenophon paradigm in the pages of the press.[18]

To compare Sherman with Xenophon was to raise the question of how Sherman's march would come to be portrayed in writing. Would Sherman's anabasis give rise to an American *Anabasis*? The importance of the shift from deeds to words is suggested by the way the misguided gloating of the *Augusta Constitutionalist* over Sherman's supposed retreat was mockingly twisted by one northern paper three months after the original article had appeared. Readers were now invited to believe that the Augusta daily had asserted that Sherman would have 'the melancholy privilege of still further imitating Xenophon', writing his history 'under the title of the "New Anabasis"'. As it was, it took ten years for Sherman to produce his *Memoirs*, but when he did so his prowess with the pen as well as the sword naturally gave rise to further comparisons with Xenophon: 'It is clear,' an early review claimed, 'that he could have conducted the celebrated march of the ten thousand and described it as well as the first.'[19]

In the months and years after Sherman's arrival at Savannah, then, the earlier southern use of the *Anabasis* to attack Sherman met with scorn in the North. That was only to be expected: the Civil War was a battle of symbols, a contest in memory, as well as a physical struggle between opposing armies; and, as in an actual battle, both sides were united in as much as they were fighting for the same symbolic territory.

Much more striking than Union resistance to Confederate assaults on Sherman's strategy was the fact that a southern writer used the *Anabasis* to attack her own side. After the capture of Savannah, with Sherman about to start on his march north through the Carolinas, Mary Chesnut, wife of a leading Confederate general, pondered in her diary the course of a campaign that was now set to threaten her own personal safety: 'You do Anabasis business when you want to get out of the enemy's country. And the Thermopylae business when they want to get into your country. But we retreated in our country – and we gave up the mountain passes without a blow.' Chesnut was here looking back a few months to Sherman's gradual advance from Chattanooga to Atlanta. Perhaps influenced by the later southern use of the *Anabasis* to describe Sherman's 'retreat' from Atlanta, she was implying that the Confederate army had got its ancient paradigms wrong in its response to Sherman's advance: it had done the Anabasis business instead of the Thermopylae business.[20]

Mary Chesnut's historical vision was shared by John Bell Hood, the dynamic general chosen to replace Joe Johnston when he was sacked for failing to prevent Sherman's advance. In his strongly defensive memoir *Advance and Retreat*, posthumously published in 1880, Hood complained that 'the Confederate commander, with seventy thousand available men, surrendered *the Thermopylae of the South* without risking a general battle'. Hood was here conceiving of the American Thermopylae not as a single pass but as the whole range of mountains in Georgia. He was implying that there were a number of mountain fastnesses where Johnston could have taken his stand – and excusing his own subsequent failure to defend Atlanta, the city down on the plain.[21]

Mary Chesnut would have us believe that she had already used Xenophon to criticize the sluggish Johnston back in May 1864, as Sherman was beginning his advance on Atlanta. Noting that Johnston 'gives up one after another of those mountain passes where one must think he could fight and is hastening down to the plain', she complains that 'every newspaper (except some Georgia ones) in the Confederacy is busy as a bee, excusing Joe Johnston's retreats'. She then looks back to Johnston's earlier record in the campaign around Richmond, Virginia, two years earlier: 'John Witherspoon says [the] president did wrong once when he did not arrest Joe Johnston before Seven Pines. Our Xenophon was then in full retreat *through* Richmond.' Johnston, she was implying, was once again proving himself the Confederate Xenophon by retreating through his own country.[22]

Whether Chesnut did write any of these words at the time is open to question. The diary as we have it has been renowned for its literary polish since its partial posthumous publication as *A Diary from Dixie*. More recently scholars have discovered that the diary was rewritten in the 1870s and again in the 1880s; the original version survives for parts of the Civil War but not for the period of Sherman's march. By calling Johnston 'our Xenophon' already in her entry for May 1864, Chesnut was anticipating her later contrast between 'Anabasis business' and 'Thermopylae business'. And she had even anticipated those terms right at the beginning of the war when she referred to a former schoolfriend, now wife of a plantation-owner, doing the 'patriotic Moscow business' by burning cotton-gins to prevent them falling into Union hands: precisely the sort of self-sacrifice that the South failed to perform in response to Sherman's threat. Shaped as it is by knowledge of what was to come, Chesnut's vivid critique of Johnston may tell us as much about later quarrels in the South over responsibility for the defeat as about contemporary perceptions of the failure to stop Sherman.[23]

*

'Anabasis business', 'Thermopylae business', 'He will either be a Xerxes or a Xenophon' – lurking behind the praise-and-blame game during the march through Georgia and in the years to come is the figure we caught earlier glancing back at the glistening columns of the Army of the West: Sherman himself. Did Sherman ever think of Xenophon? How *did* he come to conceive the campaign that caused so much surprise and uncertainty to contemporary onlookers? As he cut loose from Atlanta, followers of the war around the world felt that Sherman was attempting something unusual and exciting. The preface to the British edition of one of the first accounts of the march described it as the 'most interesting event of the war to Englishmen', and this was not empty self-promotion: Sherman too noted in a letter to his wife 'the importance attached to it in England', and the American historian Henry Adams, who was in London during the Civil War, claimed that 'the name of Sherman has of late placed us who are abroad, in a very commanding position'. Later military historians, notably Sir Basil Liddell Hart, have boosted Sherman's reputation further, claiming that he was a master of 'indirect warfare' and an influence on the *Blitzkrieg* tactics used to such effect by the Germans in the Second World War. Portrayed in these terms, Sherman's march seems to have left the world of Xenophon a long way behind – even if Liddell Hart himself evokes ancient precedent by speaking of Sherman's campaign as 'the "March of the Sixty Thousand"'.[24]

Some of Sherman's own contemporaries were curious whether Sherman thought of his achievements in terms of Xenophon. After the publication of Sherman's *Memoirs*, a former member of the Confederate cabinet wrote in a letter to Jefferson Davis that Sherman had boasted 'in his vainglorious book of his grand campaigns' that his march to the sea was 'superior to that of Xenophon'. But Sherman did not make that claim anywhere: the (deliberate?) mistake smacks of lingering southern resentment. Nonetheless, Sherman, himself well-educated and head of a Louisiana military academy when the war broke out, was certainly aware of the force of the Xenophon parallel. In a letter to his wife, he wrote that the march would be 'more appreciated in Europe than in America': 'I warrant your father will find parallel in the history of the Greeks and Persians, but none on our continent.' The telling phrase here is 'Greeks and Persians'. We would expect to find 'Greeks and Romans': Sherman's phrase hints at Alexander, perhaps, but above all at Xenophon, who (unlike Alexander) had been forced to live off the land in the absence of a supply base. But Sherman was still keen to distance himself from any suggestion that he had actually been influenced by Xenophon. When he was invited to address the cadets at West Point in 1869, he reported that he had 'oftentimes been asked by friends familiar with Xenophon, Hume, and Jomini, in which of these books I had learned the secret of leading armies on long and difficult marches' – 'and they seemed surprised when I answered that I was not aware that I had been influenced by any of them'. Sherman stressed instead the military value of his own earlier experiences in the West, where he had watched long caravans of emigrants traversing the plains.[25]

It would be rash to take Sherman's speech at West Point as a straightforward expression of his views. He was subscribing to what would come to be known as the 'frontier theory': that is, the idea that the cardinal American values of independence and self-reliance had been forged through encounters with the ever receding American wilderness. This thesis fitted the broader message he wanted to impart to the graduating cadets as they prepared themselves for service in military outposts across the land, protecting, perhaps, the engineers building the new continental railroads from Indian incursions.

Sherman was also living up to his image as a resilient American. One newspaper, decrying the tendency to look to classical antiquity for precedents, fancied that it would 'be enough for the brave soldier himself ... dispensing with these ornaments of Greek and Roman fame, to feel that his country hails him as the most dashing, keen-sighted, and successful of

American commanders'. Sherman's Americanness was especially brought out in physical descriptions: he was *'par eminence* the American general' or 'the most American looking man I ever saw'; or again, as he smoked a 'fragrant cigar' in his 'plain linen duster', he was 'simply a plain American gentleman'.[26]

Sherman's self-cultivated image of hardy self-reliance could not dispel questions over the inspiration for the march to the sea. In a volume in Scribner's 1880s *Campaigns of the Civil War* series, one of Sherman's officers complained that people had 'disputed the priority of the idea, as if it were a patent right'. He was thinking of the outcry that followed the publication of Sherman's *Memoirs* in 1875: a journalist and former army officer published a bitter critique of Sherman's alleged falsehoods in which he argued that Grant (overall commander of the Union armies and by then President) rather than Sherman was responsible for planning the march to the sea. Sherman himself thought that the author of this hatchet job had been hired by Grant's personal secretary, and paid for his brother-in-law to publish a rebuttal.[27]

Sherman's own correspondence with Grant makes clear that the idea of the campaign as it was eventually realized developed gradually. The anabasis model, whether taken to imply an advance or a retreat, does not do justice to the complexity of Sherman's thinking. Right from the start of the advance on Atlanta Sherman was aware of the prospect that the army could be forced to live off the land in Georgia. He was also confident that it could do so. If the abandonment of Atlanta can be called a retreat, then Sherman anticipated this retreat from the start. But even at Atlanta he was still weighing up a range of options – and above all keeping his eye on the movements of his adversary Hood. It was only when Hood broke towards Tennessee, expecting Sherman to follow, that he felt secure enough to set off for the coast – 'and make Georgia howl!'[28]

Pervading Sherman's later accounts of the thinking behind his march to the sea is an impatience with the romantic aura that had been attached to the march. Right at the time when he was first in control of Savannah, he expressed to his brother a fear that 'an exaggerated faith will be generated in my ability, that no man can fulfil'. He sought subsequently to dampen the excitement created by the march. In a short account of the campaign for the series *Battles and Leaders of the Civil War*, he wrote that 'the great Napoleon' had formulated the general principles of his strategy: 'the fundamental maxim for successful war is "to converge a superior force on the critical point at the critical time".' And in his *Memoirs* he insisted that the march to the sea had simply been a shift of base and far less significant than the subsequent march through the Carolinas. It was that later march that had threatened to trap the Confederate army in Virginia, and it had been made in much worse weather and through much more difficult terrain.[29]

And yet Sherman's letters and *Memoirs* reveal that this downgrading of the march to the sea is not the whole story. In a letter to General Thomas, commander of the army that finally beat Hood near Nashville, Sherman wrote that he proposed 'to demonstrate the vulnerability of the South and make its inhabitants feel that war and individual Ruin are synonymous terms'. That is, the march through Georgia was meant as a psychological blow. And Sherman was also alert to the psychology of his own troops. One of the reasons he wanted to press on to the coast rather than follow Hood about was to 'keep up the *morale* of the offensive'. Sherman wanted to advance rather than retreat – to show that he could cross the Confederate heartland unopposed. As a psychological demonstration, his march through Georgia does come to resemble Xenophon's retreat through Asia – at least according to the terms in which that retreat has generally been interpreted since antiquity. Xenophon's anabasis was thought to demonstrate the weakness of Persia: Persia fell seventy years later. Sherman's march demonstrated the weakness of the Confederacy: the Confederacy fell four months later.[30]

*

'How did the century envisage its own movement, its trajectory?' When the French philosopher Alain Badiou posed the question, the century he had in mind was the twentieth century – and in particular the twentieth century as experienced in Europe. For Badiou, the answer could be expressed in terms of the ambiguities of a single world: 'anabasis' – 'a re-ascent towards the source, an arduous construction of novelty, an exiled experience of beginning ...'. He went on to elucidate this cryptic answer by offering a reading of two very different poems that both bore the title 'Anabasis'.[31]

Badiou first discusses the famous *Anabasis* written in the early 1920s by the French Nobel Laureate Saint-John Perse (see Chapter 2). For Badiou, Perse's poem, with its lyrical intimations of a long journey across the expanse of Asia, is still instinct with the nineteenth-century European desire for imperial self-realization in foreign lands, yet haunted by a sense of absence and void. Badiou's second poem is a short piece by Paul Celan, a survivor of the Nazi labour camps, published in 1963, a few years before the author's suicide. By contrast with the flowing lines and rich images of Perse's poem, Celan's 'Anabasis' is spare in style and broken in syntax: 'This / narrow sign between walls / the impassable-true ... .' While Perse luxuriated in openness ('Roads of the world, we follow you'), Celan's path is narrow and impassable. The contrasts Badiou finds in the two poems tell the story of the fracturing of European identity in the twentieth century: 'Having departed for the anabasis in Saint-John Perse's sense, the century foundered upon a darkness so real that it was forced to change the *direction* of the movement, as well as the resonance of the words that could articulate it.'[32]

184

Badiou explains how 'anabasis' comes to have so large a range of meanings by reference to the original Greek verb from which the noun is derived: 'the verb *anabano* ("to anabase", as it were) means both "to embark" and "to return".' The problem is that Badiou is wrong about the Greek – and not just about the form of the verb (it should be *anabaino*). The Greek verb means to 'mount' a ship or horse, to 'march up' from the coast, to 'ascend' or 'rise' or 'shoot up'. The ambiguity Badiou detects and explores in 'anabasis' is nonetheless a real one. It lies, however, not in the Greek word itself but in the way later centuries have responded to the story Xenophon chose to call *Anabasis*.[33]

The ambiguity that Badiou sees as inherent in the word 'anabasis' is well exemplified by contemporary responses to Sherman's march. Anabasis was first a term of abuse in the southern states and in England. But the same term was then used by the Union side to elevate Sherman's march, with the modern American general typically seen as equalling or improving on one of the great exploits of antiquity. Sherman's anabasis paradoxically became one of the Civil War's compensatory myths of glory.

The foundering of the American anabasis was made manifest in small incoherences, puzzling contradictions. Consider the way one northern paper in February 1865 tried to mock British reluctance to reach a verdict on Sherman's plans: 'Some of these writers, in a fit of oracular reserve, were fain to let the issue determine the character of the enterprise. If it failed then was Sherman to fall into the place of a beaten leader with Xenophon and Xerxes; if successful he must forthwith take rank as master in the art of war with Caesar and Napoleon.' A long historical overview then showed that long marches away from home normally meet with disaster: 'Military history has yet to furnish a parallel to such a movement, whatever may be its results.' American exceptionalism is here established in the military sphere: Sherman's achievements are unparalleled, not to be lumped with Asian or European expeditions, ancient or modern. Yet in the process of rebuking British obliqueness the writer's memory slips: in the original *London Herald* article, Xenophon and Xerxes were an alternative, not coupled together. A negative image of the beaten Xenophon taken from the London *Times* and other pro-southern papers has displaced the ideologically pointed opposition between the doomed Persian king and the heroic Greek defender of freedom.[34]

These contradictions are also caught by responses to one of the first books devoted to the march, *The Story of the Great March*, written by G.W. Nichols, himself a participant. One American newspaper claimed that there had been nothing equal to Sherman's march 'since the famous retreat of the ten thousand, which Xenophon has immortalised' – and was glad 'to see an authentic narrative of it from the pen of one, who, like Xenophon, participated in what he describes'. Across the Atlantic the *Examiner* took a similar line – though it could not resist a knock at Nichols'

style: 'though the periods of Xenophon and the eloquence of Segur may be
wanting', *The Story of the Great March* 'may fairly take rank in the
category to which the works of the ancient Greek and the modern Gaul
belong' (the allusion was to Philippe de Ségur's account of Napoleon's
Russian campaign). A very different line was then taken by a writer in the
North American Review who chose to pick up the remarks made in the
British journal. Only recently, he wrote, the *Examiner* had been complain-
ing about Sherman's brutal proceedings – but now it 'searches history to
know on what shelf to place the Major's book, and determines to rank it in
the category to which Xenophon and Ségur belong'. After this sarcastic
swipe at the search for European terms of comparison, the reviewer went
on to remark that 'Xenophon will certainly be pleased' – 'and the Examiner
may be forgiven too for a simile which, after all, only shows its loyalty to
the old theory, – that the Major ran away from Hood, and attempted to fall
back on Washington through Savannah'. For this reviewer at least, a
reference to the *Anabasis* could still be taken as an attack on Sherman for
retreating from Atlanta. This was a blatant distortion of the *Examiner*'s
message – which had called Sherman's march 'one of the most daring and
successful enterprises that military skill has ever yet attempted'. Or
perhaps it was a deliberate misreading – the chance to knock English
hypocrisy proving too hard to resist.[35]

The ambiguities of the American anabasis are strengthened if we read
Sherman's march to the sea against the long march of Alexander
Doniphan and his Missouri volunteers. Both Sherman and Doniphan were
hailed as modern Xenophons, with Xenophon conveniently extracted from
any narrow historical context, yet still firmly embedded in the key myth
of the West, the transfer of cultural authority and imperial power from
Greece to Rome and ultimately to the United States. Both Sherman and
Doniphan were icons of progress, advancing rather than retreating – but
Sherman's movements were harder to read, disputed in both the North
and the South, less easy to exploit for the myths of American nationhood
at a time when American nationhood was itself divided. Doniphan managed the coup of combining Anabasis and Thermopylae business: Mary
Chesnut restored them to their proper opposition as she railed against the
Confederate's general's failure to stop Sherman's advance.

How, then, did the American nineteenth century envisage its own
movement, its trajectory? The trajectory from one anabasis to another can
be read as tragic – a movement from fraternity to disunion, from progress
to retreat, from expansion to self-mutilation. As was feared at the time,
the Mexican anabasis proved to be poisonous. Or the very tragedy of the
American anabasis can be taken as a form of progress: a movement from
an unwarranted attack on a foreign land to a march of freedom, with the
qualities necessary to preserve freedom prepared and tested during the
war on Mexico. A third possibility is to deny the very notion of movement.
The century was marked by dull repetition as the mantle of the modern

Xenophon passed blindly from one general to another. The very christening of a new Xenophon was an act of cultural amnesia, the winds blowing the sands into new shapes. Or else the apparent act of amnesia can be taken as a wilful re-appropriation, the very replaying of the anabasis trope – the reception of a reception of a reception – itself asserting the expansiveness of the landscape of American heroism. Unifying these disparate trajectories, these conflicting readings, is the sense of anabasis as return: advance or retreat, the American anabasis was still always in one sense a move backwards, a return to the source, a return to the power and prestige of Greece and Rome.

And yet the American century did move on, from the self-destruction of the Civil War to the facade of reconciliation. It attempted to construct a new myth of progress from the path of violence and destruction that Sherman beat from Atlanta, 'smashing things to the sea'. And the work of myth-making was strangely helped by the very boldness of Sherman's strategy. Without Sherman's march to the sea and up through the Carolinas, there would probably have been no grand review of the two Union armies on successive days at the end of the war: the review only took the form it did because the Army of the West ended the war within striking distance of the capital. And after Sherman had ridden through the streets of Washington and heard the acclaim for the romantic Army of the West match or even outstrip the previous day's celebration of the Army of the East, there was a brief but pointed foreshadowing of the role that his march would come to play in the difficult reunion of North and South. As Sherman came up on to President Johnson's stand he refused to shake hands with Secretary of War Stanton, who had led a personal assault on Sherman for the generous peace terms he offered Joe Johnston. In years to come Sherman and his march helped to shape the way the identity of the newly reunited country was constructed and debated, and once more the distant figure of Xenophon and the anabasis trail he struck through Asia would play a prominent role on the battleground of American memory.[36]

The Brutal Romance of War:
Reconstruction and Beyond

To realize what war is, one should follow our tracks …
William Tecumseh Sherman (letter to his wife Ellen, 1864)[1]

* * *

It was nearly forty years since the end of the Civil War, but many veterans from the march that had made Sherman's name had still come to Washington for the unveiling of his statue on Pennsylvania Avenue. Congress had first approved money for the memorial in 1892, the year after Sherman's death, and many of the old soldiers converging on the capital had themselves contributed to the bronze image. Five of Sherman's children were also present for the ceremony. The statue itself was yet another general on horseback – but it had a particular poignancy in this location: it was placed at the very spot from which Sherman had looked back on his army during the parade at the end of the Civil War. The 'great triumphal march' which had surged down Pennsylvania Avenue in May 1865 was duly recalled by President Roosevelt and other speakers as the statue was unveiled. One of Sherman's former colleagues even claimed that the sculptor had tried to portray Sherman as he appeared at precisely that instant – the moment that Sherman had told him was 'the happiest and most satisfactory moment of his life'.[2]

For one of Sherman's children the unveiling ceremony was to have an unexpected and unpleasant aftermath. At a dinner that evening in the White House, it was mentioned that a corps of West Point trainees was planning to traverse Sherman's route through Georgia, and President Roosevelt proposed that Sherman's oldest surviving son, Tom, now a Jesuit priest, should accompany the troops. He agreed, but his arrival in Georgia was greeted with uproar. To have General Sherman's son go over the ground devastated by his father was bad enough. The addition of a military guard made his presence even more offensive. One Georgia newspaper responded by reawakening memories of 'one of the most shameful expeditions ever inaugurated and prosecuted under the flag of an enlightened people', while a Confederate veteran proclaimed that he would not regret it 'if some one killed young Sherman should he attempt to march through Georgia'. His escort withdrawn, young Sherman promptly abandoned the trip.[3]

9. The Brutal Romance of War: Reconstruction and Beyond

Tom Sherman's angry reception in Georgia is striking evidence for continuing resentment of his father's march in the South. This chapter will explore other ways in which Sherman's march lived on in American memory – and particularly how Xenophon continued to be used to articulate shifting perceptions of the march. Sherman had led an anabasis that had at first been derided in the South as a humiliating retreat, but then celebrated in the North as a reversal of Xenophon's original anabasis, an American advance rather than a Greek retreat. As time passed, Xenophon was used in different ways to suggest both the brutality and the romance of the march. The use of Xenophon in the battle for perceptions while Sherman was marching to the sea was itself remembered during his son's brief trip to Georgia forty years later: 'Father Sherman in full retreat', the Atlanta *Constitution* crowed, while a newspaper in Alabama mockingly alluded to his 'proposed anabasis'. The priest-son's jaunt here stands in ironic counterpoise to the soldier-father's anabasis: Father Sherman was beating a proper retreat – and it is hard not to read in the Atlanta newspaper's headline a wishful rewriting of history, a return to those war days when it could be claimed that Tom Sherman's father had been in retreat from Atlanta rather than advancing unimpeded through the southern countryside.[4]

Southern outcry at Father Sherman's mission in Georgia ran against the strong national narrative of reconciliation between South and North. Many Americans at the turn of the century preferred to remember what united them in the present rather than what had divided them in the past – and it was not least the memory of the war itself that united them: in the years following the war's end, as the historian Drew Gilpin Faust writes, 'this shared suffering would override persisting differences about the meanings of race, citizenship, and nationhood to establish sacrifice and its memorialization as the ground on which North and South would ultimately reunite'. With the passing of time Xenophon too would come to be as readily exploited in the cause of reunion as for the expression of lingering pain. But as the victorious North imposed the tough terms of Reconstruction on the South at the end of the war, it was pain that was uppermost in southern minds as they contemplated their humiliating failure to oppose Sherman's path of destruction and turned to Xenophon to undermine his triumph.[5]

*

These chaps were industrial-age killers … . Their war was so impersonally murderous as to make quaint anything that had gone on before.

Yet some of the ancient military culture endured. The brutal romance of war was still possible in the taking of spoils. Each town the army overran was a prize. In this village was an amazing store of wine, in that a granary brimming to the rafters, a herd of beef here, an armory there, homes to loot, slaves to incorporate. There was something undeniably classical about it …

E.L. Doctorow, *The March* (2005)[6]

189

Twenty years after the end of the Civil War, Zebulon B. Vance, Governor of North Carolina for most of the war and now a Senator, was invited to address the Association of the Maryland Line (part of the Confederate army) at its third annual reunion in Baltimore. This was one of a growing number of Confederate reunions in the 1880s – a sign of the South's growing confidence in openly embracing its lost cause. Vance's long oration was admirably suited for its audience of embittered veterans. Taking as his theme 'The Last Days of the War in North Carolina', he launched into an attack on the behaviour of Sherman's troops during their march through the South and on Sherman himself as their leader. After reviewing the damage to both public and private property (including, he sardonically noted, pianos 'on which perhaps rebel tunes had been played'), he arrayed against Sherman an impressive range of citations on the practice and theory of war. He contrasted Sherman's troops with the British army in North Carolina in the Revolutionary War and the 'followers of Mahomet, cruel and bloodthirsty as they were', and then cited the pronouncements on war made by Chancellor Kent, 'the great American authority on international law'. Vance also turned to the evidence of 'the great Xenophon' – not the *Anabasis*, however, but the *Cyropaedia*, Xenophon's didactic and fictionalized account of the rise to power of the first Cyrus, founder of the Persian empire: Xenophon, he noted, 'puts in the mouth of his hero Cyrus, the Prince of Persia, an order directing that his army, when marching upon the enemy's borders, should not disturb the cultivators of the soil'. Vance concluded by opposing Sherman to both 'the Arab chieftain who denied Christianity and the old Greek pagan who had never heard of Christ'.[7]

Vance's citation of 'the great Xenophon' was especially cutting because it was turning against Sherman the ancient hero who had been used to elevate his achievements twenty years earlier. This move had in fact already been made by critics of Sherman at the end of the war. In 1866, a New York monthly had contrasted Sherman's tolerance of plundering with Xenophon and Wellington's ability to restrain their troops. The direct source of Vance's invective, however, was a book on *The Last Ninety Days of the War in North-Carolina* written in 1866 by an acquaintance, Cornelia Phillips Spencer, whose researches he had encouraged.[8]

Spencer, a poet and journalist who also played an active role in university affairs at Chapel Hill in the Reconstruction era, began her critique by citing a letter in which Sherman had told his Confederate adversary Wade Hampton that 'the right to forage is older than history'. While acknowledging that it was impossible to discover 'the precise character of this right among barbarians in the morning twilight of civilization', Spencer went on to adduce 'clear historic evidence' that 'long before the coming of the Prince of Peace, in the earliest ages of profane history, among civilized nations the "right to forage" did not mean a right to indiscriminate pillage': 'More than twenty centuries ago, Xenophon, at the head of the Ten

190

Thousand, accomplished his famous retreat from Babylon to the sea. The incidents of that great march are given by himself in a narrative, whose modesty, spirit, and elegance have charmed all subsequent ages. His views as to the right to forage are clearly stated in the following passage ... .' Xenophon's view then emerges in a long extract on plundering which Spencer quotes from the same standard legal textbook that Vance later cited – Kent's *Commentaries on American Law*, 'an authority that was studied by General Sherman at West-Point': 'We may infer', Kent had argued, 'the opinion of Xenophon on this subject, (and he was a warrior as well as a philosopher,) when he states, in the *Cyropaedia*, that Cyrus of Persia gave orders to his army, *when marching upon the enemy's borders*, not to disturb the cultivators of the soil; and there have been such ordinances in modern times for the protection of innocent and pacific pursuits.'[9]

Spencer's argument shows that Kent's prestigious work was also the ultimate source for Vance's appeal to 'the great Xenophon' at the Baltimore reunion in 1885. And yet had Spencer or Vance turned to the *Cyropaedia* itself they might have seen that Kent's use of Xenophon was based on a misreading of the passage he cited. In this passage Xenophon portrays Cyrus leading an expedition against the king of Assyria. Cyrus has been helped by defections from the Assyrian side, but he realizes 'that those who had revolted to his side but lived near Babylon would suffer severely unless he himself were always present'. So he sends a message to the Assyrian king suggesting that they make an agreement that Cyrus should not harm the cultivators of the king's land as long as the king does not harm the defectors while they work the land.

Kent's appeal to the *Cyropaedia* is problematic firstly because the work itself is a historical fiction. Cyrus' agreement with the Assyrian king does not fit the conditions Xenophon himself was familiar with in Greece, where there was no clear separation between soldiers and farmers. It is also dangerous to assume that orders given by Cyrus reflect Xenophon's own views. Kent ignores the fact that Cyrus' suggestion to the Assyrian king is a cynical manoeuvre. Cyrus claims that the agreement will benefit the Assyrian more, since his land is larger than that of the defectors. But he really wants to protect his new allies. Xenophon goes on in any case to note that Cyrus did allow his army to plunder the Assyrian's land freely, 'in order that the campaign might be more pleasant for the allies' and also 'to lighten the burdens of the campaign' by feeding off the enemy. The rest of the work confirms that it was normal to exploit the enemy's land for both food and plunder: at one point Cyrus tells his army to be sure to bring hand-mills when they are invading a hitherto unravaged land.[10]

Kent's neglect of the context of the *Cyropaedia* passage he adduced is typical of the nineteenth-century tendency to idealize and simplify Xenophon. The same trend is revealed by the passage's later exploitation by Spencer and Vance: they were both confident that their audiences would take Kent's reading on trust – just as they had done themselves. The simplification of Xenophon was indeed part of the idealization: the text's complexity was sacrificed so that a pure gnomic message could be extracted from it and made to represent Xenophon's own voice – a voice that could then undermine the equally rosy image of Sherman as a modern Xenophon that was being propagated by his defenders.

*

Had Cornelia Phillips Spencer and Zebulon Vance turned to Xenophon's first-hand account of a real expedition in the *Anabasis* rather than to a second-hand report of the imagined expedition described in the *Cyropaedia*, they might have been less willing to use Xenophon to knock Sherman. Spencer went to some lengths to boost the authority of the *Cyropaedia* as evidence by reflecting on Xenophon's greatness as leader and as author of the *Anabasis*. Yet the *Anabasis* itself contains descriptions of many acts of destruction that do not sit easily with Spencer's eulogy. It also contains some overt hints that Xenophon felt the need to defend some of the troops' actions – and we know from a speech by the Athenian orator Isocrates that the Ten Thousand could be cast in a bad light. The *Anabasis* can be placed at the start of a tradition of apologetic writing by military leaders that includes Sherman's *Memoirs*, first published in 1875, ten years after the end of the Civil War. Sherman was writing partly to settle scores with other Union generals, but, like Xenophon, he shows that he was conscious of the controversy caused by his march: even before reaching Savannah he had become aware that southern newspapers were portraying the conduct of his men as 'simply infamous', alleging that 'we respected neither age nor sex', 'burned every thing we came across', and 'ravished the women and killed the men'. By exploring briefly how Xenophon and Sherman portray – and excuse – the brutality of war in their famous memoirs, we can get a sense of the ideologically charged selectivity of memory involved in using Xenophon to condemn – or even to praise – Sherman.[11]

A particularly shocking episode in the Greeks' retreat occurs soon after their arrival at the Black Sea. At first the soldiers are able to buy supplies at the Greek city of Trapezus while also negotiating with the nearby Colchians. But when they find that there is not enough for sale and that they do not have enough money anyway, the generals organize raiding parties. Soon, when there are no provisions to be had close by, the Trapezuntians lead them against some more distant enemies of theirs, the Drilae. The Drilae respond by gathering in a stronghold surrounded by a deep gully. After a bold attack, the Greek soldiers plunder the stronghold while the enemy take refuge on its acropolis. But the Drilae attack again when the Greeks start to withdraw – until, Xenophon writes, 'one of the gods offered them a means of safety: one of the houses on the right, which had presumably been set alight by someone or other, suddenly blazed up',

26. 'Here was Aetna ...': Columbia in flames.

making the attackers flee; and 'when Xenophon heard about this gift from Fortune, he ordered the houses on the left to be set alight too; the wooden houses were soon ablaze', and, after Xenophon had had wood piled up and set alight, 'the whole town burnt to the ground – the houses, the towers, the palisade, and everything except the acropolis'.[12]

The sad fate of this Pontic town finds a parallel in Sherman's march in the burning of Columbia, state capital of South Carolina, where the rebellion had started. In a series of articles originally published soon after the fire in the pointedly-named Columbia *Phoenix*, the poet and novelist William Gilmore Simms portrayed the fire that consumed the glorious city as 'a scene for the painter of the terrible', with 'a range of burning mountains' stretching 'in a continuous series for more than a mile': 'Here was Aetna, sending up its spouts of flaming lava; Vesuvius, emulous of like display ...; and Stromboli, struggling, with awful throes, to shame both by its superior volumes of fluid flame.' Simms drew on natural marvels familiar from accounts of picturesque travels in southern Italy to condemn the destruction supposedly wrought by Sherman's troops. Sherman's own account of the fire is a riposte to the bitter attacks of Simms and other southerners: he laid the blame for the fire directly on the retreating Confederate generals, who he alleged had set fire to some cotton bales. In the rest of his *Memoirs*, Sherman found other ways of justifying damage that could not be blamed on the enemy: while admitting that the troops were attracted by the 'charm' of foraging, he argued that because Georgia was sparsely settled there was no possibility of an orderly system of requisitions as in Europe; he also mitigated the destruction of private

193

property by claiming that it was particularly aimed at those responsible for the war (Confederate politicians and generals) and at those who tried to impede his advance by destroying crops and removing livestock and provisions. Ten years later, Sherman strengthened his defence by embellishing the second edition of his *Memoirs* with an appendix of letters written in response to the original publication and with extracts from the official enquiry into the burning of Columbia. His autobiography took its place in the increasing number of participant narratives that were similarly disposed to excuse the army's conduct, even if they did not always advance quite the same excuses – and one memoir rather spoilt the message by entitling its chapter on the Columbia fire 'Delenda est Carthago', after the elder Cato's famous injunction to destroy Rome's old enemy.[13]

While Sherman took care to remove himself from any responsibility for the burning of Columbia, Xenophon openly proclaims that he gave the order to start the fire that burnt the Drilian stronghold. He does at least bring out that the initial attack was made only when the army had exhausted other ways of getting provisions, but a shocking gulf still remains between the army's need for provisions and the horrific destruction involved in the remedy. Xenophon's stress on divine aid, while primarily emphasizing the Greeks' unexpected rescue, could be thought to provide some justification for the fire. Yet the tone of Xenophon's account remains hard to read. Is it because the Drilae were a remote non-Greek people (and enemies of the Greeks of Trapezus) that Xenophon does not do more to justify the fire? Or is the very scale of the fire a pained reflection on the damage that the Greeks were forced to inflict on people who had done them no harm? At least Xenophon did not shirk from telling the story – and from other hints, too, of the destruction the march involved. Early in the retreat the Greeks plunder villages belonging to Cyrus' mother Parysatis – an action permitted by the Persians as a way of mocking the dead Cyrus; after relations deteriorate, the Persians scorch villages to prevent the Greeks provisioning from them; and later the Greeks remove food (but not bronze utensils) from Carduchian villages, 'since they had no choice'. And as the army advances along the Black Sea coast Xenophon also presents a broader defence of the Greek soldiers in a speech answering complaints about their treatment of Greeks living on the coast: 'whether the land was occupied by barbarians or by Greeks', the army had taken supplies whenever it was 'not offered provisions for sale', 'prompted not by arrogance but by sheer necessity'; and at Trapezus, the army had not only paid for its supplies but also 'repaid the people there in kind for the honours they bestowed upon us and the gifts they gave in friendship to the army'. The justification implicit in the earlier narrative is here openly staged in front of a Greek audience – and the horrific aftermath of the attack on the Drilae is concealed by the honourable language of reciprocity (as if the raid had been carried out solely to help Trapezus).

Xenophon's staging of the army's defence is itself conditioned by the rhetorical needs of the situation and so not necessarily a clue to his real feelings about that brutal assault. Many readers have nonetheless been prepared to accept the defence: the suffering of the Drilae and other victims of the march has generally been silenced in eulogistic rewritings of Xenophon's story – and one nineteenth-century American general even cited Xenophon's failure to take the Drilian stronghold to excuse his own failure to capture a mill from its heavily outnumbered British defenders.[14]

The selectivity of the image of the *Anabasis* projected in American public discourse can also be shown by looking at how Xenophon and Sherman present the total scale of the destruction caused by their marches to the sea. Xenophon reports that the Greeks held a review under arms at Cerasus on the Black Sea coast and discovered their total to be 8,600 – roughly two-thirds of their original strength. He makes no attempt to estimate the overall scale of the physical damage the troops had done, but he does at this point give a chilling hint of the human cost of the march for those who opposed it: at Cerasus the Greeks also 'distributed the money that had been raised by selling the prisoners of war', reserving a tithe for Apollo and Artemis of Ephesus. Xenophon does not, however, reveal how many prisoners were sold or how much they raised. The soldiers were simply following the common Greek practice of selling prisoners as slaves. But this was a practice generally ignored by the newspapers and orators who hailed Sherman's march – which brought freedom to the black slaves working the Georgia plantations – as a modern anabasis.[15]

Like Xenophon, Sherman pays attention to the human cost of his campaign. He closes his account of the march to Savannah with 'a tabular statement of the losses during the march, and the number of prisoners captured'. Unlike Xenophon, however, he also addresses the destruction to property: 'The property captured consisted of horses and mules by the thousand, and of quantities of subsistence stores that aggregate very large, but may be measured with sufficient accuracy by assuming that sixty-five thousand men obtained abundant food for about forty days, and thirty-five thousand animals were fed for a like period, so as to reach Savannah in splendid flesh and condition.' Here we do at least have an attempt at a global view of the damage inflicted on Georgia – even if the studied vagueness of 'sufficient accuracy' contrasts with the precise enu-meration of human casualties. Yet if Sherman thinks the total damage to Georgia worth estimating, that is not least because it was his army's treatment of white civilians that made his march so notorious. Far worse horrors were committed by American troops in wars against Mexico and the Plains Indians, but it was a march through the rich plantations of Georgia that became the emblem of a new mode of total war. Sherman's *Memoirs* as a whole point to the same racial logic found in contemporary responses to Xenophon.[16]

Following the *Anabasis* through to its end makes the selectivity of the

American memory of Xenophon even more clear. As the Greeks slowly make their way along the Black Sea coast, Xenophon is repeatedly critical of the behaviour of some of the troops in their greed to make as much profit as they can before they return to Greece. Yet he closes the *Anabasis* as a whole with an extraordinary demonstration of his own greed. At this point Xenophon is leading the remnants of the army to take up service with the Spartans. In Pergamum he is entertained by a woman called Hellas ('Greece'!), who informs him of a wealthy Persian, Asidates, living nearby with plenty of livestock. After a favourable sacrifice, Xenophon gathers some friends for an attack on Asidates, trying to keep the raid secret to stop other soldiers from coming along and claiming a share in the booty. When Xenophon's men arrive at Asidates' estate, however, they find it impossible to penetrate his well-fortified tower, and many are injured in the attack and the subsequent withdrawal. The next day Asidates abandons his tower in fear that Xenophon may return with a larger army – only to stumble into Xenophon's hands as he tries to escape. Xenophon gets to choose his share of the booty, and he closes by revealing that 'he was at last in a position even to do someone else a favour'.[17]

A journey into the plain to attack a Persian, a tough withdrawal – and then a windfall: Xenophon's closing account of the attack on Asidates reads like a comic resumé of the *Anabasis*. He tries to present the attack as the work of a select unit, but it still resembles the sort of private looting raid that he condemns earlier in the work, before the troops have signed up to work for the Spartans. And it was this desire for profit that created tensions both among the Ten Thousand themselves and between them and the Greeks living on the Black Sea coast. It cost some of them their lives – most strikingly an Arcadian soldier named Aeneas who tried to grab hold of a finely-clad Taochian who was about to throw himself down from a mountain stronghold, but got dragged down with him. Xenophon's own greed is cloaked in the language of reciprocity: he is not interested in profit for its own sake, but as a means of helping others. And like the burning of the Drilian stronghold his greed was supported by favourable signs from the gods. Early in his march Xenophon heard a perched eagle cry to his right – 'not an omen of profit', in his seer's view, 'because the eagle generally got its food on the wing'; at the end of the march it turns out that the seer had been overly pessimistic. The *Anabasis* ends as a tale of Xenophon's own manifest destiny.[18]

Reading Xenophon's account against Sherman's *Memoirs* suggests that it was doubly unfortunate for Cornelia Phillips Spencer and Zebulon Vance to appeal to Xenophon in order to lambast Sherman's depredations. It is not just that they were following a tradition of misusing Xenophon's *Cyropaedia*: they were also blind to the fact that Xenophon himself does not even seem to see the need to excuse certain actions that would have seemed to them more shocking than Sherman's supposed crimes. The moral and legal lesson Spencer drew from Xenophon's *Cyropaedia* could have been turned against Xenophon himself: 'If the conqueror ... seizes private property of pacific persons, for the sake of gain, ... he violates the modern usages of war, and is sure to meet with indignant resentment, and to be held up to the general scorn and detestation of the world.' As it was, the selective memory of the Greek classics in American culture made Xenophon a fitting witness in her virtual tribunal. In years to come, Xenophon would be used in many different ways as attempts were made to blot out the divisive legacy of Sherman's march and forge a stronger sense of national unity. What remained constant was the basic racial ideology seen in appeals to Xenophon to criticize Sherman: in public discourse the *Anabasis* was taken to be the story of a heroic Greek retreat, with scant regard for the stories of the peoples the Greeks attacked.

*

Though this march is done, and well accomplished, I think of it now, God help me, with longing – not for its blood and death but for the bestowal of meaning to the very ground trod upon, how it made every field and swamp and river and road into something of moral consequence, whereas now, as the march dissolves so does the meaning, the army strewing itself into the isolated intentions of diffuse private life, and the terrain thereby left blank and also diffuse, and ineffable ...

And why is Grant so solemn today upon our great achievement, except he knows this unmeaning human planet will need our warring imprint to give it value, and that our civil war, the devastating manufacture of the bones of our sons, is but a war after a war, a war before a war ...

E.L. Doctorow, *The March* (2005)[19]

The continuing imprint of the *Anabasis* on Sherman's campaign in the decades to come was especially clear in speeches celebrating and commemorating the march. At an early army reunion the march was remembered as a 'modern Anabasis', and that term was used again fifty years later, when it could still be claimed that its 'Xenophon has not yet appeared' – despite the countless memoirs that had been published in the meantime. A Colonel at an 1890s reunion who proclaimed that it would be 'tedious' to offer 'a resume of the marches and countermarches of the "Ten Thousand" on their famous retreat', even if 'illuminated by stereopticon', was still paying homage of sorts to the march's classic status. That status was more positively affirmed by allusions to Xenophon's role in the classroom: at a memorial meeting for Sherman the New York businessman Chauncey M. Depew proclaimed that 'Sherman's March to the Sea, like the retreat of Xenophon and his ten thousand Greeks, will arouse through all ages the enthusiasm of the schoolboy'; and a governor of Indiana went even further when he told veterans that Sherman's name would 'live in the memory of the Indiana school-boy long after Xenophon's memorable march shall have been forgotten by scholars' (and that would itself presumably be long after Xenophon was no longer studied by schoolboys). The same distant perspective was summoned by Chauncey Depew after Grant's death at a dinner to celebrate the anniversary of his birth – and here Depew agreed that the verdict of history would favour Sherman: Grant, he argued, 'knew and was glad' that Xenophon's march, 'the inspiration of armies for over two thousand years', would be 'replaced, for the next two thousand, by the resistless tramp of Sherman and his army'. As the protagonists of the Civil War passed away, the very survival of the classical paradigms was increasingly seen as promising the future fame of the modern American feats that equalled or surpassed them.[20]

Xenophon's role in the continuing conflict over the meaning of the Civil War can best be seen in a book-length poem on *The March to the Sea* published in 1896, five years after Sherman's death. The poem's origins can be traced back thirty-one years to Sherman's arrival at Columbia on the day the city was to be ravaged by fire. As Sherman entered the packed market-square, he saw some men pressing through the crowd to speak to him. They were Union officers who had been taken prisoner earlier in the war and escaped, and when Sherman called them up one of them handed him a folded piece of paper to read at his leisure. That afternoon Sherman opened his pockets, as usual, to look through the various notes he had stuffed in it during the day. And it was then that he read for the first time the song that, he later claimed, gave his campaign a glamour of 'romance' for the 'unmilitary public'.[21]

The song, entitled 'Sherman's March to the Sea', traced Sherman's progress in five stanzas, starting with a scene in camp before the march began:

> Our camp-fires shone bright on the mountain
>   That frowned on the river below,
> As we stood by the guns in the morning,
>   And eagerly watched for the foe;
> When a rider came out of the darkness
>   That hung over mountain and tree,
> And shouted, 'Boys, up and be ready!
>   For Sherman will march to the sea!'

And so it continued until the capture of Savannah, 'And the stars in our banner shone brighter / When Sherman marched down to the sea.' The catchy tune became a hit: more than a million copies of the sheet music were sold; the lyrics were reprinted in numerous patriotic collections; and the song was sung right up to the end of Sherman's life at army reunions, when toasts at dinner would consist of successive stanzas. It was also widely credited with giving the campaign the name by which it was generally known.[22]

The song was written by a Union soldier, Samuel Byers, while he was being held in Columbia. He had been able to follow news of the march from newspapers stuffed inside loaves of bread, and had then had his words set to music by another prisoner. Sherman rewarded him by attaching him to his staff for the rest of the war – and Byers became a devotee of Sherman for the rest of his life: his memoir of his *Twenty Years in Europe* as consul in Switzerland is full of letters from Sherman and also includes a scene where Sherman traces for Swiss officers the route of the March to the Sea ('It was a picture for an artist').[23]

Victor Davis Hanson has recently suggested that the title Byers gave to Sherman's march was 'perhaps deliberately reminiscent of Xenophon's *Anabasis*'. Given that the march was glorified at the time as an 'anabasis', Hanson's proposal is understandable: the title would then be another way of endowing the march with the same status. The problem with the suggestion, however, is that Xenophon's expedition was not known at this time as 'The March to the Sea'. The *New York Times* in 1866 could refer to Sherman as a soldier 'whose "march to the sea" will be remembered as long as Xenophon's "retreat of the ten thousand"', while a speaker at an army reunion three years later could speak of how 'the "March to the Sea", like the Retreat of the Ten Thousand' would grow vivid with the lapse of time. Both sentences make no sense if Xenophon's retreat was known as a 'march to the sea' – and 'the Retreat of the Ten Thousand' was in fact the standard term used in history books. Closest to the name given Sherman's march is the phrase used by a historian in the 1840s for the advance on Trapezus: 'The March to the Sea-coast'. But even this sub-heading points up a key difference: to speak of a march to the sea-coast is to stay within the realm of military strategy – to suggest the possibility of a further advance either on boat or by marching along the coast; to march to the sea is to arrive at the world of the elemental.[24]

Thirty years after composing his song, Byers included it in the long poem in heroic pentameters he now wrote on *The March to the Sea* (in the meantime he had also written a shorter poem, 'The Tramp of Sherman's Army', for an army reunion in 1889, as well as magazine articles on the march). The poem offered a much more extensive narrative of the march, with further notes attached at the end. Though admired at the time for its 'spirit and sustained energy' and hailed as 'a work of unquestionable genius, destined to become a classic in American literature', it is now largely forgotten. Nonetheless, Byers' poem together with his commentary offers a glimpse of the sort of meaning that could be bestowed on Sherman's march at the end of the century – and of how Xenophon could be used to bring out the march's significance.[25]

If the title of Byers' original song was not a nod to Xenophon, by the time he wrote his poem thirty years later the phrase 'March to the Sea' had come to be applied more widely to the *Anabasis*. And comparison with Xenophon was also implicit in Byers' description of the joy of Sherman's soldiers as they neared the coast:

A sudden shouting down the lines was sent;
  They looked and cried, 'It is the sea! the sea!'
And all at once a thousand cheers were heard,
And all the army shout the glorious word ...

And all the army in one mighty song
Passed the glad news, 'It is the sea,' along.

Bronzed soldiers stood and shook each other's hands;
  Some wept for joy, as for a brother found.

The poet himself compared the soldiers' joy with the shouts when 'the great Genoese / Placed his proud feet upon a new-found world' – as if Sherman's march offered a renewal of the hope expressed in Columbus' discovery of America. But reviewers of the poem were swift to note the similarity with another famous shout. One wrote that Byers had given Sherman's army 'just such a peal of joy as the "Thalassa! thalassa!" of Xenophon's weary men'. Another went even further, noting that Byers' 'moving description might almost be taken for a paraphrase of Xenophon's immortal account ... of the first sight of the sea, and the shouts of *"Thalatta! Thalatta!"* ('The sea! The sea!"), by the Ten Thousand Greeks on their ever memorable retreat from Cunaxa'. The scene even moved the reviewer to some deeper reflections: 'How marvellously history here repeated itself, and, in spite of differences of race, and time, and clime, what a marvellous similarity there often is in the behavior of human beings under like circumstances.' These grand generalizations obscure the reason why Byers' description could easily be taken for a paraphrase of the *Anabasis*: it *was* a paraphrase. It is not just that the shout 'It is the sea! the sea!' evokes the shout of the Ten Thousand: the details of the soldiers weeping and passing the word along are also found in Xenophon's famous scene. Sherman's march had been marked at the time as an anabasis, a return to the Greeks, a metaphorical retracing of Xenophon's tracks through Asia. Thirty years on Byers was gesturing back beyond that myth-making to the origin, to the Ten Thousand's shout at the sight of the Black Sea – classic words that themselves had been made in the course of the nineteenth century to carry further traces of romantic desire.[26]

Byers' poem was not alone in linking the joy of Sherman's army at reaching Savannah with the joy of the Ten Thousand at reaching the Black Sea. Four years later, a memoir of an Indiana volunteer regiment's role in the campaign drew on Xenophon's 'ecstatic moment' to express the feelings of 'our boys' after the capture of Savannah, when 'they looked out toward the ocean, and saw the beautiful flag floating over the approaching vessels'. An allusion to Xenophon was also contained in a lavish volume produced to commemorate the unveiling of Sherman's statue in Washington in 1904: a long sketch of Sherman's career marked the climax to his most famous march with the heading 'THE SEA! THE SEA!!' Unlike

Byers' poem, this heading left it open whether the words were to be taken as a quotation from Xenophon or a shout actually uttered by Sherman's soldiers. This textual indeterminacy was perhaps pointed. Byers' Xenophontic flourish bore scant relation to any actual accounts of the army's arrival at the sea. The approaches to Savannah were swampy and flat: there were no coastal mountains with high peaks offering a single moment of joy. In any case, the hostile city of Savannah still remained to be taken. An extended paraphrase of the *Anabasis* was tolerable in Byers' poem, but in volumes meant to appeal to veterans a subtler hint of a shared emotional experience was more appropriate.[27]

Byers' broader presentation of Sherman's march also aligned it with popular perceptions of the retreat of the Ten Thousand. Just as the 'romantic interest' of Xenophon's story was thought to make it appealing to modern readers, so too Byers portrays Sherman's march as 'the romantic campaign of the war': 'It had entered the unknown interior of Georgia, with its woods and swamps, and all communication with it was cut off. That was the romance of it all.' The language of romance was a common refrain in celebrations of Sherman's achievement: 'Oh that wonderful march to the sea! / Oh that romantic march to the sea!', a Union general had exclaimed in a poem on 'The March to the Sea' recited at a 1874 reunion. Another general wrote that the march seemed 'a romantic dream more than a reality'. And, as Byers saw, the heart of Sherman's romantic appeal was that he had cut loose from all communications – like Xenophon before him. It was this parallel that struck the military historian Adam Badeau in 1881 when he recalled how Sherman's march had been compared with Xenophon's: 'the disappearance of an army for a month' and its 'final emergence with undiminished numbers and enhanced prestige' constituted, he explained, 'a romantic episode that might well dazzle the imagination of indifferent spectators'. But the shared romanticism of the two marches could also rest on broader foundations: in a letter to the *New York Times* commenting on the controversy caused by the publication of Sherman's *Memoirs*, a veteran of the march referred to it as 'the romance of war – one of those grand, heroic deeds that, like Xenophon's march of the ten thousand or the charge of the light brigade at Balaklava, will live in song and treasured story when even the war itself will have been forgotten'.[28]

Byers was again using terms that had become part of the Sherman and Xenophon myths when he employed the vocabulary of chivalry. Just as Xenophon could be described in the 1890s as 'the Knight-Errant of Hellas', so too Byers calls Sherman 'the kind, true knight'. And while Byers presents Sherman's troops as passive ('Content, if only their great leader's hand / Should guide them safely through the unknown land') by contrast with their heroic leader, Sherman himself was prepared to apply chivalrous language to his whole army, speaking of them at a 1890 reunion as 'knights errant transformed into modern soldiers'.[29]

27. 'Palmyra in the desert': Columbia after the fire.

Byers' poem was further linked to popular images of Xenophon by the language of the picturesque. As we saw in Chapter 7, the *Anabasis* could be read in the nineteenth century as a picturesque work, offering vivid depictions of life amongst the highlands of eastern Anatolia and Thrace. The association of the picturesque with people marked as backward made it easy in the aftermath of the Civil War to apply this aesthetic to the South, now figured as old-fashioned in its plantation economy and in its code of honour, and contrasted with the urban, industrial, and progressive North. This implied historical narrative explains why Byers' poem – like some other accounts of Sherman's march – could be praised as 'picturesque': a poem on Sherman's march was similar to an account of picturesque travel through backward lands. Applying picturesque terminology to the Civil War became more and more popular with passing time: in an 1875 essay on the battle of Shiloh, Ambrose Bierce reflected that it was strange that he now recalled 'with difficulty the danger and death and horrors of the time, and without effort all that was gracious and picturesque'. This language was particularly appropriate for the March to the Sea, however, because Sherman had left in his wake ruins that could evoke thoughts of visits to the classical sites of Europe and Asia: the soil of the South was described by an English tourist straight after the end of the war as 'classic ground'; Columbia had become 'Palmyra in the desert', 'a mass of charred ruins – Herculaneum buried in ashes' (following Simms' image of the fire as a Vesuvius?); while the 'beauty and pride' of Charleston were now 'as dead as the glories of Athens'. These descriptions, as a modern scholar has forcefully argued, 'provided a way of integrating the South, albeit a version of the South sanctioned for its antiquity, relics, and romance, back into an affiliation with the rest of the country', with ruins suggesting both 'an old order passing into oblivion' and 'the rest of the nation's progress'.[30]

By a striking transference, the language of the picturesque was also applied to Sherman's march. Sherman once commented to Samuel Byers that without his song 'the campaign never would have had its picturesque name'. Byers later went further by referring in a magazine article to the march as 'the most picturesque as well as the most important campaign of the civil war'. And a biography of Sherman published in 1899 even began by calling him 'the most picturesque figure in the civil war'. While popular photographs of Sherman's rugged features may have contributed to that judgement, the notion of the march as picturesque suggested another point of similarity with the retreat of the Ten Thousand, eliding all differences of time and space: a magazine editorial after Sherman's death asserted that the March to the Sea was 'the most romantic and pictur-esque of the many renowned events' of the Civil War and that it already had 'a distinctive character, like that of the Greeks in Xenophon's story of the Ten Thousand'. It was as if its picturesqueness gave it an instant historical pedigree. Indeed, soon after the end of the war Sherman's own official reports on the march had been lauded for being 'as clear as those in which Caesar tells how he waged his Gallic wars, and almost as picturesque as the immortal pages in which Xenophon describes the march of the famous Ten Thousand'.[31]

Byers did oppose one popular image of life on the march when he denied that Sherman's campaign was 'one long great holiday'. An American teacher was later to call Xenophon's march a 'holiday expedition'. Similar phrases came far more often to the lips of Sherman's soldiers: the march had given the 'impression of a vast holiday frolic' or seemed a 'delightful picnic' or 'gala day festival'. For the Union side, these terms were a way of underlining southern inferiority: Sherman had been free to go as he pleased. It was, however, the use of these terms by Confederate critics that Byers was seeking to undermine: for southerners, to call the march a 'holiday excursion' or 'pleasant walk' was a way of dampening enthusiasm for Sherman's 'consummate military skill and valor' – and undermining his supposed boast about his more-than-Xenophontic success.[32]

Byers' presentation of Sherman's march is driven by the overarching goal of national reconciliation. His narrative of the march ends at the grand parade in Washington, with the Armies of the East and the West united, their 'long blue columns' pictured as 'one sea of sloping steel'. Byers does underline at this point the cause for which the war was fought: he contrasts the review with a Roman triumph, as Sherman's march has brought freedom rather than enslavement, and in his notes he compares the joy of freed slaves with the return of the children of Israel – another hint that the march has restored America to her place as the new promised land. But Byers adds to this depiction of the campaign as a march for freedom an epilogue that offers a broader historical perspective. The epilogue presents a pastoral vision of a South that has now recovered from the ravages of war: 'roses line the lanes again / Where Sherman's troopers rode.' It also celebrates the bravery of the Confederate soldiers irrespective of their cause: 'What matters now if they were wrong? / They were our own kith and kin'; 'North or South, 'tis all the same / ... / One starry banner guards the fame / Of blue coat and of gray.' This note of reconciliation was also implicit in Byers' earlier presentation of the march: the language of romance and chivalry, evoking noble images of medieval valour, deflected attention from the reality of physical destruction.[33]

Byers' stress on national unity fitted the trends of the closing years of the century. After the difficult years of Reconstruction, the Civil War became increasingly to be seen not as a battle for the emancipation of black slaves but as a tragic but noble conflict from which the country had emerged stronger: it was with approval that a reviewer of Byers' poem noted that 'not a line of the poem ... indicates a narrow or sectional spirit'. The courage of soldiers on both sides was now widely celebrated, and there were reunions with veterans from both sides present. The new meaning attached to the war was well expressed by a speaker at a memorial meeting after Sherman's death: 'we can say of all the combatants, as did the Greek historian of those who engaged in the civil war of that famous State, "There were no mean thoughts on either side". It was a war of giants, and it has led to results in which all acquiesce and rejoice.' The catastrophic war between the states was here salvaged by citation of Thucydides' description of the participants in the Peloponnesian War. The rhetoric of greatness ('It was a war of giants') obscured the fact that the results in which 'all' were said to acquiesce were by no means universally applauded: the newly enfranchised blacks in the South were subjected to segregation and frequently to mob violence.[34]

At the time Byers was writing, the ideology of national unity had itself led to further shifts in the way the memory of Xenophon could be applied to the Civil War. A history of the Confederate Missouri brigades published in 1879, just after the end of the Reconstruction era, began with the claim that 'the heroism of the Anabasis recounted by Xenophon, which has been crystallized in history and in song, was not one whit more worthy of that distinction than was the prowess, the patriotism and the daring of the Missouri Brigades in behalf of the wavering fortunes of the "Lost Cause"'. The same confident strain in reclaiming Xenophon for the Confederate cause appeared in a memorial address for Sherman's old adversary Joe Johnston. Johnston had marched with head uncovered among the Union generals when Sherman was buried in New York on a cold and wet day in February 1891. When he himself died a month later, he was praised for 'the masterly, strategic defence' that had retarded Sherman's advance and for conducting 'an orderly retreat' that would 'take its place in future history with that of the famous Ten Thousand under Xenophon'. With these words Johnston was posthumously restored to the stature of a hero from antiquity – a far cry from the Xenophon in flight scorned by angry southern matrons like Mary Chesnut.[35]

An even more striking change in the American appropriation of the *Anabasis* occurred during the subjugation of the Plains Indians. The spread of railroads in the West and the increasing number of settlers led to a more active policy of pacifying the Indian tribes, spearheaded by Sherman himself as head of the army after Grant became President. One Indian tribe that had maintained relatively friendly dealings with the United States was the Nez Percés, inhabitants of a beautiful highland area in Montana. In 1877, however, when ordered to leave their tribal homeland for a reservation, they resisted. Pursued by federal forces, they began a long march in the hope of reaching Canada. They outmanoeuvred the army on several occasions, but were finally overcome by cold and hunger after a journey of some 1,500 miles.[36]

Xenophon soon became a fixed part of the way the long march of the Nez Percés was remembered. Their journey was compared in Congress with Xenophon's retreat and celebrated in American publications as an 'anabasis', with their leader, Chief Joseph, designated for years to come as 'the Indian Xenophon', 'the modern Xenophon', 'the Xenophon of the Nez Perces', even a 'swarthy Xenophon'. One of the army officers involved in the pursuit avowed that 'Xenophon did no more than he'; a later author agreed that Xenophon would have given the retreat its 'true place, as the most famous in history', for Xenophon had 'covered but half the distance' (true at least as his retreat was restricted to the section between the river Zab and the Black Sea), and that while 'burdened with no host of women and children' (not quite true) and encountering 'only rude mountaineers, to whom they were vastly superior in arms and discipline'.[37]

The cult of heroism constructed around the figure of Chief Joseph ultimately served the interests of the American republic. In the 1830s, as we saw in Chapter 3, it had been a telling racial argument to praise the courage of native Americans fleeing to Canada from white oppression by comparing them with the Ten Thousand – and to suggest that runaway black slaves were equally heroic. Now that the threat from the Indians was passing, it was safe to apply more widely to a noble but doomed Indian leader the sort of rhetoric that had been applied by earlier panegyrists to Doniphan and Sherman. And yet (as noted in Chapter 7) there was a subtle difference between applying classical paradigms to Chief Joseph and applying them to American army generals. However genuine the admiration for Chief Joseph, invoking Xenophon was a way of suggesting that he was a heroic relic rather than an heir to Greek virtue; it also simplified the structure of command in the Nez Percé march by focusing on a single exceptional leader. In any case, the praise bestowed on Chief

28. 'The Xenophon of the Nez Perces': Chief Joseph.

Joseph did not stop an army general from comparing the American troops' pursuit of the Nez Percés with the march of the Ten Thousand – much as the 1874 Black Hills Expedition through Sioux territory had been proclaimed in headlines as 'Custer's Anabasis'. The liberality with which the Xenophon comparison could be applied to victor and victim alike was a sign of the expansive confidence of a nation newly strengthened by its emergence from the war that had almost torn it apart. It would have taken much more than allusions to Xenophon to relieve the anger felt in some quarters over the treatment of the South and the American Indians, but the causes for which patriotic Confederates and noble Indians had fought were slowly disappearing in the concordant mists of memory.[38]

*

If Samuel Byers' *March to the Sea* reflects this same tendency to focus on the nobility of the fighters on both sides in the Union's triumphant wars, then it can also be read as part of a concerted effort to ward off the danger that the meaning bestowed by Sherman's march might be dissolved – even if the march's meaning necessarily shifted in the process. The poem was a striking addition to Byers' service in Sherman's cause, but its most telling contribution to this effort lay in its title, derived from the song that Byers had originally composed while still a prisoner in Columbia. Byers' song and poem on the March to the Sea together followed – and fostered – the most significant trend in the development of the Sherman legend: the practice of focusing on the march through Georgia rather than on the subsequent Carolinas campaign. The same trend was reflected by the other famous song to emerge from the campaign, 'Marching through Georgia'. And ten years after Byers' poem was published, it was Sherman's path through Georgia that was followed by the West Point cadets whom Father Tom Sherman briefly accompanied – and it was the same tracks that have been followed by so many in the imagination and on the ground in the century since.

The priority given to the March to the Sea did meet some resistance. When Zebulon Vance spoke on Sherman's impact on North Carolina, for instance, he snidely dismissed 'all the partisan songs which have been sung, or orations which subservient orators have spoken, about that great march to the sea'. For Vance, to speak of Sherman's March to the Sea was to neglect the damage the army had done in the Carolinas. And, as we saw in the last chapter, Sherman himself promoted the Carolinas campaign for an entirely different reason: he regarded the later sections of the march as far more difficult and strategically important than the march from Atlanta to Savannah. Indeed, the vehemence with which he insisted on this point was already a response to the romanticization of the march through Georgia. And for some of his followers it would be a point of honour to make the same distinction: in a 1908 address to the veterans of the campaign, Sherman's son Philemon chose to apply the usual Xenophon paradigm ('a march ... that for distance and difficulties surmounted has never been surpassed, unless by the armies of Xenophon and Hannibal') to the Carolinas rather than the Georgia campaign.[39]

The ideologically pointed practice of celebrating a curtailed version of Sherman's march is matched by nineteenth-century responses to the retreat of the Ten Thousand. The *Anabasis* was regularly read as a triumphant return to the sea: in re-tellings and dramatizations of Xenophon's story, far more attention was paid to the march upcountry and the subsequent retreat to Trapezus (covered in the first four books) than to the troubled journey along the Black Sea coast to Byzantium (covered in the final three books); and it was the first four books – ending with the euphoric arrival at the sea – that were often set as entrance requirements for college. This tendency to abridge Xenophon was even promoted by the Sherman legend: as we have seen, it was only after Sherman's campaign had come (thanks to Byers' song) to be known as the 'March to the Sea' that this name was attached to Xenophon's retreat. And Samuel Byers himself came to subscribe to the idealized reading of Xenophon in his poem by echoing the Greek soldiers' united shout of rapture: "It is the sea! the sea!".' Sherman's march helped to change the way Xenophon was read.[40]

As with Sherman's campaign, a potentially much more disturbing story was suppressed by the attention on the March to the Sea. Beyond the sea, Xenophon portrays the Greek soldiers moving from the relative unity they have shown in the face of a common danger to increasing disunity as they try to gain profit for themselves and also as they face the problem of dealing with the Greek cities along the coast and the imperial power of Sparta. Expressive of these growing tensions is a shift in rhetorical appeals to the past: when the Greeks are cut off in Asia, Xenophon presents himself appealing to the memory of the Greek victory over the Persian invasions in 490 and 480-79 BC; as they approach Greece, Xenophon warns the troops of the threat from Sparta by reminding them of the Spartan victory in the Peloponnesian War (431-404 BC). As the Ten Thousand themselves move from harmony to internal bickering, their journey begins to seem like a mirror of the experience of the Greeks at large over the previous few generations. If the nineteenth-century American anabasis beat a path from a united war against Mexico to a war of disunion, then Xenophon's *Anabasis* contains within itself the same shift from union to disunion.[41]

The general suppression in popular memory of the subversive story told by the *Anabasis* as a whole has gone hand in hand with a failure to confront the circumstances in which Xenophon wrote his account of the Greeks' journey. Xenophon is generally thought to have written the *Anabasis* in the 360s BC – over thirty years after the Greeks' return and at the same temporal remove from his march as Samuel Byers when he wrote his romantic poem on *The March to the Sea*. When his account has been exploited in the modern world for patriotic ends, this temporal distance has been ignored: indeed, not just Xenophon's writing but also the march itself have been removed from their historical contexts and made to stand in isolation as pure expressions in word and deed of an archetypal Hellenism, the ancestral spirit of western culture. The dehistoricizing of the original context of the account and of the event it commemorated was necessary for them both to be recontextualized under the banner of American power. And yet, like Byers' poem about Sherman, like all stories for that matter, the tale Xenophon tells is itself a reconstruction, an imaginative recreation written at what Xenophon himself saw as a time of unparalleled convulsion in the Greek world – a time of waning Spartan power after their defeat at Leuctra in 371 BC. As we confront the way Xenophon's story was transfigured by the workings of American memory in the interests of American hegemony, we need also to recognize that Xenophon's story is itself a transfiguration of experience – a reconstruction which we have little hope of moving beyond, for we do not have other accounts, other reconstructions, to weigh it against. Rather than succumbing blindly to the power of ancient and modern myth-making, we must face the fact that to speak of the *Anabasis* – of any anabasis – is always to speak of an interpretation of the march of history that is constituted by a culture of longing, a longing for the bestowal of meaning, a longing to make every step, in E.L. Doctorow's poignant phrase, 'something of moral consequence'.

Conclusion

Anabasis Investments

I would simply like, some day, to have the privilege of leading an 'undertaking' the way an Anabasis *is conducted by its leaders. (That very word seems to me so beautiful that I should like to come across the work worthy of such a title. It haunts me.)*

Saint-John Perse, *Letters* (1911)

When Phisterer drew himself up to salute, the Colonel brought out a leather volume: the Anabasis. *'I bought it in Heidelberg,' Carrington said. 'I have carried it with me every since. I thought ... since we both ...' Phisterer looked up from the Greek text and saw, to his embarrassment, that the Colonel was weeping ...*

Michael Straight, *Carrington* (1960)

This time, the sequel was corporate: Anabasis Investments NV, which owned the rights to the Rambo movies, offered to buy $55 million in stock and warrants ...

New York Magazine (1987)[1]

* * *

Soon after joining the Marines in 1988, at the age of eighteen, Anthony Swofford was sent on a training tour to Okinawa. He was approached there by a corporal from a platoon of Scout Snipers who had heard that he was 'a hard bastard' – and also that he spent time in the library when he was not in the gym: 'He looked over my stack of books, *The Myth of Sisyphus, The Anabasis, The Portable Nietzsche, Hamlet,* and said, "I don't know what the fuck any of these books are, and I don't care ...".' Despite his apparent disdain for literature, the corporal was persuasive enough: it was as a sniper that Swofford subsequently served in the Gulf War.[2]

What effect is Swofford aiming for as he recounts this episode in his memoir *Jarhead*? Swofford's often unflattering portrayal of himself and of life in the Marines has aroused both acclaim and disgust: one of the lead reviewers in the *New York Times* praised the book as 'a searing contribution to the literature of combat', while Bing West dismissed it in the *Wall Street Journal* as 'an insult to the American infantryman'. In itself, Swofford's account of the corporal's studied indifference to reading seems an obvious way of conveying the bleak image of Marines culture that upset

211

Bing West. More surprising, perhaps, is Swofford's equally studied list of books – above all the inclusion of the *Anabasis* alongside three classics of adolescent alienation. Is the *Anabasis* the odd-one-out – a joke at the expense of the corporal, who should have been aware that a military classic (full of Kurdish snipers) lurks amidst more philosophical matter? Or is Xenophon's presence a nod to Swofford's own coming adventures on the borders of Kuwait and Iraq? Or does Xenophon deserve a place in his own right alongside Camus, Nietzsche, and Shakespeare – as author of a more questioning work than the triumphalist classic beloved of military historians? Xenophon's inclusion remains a riddle: the bookish Swofford does not even reveal whether he ever read the *Anabasis*.[3]

This book has been more concerned with public commemoration than with private reading. In the final stage of this anabasis, however, we will explore a number of other private responses to Xenophon that help to draw the main themes together – and also to transcend the temporal structure of the story that has been told in the earlier chapters. We will close by reflecting on two distinctive elements in the American experience of anabasis: the haunting power of the word itself and readers' emotional investment in the very materiality of their copies of Xenophon.

We may start with a famous American family. During the First World War Kermit Roosevelt (son of Theodore) read a translation of the *Anabasis* while serving as an Honorary Captain with the British army in Mesopotamia. In his memoir *War in the Garden of Eden* he recalls that he had spent time at school 'plodding drearily' through the original – but he 'found it a very different book now' as he lay reading during stops in the shade of his car's turret: 'Here it was all vivid and real before my eyes … . On the ground itself one could appreciate how great a masterpiece the retreat really was.' While his written account deals with his changing perceptions of Xenophon on a purely personal level, Roosevelt was also sending out a more public signal by revealing that he read the *Anabasis* in Mesopotamia in 1918 – a similar signal to modern allusions to Xenophon before and during the invasion of Iraq. He himself acknowledges that reading was bound up with power when he reports that he was worried that he would have nothing new to read on the march to Tikrit – until an ex-master at Eton now serving in the Royal Flying Corps arranged to drop him a copy of Plutarch's *Lives* the next time he flew over. By reading two of the most famous expressions of classical heroism, he was establishing a genealogical link with the Greek soldiers who had penetrated Mesopotamia over two thousand years earlier and with Plutarch's heroes, including Alexander, whose path he was also following. And his bond with antiquity would be further promoted by the advertising for his book – a 'stirring modern Anabasis, frequently reminiscent of that earlier record of Xenophon's intrepid band'.[4]

Fifteen years earlier Kermit Roosevelt's father is recorded as reading the *Anabasis* while President – on a long trip by train across the American

West. It was a tour of self-promotion a year before the 1904 election, covering 6,000 miles in two months, and there was plenty of time for reading in between making speeches, hunting bears, and waving at farmers. But we can only speculate about what Theodore Roosevelt made of the *Anabasis* itself. Perhaps it appealed to him as an earlier adventure in the winning of the West, written by another keen devotee of the strenuous life – with Xenophon riding up the slopes of Asian mountains to face the enemy ahead evoking his own famous charge up San Juan Hill five years earlier. Whatever memories of his Rough Riders Xenophon's tale may have triggered, Roosevelt was also aware that it had had a profound influence on responses to the conquest of the American West: in his 1887 biography of Thomas Hart Benton, he had given particular praise to Benton's speech welcoming the Missouri volunteers back to St Louis – the speech where their expedition was said to have exceeded the march of the Ten Thousand by 2,000 miles. As he now travelled in his special train from St Louis across the plains to Santa Fé and on to California, Roosevelt was crossing terrain that had been won in part by the exertions of those Missouri troops and of another explorer who had been hailed as a Xenophon, John Charles Frémont.[5]

Roosevelt father and son together capture the trajectory that has been traced in this book. A decade and a half separate Theodore reading the *Anabasis* in the American West from Kermit reading it in Mesopotamia: a century and a half separate the anabasis of the Missouri volunteers to Mexico from the American anabasis in Iraq – and yet the trail we have ourselves followed back from Iraq to Mexico has revealed some notable continuities. Both in the mid-nineteenth century and more recently Xenophon has been used to project an image of American power abroad – an image of democratic forces bringing the light of freedom to benighted lands. Accounts of the invasion of Mexico by American forces in the 1840s bear striking similarities to contemporary accounts of the Iraq War in their dismissiveness towards foreign lands and peoples and in their use of the same ancient models to celebrate US military power. American troops have been figured as the Ten Thousand battling their way out of Asia or again as their mirror image, the 300 Spartans resisting Asiatic invaders at Thermopylae. This imperialist exploitation of antiquity has been accompanied by a highly uncritical presentation of the ancient Greeks in popular history. The creation of the myth of America has been paralleled by the creation of an equally buoyant image of Greek democratic courage and discipline.

The image of Xenophon propagated both in the rhetoric of American militarism and in popular re-writings of antiquity has been highly selective. The details of the march have been displaced by the repetition of a limited range of tropes glorifying the similar or greater achievements of American armies. Time and time again it has been claimed that American generals have led their armies further, and with better aims and results,

213

than Xenophon and the leaders of other famous marches (Hannibal, Napoleon). Some American armies have even shared the feelings of Xenophon's troops after marching for far smaller distances. Bolstered by blatant distortion (the most widely-reproduced panegyric of Doniphan's soldiers reduced the number of Xenophon's soldiers to 500), these public fantasies also seeped into private jottings: a soldier in the 44th Indiana during the Civil War evoked the Retreat of the Ten Thousand to express the privations suffered by his regiment while crossing the Cumberland mountains.[6]

This book has tried to write Xenophon back into the Anabasis story. Analysis of how the *Anabasis* has been interpreted or used to promote and celebrate American expansionism has throughout been set against a reading of Xenophon's original as a work that deflates the Greek archetypes that lie behind its appeal to the modern imperial imagination. This book has raised further questions about the status of Xenophon's narrative by exploring the conflicting accounts of key scenes in Doniphan's expedition. As the first surviving war memoir and the only proper source for the Greek march, the *Anabasis* has had the allure of innovation and authenticity. Its air of simplicity and its apparent timelessness have made it an all too perfect fit for the march it describes – which has itself often been removed from its place in Greco-Persian relations and made to stand as an isolated anticipation of Alexander's conquests two generations later. In the course of this book, we have focused on some important scenes that have generally been extracted as illustrations of timeless truths about the Hellenic spirit, and read them instead as part of an artful and developing narrative. The *Anabasis* should not be cast as a pure 'original' – not least because of Xenophon's own circumstances at the time he wrote it. His participation in Cyrus' expedition and the subsequent retreat proved highly controversial: the *Anabasis* itself hints at his later exile from Athens (caused by his dealings either with Cyrus or with the Spartans); it includes scenes where Xenophon openly defends himself against attacks on his leadership; and a strong element of self-defence has often been detected in other sections. The issues raised by Xenophon's self-presentation were so delicate that he seems to have concealed his authorship by a pseudonym. The very tendentiousness of the *Anabasis* is not the least part of its interest – and yet its contours have frequently been flattened out in American reworkings.

By its critical focus both on Xenophon's own writings and on their use in the US, this book has aimed to offer insights into an often neglected aspect of American imperialism – the increasingly militaristic use of antiquity from the time of the Mexican War, with more emphasis now put on classical military rather than civic virtue and with an increasing focus on Greece rather than Rome. It should be stressed, however, that the critique that has been offered of this highly partial and selective appropriation of Greek militarism has not sought merely to recast the myth of

American exceptionalism. The United States has not been alone in drawing on Xenophon's symbolic capital – and we have in fact had glimpses of his nationalistic exploitation in other countries (the Czech Anabasis through Siberia, the anabasis of German revival after the First World War). It would also be interesting to compare how the *Anabasis* was read during the expansion of the other great nineteenth-century land empire, Russia (Tolstoy confessed that it made a great impression on him). It remains true, nonetheless, that the United States has always had a distinctively strong investment in Greece and Rome. Certainly no other country has been as prolific in giving towns and people classical names: there were even quite a number of Xenophons born in nineteenth-century America, one of whom became a Senator, another a Federal Judge. And the more general American identification with antiquity has been helped by three factors in particular: the nation's status as a republic, its lack of an established church, and its self-conscious newness, often asserted precisely by reference to the ancient models that it hoped to assimilate and transcend (even the Great Seal hailing a 'novus ordo seclorum' evokes the golden age vision of Virgil's fourth *Eclogue*).[7]

Our restricted focus on anabasis as an emblem of American expansion may also seem to blur synchronic and diachronic differences. Grand monolithic definitions of American ideology have rightly gone out of fashion: America, after all, is too immense and diverse to be summed up by any single word – even 'America'. The danger of oversimplification is particularly great because the idea of anabasis panders to the popular vision of American history as a movement from east to west: a periodical writer in 1890, for instance, spoke of the 'great migration westward over the Blue Ridge' as 'that romantic *anabasis* which has ... added to our biography such names as Clay, Benton, Jackson, Taylor, Houston, Lincoln'. Yet the notion of a linear progress across the American continent is itself a mythic conception of space, fostered by the vision of the frontier developed by Theodore Roosevelt and Frederick Jackson Turner – a vision of the West as a nursing-ground for rugged individualism. Historians now tend to focus on the economic interests that were served by the myth of the frontier: the rhetoric of unity and egalitarianism implicit in allusions to the *Anabasis* and in the broader ideology of the frontier glossed over class divisions and the specific networks of profit involved in America's westward expansion. Historians also prefer now to see the American continent as a 'middle ground', a site of both conflict and interaction between different ethnic groups, rather than as a wilderness that was slowly filled from east to west. And they also pay attention to movement by water as well as by land: in Felipe Fernández-Armesto's telling phrase, they regard American culture as 'produced by odyssey as well as anabasis'.[8]

If a rich vision of history has nonetheless emerged from our American anabasis, then that is testimony to the complexity that the idea of anabasis has been made to carry. Though seemingly repetitive and predictable, allusions to Xenophon could still be contested – and never more so than during the Civil War, when very different visions of Xenophon were applied to Sherman's march in the northern and southern states as well as by observers across the Atlantic. In the final decades of the nineteenth century the racial hierarchy implicit in the notion of anabasis also began to be upset when Chief Joseph was hailed as a new Xenophon for leading the Nez Percés in a doomed attempt to avoid being confined in a reservation. This process continued when the anabasis label was attached in retrospect to a long Indian march undertaken in 1878 – this time, an equally doomed attempt by the northern Cheyennes to return from a reservation to their original homeland. While some officers made the comparison with Xenophon in private journals at the time, it only became prominent in the twentieth century. A historian of the West claimed in 1915 that 'men who were stationed on the plains forty years ago are likely to tell you … that there never was such another journey since the Greeks marched to the sea'. And in time this way of commemorating the Cheyennes became part of a strong critique of the ethos of white expansion rather than a nostalgic celebration of faded Indian glory: particularly influential was Mari Sandoz' 1953 novel *Cheyenne Autumn* (later filmed by John Ford), which was widely promoted with a quotation from the western novelist and poet Struthers Burt – 'the march of Xenophon and his Ten Thousand was nothing compared with it'.[9]

More complex readings of the American past have also led to an inversion of the anabasis paradigm. 'The Katabasis' – the Greek word for a march downcountry – appears as one of the section headings in Cormac McCarthy's bleak 1985 novel *Blood Meridian*, widely considered one of the masterpieces of twentieth-century American fiction. The section describes part of the journey of the novel's central characters – a violent group of filibusters and scalp-hunters in the South-West and Mexico soon after Doniphan's conquests. By labelling part of their journey a 'katabasis', McCarthy overturns the myth of the conquest of the West as an 'anabasis' while also gesturing to the epic pattern of katabasis as descent to the land of the dead.[10]

Paradoxically the work that has most strongly disrupted the conventional image of the *Anabasis* is also now 'the Ten Thousand's best-known legacy': Walter Hill's cult classic *The Warriors* (1979), a reworking of Xenophon's story in which a New York gang battles its way back from the Bronx to Coney Island after being falsely accused of murdering a gang leader, Cyrus. Controversial at its release for its supposed promotion of violence, the film has grown in stature over the years: a video game based on the film was released in 2005, and a remake by Tony Scott is promised, continuing the westward course of Xenophon's story by shifting the action to Los Angeles. The popularity of Hill's film stems partly from its garishly coloured, almost comic-book, vision of New York – an appropriate setting for its deliberately unrealistic portrayal of gang violence (allusions to Xenophon are bolstered by Odyssean echoes). And by transferring the story to adolescent American gangs it also invites a striking re-evaluation of the praise generally bestowed on Xenophon's Greek soldiers – making us ask, as the reviewer Patrick French wrote, whether they are 'superior to any New York street gang, save in the way their deeds are commemorated'. 'I'd like to see [Hill] tackle a Western', French added – and yet in a sense *The Warriors* is already a western, moving the frontier to the city and muddling the conventional roles: the eponymous gang plays on the traditions of savage warfare by having a 'warchief' and Indian regalia and by bestowing an Indian name on one member. In this way Hill's film, while in some ways closer to Xenophon's original than the 1965 novel by Sol Yurick on which it is based, does justice to the novel's epigraph – a speech where Xenophon urges his troops into battle against yet another tribe blocking their path by telling them that they must 'find a way to eat them alive'.[11]

The Warriors owes much of its power to the fact that it preserves the ambiguity of Xenophon's vision in the *Anabasis*. Xenophon, like Walter Hill, has been accused of promoting violence – in Xenophon's case, Alexander the Great's march of destruction to Persia and beyond. That accusation is based on a very superficial reading of the *Anabasis* – and yet, as we have seen, Xenophon's memoir maintains an unresolved tension between commemorating heroism and reporting brutality. *The Warriors* also preserves the ambiguity of Xenophon's ending. The film leaves the gang members on a Coney Island beach, vindicated and respected, yet disillusioned by the place they have battled to regain. Similarly Xenophon undermines any simple sense of heroic escape or homecoming. He ends with his warriors starting on a new cycle of violence as they enlist for the Spartans. He hints too at the cloud of double exile under which he wrote the work – cast out from both his native Athens and the delightful estate at Scillus where he had settled on his return to Greece, passing the time hunting in the meadows and wooded glens nearby. And he complicates the idea of anabasis even further by the tragic structure he imposes on his work, with the soldiers' shift from unity to disunity echoing the shape of Greek history after the Persian Wars and undoing still more the heroic deeds of the greatest generation. He wrote an *Anabasis* that is not simply fit to stand comparison with a gang's violent journey back to Coney Island, but can also become a metaphor for the advances and retreats of human history – for the trajectory of mid-nineteenth-century America as the country's vast westward expansion led inexorably to civil war.[12]

*

In the original novel of *The Warriors* Sol Yurick archly alludes to the source from which the work was drawn by having the youngest gang-member read through a comic several times in the course of the night – looking at one point at a panel 'where the Greek warrior, muscled and big-chested, was putting the spear point to the enemy's gut', and fantasizing himself about 'putting the spear point to the enemy cops'. The identity of the Greek warriors, 'the hardest men in a hard world', is never revealed openly, but readers can easily recognize that they are Xenophon's Ten Thousand – a distant emblem of longing for the young man, yet in other ways all too close to his own world.[13]

Yurick's inclusion of a comic version of the *Anabasis* also suggests a more general point about Xenophon's hold on the American imagination. Throughout this book, we have seen that the *Anabasis* has often been received second- or third-hand. There has rarely been direct contact with Xenophon's original – except when children have plodded wearily through it at school. And yet the *Anabasis*' former status in school and college curricula has also made it a marker of both class (the elite that read it in the original) and time (the era when 'every schoolboy' supposedly knew its story). That lost world of the classroom is implicitly recalled by Yurick's comic *Anabasis*: the picture-panels that the young gang-member follows articulate a discontinuity in Xenophon's American reception.

That distant world in which Xenophon was a material presence in the classroom is made fully present in a 1921 poem by John Elliot Bowman entitled 'Anabasis'. Published in *The Youth's Companion*, an old Boston-based family paper, with a frame displaying Greek hoplites and American troops on the march, the poem is similar to many recent accounts of the Iraq War in its promotion of a continuity between ancient and modern military values. Where it differs is that it grounds that continuity in a further link between the soldiers' experiences in the trenches of France and their study of Greek in the schoolrooms they had so recently left. After an initial narrative of the Greek expedition down to the shout of 'The Sea! The Sea!', the poem breaks off to reflect on the form in which the Greeks' exploits survive: 'March, bivouac, battle, all to fill the page / Wherein the schoolboy learns from age to age, / The speech of Hellas! This and nothing more?' It then turns to the readers themselves – the 'lads' who 'laid down the long familiar book / That tells of the Ten Thousand's strife and toil' and:

> Have made the Great Adventure, lived again
> The life of the Ten Thousand in the trench.
> Facing Cocytus vapors and the wrench
> Of deadly shell fire; and I see in them
> That earlier host incarnate, multiplied.
> The lads who at their task read Xenophon
> Have breathed through death new life into his words.

No attempt is made to separate soldiers who had read Xenophon in Greek from the far greater numbers who had not. Blood for the ghosts, every soldier dying in the trenches here reaffirms the status of the Ten Thousand as timeless symbols of heroism. And the modern troops come to share in that timelessness in the short final stanza: 'They wrought, they strove, / They sail a sunlit sea.' The closing image strengthens the religious language of 'that earlier host incarnate': after their katabasis amidst the 'Cocytus vapors' of the trenches, the soldiers have made their ascent to a bright world of heavenly calm – and revivified by their sacrifice the most famous words from a 'long familiar book'.[14]

While Bowman's poem presents antiquity and modernity in equilibrium, with the deaths of soldiers in the First World War giving new life to the values expressed in a dead language, more recent writers have recreated nineteenth-century readings of the *Anabasis* as a way of suggesting the same chronological rupture that is intimated in *The Warriors*. As we noted in Chapter 1, Anne Nelson in her 2006 play *Savages* places a copy of the *Anabasis* in the pocket of a general court-martialled for ordering atrocities during the American occupation of the Philippines. As he reads from that copy, Xenophon's story is made to stand for an ideal of heroic conduct that has been perverted by American war-crimes. And while in one way Xenophon's text is used to hint at similarities between American behaviour in the Philippines and Iraq, the power of Nelson's fictional reading also comes from the setting of the play in a past era that is being stripped of its reassuring myths. While Yurick's novel presents a contemporary world where the *Anabasis* is read as a comic, Nelson's play lightly evokes a distant time when American officers could still be expected to read ancient history in the original – rather than encountering it in novels (*Gates of Fire*) or children's books (*The Exploits of Xenophon*), or dismissing it altogether, like Anthony Swofford's corporal on Okinawa.[15]

A lost era of Xenophon-reading is also portrayed in Michael Straight's *Carrington* (1960), a well-received historical novel set in the American West immediately after the Civil War. Here the real-life American officer who is made to read Xenophon is the eponymous hero, Colonel Henry B. Carrington, a Yale-educated former abolitionist who is now in command of an army fort – and doing his best to calm tensions between his troops and the local Indians. Owner of a leather-bound edition of the *Anabasis* bought in Germany, Carrington sees himself in its hero – 'Xenophon, born a gentleman, who came late to the Army as I did; who triumphed where the professionals failed'. His adjutant sees through Carrington's self-image – recognizing that he is more like Xenophon's friend Proxenus, a general 'more afraid of being disliked by his men than his men were of disobeying him'. As the adjutant leaves, he 'looked out and saw in the ghostly rows of tents the camp of the Greek army huddled on the windy plains of Tarsus, surrounded by the barbarian hordes, and far from home'. And those hordes triumph when an impetuous subordinate disobeys his vacillating commander and leads over eighty soldiers into a deadly ambush – setting in motion the violent pattern of Plains warfare for the next generation. Xenophon's story functions in *Carrington* as part of the novel's reflections on the myths surrounding the history of the American West – but it has meaning only for the commander and his equally educated adjutant (a German immigrant). By making the *Anabasis* in part a symbol of an elite, the novel fails to do justice to its extraordinarily wide dispersal during the actual conquest of the American West. At the same time, however, it points to the genuine class-divisions that were concealed by the universal application of classical paradigms in contemporary American newspapers.[16]

Allusions to Xenophon again dramatize a class-gap between a leader and his subordinates in *Comanche Moon* (1997), the final part of Larry McMurtry's *Lonesome Dove* tetralogy. Set in the 1850s, the novel depicts a group of Texas Rangers pursuing a Comanche horse thief and a Mexican bandit. The band's captain, Inish Scull, is a Harvard-educated New Englander who has achieved distinction in the Mexican War. He has a passion for military history but a preference for making history rather than teaching it – and he is ambitious to achieve further glory as a path to high command in the coming Civil War. Scull imposes his authority on his band by mapping their experiences in terms of the classical past: a hill becomes Hannibal's Alps, and though the band itself is only twelve men, he confesses that 'when I read Xenophon I can imagine that we're ten thousand'. He even reads out some of the *Anabasis* in Greek to his men, impressing an Indian scout by the way he follows 'an even harder and more elusive track' – 'the tiny, intricate track that ran across the pages of a book'. And while one of his subordinates does not like hearing the Greek, he 'can still wonder about that war' – about how many fought on the side that won. Scull's use of the classics as an exercise in power is later given a twist when he is captured by the sadistic bandit and suspended in a cage – from which he carves thirteen Homeric hexameters in Greek on the cliff face, 'words hard and clear, to remind him that brave men had battled before', winning for himself 'a victory, of sorts'. As in *Carrington*, the portrayal of an officer addicted to antiquity suggests that the traditional classical curriculum reinforced class-divisions as well as providing positive role-models. Xenophon is again used as a figure of nostalgia – as if the contribution of classical paradigms to the forging of the myths of the American West sprang from a pure contact with the text itself, the twisting Greek letters that dazzle the Indian scout, the lines of Homer scratched on a cliff-face in Mexico.[17]

The image of a single elite officer with his copy of Xenophon may seem an attractive way to evoke a distant era of incipient Anglo-Saxon domination over the American West, but it does not capture the technological transformations through which the *Anabasis* was actually exploited during the nineteenth century. It was American investment in the transport and communications revolutions in the first half of the century that made it possible for Xenophon to become part of a cult of military celebrity. The image of reception that has emerged from this book is not the solitary captain, educated at Harvard or Yale and now surrounded by savages in the West and clinging to his copy of Xenophon as a token of East Coast civility. It is, rather, the scene in St Louis in July 1847 as a vast crowd gathers to hear Thomas Hart Benton mention the Ten Thousand in his hour-long

29. Richard Caton Woodville, *War News from Mexico* (1848).

speech welcoming the Missouri volunteers home; or again, it is the scene depicted in Richard Caton Woodville's 1848 painting *War News from Mexico* (Fig. 29, also a popular engraving) – the porch of a post office emblazoned with the American eagle and thronged with white men listening eagerly to a figure in the centre reading from a newspaper. It was in public contexts such as these that allusions to Xenophon were used to unify the diverse American public in the belief that the contemporary achievements of their nation were equal or superior to the greatest deeds of antiquity.[18]

The public language of heroism promoted in orations and newspaper articles could easily clash with the private experience of war. When a

221

young Union staff officer in the 57th New York reflected early in the Civil War on a 'terribly long night' battling through a swamp, he 'thought of Zenophon and his nine hundred and all the other notable retreats I could think of, and wondered whether they were any better soldiers than we, or capable of making greater efforts'. The private diary offers a glimpse of the dark underside to the public cult of celebration: far from being easily surpassed by trite boasts, the heroic endeavours of antiquity seem remote and almost other-worldly, posing painful questions to the writer as he endures the toils of a gruelling campaign. The officer's musings are perhaps the more poignant for his glaring error about the number of Xenophon's troops. But that error may make this officer a more typical figure than the fictional captain lovingly preserving his leather-bound *Anabasis* as the Sioux run wild on the plains.[19]

If our experience of the *Anabasis* is necessarily mediated through the memory of its physical presence in the schoolroom, this very second-handedness can itself be put to aesthetic advantage. The process of reflecting on the journey that the *Anabasis* itself has undertaken is implicit in some of the American poems that have adopted Xenophon's title or alluded to his texts in other ways ('the nostalgic sea / sopped with our cries / Thalassa! Thalassa!'). But it has been captured most remarkably in a series of drawings by an American artist famous for his use of writing – Cy Twombly. Born in 1928, Twombly migrated to Italy in 1959, and it is largely in Rome and its surroundings that he produced in the ensuing decades the work that has established him as one of the most prominent contemporary artists. That work has included deceptively simple white sculptures, drawings on paper, and many large canvases. Varying over the years in their use of colour and texture, the paintings have typically been covered with recurring scrawls as well as with isolated words and sentences – many of them inspired by the classical world ('Achilles', 'Apollo', 'Aphrodite Anadyomene') and inviting reflection on the aesthetics and politics of transmission inherent in all modern appropriations of antiquity. Love it or loathe it, Twombly's oeuvre will form a fitting end to this book.[20]

*

The critic I dream of, the critic who takes on the task of restoring and recreating ... that critic is himself a poet, or he risks being nothing at all. He 'imagines' himself no less than the poet, since he must restore to the work its entire careening, that is, the whole world that supports it; nor can he avoid personal revelation, since he, too, 'investigates' from within. It is in that way, it seems to me, by the use of interrelating and by a play of analogies, that criticism can accomplish a unique service and cease to be parasitism, becoming instead an itinerant apprenticeship – an 'anabasis', if you will, or return to the sea, to that all-embracing sea whence the work was drawn (in its definitive, and perhaps cruel, singularity).

Saint-John Perse, *Letters* (1910)[21]

Cy Twombly's Anabasis began in 1980 with a sculpture and continued over the next three years with a series of drawings on paper. The *Anabasis* sculpture is a slightly off-white box supporting what slowly reveals itself as a thin wedge – 'a chariot on gummed-up castors whose two rising sides, made of plywood trapezoids, meet at an acute angle'. The *Anabasis* series on paper was first exhibited in 1984 – fifteen works (all 100 cm high and 70 cm wide) with 'Anabasis' the most prominent of a number of repeating motifs. The drawings on paper link with the earlier sculpture by featuring chariots, either shown as simple bodies with loosely drawn wheels or else represented by wheels alone. These chariots and wheels have cryptic phrases inscribed above them: 'SYLVAE' in the first three pieces, for instance, and 'VIRGILIAN VIEWS' in the first two, with 'anabasias' (*sic*) scrawled above 'VIRGILIAN' in the first two and above 'SYLVAE' in the third. As the series progresses, Xenophon takes over from Virgil: in one drawing (Fig. 30), 'ANABASIS' is written in red at the top of the sheet (in another it is misspelt 'ANBASIS'), with the As formed as triangular Greek deltas; below this heading 'XENOPHON' is faintly visible, and below this the artist's initials ('C T') and a date ('NOV 20 83') are roughly scribbled. The space below the words in this, the most commonly shown drawing in the *Anabasis* series, is dominated by a large spoked wheel which is itself covered with squiggles – dark brown lines running strongly across as well as paler concentric circles – and partly occluded at top and bottom by bold red smudges that dash out to the right. The series continues with two drawings inscribed '*NIKE Androgyne*' and then with a number of blurred circles of paint with some new motifs ('LYCIAN', 'FORMIAN dreams & actuality', 'PROEM') as well as faint traces of the older Virgilian and Xenophontic ones.[22]

Twombly's technique of scribbling words such as 'Anabasis' has divided critics. While all agree that Twombly's images challenge conventional expectations of visual and narrative coherence, some condemn his 'pretentious (and tiresome) name-dropping'. Other critics see the words as 'the allusive signs of a vast, branching culture suddenly condensed on the surface of a canvas in a heap of broken images'. Many have been enraptured by the mysterious way in which Twombly produces lines that seem, in Roland Barthes' terms, 'extremely elegant', yet also 'childlike' and 'inimitable': one critic even reports in detail on an unsuccessful attempt to imitate the 'Anabasis' drawing. Twombly's work has invited grand totalizing claims ('the essence of the work is the traced process of its own making') while also challenging the very idea that it has an essence.[23]

Some critics have responded to the challenge of the *Anabasis* series by suggesting that the artist had a psychological investment in Xenophon's story. Given at birth his father's name – Edwin Parker Twombly – he also took on his father's nickname, Cy – after the baseball player Cy(clone) Young. When he became a father himself he gave his son the forenames Cyrus Alessandro. And he also produced works with titles such as *Cyclops*

30. Cy Twombly, *Anabasis* (1983).

and *Cycnus* – word games that 'incessantly inscribe the artist's name on his works'. The *Anabasis* drawings have been seen as part of the same game: they evoke the expedition of Cyrus the Younger, namesake of the baseball legend who gave Twombly and his father their nicknames, and the red slashes jutting from the wheel also help the verbal play if they can be interpreted as scythes. However convincing, this type of bio- graphical explanation is at least fitting for a drawing whose source text, written after Xenophon was forced to leave the Virgilian views of his sylvan estate at Scillus, involved similar games with names (or at least a pseudonym).[24]

One issue that is central to Twombly's engagement with the classical past is the process of survival and transmission. His art continually explores his role as an American artist living in Italy at a time when military and artistic power has passed to the United States. In the *Anabasis* series, reflection on Twombly's status is implicit in the word 'Roma' (presumably marking the artist's location) and in the phrases 'Virgilian views' (evoking the author of the *Aeneid*, the dominant expres- sion of the idea of a shift of power from east to west) and 'Formian dreams' (evoking the site of one of Cicero's villas, close to another of Twombly's workplaces). Similar reflections are also suggested by the repetition of 'Sylvae': while this word may allude to the pastoral views found in another of Virgil's works, the *Eclogues*, it has also been used as a term for poetry anthologies – notably John Dryden's *Sylvae*, a collection of translations from Latin poetry (mainly from Lucretius, Virgil, and Horace) whose preface is one of Dryden's most important statements on the practice of translation. The *Anabasis* drawings take this self-reflexivity further by shifting the focus further east – to another of Twombly's obsessions: the great narratives of conflict between Europe and Asia. Twombly has at various times exploited the Trojan War (the ten large panels depicting *Fifty Days at Iliam*), the Persian Wars (the *Thermopylae* sculpture), the *Age of Alexander* (a large canvas painted soon after the birth of Cyrus Alessandro), and the wars against the Turks (the *Lepanto* series). He has also exploited literary accounts of the Hellespont (the *Hero and Leandro* paintings, alluding to poems by Marlowe and Keats) and of Asia Minor (*Say Goodbye, Catullus, to the Shores of Asia Minor*) – and in interviews he has confessed that these titles are tinged with romanticism: 'The sound of "Asia Minor" is really like a rush to me, like a fantastic ideal.' The same self-aware romanticism appears in Twombly's use of 'Anabasis': as scrawled by Twombly, that word seems to evoke and question the long history of western desire for the orient.[25]

Twombly does not shrink from suggestions of the violence that has marked the conflict between East and West. The chariot wheel stands for battle, and the two reddish smears dashing diagonally out from it are like splashes of blood as well as scythes – the corporeality enhanced by Twombly's technique of squeezing paint directly from the tube and rubbing it with a finger. There is also a hint of violence in the red inscription 'Anabasis': for Twombly, the letter A has a 'phallic aggression' (he even named his Trojan cycle *Fifty Days at Iliam* rather than *Ilium* because he wanted 'the A for Achilles'). If Twombly's *Anabasis* condenses Xenophon, then it is a reduction that emphasizes the masculine aggression of battle. And yet the series as a whole moves beyond the violence of the main *Anabasis* works to a more fluid conclusion that embraces *Nike Androgyne* – 'the victory of sexual wholeness at the end of a journey upcountry'.[26]

Twombly's *Anabasis* plays on the strange power of a single Greek word – the word that haunted Saint-John Perse. That word's complex resonance is further suggested by Perse's self-confessed longing to lead 'an "undertaking" the way an *Anabasis* is conducted by its leaders' – and in responses to the *Anabasis* that he did undertake: T.S. Eliot initially wanted to print his translation of Perse with the title written in capital Greek letters – as if to root the poem even more strongly in the soil of ancient Hellas. The power of anabasis, as this book has shown, is equally evident in its hold on the military imagination. Something of the longing that made Eliot want to Hellenize Perse's title fully is paralleled in a letter to the *Washington Post* by the official Marines historian Lynn Montross. Responding to an account of the Marines' withdrawal from the Chosin Reservoir, she objected that 'the word "retreat" hardly describes one of the greatest fights Americans have put up against numerical odds' – and closed with a tentative variant: 'Perhaps "anabasis" is the word.' That tentativeness is a stronger expression of the word's power than bravado self-assertion: it signals a self-consciousness about drawing on Xenophon – but an acceptance that the almost mythical register of 'anabasis' may still be inescapable.[27]

Twombly's drawing derives its strength in part from the gap between the letters 'Anabasis' inscribed in red and the range of significations those letters have been made to carry in the centuries since Xenophon wrote of Cyrus' doomed march upcountry. In the American tradition, anabasis has been a highly ambiguous symbol, useful for articulating – or disrupting – the sometimes violent march of American destiny. Within Twombly's drawing that ambiguity is expressed not just by the letter-forms that we read as 'Anabasis' but also by the lines that advance and retreat in a frenzy of whirling and eddying on the page below – the wheel of progress that is traced over by the signs of its own destruction, but that still generates from the creative tension of Twombly's hand-work an explosive orgy of red, a bloody Bacchic smear of raw violence. Twombly invites the viewer to share in the same process as Saint-John Perse's ideal poet-critic. As he creates a new piece of art from the all-embracing sea of history and its images, the violence of his creativity produces a work whose cruel singularity still opens itself to a multiplicity of new readings – to the unceasing anabasis of interpretation. And in this way he pays a peculiarly appropriate homage to Xenophon's 'original' *Anabasis* – a work that in all its elegance, in all its simple and even childlike charm, has also opened itself up to strong misreadings from the age of Alexander to the age of Bush. Passionately engaging with both the ancient and the modern worlds, Twombly draws our American anabasis to a close.[28]

Notes

Full bibliographical references are given when items are first mentioned, and in the Select Bibliography in the case of items mentioned more than once.

Introduction: The Anabasis Project

1. Anabasis project: M. Isikoff and D. Corn, *Hubris: The Inside Story of Spin, Scandal, and the Selling of the Iraq War* (New York, 2006), 3, 6; see pp. 6-9, 153-62, 211-12 n. for more details of the plan, and 440 for their sources; some details (but not the name) are also found in B. Woodward, *Plan of Attack* (New York, 2004). Cf. NATO's Operation Achilles in Afghanistan in 2007.

2. I shall generally use the term 'Indians' in this book because it reflects the usage of the authors I will be discussing and because no other term embracing all the tribes (e.g. 'Native Americans') is free from problems of its own.

3. On Classics in the US, see esp. M. Reinhold, *Classica Americana: The Greek and Roman Heritage in the United States* (Detroit, 1984); C.J. Richard, *The Founders and the Classics: Greece, Rome, and the American Enlightenment* (Cambridge, MA, 1994). More recently there has been a shift of focus: see C. Winterer, *The Culture of Classicism: Ancient Greece and Rome in American Intellectual Life, 1780-1910* (Baltimore, 2002), and *The Mirror of Antiquity: American Women and the Classical Tradition, 1750-1900* (Ithaca, NY, 2007); C.J. Richard, *The Golden Age of the Classics in America: Greece, Rome, and the Antebellum United States* (Cambridge, MA, 2009); M. Malamud, *Ancient Rome and Modern America* (Malden, MA, and Oxford, 2009). Note also (on the South) E. Fox-Genovese and E.D. Genovese, *The Mind of the Master Class: History and Faith in the Southern Slaveholders' Worldview* (Cambridge, 1995), 249-304, with 745-6 on Xenophon.

4. Sunium: H. Taine, *Essai sur Tite-Live* (2nd edn; Paris, 1860; orig. pub. 1854), 322.

5. I should stress that there are more subtle recent treatments: e.g. W.E. Higgins, *Xenophon the Athenian: The Problem of the Individual and the Society of the Polis* (Albany, NY, 1977), 82-98; J. Dillery, *Xenophon and the History of his Times* (London, 1995), 59-98; the essays in R. Lane Fox (ed.), *The Long March: Xenophon and the Ten Thousand* (New Haven, 2004); R. Waterfield, *Xenophon's Retreat: Greece, Persia and the End of the Golden Age* (London, 2006).

1. Dubya Anabasis: Xenophon and the Iraq War

1. F.J. West and R.L. Smith, *The March Up: Taking Baghdad with the 1st Marine Division* (New York, 2003): for reviewers' comments, see www.west-write.com (accessed February 2008); this website also has details on Bing West's other writings (including a 2003 novel with the archetypal plot of marines disobeying orders to rescue a kidnapped colleague in Serbia). Cf. also R.D. Kagan, *Imperial Grunts: The American Military on the Ground* (New York, 2005), 308.

229

2. Quotations from West and Smith, *March Up*, 2-3, 5, 244-5.

3. Grass: West and Smith, *March Up*, 259 n.; email from Bing West dated 26 February 2008; G. Household, *The Exploits of Xenophon* (New York, 1955) – where a faithful paraphrase of Xenophon's speech is offered (p. 50). Hack: G. Household, *Against the Wind* (London, 1958), 232.

4. Hacking: West and Smith, *March Up*, 2.

5. Quotations from West and Smith, *March Up*, 181-2, 232, 244. Rifle as body: cf. E. Scarry, *The Body in Pain: The Making and Unmaking of the World* (New York, 1985), 66-7, on the humanization of weapons; also K. Theweleit, *Male Fantasies*, ii: *Male Bodies: Psychoanalyzing the White Terror*, trans. E. Carter and C. Turner (Minneapolis, 989; Germ. orig. 1978), 179-80, 283, for a psychoanalytical approach, based on the writings of right-wing post-WWI fighters. Fascist aesthetics: S. Sontag, 'Fascinating Fascism', in *Under the Sign of Saturn* (New York, 1991; orig. pub. 1980), 73-105, is a classic.

6. Spartan: West and Smith, *March Up*, 244-5. Cartledge: *The Times* (London), 27 August 2008. American Spartans: J.A. Warren, *American Spartans: The U.S. Marines: A Combat History from Iwo Jima to Iraq* (New York, 2005), 1; D.J. Danelo, *Blood Stripes: The Grunt's View of the War in Iraq* (Mechanicsburg, PA, 2006), esp. pp. iii, iv, 3-4, 12-13, 44, 66-7. Athens: Danelo, *Blood Stripes*, 312 (cf. 313-14); C.M. Mullaney, *The Unforgiving Minute: A Soldier's Education* (New York, 2009), 195, in a chapter entitled 'From Athens to Sparta' (Mullaney is currently an important adviser on Central Asia policy at the US Department of Defense); contrast S.P. Huntingdon, *The Soldier and the State* (Cambridge, MA, 1957), 465, on West Point as 'a bit of Sparta in the midst of Babylon'.

7. Quotations from N.C. Fick, *One Bullet Away: The Making of a Marine Officer* (Boston, 2005), 4, 33. Since June 2009 Fick has been CEO of a Washington think-tank, the Center for a New American Security; he was co-author of an influential paper on Afghan policy.

8. Bible: Danelo, *Blood Stripes*, 13 (this book has a foreword by Pressfield). Heroism: Fick, *One Bullet Away*, 48, citing S. Pressfield, *Gates of Fire: An Epic Novel of the Battle of Thermopylae* (New York, 1998), 112; E.J. Weis, 'Quiet Leadership', in D. Crandall (ed.), *Leadership Lessons from West Point* (San Francisco, 2007), 206-17, at 216; N. Fick, 'Books and Battles', *Washington Post*, 17 July 2005 (confirmed by E. Wright, *Generation Kill: Devil Dogs, Iceman, Captain America, and the New Face of American War* (New York, 2004), 20, a book in which Fick plays a prominent role).

9. Means: S. Jeffords, *The Remasculinization of America: Gender and the Vietnam War* (Bloomington, 1989).

10. Fantasy: S.Žižek, *The Art of the Ridiculous Sublime: On David Lynch's Lost Highway* (Seattle, 2000), 34; cf. similar remarks in Walter Benjamin's 1930 review of *War and Warrior*, a collection of essays edited by Ernst Jünger ('Theories of German Fascism', trans. J. Wikoff, *New German Critique* 17 (1979), 120-8); for suspicions of modern warfare, above all based on the nature of the 1991 Gulf War, see J. Baudrillard, *The Gulf War did not Take Place*, trans. P. Patton (Bloomington, 1995; Fr. orig. 1991); for an analysis of the contrast between the bureaucratic and technological language of war and the perspective offered by soldier narratives, see J.W. Gibson, *The Perfect War: TechnoWar in Vietnam* (Boston, 1986). For the tradition, cf. e.g. M. Cunliffe, *Soldiers and Civilians: The Martial Spirit in America, 1775-1865* (Boston, 1968), 52-3, on the 1815 Battle of New Orleans (hailed as a victory for the backwoodsman, not for artillery technology).

11. Traffic: West and Smith, *March Up*, 254, 253, 244. Odyssey: P.R. Mansoor, *Baghdad at Sunrise: A Brigade Commander's War in Iraq* (New Haven, 2008), 339. Chosin: Warren, *American Spartans*, 168, citing 4.2.25-6; the comparison is also made in an official history, L. Montross and N.A. Canzona, *The Chosin Reservoir Campaign*, p. iii, 333 (vol. iii of *U.S. Marine Operations in Korea, 1950-1953* (5 vols; Washington, DC, 1955-71)), and has been repeated elsewhere (e.g. by Montross herself, review of E. Frankel, *Band of Brothers, Washington Post*, 2 November 1958; B. Alexander, *Korea: The First War We Lost* (New York, 1986), 320 – from a chapter entitled 'The March to the Sea'); cf. already *Time Magazine*, 18 December 1950 (article on 'The Retreat of the 20,000', with Bataan, Anzio, Dunkirk, and Valley Forge thrown in as well as the *Anabasis*).

12. Quotations from West and Smith, *March Up*, 145, 2, 146 (alluding to *Apocalypse Now*), 140; for rivers, cf. Chapter 3 n. 15.

13. Ozymandias: West and Smith, *March Up*, 244. 'Nothing': continuation of the Shelley quotation (also quoted in West and Smith).

14. Geographical links: West and Smith, *March Up*, 2, 248; for the British in WWI, see *The Sea! The Sea!*, 36-41; and cf. 'Conclusion', n. 4, on Kermit Roosevelt. Nimrud: M. Walker (ed.), *The Iraq War as Witnessed by the Correspondents and Photographers of United Press International* (Washington, DC, 2004), 83. Fallujah: M. Tucker, *Among Warriors in Iraq: True Grit, Special Ops, and Raiding in Mosul and Fallujah* (Guilford, CT, 2005), 89. Cf. e.g. R. Atkinson, *In the Company of Soldiers* (New York, 2004), 294-5; T.E. Ricks, *Fiasco: The American Military Adventure in Iraq* (New York, 2006), 12.

15. Decisive battles: P. Cartledge, *Thermopylae: The Battle that Changed the World* (London, 2006), which expressly notes the increased urgency of its theme in light of the 9/11 and 7/7 attacks (though it is also much more nuanced in its portrayal of the Greece/Persia opposition than its subtitle suggests); B. Strauss, *The Battle of Salamis: The Naval Encoutner that Saved Greece – and Western Civilization* (New York, 2004); the subtitle of the British edition of Strauss' book is *The Greatest Battle of the Ancient World, 480 BC*.

16. Dedication: K.W. Krüger, *Xenophon: Kyrou Anabasis* (Halis Saxonum, 1826), p. iii (Robert Parker alerted me to this); cf. *The Sea! The Sea!*, 103-4, on Shelley's *Hellas*. Charles V: see my article 'Panhellenism and Self-Presentation: Xenophon's Speeches', in R. Lane Fox (ed.), *The Long March: Xenophon and the Ten Thousand* (New Haven, 2004), 305-29, at 305. Antony: Plutarch, *Antony* 45.12.

17. Alexander: Eunapius, *Lives of the Sophists* 1.1; Polybius 3.6.9-12. Saviour: W.F. Ainsworth, *Travels in the Track of the Ten Thousand Greeks: Being a Geographical and Descriptive Account of the Expedition of Cyrus and of the Retreat of the Ten Thousand Greeks, as Related by Xenophon* (London, 1844), p. v; cf. F. Arnold, *A History of Greece* (London, 1871), 393. Panhellenism: Isocrates 4.145-9, 5.90-2.

18. Dangerous: V.D. Hanson, 'Iraq's Future – and Ours', *Commentary*, January 2004; reprinted in G. Rosen (ed.), *The Right War? The Conservative Debate on Iraq* (Cambridge and New York, 2005), 7-17, at 9. Hanson is the only author to have two pieces in this collection of essays by leading conservatives.

19. Western supremacy: V.D. Hanson, *The Western Way of War: Infantry Battle in Classical Greece* (2nd edn; Berkeley, Los Angeles and London, 2000; orig. pub. 1989), esp. 9-18; *Carnage and Culture: Landmark Battles in the Rise of Western Power* (2nd edn; New York, 2002; orig. pub. 2001), 24, 443, 456-61. Keegan wrote the preface to *The Western Way of War*; cf. also his *A History of Warfare* (2nd edn; London, 2004; orig. pub. 1993), 73, on Hanson's 'breathtakingly original' thesis.

20. Thugs: Hanson, *Carnage and Culture*, 1, 3.

21. Quotations from Hanson, *Carnage and Culture*, 1, 3, 4.

22. Reviews: F. McLynn, *Independent*, 13 October 2001; Hanson, *Carnage and Culture*, 462. For an academic military historian's critique of the concept of a western way of war, see J. Lynn, *Battle: A History of Combat and Culture* (Boulder, 2003), 12-27; cf. already the criticisms made by reviewers of *The Western Way of War* (E.L. Wheeler, *Journal of Interdisciplinary History* 21 (1990), 122-5; J. Lazenby, *Journal of Hellenic Studies* 112 (1992), 203-4).

23. Review: E. Rothstein, *New York Times*, 1 December 2001.

24. Horses: 3.2.18, 3.8-10, 16. The first passage is one of the parts of the *Anabasis* Emerson most admired: R.W. Emerson, *The Journals and Miscellaneous Notebooks of Ralph Waldo Emerson*, ed. W.H. Gilman et al. (16 vols; Cambridge, MA, 1960-82), v. 246.

25. Orphaned: V.D. Hanson, 'The Fighting over the Fighting', *National Review Online* (http://www.nationalreview.com, accessed March 2008), 17 November 2006.

26. Dubya: R.M. Peabody, 'Dubya Anabasis', in T. Swift (ed.), *100 Poets against the War* (http://www.nthposition.com/100poets0.pdf, accessed 17 February 2008), 37 (reprinted in R.M. Peabody, *Last of the Red Hot Magnetos* (Arlington, VA, 2004), 12); for download details, see the interview with Todd Swift at http://www.poetrykit.org/pkmag/pkmag3/031.htm (accessed 4 March 2008).

27. Schweik: J. Hašek, *The Good Soldier Švejk and his Fortunes in the World War*, trans. C. Parrott (London, 1993; orig. pub. 1973; Czech orig. 1921-3), 258-331; cf. M. Kundera, 'The Czech Wager', *New York Review of Books* 27 (22 January 1981), and, more specifically on the ironic use of 'anabasis', V.H. Brombert, *In Praise of Antiheroes: Figures and Themes in Modern European Literature, 1830-1980* (Chicago, 1999), 72; C. Kiebuzinska, *Intertextual Loops in Modern Drama* (Madison and London, 2001), 155. Anabasis, Hitler: B. Brecht, 'Schweyk in the Second World War', in *Collected Plays*, vii, trans. M. Knight and J. Fabry (New York, 1974), 284, 132; cf. P. Werres, 'The Brecht-Hašek Connection', in J.K. Lyon and H.-P. Breuer (eds), *Brecht Unbound* (Newark, DE, and London, 1995), 211-26, at 216.

28. Walking: S. Brennan, *In the Tracks of the Ten Thousand: A Journey on Foot through Turkey, Syria and Iraq* (London, 2005), 308; T. Macintosh Smith, 'Foreword', in Brennan, *In the Tracks of the Ten Thousand*, pp. ix-x, at p. x. For another Irish work that uses Xenophon in a critique of the Iraq war, see Colin Teevan, *How Many Miles to Basra?* (BBC Radio 3, 2004; revised version staged at West Yorkshire Playhouse, 2006) – a play which Edith Hall kindly drew to my attention, but too late for discussion in this book.

29. Quandary: I. Wilson, 'America's Anabasis', in T.G. Mahnken and T.A. Keaney (eds), *War in Iraq: Planning and Execution* (London and New York, 2007), 9-21, at 9. Postmodern: I. Wilson, *Thinking Beyond War: Civil-Military Relations and Why America Fails to Win the Peace* (New York and Basingstoke, 2007), 68.

30. Retreat: W.S. Lind, 'On War #211: Operation Anabasis', published on the website *Defense and the National Interest* 27 March 2007 (http://www.d-n-i.net/lind/lind_3_29_07.htm); cf. 'Operation Xénophon', codename of the French plan to evacuate Dien Bien Phu in Vietnam in 1954 (H.R. Simpson, *Dien Bien Phu: The Epic Battle America Forgot* (Washington, DC, 1994), 40).

31. Warning: N.D. Kristof, 'Under Bush's Pillow', *New York Times*, 4 February 2007, 'Week in Review', p. 18 (thanks to Martin Margulis for alerting me to this column).

32. Babylon: J.W.I. Lee, *A Greek Army on the March: Soldiers and Survival in*

Xenophon's Anabasis (Cambridge, 2007), p. ix. Film: www.variety.com, 31 July 2008 (accessed August 2008).

33. Other conflicts: e.g. for World War I, O.L. Spaulding and J.W. Wright, *The Second Division American Expeditionary Force in France, 1917-1919* (New York, 1937), 227; 'Conclusion', n. 14. Anabasis: J. Cushman, 'James Webb's New "Fields of Fire"', *New York Times*, 28 February 1988. Pitch: T. Holland, 'Over the Cliff', *Times Literary Supplement* 5334 (24 June 2005), 9. Cf. also D.A. Strickland, *The March Upcountry: Deciding to Bomb Hanoi* (Wilmette, IL, 1973), esp. p. v, 31-2, a tract on the escalation of the Vietnam war; and n. 30 for a French usage in the defeat that led to American involvement in Vietnam. Korea: see n. 11. Burma: *Time Magazine*, 26 February 1945. Cf. also the influence of the *Anabasis* on James Dickey's 1993 novel *To the White Sea*, which focuses on an American soldier in Japan in World War II, and was at one time to be entitled *Thalatta* (I am grateful to Ward Briggs for the reference).

34. Play: A. Nelson, *Savages* (New York, 2007), 28-9, 34, 7.

35. Eaton: A. Johnson, *Jefferson and his Colleagues: A Chronicle of the Virginia Dynasty* (New Haven, 1921), 52-3 ('modern *Anabasis*'); C. Moran, *The Sea of Memories: The Story of Mediterranean Strife, Past and Present* (New York, 1942), 158 ('American'); M. Minnigerode, *Lives and Times: Four Informal American Biographies* (New York and London, 1925), 81 ('blue-eyed'); for classical paradigms applied at the time ('the modern Africanus', 'Spartan band', contrast with desert marches of Alexander and Cambyses), see L.B. Wright and J.H. Macleod, *The First Americans in North Africa: William Eaton's Struggle for a Vigorous Policy Against the Barbary Pirates, 1799-1805* (Princeton, 1945), 188-9.

36. Indian warfare: see e.g. R.M. Drinnon, *Facing West: The Metaphysics of Indian-Hating and Empire Building* (Norman, OK, 1997; orig. pub. 1980), and R. Slotkin's renowned trilogy (*Regeneration through Violence: The Mythology of the American Frontier, 1600-1860* (Middletown, CT, 1973); *The Fatal Environment: The Myth of the Frontier in the Age of Industrialization, 1800-1890* (New York, 1985); *Gunfighter Nation: The Myth of the Frontier in Twentieth-Century America* (New York, 1992)) – though these works have been criticized for too monolithic a view of myth and for blurring some historical differences. 'Indian country': for Vietnam, see e.g. Slotkin, *Gunfighter Nation*, esp. 494-6, 524-5, 546-7; M.J. Bates, *The Wars We Took to Vietnam: Cultural Conflict and Storytelling* (Berkeley, Los Angeles and London, 1996), 9-47; for Iraq, see e.g. S. Faludi, *The Terror Dream: Fear and Fantasy in Post-9/11 America* (New York, 2007), esp. 4-5; A. Carroll, *Medicine Bags and Dog Tags: American Indian Veterans from Colonial Times to the Second Iraq War* (Lincoln, NE, 2008), 198-206. Cheyenne: T.E. Ricks, *The Gamble: General David Petraeus and the American Military Adventure in Iraq, 2006-2008* (New York, 2009), 153-4.

2. Look Homeward: The Idea of America

1. Anabasis: St.-J. Perse, *Anabasis*, trans. T.S. Eliot (London, 1959; orig. edn 1930; Fr. orig. *Anabase* published 1924), 51 ('Un pays-ci n'est point le mien. Que m'a donné le monde que ce mouvement d'herbes? ... / Jusqu'au lieu dit de l'Arbre Sec: / et l'éclair famélique m'assigne ces provinces en Ouest'); W.S. Merwin, *A Mask for Janus* (New Haven, 1952), 8.

2. Frontier: F.J. Turner, *The Frontier in American History* (Tucson, 1986; orig. pub. 1920), 37.

3. La Salle: L.P. Kellogg, 'Wisconsin Anabasis', *Wisconsin Magazine of History*

7 (1924), 322-39. Clark: H.N. Dick, *Clark's Anabasis and The Hymn of Deborah* (Cynthiana, KY, 1944), 1 (with pp. vii-viii for his comments on style and patriotic purpose); cf. already C.W. Alvord, 'Virginia and the West: An Interpretation', *Mississippi Valley Historical Review* 3 (1916), 19-38, at 19, for Clark's march as anabasis. Young: L.M. Beebe and C. Clegg, *The American West: The Pictorial Epic of a Continent* (New York, 1955), 352 (cf. 255, 295, for 'anabasis' of the California Gold Rush and of a Rocky Mountains expedition), also adducing the Lewis/Clark expedition, for which cf. V. Fisher, *Tale of Valor: A Novel of the Lewis and Clark Expedition* (Garden City, NY, 1958), 355 ('"The ocean!" they shouted. "The OCEAN!"': cf. J.G. Taylor (ed.), *The Literature of the American West* (Boston, 1971), 26 – F. Manfred on this novel as reminiscent of the *Anabasis*); also *The Sea! The Sea!*, 23. The same trope in e.g. R. Vaughn, *Then and Now: or, Thirty-six Years in the Rockies* (Minneapolis, 1900), 267 (pioneers' journeys more perilous than Xenophon's); C.M. Harvey, 'The Story of the Santa Fé Trail', *Atlantic Monthly* 104 (1909), 774-85, at 782 (the trader Josiah Gregg as 'the Xenophon of this Anabasis'); J. Lembke, 'The Reports from the River Styx', *The Southern Review* 30 (1994), 596-614, at 604 ('anabasis' of an eighteenth-century surveyor whose journal mirrors Xenophon's repetitive parasang-style).

4. Schoolboy: Kellogg, 'Wisconsin Anabasis', 322.

5. Inauguration: http://www.whitehouse.gov/blog/inaugural-address/ (accessed May 2009). Hercules: Xenophon, *Memorabilia* 2.1.21-33; cf. a New Zealand blogger's discussion (http://bowalleyroad.blogspot.com/2009/01/choice-of-hercules_23.html, accessed May 2009).

6. War-cry: R.J. Hendricks, *Innnnnnng Haaaaaaa! Savage Warfare, Southern Chivalry, Facts Stranger'n Fiction; The War to End the White Race; Soul of Philip Knot with Soul of David* (Salem, OR, 1937); he continued the pioneer theme in *The West Saved America and Democracy* (Salem, OR, 1939), styled as 'a continuation of the trilogy in the anabasis of the westernmost West'. Sioux: J.A. Altsheler, *The Great Sioux Trail* (New York, 1918), 215.

7. Aryan: H.A. Covington, *The March Up Country* (Liberty Bell Publications; Reedy, WV, 1987), p. vii; on Covington, see J. Kaplan, *Encyclopedia of White Power: A Sourcebook on the Radical Racist Right* (Walnut Creek, CA, and Lanham, MA, 2000), 76-90; J.W. Gibson, *Warrior Dreams: Paramilitary Culture in Post-Vietnam America* (New York, 1994), 214-15.

8. *Anabasis*: 3.1.42 (literally 'numbers and strength' rather than 'strength and weapons'; and 'with the help of the gods' is omitted in the 'When ...' clause). Quotations from Covington, *March*, 141-3.

9. Cunaxa: Covington, *March*, 143. Covington also sets himself up as the Xenophon of the march-to-come as he ends by noting that Xenophon wrote the *Anabasis* on his return home – and 'most Greek scholars today translate this as "The March Up Country"'.

10. German anabasis: F. von Notz, *Deutsche Anabasis 1918: Ein Rückzug aus dem bulgarischen Zusammenbruch in Mazedonien* (Berlin, 1921), 63-4 ('Der Ausstieg, der Aufstieg, die Auferstehung!'). Ratzel: M. Bassin, 'Friedrich Ratzel's Travels in the United States: A Study in the Genesis of his Anthropogeography', *History of Geography Newsletter* 4 (1984), 11-22. German East and US West: D. Blackbourn, '"The Garden of our Hearts": Landscape, Nature, and Local Identity in the German East', in id. and J.N. Retallack (eds), *Localism, Landscape, and the Ambiguities of Place: German-Speaking Central Europe, 1860-1930* (Toronto, 2007), 149-64, at 155-7.

11. Reception in Germany: W.W. Pusey, 'The German Vogue of Thomas Wolfe',

Germanic Review 23 (1948), 131-48 (142 for the 'epic' quotation); C.I. Johnston, *Of Time and the Artist* (Columbia, SC, 1996), 58-61, 115-19, 155-8 (59 for Hesse, 60 the 'elemental' quotation, from a party-line critic, A.E. Günther).

12. Orestes: D.H. Lawrence, *Studies in Classic American Literature*, ed. E. Greenspan, L. Vasey, and J. Worthen (Cambridge, 2003; orig. pub. 1923), 43 (with 'Introduction', pp. lix-lxvi, for its American reception and context); S. Stutman (ed.), *My Other Loneliness: Letters of Thomas Wolfe and Aline Bernstein* (Chapel Hill, 1983), 102 (letter of 25 October 1925), and cf. the Orestes section in Wolfe's novel *Of Time and the River*. For the 1920s context, cf. D.R. Shumway, *Creating American Civilization: A Genealogy of American Literature as an Academic Discipline* (Minneapolis, 1994).

13. Quotations from T. Wolfe, *The Autobiographical Outline for Look Homeward, Angel*, ed. L. Conniff and R.S. Kennedy (Baton Rouge, LA, 2004; orig. pub. 1991), 3 (born), 72 (Harvard).

14. Rustling: Wolfe, *Autobiographical Outline*, 6. Dickensian: T. Wolfe, *The Letters of Thomas Wolfe*, ed. E. Nowell (New York, 1956), 113 (letter of 3 September 1926). Picture: Wolfe, *Letters*, 115. Wandering: T. Wolfe, *The Autobiography of an American Novelist*, ed. L. Field (Cambridge, MA, and London, 1983), 28-9. Perkins: A.R. Cotten (ed.), *'Always Yours, Max': Maxwell Perkins Responds to Questions about Thomas Wolfe* (Thomas Wolfe Society, 1997), 1-2.

15. Cow bells: Wolfe, *Autobiographical Outline*, 26; for Wolfe's school Xenophon, see R.S. Kennedy, *The Window of Memory: The Literary Career of Thomas Wolfe* (Chapel Hill, 1962), 33. For reasons that will become clear, I base my discussion on Wolfe's initial typescript, *O Lost*, which was first published in 2000 (T. Wolfe, *O Lost: A Story of Buried Life*, ed. A. and M.J. Bruccoli (Columbia, SC, 2000)); I am indebted to the discussion of the use of Xenophon in *O Lost* by L.K. Kerr, 'Climbing Parnassus: Thomas Wolfe's *O Lost* as Künstlerroman', PhD thesis, University of South Carolina (2002), 34-43, and 'Journey to the Interior: The Influence of Xenophon's *Anabasis* on Thomas Wolfe's *O Lost*', *Thomas Wolfe Review* 31 (2007), 5-10, but the details of our discussions differ in many ways; cf. also R.S. Kennedy, 'Wolfe's *Look Homeward, Angel* as a Novel of Development', in P. Reeves (ed.), *Merrill Studies in Look Homeward, Angel* (Columbus, 1970), 82-90, at 84 (reprinted from *South Atlantic Quarterly* 63 (1964), 218-26), on Xenophon in relation to the theme of development.

16. Senses: Wolfe, *O Lost*, 460-1.

17. Sea: Wolfe, *O Lost*, 565.

18. School: Wolfe, *O Lost*, 247-8.

19. Parasangs: 1.4.1; A. Pretor (ed.), *The Anabasis of Xenophon: Book VII* (Cambridge, 1880), 19. Plumber: Wolfe, *O Lost*, 248.

20. Cyrus: Wolfe, *O Lost*, 248-9. Wolfe had jotted the opening sentence down correctly in his notebook in February 1927: 'Darius and Parysatis had two sons, the older, Artaxerxes, the younger Cyrus' (T. Wolfe, *The Notebooks of Thomas Wolfe*, ed. R.S. Kennedy and P. Reeves (Chapel Hill, 1970), 108); in the published text, 'Cyrus' should perhaps be corrected to 'Darius', but the mistake could be satire against Mr Leonard (Arlyn Bruccoli, email, 5 May 2008). In quoting Longfellow, Wolfe runs together the first and last lines of the first stanza of the poem: 'The shades of night were falling fast, / As through an Alpine village passed / A youth, who bore, 'mid snow and ice, / A banner with the strange device, / Excelsior!' He also (as often) made a slight mistake, changing 'night' to 'eve' (more satire?). For 'from there ...' (*enteuthen exelaunei*), cf. e.g. J. Dos Passos, *Orient Express* (New York, 1930), 149 (Syrian travels, appropriately); Spaulding and Wright, *Second*

Division American Expeditionary Force, 227; A. Young, *The Women and the Crisis: Women of the North in the Civil War* (New York, 1959), 318 – chapter epigraph, in Greek, for Sherman's 1864 campaign, cf. Ch. 8; for school debate, R.L. Perkins, 'Enteuthen Exelaunei', *Journal of Education* 27 (21 June 1888), with title in Greek font, answering W.S. Scarborough, 'Xenophon or Andocides, – Which?', *Journal of Education* 27 (17 May 1888), 311, who objected to the repetition of *Kuros elaunei*.

21. Joyce: Wolfe, *O Lost*, 248-9; *Letters*, 115; *Notebooks*, 112; *Letters*, 586; cf. e.g. *Autobiographical Writings*, 8, 121, for his admiration for Joyce at this time. J. Joyce, *Ulysses* (Paris, 1922), 403 (see further *The Sea! The Sea!*, 162-7, for Joyce's use of Xenophon). For Wolfe and Joyce, see e.g. N.L. Rothman, 'Thomas Wolfe and James Joyce: A Study in Literary Influence', in R. Walser (ed.), *The Enigma of Thomas Wolfe: Biographical and Critical Selections* (Cambridge, MA, 1953), 263-89; J.C.S. Durr, '*Look Homeward, Angel*, Thomas Wolfe's *Ulysses*', *Southern Studies* 24 (1985), 54-68; M.M. Harper, *The Aristocracy of Art in Joyce and Wolfe* (Baton Rouge and London, 1990).

22. On the issue of point of view, see F.C. Watkins, 'Thomas Wolfe's High Sinfulness of Piety', *Modern Fiction Studies* 2 (1956-7), 197-206; M.D. Hawthorne, 'Thomas Wolfe's Use of the Poetic Fragment', *Modern Fiction Studies* 11 (1965), 234-44; J.R. Blackwelder, 'The Dimensions of Literature in *Look Homeward, Angel*', PhD thesis, Emory University, 1968, which includes a useful list of Wolfe's literary allusions.

23. Quotations from Wolfe, *O Lost*, 329, 330-1, 565.

24. Hunger: Wolfe, *O Lost*, 461, 544.

25. Quotations from Wolfe, *O Lost*, 368, 361; 'the life so short ...' is a quotation of the opening line of Chaucer's *Parliament of Fowls*, itself based on a Hippocratic apophthegm.

26. Whistles: D.G. Kehl, 'Writing the Long Desire: The Function of *Sehnsucht* in *The Great Gatsby* and *Look Homeward, Angel*', *Journal of Modern Literature* 24 (2000-1), 309-19, at 317, counts fifteen. Incursion: L. Marx, *The Machine in the Garden: Technology and the Pastoral Ideal in America* (New York, 1964), esp. 13, 15, 17, 344. Quotations from Wolfe, *O Lost*, 346, 613, 564.

27. Trains: Wolfe, *Notebooks*, e.g. 54, 342 ('The train! The train!'), 806-7 (a list of train trips); M. Perkins, 'Thomas Wolfe: A Writer for the People of his Time and Tomorrow', in M.J. Bruccoli (ed.), *The Sons of Maxwell Perkins: Letters of F. Scott Fitzgerald, Ernest Hemingway, Thomas Wolfe, and their Editor* (Columbia, SC, 2004), 339-42, at 339, 341 (originally in *Wings* (the journal of the Literary Guild), October 1939); Cotten, *Always Yours, Max*, 94; H.M. Ledig-Rowohlt, 'Thomas Wolfe in Berlin', in H. Haydn and B. Saunders (eds), *The American Scholar Reader* (New York, 1960), 275-90, at 277, 282 (originally in *The American Scholar* 22 (1953), 185-201).

28. Railroad: Rev. C. Colton, *A Lecture on the Railroad to the Pacific: Delivered August 12, 1850, at the Smithsonian Institute, Washington, at the Request of Numerous Members of Both Houses of Congress* (New York, 1850), 16. Pictures: see in general W.H. Truettner (ed.), *The West as America: Reinterpreting Images of the Frontier, 1820-1920* (Washington, DC, and London, 1991), index s.v. 'railroads' (adding 167-8); note esp. illustrations 109, 114, 122, and 123 (Thomas P. Otter, *On the Road* (1860); Fanny Palmer, *Across the Continent: 'Westward the Course of Empire Takes Its Way'* (1868); John Gast, *American Progress* (1872); Domenico Tojetti, *Progress of America* (1875)), and also 143 (Theodor Kaufmann, *Westward the Star of Empire*, 1867), in which (as in Fig. 3) a train with strong headlights runs straight towards the viewer. 'A Prologue to America': in F.E. Skipp (ed.), *The*

Complete Short Stories of Thomas Wolfe (New York, 1987), 409-19, at 409-10 (orig. pub. in *Vogue*, 1 February 1938); cf. *Notebooks*, 769-70, for an earlier draft.

29. Triumph: Wolfe, *O Lost*, 265-6. Moment: J.P. Bishop, 'The Sorrows of Thomas Wolfe', in *Collected Essays*, ed. E. Wilson (New York, 1948), 131-2 (orig. *Kenyan Review* 1 (1939), 7-17).

30. President: Wolfe, *Notebooks*, 114. King: Wolfe, *Autobiography*, 140 (alluding to Marlowe's *Tamerlane*).

31. Reading: Wolfe, *Notebooks*, 79-80; *Autobiographical Outline*, 18, 6; *O Lost*, 114-15. Cf. S. Holliday, *Thomas Wolfe and the Politics of Modernism* (New York, 2001), 9-24.

32. Ridpath: Wolfe, *O Lost*, 85-6; on Ridpath, see G.M. Pfitzer, *Popular History and the Literary Marketplace, 1840-1920* (Amherst, 2008), 1-5 (on sales techniques), 123-78.

33. Cyrus: J.C. Ridpath, *Cyclopaedia of Universal History: Being an Account of the Principal Events in the Career of the Human Race, from the Beginning of Civilization to the Present Time* (3 vols; Cincinnati, 1885), i. 362.

34. Farm: W. Peirce, 'Classics on the Farm', *The Yale Review* 15 (1925-6), 353-63, at 353-4, 357-8; reprinted in O. Shepard and R. Hillyer, *Essays of Today (1926-1927)* (New York and London, 1928), 210-22.

35. Quotations from Ridpath, *Cyclopaedia*, i. 6, 364, 366, 369.

36. Prologue: Kennedy, *Window of Memory*, 160 n. 11, noting that it was written in a ledger bought in New York after 3 October 1927. Movements: Newell, *Letters*, 129 (from the 'Note for the Publisher's Reader'). The editors of the excellent first published edition of *O Lost* print 'Anabasis' only as heading of a sub-unit, after 'Prologue' (in larger type) and three asterisks (Wolfe, *O Lost*, 5). Wolfe's manuscript in fact makes clear that 'Anabasis' is the heading of the whole opening section: he first wrote 'Part I (Anabasis)' but at some point he crossed out 'Part I' and the parentheses (see *O Lost*, p. xxxviii, for a reproduction of the opening page of the 'Anabasis' section). I am very grateful to Arlyn Bruccoli for confirming that she would now prefer 'Anabasis' to 'Prologue' as section head and for the running heads (email, 4 January 2008).

37. 'Exciting': Cotten, *Always Yours, Max*, 3. Quotations from Wolfe, *O Lost*, 10, 12, 6, 26, 35, 36. Civil War: J.W. Clark, 'The War between the Gants', *Thomas Wolfe Review* 10 (1986), 58-63.

38. Lost: Wolfe, *O Lost*, 5, 565. Flourish: Harper, *Aristocracy of Art*, 89.

39. Quotations from Wolfe, *Notebooks*, 65; *O Lost*, 562, 662.

40. Death: A. Tate, 'The Anabasis', in *Poetry* 40 (1932), 74 (reprinted in *Poems 1922-1947* (New York, 1949), 132-3). Anabasis I and II: Merwin, *Mask for Janus*, 1-4, 5-8 (quotations from 7-8); for discussion, see G. Cambon, *Recent American Poetry* (Minneapolis, 1962), 17-19; E. Brunner, *Poetry as Labor and Privilege: The Writings of W.S. Merwin* (Urbana, 1991), 6-7.

41. Influence: C. Rigolot (ed.), *Lettres atlantiques: Saint-John Perse, T.S. Eliot, Allen Tate, 1926-1970* (Paris, 2006), for Tate; R. Howard, *Alone with America: Essays on the Art of Poetry in the United States since 1950* (New York, 1969), 355, on Merwin. Whitman: A.H. Patterson, *Race, American Literature and Transnational Modernisms* (Cambridge, 2008), 66-7 (with 62-78 for the American context). Mexico: C. Rigolot, *Forged Genealogies: Saint-John Perse's Conversations with Culture* (Chapel Hill, 2001), 65, citing Marcelle Auclair. Conquistador: M. Turnell, 'A New Life Emerging', *New York Times*, 19 April 1953; it is at least certain that Perse directly inspired A. MacLeish, *Conquistador* (Boston and New York, 1932). Tree: Rigolot, *Forged Genealogies*, 81-2. Imperialism: S. Edmunds, *Out of Line:*

History, Psychoanalysis, and Montage in H.D.'s Long Poems (Stanford, 1994), 6. Spiritual: quoted by S. Winspur, *Saint-John Perse and the Imaginary Reader* (Geneva, 1988), 54 n. 54. Frontiers: Perse, *Anabasis*, 51 ('les frontières de l'esprit'); same phrase about a trip to Mongolia in St.-J. Perse, *Letters*, trans. and ed. A.J. Knodel (Princeton, 1979), 358 (letter to mother, 5 June 1920). Navigator: Perse, *Anabasis*, 65 ('Terre arable du songe! Qui parle de bâtir? – J'ai vu la terre distribuée en de vastes espaces et ma pensée n'est point distraite du navigateur'). On the ambiguity of Perse's 'anabasis', see K.R. Srinivasa Iyengar, 'St-John Perse's "Anabase": A Study', *The Aryan Path* 33 (1962), 15-18; J.-P. Richard, *Microlectures* (Paris, 1979), 195-8.

42. Loss of the encyclopedic: M.S. Mills, 'From *O Lost* to *Look Homeward, Angel*: A Generic Shift', *Thomas Wolfe Review* 10 (1986), 64-72.

43. Idea: Wolfe, *Notebooks*, 49. Truth: Bishop, 'Sorrows', 129. Escape, romantic: Wolfe, *Autobiography*, 113, 120. Loathe: Wolfe, *Notebooks*, 919.

44. Berlin: Wolfe, *Notebooks*, 912-13, cf. 905-6. The description of the Olympics is taken from a response (never sent) to a request for Wolfe's position on the Spanish Civil War, and was used (with adjustments) in T. Wolfe, *You Can't Go Home Again* (New York, 1940), 626-7 (a posthumous novel edited by Edward Aswell); it cannot of course be taken as a straightforward account, as the uncritical description of German militarism prepares for Wolfe's about-turn. 'I Have a Thing to Tell You': originally in three instalments in *The New Republic* (March 1937); reprinted in C.H. Holman (ed.), *The Short Novels of Thomas Wolfe* (New York, 1961), 236-78; for Wolfe and Nazism, see B. Kussy, 'The Vitalist Trend and Thomas Wolfe', *Sewanee Review* 50 (1942), 306-24 (reprinted in C.H. Holman (ed.), *The World of Thomas Wolfe* (New York, 1962), 101-11). You can't go home: Wolfe, *Notebooks*, 939; used by Aswell in *You Can't Go Home Again*, 706; cf. also *Notebooks* 904, 910; *Autobiography*, 151.

45. Miles: Wolfe, *Notebooks*, 971, 980.

46. Credo: Wolfe, *You Can't Go Home Again*, 741. 'Gone home': my formulation is indebted to H.J. Muller, *Thomas Wolfe* (Norfolk, CT, 1947), 11. Magnificence: Wolfe, *Notebooks*, 981.

3. The American Xenophon: Doniphan in Mexico

1. Quotations from J. Hughes, *Doniphan's Expedition and the Conquest of New Mexico and California*, ed. W.E. Connelley (Kansas City, 1907; orig. pub. 1847), 154; F. Edwards, *A Campaign in New Mexico with Colonel Doniphan* (Albuquerque, 1996; orig. pub. 1847), 76.

2. Poffenburgh: W. Irving, *A History of New York*, ed. M.L. Black and N.B. Black (Boston, 1984; orig. pub. 1848; 1st edn 1809), 196.

3. Adams: R.J. Taylor (ed.), *The Papers of John Adams: Volume I* (Cambridge, MA, 1977), 77 (letter of 29 August 1763). Hercules: Richard, *Founders*, 49. Whig: J. McLachlan, 'The *Choice of Hercules*: American Student Societies in the Early Nineteenth Century', in L. Stone (ed.), *The University in Society* (2 vols; Princeton, 1974), ii. 449-94. Arnold: T.A. Desjardin, *Through a Howling Wilderness: Benedict Arnold's March to Quebec, 1775* (New York, 2006), 189 (letters from Thomas Jefferson and James Warren); also P.H. Smith (ed.), *Letters of Delegates to Congress* (26 vols; Washington, DC, 1976-2000), ii. 519 (letter of Samuel Ward: 'Some say it equals Xenophons') – these letters were all written when it was still thought that Arnold could capture Quebec; *An Impartial History of the War in America, between Great Britain and the United States* (3 vols; Boston, 1781-4), i.

400. Delaware: G. Chalmers, *Life of Thomas Pain* (London, 1791), 15; cf. C.E. Lester, *Lester's History of the United States* (New York, 1883), 304 (also in the introduction, n.p.). Yorktown: J.B. Romeyn, *A Funeral Oration, in Remembrance of George Washington: Delivered At Rhinebeck Flats, February 22* (Poughkeepsie, NY, 1800), 5 ('like another Xenophon'); J.G. Brainard, *An Oration, Commemorative of the Virtues and Services of General George Washington, Spoken in the Presbyterian Church in the City of New-London, February 22d, 1800* (New London, CT, 1800), 9-10 (better than Xenophon and Hannibal). Cf. also R.W. Emerson, *The Early Lectures of Ralph Waldo Emerson*, ed. S.E. Whicher and R.E. Spiller (3 vols; Cambridge, MA, 1959-72), iii. 231 (on reading 'Washington's Campaigns or Xenophon's'); and a character's comic reference to 'George Washington Xenophon, beloved wife of Alexander the Great' (C.A. Washburn, *Gomery of Montgomery: A Family History* (2 vols; New York, 1865), i. 93-4).

4. Cooper: J.F. Cooper, *Wyandotté, or The Hutted Knoll* (London, 1856; orig. pub. 1843), 143, 224; *The Pathfinder*, in *The Leatherstocking Tales*, ii (Library of America; New York, 1985; orig. pub. 1840), 331; *Satanstoe, or The Littlepage Manuscripts* (New York, 1867; orig. pub. 1845), 281; cf. similar inflated uses in *New-Hampshire Statesman and Concord Register,* 5 January 1828 (retreat from shop); *Indiana Journal* (Indianapolis), 29 June 1839 (retreat from gambling den); 'J.B.', *Wolfsden* (Boston, 1856), 471 (flight from a 'palace of seduction'); and in Irving's vein, a humiliating retreat (in trains) by 800 Fenians after an attempt to invade Canada headlined as 'The New Anabasis: Great Retreat of the Modern Ten Thousand' (*New York Times,* 11 June 1866), or German colonists in Colorado 'riding in Federal ambulances and eating Government rations' compared with the Ten Thousand (*Colorado Chieftain,* 10 March 1870, quoted in J.F. Willard (ed.), *Experiments in Colorado Colonization, 1869-1872* (Boulder, 1926), 77: 'Where then shall we find a Xenophon to write the Anabasis ...'). On the significance of American captivity narratives, see e.g. Slotkin, *Regeneration through Violence* (with 484-508 on Cooper); E.J. Sundquist, 'The Literature of Expansion and Race', in S. Bercovitch (ed.), *The Cambridge History of American Literature*, ii: *1825-1865* (Cambridge, 1995), 125-328, at 218-26; and for a more global perspective, L. Colley, *Captives: Britain, Empire and the World, 1600-1850* (London, 2002), 137-238.

5. Syllabus: see e.g. *Catalogue of the Officers and Students of Bowdoin College, Maine* (Brunswick, ME, 1834), 10 (ctr. 1832 edn, 20, for use of *Graeca Majora*); *Harvard University Catalog* 1833 and 1834 for shift from *Graeca Minora*; cf. Winterer, *Culture of Classicism*, 32-3, 189 n. 97, for the decline of *Graeca Majora*. Moral: C.C. Felton, *A Greek Reader, for the Use of Schools* (Hartford, CT, 1840), p. vi. School editions were published by e.g. C.D. Cleveland (1830), J.J. Owen (1843), A. Crosby (1844), C. Anthon (1847), J.R. Boise (1860) – also prose composition book adapted to *Anabasis* (1850), A.C. Kendrick (1873); I give the earliest dates known to me – there were often many editions; see also A. Rijksbaron, 'The Xenophon Factory: One Hundred and Fifty Years of School Editions of Xenophon's *Anabasis*', in R.K. Gibson and C.S. Kraus (eds), *The Classical Commentary: Histories, Practices, Theory* (Leiden, Boston and Köln, 2002), 235-67 – but the data for American editions is very incomplete. 4+3: e.g. A. Zimmern, *Methods of Education in the United States* (London and New York, 1894), 171 (on Yale); *New York Times,* 16 September 1895, p. 10 (Union College); C. Pharr, *Homeric Greek: A Book for Beginners* (Boston, 1925), p. xxxiii. College attendance: Winterer, *Culture of Classicism*, 44. Memorable: E. Willard, *A System of Universal History, in Perspec-*

tive (Hartford, CT, 1835), 54. Greatest: D.J. Jordan, 'Xenophon', *African Methodist Episcopal Church Review* 9 (1892), 167-9, at 169.

6. Reading: Emerson, *Journals*, v. 246. Wood-chopping: 4.4.11-12 (a paraphrase rather than a translation as Emerson's quotation marks imply); R.W. Emerson, *Essays: First Series*, in *Essays & Lectures* (Library of America; New York, 1983), 247-8; cf. Emerson, *Early Lectures*, ii. 134 (cf. also n. 3 for further use of the *Anabasis*); and for Greeks and childhood, *Journals*, v. 244 ('Every child is a Greek').

7. Hellenism: see esp. Winterer, *Culture of Classicism*, 44-76; for travel, S.A. Larrabee, *Hellas Observed: The American Experience of Greece, 1775-1865* (New York, 1957). Wood: Truettner, *West as America*, 72 (pediment), cf. 115, 131. Lincoln: see all accounts of his childhood; also H. Melville on how he 'shook hands like a good fellow – working hard at it like a man sawing wood at so much per cord' (quoted by R. Castronovo, *Fathering the Nation: American Genealogies of Slavery and Freedom* (Berkeley, 1995), 141).

8. Tarrying: H. D. Thoreau, *A Week on the Concord and Merrimack Rivers* (Princeton and Oxford, 2004; orig. pub. 1849), 216.

9. Fugitive: *The Anti-Slavery Record* 3 (July 1837), 1; cf. M. Wood, *Blind Memory: Visual Representations of Slavery in England and America* (Manchester, 2000), 94-5; for a similar use of antiquity in anti-slavery polemic, cf. D. Walker, *Walker's Appeal* (Boston 1830; orig. pub. 1829), 33-4, 35, 37. Florida: *Daily National Intelligencer*, 26 February 1838 (originally from the *Richmond Whig*). For tensions between Christianity and classicism, see Richard, *Golden Age*, 152-80.

10. Toads: 'D. Knickerbocker', *A History of New York from the Beginning of the World to the End of the Dutch Dynasty* (2 vols; New York, 1809), ii. 62. Account: e.g. *History of New York* (2 vols; New York, 1826), ii. 70. Failure: J. Wilkinson, *Memoirs of My Own Times* (3 vols; Philadelphia, 1816), iii. 455. Press coverage: R.W. Johannsen, *To the Halls of the Montezumas: The Mexican War in the American Imagination* (New York, 1985), 16-20; S. Streeby, *American Sensations: Class, Empire, and the Production of Popular Culture* (Berkeley, 2002), 11, for the number of papers; on newspapers and nationalism, see the classic study of B. Anderson, *Imagined Communities: Reflections on the Origins and Spread of Nationalism* (3rd edn; London and New York, 2006; orig. pub. 1983), esp. 32-6.

11. St Louis reception: the most detailed account is J.T. Scharf, *History of St Louis City and County* (Philadelphia, 1883), i. 379-85.

12. Fervent: R. Horsman, *Race and Manifest Destiny: The Origins of American Racial Anglo-Saxonism* (Cambridge, MA, 1981), 89; for Benton and Mexico, see E.B. Smith, *Magnificent Missourian: The Life of Thomas Hart Benton* (Philadelphia, 1958), 210-11; W.N. Chambers, *Old Bullion Benton, Senator from the New West* (Boston, 1956), 305-8.

13. Roosevelt: T. Roosevelt, *Life of Thomas Hart Benton* (Boston and New York, 1887), 316. Benton: T.H. Benton, *Thirty Years' View: Or, A History of the Working of the American Government for Thirty Years, from 1820 to 1850* (2 vols; New York, 1858), ii. 684-8. The speech was also published as a pamphlet (with Doniphan's) and re-printed in full or in part in numerous newspapers and books (see J.G. Dawson III, *Doniphan's Epic March: The 1st Missouri Volunteers in the Mexican War* (Lawrence, KS, 1999), 282 n. 20).

14. Ten Thousand: Benton, *Thirty Years' View*, 687; this part of the speech was also cited (in addition to the sources mentioned by Dawson, see previous note) in R.S. Elliott, *Notes Taken in Sixty Years* (St Louis, 1883), 245-6 (the memoir of a participant in the first part of the expedition).

15. Teleboas: 4.4.3; J.G. Shea, *Discovery and Exploration of the Mississippi Valley: With the Original Narratives of Marquette, Allouez, Membré, Hennepin, and Anastase Douay* (New York, 1853), 39 n. (quoting Stoddard); for rivers, cf. also H.N. Smith, *Virgin Land: The American West as Symbol and Myth* (2nd edn; Cambridge, MA, 1970; orig. pub. 1950), 11; Larrabee, *Hellas Observed*, 261, 270; S. Rainey, *Creating Picturesque America: Monument to the Natural and Cultural Landscape* (Nashville 1994), 227 (the Mississippi was worth 'countless Rhines and many Danubes'). Niagara: quoted by R.M. Elson, *Guardians of Tradition: American Schoolbooks of the Nineteenth Century* (Lincoln, NE, 1964), 37. For American rejection of tradition, cf. M. Kammen, *Mystic Chords of Memory: The Transformation of Tradition in American Culture* (New York, 1991), 40-62.

16. Gallatin: Dawson, *Doniphan's Epic March*, 193. Independence: Hughes, *Doniphan's Expedition*, 498-503.

17. Alexander: see ch. 7 n. 54. Other comparisons: Dawson, *Doniphan's Epic March*, 199, 194.

18. Comparisons: *New Orleans Delta* 7 and 14 May 1847 (but see Ch. 4 n. 2 for an earlier implicit allusion); *Daily Republican & Argus* (Baltimore), 15 May 1847; cf. Dawson, *Doniphan's Epic March*, 198-9.

19. Sobriquets: *Niles National Register* (Baltimore), 12 June 1847; *Boston Evening Transcript*, 21 June 1848 (as article heading; also 29 June 1848, and *New York Herald*, 23 June 1848; *Massachusetts Ploughman*, 1 July 1848; *Spirit of the Times*, 20 January 1849); *Merchants' Magazine and Commercial Review* 18 (1848), 127; *Boston Daily Atlas*, 25 July 1848; *North American and United States Gazette* (Philadelphia), 7 August 1848 (the same paper on 6 June 1848 called Doniphan 'the Xenophon of the New Mexico war'); P.H. Burnett, *Recollections and Opinions of an Old Pioneer* (New York, 1880), p. iii (a dedication to Doniphan). Cf. Dawson, *Doniphan's Epic March*, 194-5. Pseudonyms: E. Shalev, 'Ancient Masks, American Fathers: Classical Pseudonyms during the American Revolution and Early Republic', *Journal of the Early Republic* 23 (2003), 151-72; G. Wills, *Cincinnatus: George Washington and the Enlightenment: Images of Power in Early America* (Garden City, NY, 1984), esp. 13-16, 36-7.

20. 'Xenophon and Doniphan': *New York Evening Post*, 25 June 1847; reprinted in full e.g. in the *Ohio Statesman*, 2 July 1847; *New Hampshire Sentinel*, 15 July 1847; *Barre Gazette* (Maine), 16 July 1847; *Vermont Journal*, 30 July 1847; and summarized e.g. in the *Baltimore Sun*, 30 June 1847; *The Age* (Augusta, ME), 9 July 1847; *The National Union*, (Nashville), 14 July 1847; *The Semi-Weekly Natchez Courier* (Natchez, MS), 16 July 1847; *The Floridian*, 24 July 1847. Later that year the *Evening Post* managed to refer to Cortez' conquests 'three thousand', rather than three hundred, years ago (quoted by F. Merk, *Manifest Destiny and Mission in American History* (New York, 1963), 158).

21. Equal: *Floridian*, 24 July 1847.

22. Parallel: Hughes, *Doniphan's Expedition*, 492, 506-7; the second passage is among a number of passages from Hughes that are repeated without acknowledgement in I. George, *Heroes and Incidents of the Mexican War* (Greensburg, PA, 1903).

23. Old age: W.C. Kennerly, *Persimmon Hill: A Narrative of Old St Louis and the Far West* (Norman, OK, 1948), 208; for another much later (implicit) allusion, see F.W. Seward, *Seward at Washington, as Senator and Secretary of State: A Memoir of his Life, with Selections from his Letters 1846-1861* (New York, 1891), 59. Reprintings: J. Frost, *Life of Major General Zachary Taylor* (New York and Philadelphia 1847), 157-9; Edwards, *Campaign*, pp. xxiii-xxvi.

24. Macedonia: *Ohio Statesman*, 2 August 1847 (letter dated 17 July); *Henry V*, Act 4 scene 7, with the discussion of D. Quint, "'Alexander the Pig": Shakespeare on History and Poety', *Boundary 2* 10 (1982), 49-67. The Macedon/Monmouth comparison may in fact have been inspired by a passage in Xenophon's *Anabasis* – but that is for another time.

25. Chivalry: G. Lippard, *Legends of Mexico* (Philadelphia, 1847), 96. Rowdy: G.F. Ruxton, *Adventures in Mexico and the Rocky Mountains* (New York, 1848), 303-4.

26. Reviews of Edwards: *Athenaeum* 1094 (October 1848), 1025 (reprinted in *The Daguerrotype*, 9 December 1848); *Examiner* 2125 (21 October 1848), reprinted in *Spirit of the Times*, 18 November 1848, and *Littell's Living Age*, 9 December 1848. Cf. W.H. Bartlett, B.B. Woodward and C. Mackay, *The History of the United States of America* (2 vols; London, 1861), ii. 400, for a similar British critique of an earlier episode, the 1842 Mier filibusters: 'this Texian "Anabasis"', 'this western Xenophon'.

27. West Point: *New York Herald*, 18 June 1848 (the speeches were also published as a separate pamphlet); Dawson, *Doniphan's Epic March*, 201. More allusions: J.S. Jenkins, *History of the War between the United States and Mexico* (New York, 1850), 320; *Weekly Era Southwestern* (Santa Fé), 5 August 1880 – an interview with Doniphan quoted in Hughes, *Doniphan's Expedition*, 586; *Daily Evening Bulletin* (San Francisco), 8 October 1883; *Rocky Mountain News* (Denver), 30 January 1887 (with an allusion to the Bryant editorial); for the comparison in an honorific context after his death, cf. *Proceedings in Congress upon the Acceptance of the Statues of Thomas H. Benton and Francis P. Blair presented by the State of Missouri* (56th Congress, 1st Session, 1900), 25. Later historians: e.g. E.A. Powell, *The Road to Glory* (New York, 1915), 237-8; B.A. De Voto, 'Anabasis in Buckskin', *Harper's Magazine* 180 (1939-40), 400-10 (also 'Anabasis in Homespun', ch. 14 of his *The Year of Decision, 1846* (Boston 1943)); T.L. Karnes, *William Gilpin, Western Nationalist* (Austin, TX, 1970) – 'Xenophon's March' as title of ch. 6; Dawson, *Doniphan's Epic March* – 'American Xenophon' in title to ch. 9 (cf. his earlier article 'American Xenophon, American Hero: Alexander Doniphan's Homecoming from the Mexican-American War as a Hallmark of Patriotic Fervor', *Military History of the West* 27 (1997), 1-31); J. Wheelan, *Invading Mexico: America's Continental Dream and the Mexican War, 1846-1848* (New York, 2007) – 'America's Xenophon' as title of ch. 16.

28. Praise: *Ohio Statesman*, 22 September 1847. Scott: *American and Commercial Daily Advertiser* (Baltimore), 22 October 1847 (cited in *General Scott and His Staff* (Philadelphia, 1848), 75-6); *Raleigh Register and North-Carolina Gazette*, 6 May 1848, reporting a speech in Congress that suggested Prescott write the history of Scott's march ('He might render not less famous in after ages the advance of the ten thousand Americans than was the retreat of the ten thousand Greeks rendered immortal by the pen of Xenophon'). Wool: F. Baylies, *A Narrative of Major-General Wool's Campaign in Mexico* (Albany, NY, 1851), 22.

29. Advert: *Richmond Enquirer*, 16 July 1847.

30. Jugurtha: 'War and its Incidents', *Southern Quarterly Review* 13 (1848), 1-54 (though see Ch. 4 n. 6 for Metellus). Patriotism: cf. e.g. *Vermont Chronicle*, 16 August 1848 (Commencement oration at Middlebury); 25 June 1864 ('The intense pride of every Athenian citizen in his own splendid capital ... is familiar to any one who remembers the soldierly summons of Xenophon on his retreat').

31. Bryant: n. 20 above. Wool, Scott: n. 28 above (in the Baltimore *American* as well as the Congress speech); also the similar allusions to Xenophon and Mexico in C.E. Pickett, *Oration Delivered in the Congregational Church, Sacramento, California, July 4, 1857* (San Francisco, 1857), 23 ('retreat' vs. 'advance'), and J.L. Denison, *A Pictorial History of the Wars of the United States* (New York, 1859), 521 ('offensive' vs. 'defensive'); cf. *Daily National Intelligencer* (Washington, DC), 9 February 1848, for a citation in Congress of the Retreat of the Ten Thousand as the fate that the US troops in Mexico must avoid. Santa Anna: *The Weekly Nashville Union*, 27 January 1847. Benton: n. 13 above. 'Battle Hymn': E.L. Tuveson, *Redeemer Nation: The Idea of America's Millennial Role* (Chicago and London, 1968), 198-9, sets the hymn in its ideological context. For America's sense of superiority to antiquity, cf. Richard, *Golden Age*, 106-12.

    32. Republic: H. Taine, 'Xénophon: *L'Anabase*', in *Essais de critique et d'histoire* (Paris, 1887; orig. publ. 1858), 49-95, at 50 (my translation); note that the second (1866) edition of this work was the first to include the Xenophon essay (first published in *Revue de l'instruction publique*, 3 and 10 July 1856). Hanson: see Ch. 1 n. 21. Volunteers: Benton, *Thirty Years' View*, 688.

    33. New World: Taine, 'Xénophon', 50, 54.

4. East and West: Promised Lands

    1. Bible times: J. Crawford, *The Last True Story I'll Ever Tell: An Accidental Soldier's Account of the War in Iraq* (New York, 2005), 213-14; J.C. Hartley, *Just Another Soldier: A Year on the Ground in Iraq* (New York, 2005), 77-8.

    2. Arkansas: F. Parkman, *The Oregon Trail* (Oxford, 2000; orig. pub. 1849), 311. Anabasis: Hughes, *Doniphan's Expedition*, 141 n. Scenery: G.R. Gibson, *Journal of a Soldier under Kearny and Doniphan*, ed. R. P. Bieber (Glendale, CA, 1935), 127. Jaunt: Elliott, *Notes*, 222.

    3. Depiction of country: e.g. review of Edwards, *Campaign*, quoted in an advertisement in the *Examiner* 2108, 24 June 1848 (from 'Douglas Jerrold's Newspaper'). Travel: J. Rennell, *Illustrations, (Chiefly Geographical,) of the History of the Expedition of Cyrus, from Sardis to Babylonia, and the Retreat of the Ten Thousand Greeks, from thence to Trebisonde and Lydia* (London, 1816), p. ii; the same sentence (with 'travel' for 'travels') in Ainsworth, *Travels*, p. vi.

    4. Domination: H. Henderson, 'Travel Writer and the Text: "My Giant Goes With Me Wherever I Go"', in M. Kowalewski (ed.), *Temperamental Journeys: Essays on the Modern Literature of Travel* (Athens, GA, 1992), 230-48, at 245. Privilege: R. Davidson, 'Against Travel Writing', *Granta* 72 (2000), 248-54, at 254.

    5. Caesar: Elliott, *Notes*, 231.

    6. Quotations from Hughes, *Doniphan's Expedition*, 135, 141-2, 157, 171-2, 173, 176, 183-4.

    7. Israelites: Gibson, *Journal*, 151. Santa Fé: Elliott, *Notes*, 238, 241-2; cf. J. Gregg, *Commerce of the Prairies* (Norman, OK, 1954; orig. pub. 1844), 144, on 'Moorish castles'.

    8. Asiatic: Benton, *Thirty Years' View*, 581.

    9. Asia: D. Jackson and M.L. Spence (eds), *The Expeditions of John Charles Frémont* (3 vols in 4; Urbana, 1970-80), i. 671 (quoted by P.N. Limerick, *Desert Passages: Encounters with the American Deserts* (Albuquerque, 1985), 34). Bible: S. Bowles, *Across the Continent: A Summer's Journey to the Rocky Mountains, the Mormons, and the Pacific States, with Speaker Colfax* (New York, 1865), 14, 15. Bagdad: L. Giddings, *Sketches of the Campaign in Northern Mexico in Eighteen Hundred Forty-Six and Seven* (New York, 1853), 33. Matamoras, Moorish: Lippard, *Legends of Mexico*, 20, 28. Prescott: quotations from W.H. Prescott, *History* *of the Conquest of Mexico* (3 vols; London, 1850; orig. pub. 1843), ii. 44-5, 56-7; for the 'master of all I survey' scene, see M.L. Pratt, *Imperial Eyes: Travel Writing and Transculturation* (London and New York, 1992), 201-27 (a book that also has an important discussion of images of South America).

10. Self-definition: B.A. Harvey, *American Geographics: U.S. National Narratives and the Representation of the Non-European World, 1830-1865* (Stanford, 2001), 28. Rivers: Ch. 3 n. 15. Castles: Rainey, *Creating Picturesque America*, 227; cf. also index s.v. 'antiquities, natural features as substitute for' and 'comparisons'. Yosemite: e.g. C.C. Coffin, *Our New Way Round the World* (Boston, 1869), 482, 490.

11. Columbus: Truettner, *West*, 94 n. 55.

12. Orient: Coffin, *Our New Way*, 24; on orientalism, a vast literature has arisen in the wake of E. Said, *Orientalism: Western Conceptions of the Orient* (London, 1978) – see e.g. J.M. MacKenzie, *Orientalism: History, Theory and the Arts* (Manchester, 1995); for the American West and Latin America as oriental, see e.g. A. Cabañas, *The Cultural 'Other' in Nineteenth-Century Travel Narratives: How the United States and Latin America Described Each Other* (Lewiston, NY, 2008), esp. 41-4, 96 n. 14. Romance: Baylies, *Narrative*, 5; cf. e.g. Giddings, *Sketches*, 333; P. St. G. Cooke, *The Conquest of New Mexico and California: An Historical and Personal Narrative* (New York, 1878), p. x. Doniphan: E.D. Mansfield, *The Mexican War: A History of its Origin, and A Detailed Account of the Victories Which Terminated in the Surrender of the Capital* (New York, 1848), 103; cf. Ch. 3 on the St Louis reception. For Mexico and the past, cf. e.g. Johannsen, *To the Halls*, 158, 166; N. Leask, '"The Ghost in Chapultepec": Fanny Calderon de la Barca, William Prescott and Nineteenth-Century Mexican Travel Accounts', in J. Elsner and J.-P. Rubiés (eds), *Voyages and Visions: Towards a Cultural History of Travel* (London, 1999), 184-209; Cabañas, *Cultural 'Other'*, esp. 71; and for the continuing power of the image, D. Cooper Alarcón, *The Aztec Palimpsest: Mexico in the Modern Imagination* (Tucson, 1997).

13. Promised land: J. Davis, *The Landscape of Belief: Encountering the Holy Land in Nineteenth-Century American Art and Culture* (Princeton, 1996), 20-2. Canaan: in J.C. Frémont, *Oregon and California: The Exploring Expedition to the Rocky Mountains* (Buffalo, 1851), 4 (the words are presumably to be attributed to the publisher); cf. Truettner, *West*, 311, 314. Israelites: Hughes, *Doniphan's Expedition*, 401; cf. (but without the miracle) Giddings, *Sketches*, 114. Pioneers: quoted by D.L. Walker, *Pacific Destiny: The Three-Century Journey to the Oregon Country* (New York, 2000), 351; cf. Ch. 2 nn. 3, 6 on the Mormons and pioneers.

14. Roman fortitude: Hughes, *Doniphan's Expedition*, 168, 187, 299, 503. Mexico and Carthage: Hughes, *Doniphan's Expedition*, 187 n., 218 n.; cf. 299-300, 420-1, for Americans exceeding Hannibal.

15. Pioneers: quoted by Walker, *Pacific Destiny*, 351. Promised land: S.S. Cox, *Diversions of a Diplomat in Turkey* (New York, 1893), 137. Ridpath: see Ch. 2 n. 32. Moses: L.J. Halsey, *Life Pictures from the Bible, or, Illustrations of Scripture Character* (Philadelphia, 1860), 186 (cf. L.H. Feldman, *Josephus' Interpretation of the Bible* (Berkeley, 1998), 406, for a possible ancient parallel).

16. Rio Grande: J.C. Ridpath, *The Citizen Soldier: His Part in War and Peace* (Cincinnati, 1891), 33.

17. Euphrates: H.K.B. von Moltke, *Briefe über Zustände und Begebenheiten in der Türkei aus den Jahren 1835 bis 1839* (8th edn; Berlin, 1917; orig. pub. 1841), 246.

18. Mexico: Ridpath, *Citizen Soldier*, 33-5. For Mexico as picturesque, cf. e.g. Kennerly, *Persimmon Hill*, 201-2; Baylies, *Narrative*, 15; and see Ch. 7 on the ideology of the picturesque.

19. Lope: Edwards, *Campaign*, 13. Confusion, thrilling: Hughes, *Doniphan's Expedition*, 171. Parks: Gibson, *Journal*, 127.

20. Coronado: cited by R. Thacker, *The Great Prairie Fact and Literary Imagination* (Albuquerque, 1989), 14; cf. index s.v. 'prairie: likened to sea'. Prairie ocean: Gregg, *Commerce*, 50. Mound: J.S. Robinson, *A Journal of the Santa Fe Expedition under Colonel Doniphan* (Princeton, 1932; orig. pub. 1848), 2. Pirates: Edwards, *Campaign*, 10. Further examples in Dawson, *Doniphan's Epic March*, 55; for a stimulating reading of this motif in relation to the idea of the desert as oriental, see S. LeMenager, *Manifest and Other Destinies: Territorial Fictions of the Nineteenth-Century United States* (Lincoln, NE, 2004), esp. 54-5, 80-3.

21. Hunting: 1.5.2-3. Didactic: Edwards, *Campaign*, 13.

22. Desert as sea: 1.5.1. Prairie as sea: B. Hall, *Travels in North America in the Years 1827 and 1828* (Edinburgh, 1829), iii. 384; *Westminster Review* 11 (October 1829), 416-47, at 419.

23. Hunting and war: Xenophon, *Cynegeticus* 12.1-9. Fitness: J.M. MacKenzie, 'Hunting and the Natural World in Juvenile Literature', in J. Richards (ed.), *Imperialism and Juvenile Literature* (Manchester, 1989), 144-72, at 170. Wild ass: R.K. Porter, *Travels in Georgia, Persia, Armenia, Ancient Babylonia, &c. &c., During the Years 1817, 1818, 1819, and 1820* (2 vols; London, 1821-2), i. 461; cf. J.J. Morier, *A Second Journey Through Persia, Armenia, and Asia Minor, to Constantinople, Between the Years 1810 and 1816* (London, 1818), 200-1, 206; for the imperial resonance, also J.K. Anderson, *Xenophon* (London, 1974), 91.

24. Bennett: *New York Herald*, 25 September 1845 (cited by Merk, *Manifest Destiny and Mission*, 46); for the North/South axis, cf. e.g. *Oration of O.P. Morton, Address of Major General G.G. Meade, and Poem of Bayard Taylor, with the Other Exercises At the Dedication of the Monument in the Soldiers' National Cemetery At Gettysburg, July 1, 1869* (Gettysburg, 1870), 46. Kentuckian: review of W.S. Mayo, *Kaloolah, or, Journeyings to the Djébel Kumri: An Autobiography of Jonathan Romer*, *Athenaeum* 1134 (July 1849), 736-7, at 736. Plains: W. Gilpin, *Mission of the North American People, Geographical, Social, and Political* (2nd edn; Philadelphia, 1874; orig. pub. 1873), esp. 119-20, 222.

25. Persian empire: 1.7.6; cf. *Cyropaedia* 8.6.21. Xerxes: Herodotus 7.8; cf. M. Flower, 'Herodotus and Persia', in C. Dewald and J. Marincola (eds), *The Cambridge Companion to Herodotus* (Cambridge, 2006), 274-89, at 277, on Persian 'manifest destiny'; and on modern US and ancient Persian imperialism, see further B. Lincoln, *Religion, Empire, and Torture: The Case of Achaemenian Persia, with a Postscript on Abu Ghraib* (Chicago, 2007). Cf. the inscription on the New York Post Office (1912), taken from Herodotus' account of the message service in the Persian empire (8.98).

26. Ruins: e.g. Edwards, *Campaign*, 95; Robinson, *Journal*, 60; cf. B. DeLay, 'Independent Indians and the U.S.-Mexican War', *American Historical Review* 112 (2007), 35-68, esp. 58-9. Pecos: Edwards, *Campaign*, 22-3.

27. Annex: *Daily American Star* (Mexico City), 20 May 1848 (cited by J.M. McCaffrey, *Army of Manifest Destiny: The American Soldier in the Mexican War, 1846-1848* (New York, 1992), 200). Ravisher: *New York Herald*, 8 October 1847 (cited by Merk, *Manifest Destiny and Mission*, 123). Lotus-eaters: J.C. Jamison, *With Walker in Nicaragua* (Columbia, MO, 1909), 116 (cited by A.S. Greenberg, *Manifest Manhood and the American Empire* (Cambridge and New York, 2005), 127). For the feminizing of land, see A. Kolodny, *The Lay of the Land: Metaphor as Experience in American Life and Letters* (Chapel Hill, 1975); Greenberg, *Manifest Manhood*, 62; for visiting Mexico as like visiting the lotus-eaters, cf. W.H.B. Hall, *Across Mexico in 1864-5* (London and Cambridge, 1866), 281-2.

28. El Paso: Hughes, *Doniphan's Expedition*, 385. Onions: Robinson, *Journal*, 32. Paradise: e.g. Prescott, *History*, i. 335; Giddings, *Sketches*, 145. Eden: W.S. Henry, *Campaign Sketches of the War with Mexico* (New York, 1847), 18; cf. Johannsen, *To the Halls*, 146, 164, 166, 258, 260.

29. Wag: W.M. McGroarty (ed.), 'William H. Richardson's Journal of Doniphan's Expedition', *Missouri Historical Review* 22 (1928), 193-236, 331-60, 511-42 (orig. pub. 1847), 233-4.

30. Deserted cities: 1.5.4; 3.4.7-12.

31. Canals, paradise: 2.4.13-14. Dates, palm: 2.3.15-16; for Mesopotamian fertility, cf. Herodotus 1.193, Hippocrates, *Airs, Waters, Places* 11. Millstones: 1.5.5. Auctions: Herodotus 1.196.

32. Discordant: Porter, *Travels*, i. 171-2. Pleasure: J.M. Kinneir, *Journey through Asia Minor, Armenia, and Koordistan, in the Years 1813 and 1814, with Remarks on the Marches of Alexander and Retreat of the Ten Thousand* (London, 1818), 441. Progress: A.H. Layard, *Discoveries in the Ruins of Nineveh and Babylon: With Travels in Armenia, Kurdistan and the Desert* (London, 1853), 245; P. Nostitz, *Travels of Doctor and Madame Helfer in Syria, Mesopotamia, Burmah and other Lands*, trans. G. Sturge (2 vols; London, 1878; Ger. orig. 1873), i. 201, 275-6.

33. Anglos: M.P. Brady, '"Full of Empty": Creating the Southwest as "Terra Incognita"', in H. Michie and R.R. Thomas (eds), *Nineteenth-Century Geographies: The Transformation of Space from the Victorian Age to the American Century* (New Brunswick, 2003), 251-64, at 256. Potential: Hughes, *Doniphan's Expedition*, 394 (cf. R.D. Launius, *Alexander William Doniphan: Portrait of a Missouri Moderate* (Columbia, MO, 1997), 152-3); F.A. Wislizenus, *Memoir of a Tour to Northern Mexico* (Washington, DC, 1848), esp. 82-5. Land use: Streeby, *American Sensation*, 182-3; D. Spurr, *The Rhetoric of Empire: Colonial Discourse in Journalism, Travel Writing, and Imperial Administration* (Durham, NC, 1993), 29-32. Nineveh: Rainey, *Creating Picturesque America*, 270; cf. Smith, *Virgin Land*, 19-20; Ch. 1 n. 12.

34. Capture: 3.4.8, 12; Higgins, *Xenophon*, 95.

35. Wall: 2.4.12. Regret: C.J. Tuplin, 'Xenophon in Media', in G.B. Lanfranchi, M. Roaf and R. Rollinger (eds), *Continuity of Empire (?): Assyria, Media, Persia* (Padua, 2003), 351-89, at 385; cf. 370-85 for an invaluable discussion of the problems in Xenophon's account of Larisa and Mespila.

36. Authenticating: S. Greenblatt, *Marvelous Possessions: The Wonder of the New World* (Oxford, 1991), 30, cf. 74.

37. Cortes: Prescott, *History*, i. 340.

38. Honey: 4.8.20-1.

39. Cheering: Hughes, *Doniphan's Expedition*, 142-3. Bryant: Edwards, *Campaign*, 8. Council Grove: Gibson, *Journal*, 139.

40. Possibility of settling: 2.4.22, 3.2.23-6.

41. Lotus-eaters: Homer, *Odyssey* 9.82-104; Plato, *Republic* 560c5.

42. Cyrus: Herodotus 9.122; cf. Hippocrates, *Airs, Waters, Places* 14, for another environmental explanation of supposed Asiatic softness. *Cyropaedia* as anti-pan-hellenic: P. Carlier, 'L'idée de monarchie impériale dans la Cyropédie de Xénophon', *Ktema* 3 (1978), 133-63.

43. Isocrates: see e.g. 4.163-6, 5.120-3, 12.13-14, *Epistle* 9; cf. L. Mitchell, *Panhellenism and the Barbarian in Archaic and Classical Greece* (Swansea, 2007), esp. 23. For the similar ideology of the American West as offering a solution to metropolitan problems, see Slotkin, *Fatal Environment*, esp. 35, 47.

44. Poison: Emerson, *Journals*, ix. 430-1. Race: Streeby, *American Sensation*, 169. Aztecs: Prescott, *History*, i. 133, ii. 73, 62; cf. i. 21; D. Levin, *History as Romantic Art: Bancroft, Prescott, Motley, and Parkman* (Stanford, 1959), 149-54.

5. Spartan Courage: The Culture of Militarism

1. Quotations from A. Swofford, *Jarhead: A Marine's Chronicle of the Gulf War* (London, 2003), 20-1, 203.
2. Dust: McGroarty, 'Richardson's Journal', 346. Invincible: Hughes, *Doniphan's Expedition*, 370 and n.
3. Jefferson, Hamilton: quoted by Richard, *Founders*, 73; cf. E. Rawson, *The Spartan Tradition in European Thought* (Oxford, 1969), 368-70; P.A. Rahe, *Republics Ancient and Modern: Classical Republicanism and the American Revolution* (Chapel Hill, 1992), 254-6; Fox-Genovese and Genovese, *Mind of the Master Class*, 289-90. Bands: e.g. *Daily National Intelligencer*, 6 August 1846 (Walker); 24 October 1846; see nn. 19, 20, 22; for a Civil War example, T. Reid, *Spartan Band: Burnett's 13th Texas Cavalry in the Civil War* (Denton, TX, 2005), 54 (book title derived from a commemorative poem). Taylor: *Berkshire County Whig*, 18 June 1846; *The North American* (Philadelphia), 17 June 1846. Heroism: *Boston Daily Atlas*, 9 June 1846 (from the New Orleans *Picayune*). Mother: *Boston Daily Atlas*, 20 May 1846. Boy: *The North American* (Philadelphia), 25 June 1846.
4. Gallant, glitter: Hughes, *Doniphan's Expedition*, 371-2. Red coats: letter quoted by Launius, *Alexander William Doniphan*, 145-6. Gay: Edwards, *Campaign*, 54.
5. Churches: cf. McCaffrey, *Army of Manifest Destiny*, 71. Prescott: see Ch. 4 n. 44. Tent: Lippard, *Legends of Mexico*, 22.
6. Taylor: Lippard, *Legends of Mexico*, 23; cf. Johannsen, *To the Halls*, 199, 116; S. Streeby, 'American Sensations: Empire, Amnesia, and the US-Mexican War', *American Literary History* 13 (2001), 1-40, at 19. Ragged: Hughes, *Doniphan's Expedition*, 450; alluded to by Benton, *Thirty Years' View*, 686-7; J.S. Jenkins, *History of the War between the United States and Mexico* (Auburn, 1850), 320 n. Vermin: Ruxton, *Adventures in Mexico*, 304. Thunderstruck: Wislizenus, *Memoir*, 54. Political: T.B. Thorpe, *Our Army on the Rio Grande* (Philadelphia, 1846), 160.
7. Persian tents: 4.4.21; Herodotus 9.80, 82.
8. Pausanias: Thucydides 1.128-30; C.W. Fornara, *Herodotus: An Interpretative Essay* (Oxford, 1971), 62-6. Display: 3.2.7. Parade: 1.2.16-18; cf. E. Howell, '"Meet General X"', *Greece and Rome* 18 (1949), 1-13, at 5 ('delight in gay trappings'; also comparing Xenophon with Nelson before Trafalgar).
9. Spartan cloaks: cf. J.K. Anderson, *Military Theory and Practice in the Age of Xenophon* (Berkeley, 1970), 39. Explanations: Xenophon, *Constitution of the Spartans* 11.3; J. Davidson, *Courtesans and Fishcakes: The Consuming Passions of Classical Athens* (London, 1997), 62, with further references at 324 n. 37.
10. Persian colours: Lee, *Greek Army*, 118; Xenophon, *Cyropaedia* 6.4.1, 8.3.3.
11. Despot: Lippard, *Legends of Mexico*, 123. Muscle: Streeby, *American Sensations*, 143, quoting Ned Buntline's *The Volunteer*.
12. Size: Lippard, *Legends of Mexico*, 123. Exaggerations: Herodotus 7.185-6; Xenophon, *Anabasis* 1.7.12.
13. Lightning: Hughes, *Doniphan's Expedition*, 373. Skull-and-bones: Edwards, *Campaign*, 54. Surrender: McGroarty, 'Richardson's Journal', 346. 'Take him': letter by C.H. Kribben, published in several newspapers (e.g. *Boston Daily Atlas*,

11 March 1847; *The Floridian* (Tallahassee), 20 March 1847), and quoted in J.M. Cutts, *The Conquest of California and New Mexico by the Forces of the United States, in the years 1846 & 1847* (Philadelphia, 1847), 78; Frost, *Life*, 148.

14. Phalinus: 2.1.7-20.

15. Leonidas: Diodorus Siculus 14.25.2-3, cf. 11.5.5.

16. Unwittingly: letter by Kribben (n. 13).

17. Spartan reply: Hughes, *Doniphan's Expedition*, 457-8.

18. Spartan will: Gilpin, *Mission*, 223. Father: Gibson, *Journal*, 124. Mother: M.B. Edwards, A.S. Johnston, and P.G. Ferguson, *Marching with the Army of the West*, ed. R.P. Bieber (Glendale, CA, 1936), 242; on the image of the Spartan mother in revolutionary America, see Winterer, *Mirror of Antiquity*, 76-7.

19. Consecrate: *The North American* (Philadelphia), 11 May 1846. 300: Lippard, *Legends of Mexico*, 101. No surrender: Lippard, *Legends of Mexico*, 123. Pass: Baylies, *Narrative*, 29, cf. 28, 43, 45, also 64 ('Spartan band' in a speech); cf. e.g. Mansfield, *Mexican War*, 123.

20. Alamo: J.H. Jenkins, 'The Thermopylae Quotation', *Southwestern Historical Quarterly* 94 (1990), 299-304; the phrase 'American Spartans' (not noted by Jenkins) is found at R.P. Smith, *On to the Alamo: Colonel Crockett's Exploits and Adventures in Texas* (New York, 2003; orig. pub. 1836), 102. Cf. D. Levene, 'Xerxes Goes to Hollywood', in E. Bridges, E. Hall, and P.J. Rhodes (eds), *Cultural Responses to the Persian Wars* (Oxford, 2007), 383-403, on reflections of this myth in American films. Survivor: Herodotus 9.71.

21. 'World's Thermopylae': *New York Herald*, 25 September 1845 (later cited with alarm in the London *Times*, 21 October 1845, p. 5); for the English use, see my 'From Marathon to Waterloo: Byron, Battle Monuments, and the Persian Wars', in E. Hall, P.J. Rhodes, and E. Bridges (eds), *Cultural Responses to the Persian Wars* (Oxford, 2007), 267-97, at 268. Even more quixotic are the words of the western visionary William Gilpin in an 1867 Independence Day address at Denver: 'the mysterious crisis between the clashing continents and civilizations of the world, held and decided, three thousand years ago, by the three hundred Spartans at Thermopylae, now rests with the geographical States and people of Colorado and Utah' (*Mission*, 223).

22. Duck Creek: *Cleveland Herald*, 19 June 1848. Oration: J.C. Breckenridge, *An Address on the Occasion of the Burial of the Kentucky Volunteers who Fell at Buena Vista* (Lexington, KY, 1847), 12-13.

23. Wolfe: Ch. 2 n. 31. Schoolbooks: Elson, *Guardians*, 332. 3-to-1: Giddings, *Sketches*, 248. 5-to-1: Elliott, *Notes*, 245; cf. also Johannsen, *To the Halls*, 84, and Dawson, *Doniphan's Epic March*, 47, 105, for other examples of the theme; also M. Green, *Dreams of Adventure, Deeds of Empire* (London and Henley, 1980), 28, 348 n. 16.

24. Yankee: A. Johnson, 'On Xenophon and Dr Strauss', in L. Strauss, *On Tyranny: An Interpretation of Xenophon's Hiero* (New York, 1948), pp. vii-ix, at p. viii. Cyrus: 1.7.3. Numbers: e.g. Andocides 1.107. Men: Herodotus 7.210.2; noted by E. Spelman (trans.), *Xenophon: The Expedition of Cyrus* (2 vols; London, 1740-2), i. 74 n. 111.

25. Agony: 3.1.17. Thermopylae applied to other passes: e.g. Giddings, *Sketches*, 246; J. Frost, *The Pictorial History of the United States of America* (Boston, 1852), 465; id., *The Mexican War and its Warriors* (New Haven and Philadelphia, 1848), 319 ('country').

26. Leonidas: Plutarch, *Moralia* 225d.

27. 'Come and take him': also in Hughes, *Doniphan's Expedition*, 373; Gibson, *Journal*, 304. Hell: McGroarty, 'Richardson's Journal', 346.

28. Custer: *New York Herald*, July 1876 (cited by Slotkin, *Fatal Environment*, 462); W.W. Glazier, *Heroes of Three Wars* (Philadelphia, 1880), 446. Stalingrad: A. Beevor, *Stalingrad* (London, 1998), 380; for the German reception, cf. S. Rebenich, 'From Thermopylae to Stalingrad: The Myth of Leonidas in German Historiography', in A. Powell and S. Hodkinson (eds), *Sparta Beyond the Mirage* (Swansea, 2002), 323-49; R.H. Watt, '"Wanderer, kommst du nach Sparta": History through Propaganda into Literary Commonplace', *Modern Language Review* 80 (1985), 871-83. See in general E. Clough, 'Loyalty and Liberty: Thermopylae in the Western Imagination', in T.J. Figueira (ed.), *Spartan Society* (Swansea, 2004), 363-84; Cartledge, *Thermopylae*, 179-213.

29. Drill: Hughes, *Doniphan's Expedition*, 372. Volley: McGroarty, 'Richardson's Journal', 347. Losses: M.L. Gardner (ed.), *Brothers on the Santa Fe and Chihuahua Trails: Edward James Glasgow and William Henry Glasgow, 1846-1848* (Niwot, CO, 1993), 167, with 176 n. 3; Dawson, *Doniphan's Epic March*, 117.

30. Frolic: Hughes, *Doniphan's Expedition*, 88; Gibson, *Journal*, 308; also *Weekly Tribune* (Liberty, MO), 27 February 1847 (cited by Dawson, *Doniphan's Epic March*, 118), probably written by Hughes. Glorious: Dawson, *Doniphan's Epic March*, 118. Discipline: Gilpin, *Mission*, 139 (speaking of the whole campaign). Veterans: Gibson, *Journal*, 308. Weakness: Wislizenus, *Memoir*, 39 n.; Polybius 3.6.9-12.

31. Straight line: Gardner, *Brothers*, 167. Drill: Hughes, *Doniphan's Expedition*, 132. Worthless: Parkman, *Oregon Trail*, 311. Kearny: Dawson, *Doniphan's Epic March*, 61-2. Sahara: Hughes, *Doniphan's Expedition*, 175.

32. Whip: Gibson, *Journal*, 323. Groups: Herodotus 7.104.4.

33. Parade: 1.2.16-18.

34. Kukuanas: H. Rider Haggard, *King Solomon's Mines* (Oxford, 1989; orig. pub. 1885), 127. Solid wall: R. Kipling, *The Jungle Book* (London, 1907; orig. pub. 1894), 272-3; cited by Anderson, *Xenophon*, 87.

35. Drill: Taine, 'Xénophon', 55; Hanson, *Carnage and Culture*, 1, 4; cf. already his *Western Way of War*, 12, 15.

36. Artless: Taine, 'Xénophon', 72. Ironic pleasure: see S. Flory, 'Laughter, Tears and Wisdom in Herodotus', *American Journal of Philology* 99 (1978), 145-53, at 150, with n. 7, on Herodotus; also Thucydides 1.129.1.

37. *Proskunesis*: 1.8.21; see P. Briant, *From Cyrus to Alexander: A History of the Persian Empire* (Winona Lake, IN, 2002; Fr. orig. 1996), 222-3 (Persian images suggest that it involved bowing slightly while blowing a kiss). *Ton andra*: Ch. 2 nn. 33, 34.

38. Women: Isocrates 5.90.

39. Mountain: 1.2.25. Slingers, cavalry: Ch. 1 n. 24.

40. Shouting: 1.7.4, 2.17. Silence: 1.8.11. Slow: Thucydides 5.70 (though to the sound of flutes).

41. Carts: 1.5.8; cf. Parkman, *Oregon Trail*, 13, 30, 32; Edwards, *Campaign*, 7. Uncorrupted: cf. Porter, *Travels*, ii. 93. Shah: Morier, *Second Journey*, 198.

42. Dandies: Higgins, *Xenophon*, 85. Gardening: Xenophon, *Oeconomicus* 4.21-5; cf. Plutarch *Artaxerxes* 24.9-10 for a similar point about Artaxerxes.

43. Staff-bearer: 1.8.28-9. Gifts: 1.2.27; 'The Prospects of Persia', *British Quarterly Review* 59 (1874), at 367-96, at 369; cf. Morier, *Second Journey*, 93. Ornamentalism: D. Cannadine, *Ornamentalism: How the British Saw their Empire* (New York, 2001), 122.

44. Greek independence: Taine, 'Xénophon', 58.

6. A Wandering Democracy: Freedom on the March

1. Quotation from Swofford, *Jarhead*, 28.

2. Liberty, secret: Edwards, *Marching*, 115. Majority: M.L. Gardner and M. Simmons (eds), *The Mexican War Correspondence of Richard Smith Elliott* (Norman, OK, 1997), 30; Hughes, *Doniphan's Expedition*, 128. Cf. Dawson, *Doniphan's Epic March*, 32-3, 89.

3. No election: Gibson, *Journal*, 121. Price: Hughes, *Doniphan's Expedition*, 256-7.

4. Quotations from Parkman, *Oregon Trail*, 181, 311; Hughes, *Doniphan's Expedition*, 125, 254, 152-3.

5. Whisky: P.W. Foos, *A Short, Offhand, Killing Affair: Soldiers and Social Conflict during the Mexican-American War* (Chapel Hill, 2002), 50. British view: Ruxton, *Adventures in Mexico*, 176-7 (partly quoted in Dawson, *Doniphan's Epic March*, 109). Not congenial: Cooke, *Conquest*, 62 (quoted by Foos, *Short, Offhand, Killing Affair*, 89). Equally brave: Hughes, *Doniphan's Expedition*, 227.

6. Citizens: Benton, *Thirty Years' View*, ii. 688.

7. People: Lippard, *Legends of Mexico*, 13; Aeschylus, *Persians* 241-4 (trans. E. Hall); Herodotus 5.78 (trans. R. Waterfield, adapted).

8. Military spirit: *New York Herald*, 22 October 1847. Spartan Association: P. Adams, *The Bowery Boys: Street Corner Radicals and the Politics of Rebellion* (Westport, CT, 2005).

9. Marathon: *First Reunion of the Survivors of the Army of the Tennessee and its Four Corps* (Logansport, IN, 1892), 109 (Major. C. Townsend, of Athens, Ohio). Athens: D. Webster, *An Address Delivered Before the New York Historical Society: February 23, 1852* (New York, 1852), 13-15; quoted e.g. in *The Weekly Herald* (New York), 28 February 1852; C.C. Felton, *Greece, Ancient and Modern: Lectures Delivered before the Lowell Institute* (2 vols; Boston, MA, 1867), i. 468. For Athens and America, cf. also e.g. Elson, *Guardians*, 260 (passage cited in an 1820s school reader: 'Who shall say then, contemplating the past, that England, proud and powerful as she appears, may not one day be what Athens *is*, and the young America soar to be what Athens *was*?'); Larrabee, *Hellas Observed*, 204 (stone from Parthenon in Washington Monument); E. Cadava, *Emerson and the Climates of History* (Stanford, 1997), 74-81 (hints of America as Athens in Shelley's *Hellas*); Winterer, *Mirror of Antiquity*, 193 (discussing an 1851 article in the *Christian Review*); Richard, *Golden Age*, 117-18; contrast the hostility to Athenian democracy in eighteenth-century America (J.T. Roberts, *Athens on Trial: The Antidemocratic Tradition in Western Thought* (Princeton, 1994), 179-93).

10. Americanism: J.A. Logan, *The Volunteer Soldier of America* (Chicago and New York, 1887), 90; for Logan's pique, M. Fellman, *Citizen Sherman: A Life of William Tecumseh Sherman* (New York, 1995), 322-3. Troy: George, *Heroes and Incidents*, 249 (from an address by General Shields, 22 February 1879).

11. Freedom: 1.7.3-4; Aeschylus' *Persians* 402-5 (trans. E. Hall, adapted).

12. Autocrat: Hanson, *Carnage and Culture*, 49. Crusade: P. Gauthier, 'Xénophon et l'odyssée des "Dix-Mille"', *L'Histoire* 79 (1985), 16-25, at 21. Champion of democracy: E. Delebecque, 'Xénophon, Athènes et Lacédémone: Notes sur la composition de l'Anabase', *Revue des études grecques* 59-60 (1946-7), 71-138, at 78; cf. his *Essai sur la vie de Xénophon* (Paris, 1957), 201. Non-Greek: Dillery, *Xenophon*, 60-1.

13. Democracy: J.B. Bury, *A History of Greece to the Death of Alexander the Great* (3rd edn, rev. R. Meiggs; London, 1956; orig. pub. 1900), 526. Undisciplined:

W.C. Greene, *The Achievement of Greece: A Chapter in Human Experience* (Cambridge, MA, 1923), 200. Parliament: R.W. Livingstone, *The Greek Genius and its Meaning to Us* (Oxford, 1915; orig. pub. 1912), 62-3. Athens: Taine, 'Xénophon', 50; E. Hamilton, *The Greek Way to Western Civilization* (2nd edn; New York, 1948; orig. pub. 1930), 162.

14. Quotations from 1.7.5-7.

15. Capua: Benton, *Thirty Years' View*, ii. 686; contrast Allan Nevins on their 'Capuan excesses' (A. Nevins (ed.), *Polk: The Diary of a President* (New York, 1929), 227 n. 4). El Paso: Dawson, *Doniphan's Epic March*, 95, 121, 130. Restless: Gibson, *Journal*, 323. Matamoras, Mexico City: Foos, *Short, Offhand, Killing Affair*, 98-9, 120. Marching: Hughes, *Doniphan's Expedition*, 274, cf. 511.

16. Critical: Edwards, *Marching*, 246. Dispute: Robinson, *Journal*, 69-70 (under 3 February 1847). Delusions: *Detroit Free Press*, 22 March 1847, quoted by Dawson, *Doniphan's Epic March*, 124.

17. News about Wool: Hughes, *Doniphan's Expedition*, 77; Gibson, *Journal*, 257, 273. News in El Paso: Gibson, *Journal*, 322; Wislizenus, *Memoir*, 61; Hughes, *Doniphan's Expedition*, 391 n. Onward: Robinson, *Journal*, 70.

18. Conquer or die: Wislizenus, *Memoir*, 61; Hughes, *Doniphan's Expedition*, 395-6.

19. Vote: Connelley in Hughes, *Doniphan's Expedition*, 396 n. 102. News: Edwards, *Marching*, 251; Edwards, *Campaign*, 69.

20. Quotations from 1.2.26, 3.1.

21. Fatherland: 1.3.6. Andromache: Homer, *Iliad* 6.429-30.

22. Greek character: G. Grote, *A History of Greece from the Earliest Period to the Death of the Generation Contemporary with Alexander the Great* (10 vols; London, 1904; orig. pub. 1846-56), vii. 195-6.

23. Black flag: Kennerly, *Persimmon Hill*, 199. Drunkenness: quoted from an unpublished diary by Dawson, *Doniphan's Epic March*, 170. 'Ticklish', dispatch, 'unfit': quoted in Hughes, *Doniphan's Expedition*, 450, 360 n. 82, 455 (7 March, 4 March, 20 March).

24. Elliott: Gardner and Simmons, *Mexican War Correspondence*, 159 (letter written 24 March 1847), 158, 160, 257 n. 138.

25. High spirits: quoted in Hughes, *Doniphan's Expedition*, 450. Divided: Robinson, *Journal*, 79. Sarah: Edwards, *Campaign*, 90. Parral: Edwards, *Campaign*, 90-1 (fled); cf. Gardner, *Brothers*, 117-18; Gibson, *Journal*, 362 (Doniphan had 'heard that public property of a large amount still remained in the little town of San Geronimo and some other places' and intended 'to go as far, perhaps, as Parral, where it was said some kind of a government was kept up'); Wislizenus, *Memoir*, 61-2; Edwards, *Marching*, 277. For the report of an army, cf. McGroarty, 'Richardson's Journal', 518 (10,000 Mexicans); Edwards, *Marching*, 277 (6,000); Robinson, *Journal*, 80, Gardner, *Brothers*, 118 (both giving 5,000). 'Retrograde', 'scorn': Edwards, *Marching*, 277. Chivalric: Wislizenus, *Memoir*, 62. Hoax: Wislizenus, *Memoir*, 62; cf. Gardner, *Brothers*, 118 (letter of 6 May 1847), alleging that the source was an American merchant living in Parral who feared the competition from the merchants accompanying Doniphan's army.

26. Mexico City: H.H. Bancroft, *History of the Life of William Gilpin: A Character Study* (San Francisco, 1889), 33-4; followed by Karnes, *William Gilpin*, 180; Launius, *Alexander William Doniphan*, 177-8.

27. Secret: Launius, *Alexander William Doniphan*, 177.

28. Express: Edwards, *Campaign*, 91, and Gardner, *Brothers*, 118, place it after the return; contrast the vote recorded by John Hughes (who was a member of the express party) in his diary for 19 March: 'Council of the officers – Vote to go on carried (26 to 6)' (*Doniphan's Expedition*, 108). Gilpin: reprinted in Hughes, *Doniphan's Expedition*, 597.

29. Emergency: G.W. Burnell, 'The Development of Our Armies, 1861-1865', in *War Papers Read Before the Commandery of the State of Wisconsin, Military Order of the Loyal Legion of the United States* 2 (Milwaukee, 1896), 70-80, at 79-80 (paper delivered 2 December 1891).

30. Stranded: 3.1.2-3.

31. Disasters: Thucydides 8.1.1-2; Xenophon, *Hellenica* 2.2.3.

32. Apollonides: 3.1.30-1.

33. Freedom: 3.2.13.

34. Election: 3.1.47; Rennell, *Illustrations*, 15. Ordinary soldiers: 3.2.32. Votes: 3.2.33, 38. Muster: 3.3.20.

35. *Aporia*: 1.3.13, 3.1.2. Fear: 1.3.8, 2.5.29. Sleep: 1.3.11, 3.1.13. Guide: 1.3.14, 16, 3.1.2. Election: 1.3.14, 3.1.47.

36. Assembly: E. Gibbon, *The History of the Decline and Fall of the Roman Empire*, ed. D. Womersley (3 vols; Harmondsworth, 1994; orig. pub. 1776-88), i. 951; Grote, *History of Greece*, vii. 250-4.

37. Sneeze: 3.2.9. Profit: 3.2.29.

38. Privilege: 3.1.37; cf. *Iliad* 12.310-28 (a link drawn by J. Hawkey (trans.), *Xenophon: The Ascent of Cyrus the Younger and the Retreat of the Ten Thousand Greeks* (Dublin, 1738), 99 n.). Leaders: 3.1.38.

39. Doniphan: the speech is given in full in *Dover Gazette & Strafford Advertiser*, 7 August 1847; in part in Cutts, *Conquest*, 98-100.

40. Quotations from I. Strohm (ed.), *Speeches of Thomas Corwin, with a Sketch of his Life* (Dayton, OH, 1859), 374-5, 338.

7. The Savage State: Kurds and Indians

1. Indian country: C. Buzzell, *My War: Killing Time in Iraq* (London, 2006; orig. pub. 2005), 73; Hartley, *Just Another Soldier*, 77.

2. For my use of the term 'Indians', see Introduction, n. 2.

3. Navajos: see Launius, *Alexander William Doniphan*, 118-33; Dawson, *Doniphan's Epic March*, 176-7; and more broadly F. McNitt, *Navajo Wars: Military Campaigns, Slave Wars, and Reprisals* (Albuquerque, 1972), 95-123.

4. Reid: see Dawson, *Doniphan's Epic March*, 176-7; B. DeLay, *War of a Thousand Deserts: Indian Raids and the U.S.-Mexican War* (New Haven and London, 2008), 267-70.

5. Carduchians: 3.5.15-16.

6. Losses: 4.3.2. Valiant: 4.7.15. Cf. already Ch. 1 n. 11 on Carduchian fighting.

7. Pacificator: Hughes, *Doniphan's Expedition*, 308.

8. Reid: quoted by DeLay, *War of a Thousand Deserts*, 268. Benton: cited e.g. in *The Rough and Ready Annual: Or, Military Souvenir* (New York and Philadelphia, 1848), 212-14; this passage is strangely omitted from Benton's reproduction of his speech in *Thirty Years' View*.

9. Captivity: see Ch. 3 n. 4.

10. Kurds and Indians: J. Perkins, 'Nestorians of Persia', *Missionary Herald* 31 (May 1835), 161-9, at 167 (his slightly longer account in *A Residence of Eight Years in Persia, among the Nestorian Christians* (Andover, MA, 1843), 191, replaces 'wild' with 'rude'); G.H. Hepworth, *Through Armenia on Horseback* (New York, 1898), 230; Cox, *Diversions of a Diplomat*, 186.

11. Paris: quoted by L.E. Gelfand, *The Inquiry: American Preparations for Peace, 1917-1919* (New Haven, 1963), 243. Turks: quoted by P. Mansel, *Constantinople: City of the World's Desire, 1453-1924* (London, 1995), 421. Iraq War: Carroll, *Medicine Bags*, 176-7, 204.

12. Skull: Kennerly, *Persimmon Hill*, 203-4; cf. Wislizenus, *Memoir*, 71-2.

13. School: A. Pretor (ed.), *The Anabasis of Xenophon* (Cambridge, 1881), 421.

14. Stadial theory: see e.g. G. Dekker, *The American Historical Romance* (Cambridge, 1987), 73-98; T. Fulford, *Romantic Indians: Native Americans, British Literature, and Transatlantic Culture, 1756-1830* (Oxford, 2006), 41-8; C.W.J. Withers, *Placing the Environment: Thinking Geographically about the Age of Reason* (Chicago, 2007), 136-63 (with 263 n. 38 for further bibliography).

15. Cole: see e.g. A.L. Miller, *The Empire of the Eye: Landscape Representation and American Cultural Politics, 1825-1875* (Ithaca, NY, and London, 1993), 21-65; A. Wallach, 'Landscape and the Course of American Empire', in W.H. Truettner and A. Wallach (eds), *Thomas Cole: Landscape into History* (New Haven, 1994), 23-112, at 90-5 (with plates 103-7).

16. Navajos: Hughes, *Doniphan's Expedition*, 315. Scott: cf. D. Richards, *Masks of Difference: Cultural Representations in Literature, Anthropology and Art* (Cambridge, 1994), 129 (with 125-6 for Scots and Afghans); and more generally R. Emerson, 'American Indians, Frenchmen, and Scots Philosophers', *Studies in Eighteenth-Century Culture* 9 (1979), 211-36, esp. 213-14; for a Scottish aristocrat's identification with Indians, L. Strong, 'American Indians and Scottish Identity in Sir William Drummond Stewart's Collection', *Winterthur Portfolio* 35 (2000), 127-55; and see now C.G. Calloway, *White People, Indians, and Highlanders: Tribal Peoples and Colonial Encounters in Scotland and America* (New York, 2008).

17. Elliot: J.B. Fraser, *Mesopotamia and Assyria, from the Earliest Ages to the Present Time; with Illustrations of their Natural History* (Edinburgh and London, 1842), 310-11; on Elliot, see *The Sea! The Sea!*, 141. For the same trope, see Kinneir, *Journey*, 411 ('The chief of Sert is ... probably not very different from some of our dukes and earls six or seven hundred years ago'). Britain: A. Ferguson, *An Essay on the History of Civil Society* (Edinburgh, 1966; orig. pub. 1767), 75; cf. H. Honour, *The New Golden Land: European Images of America from the Discoveries to the Present Time* (New York, 1975), 120, for comparisons with the ancient Germans described by Tacitus. On the notion of the timeless or backward foreigner, cf. J. Fabian, *Time and the Other: How Anthropology Makes its Object* (New York, 1983); P. Horden and N. Purcell, *The Corrupting Sea: A Study of Mediterranean History* (Oxford, 2000), 463-84; R. Shiffer, *Oriental Panorama: British Travellers in 19th Century Turkey* (Amsterdam, 1999), 243-7 (on Turkey).

18. Interesting: J. Williams, *Two Essays on the Geography of Ancient Asia, Intended Partly to Illustrate the Campaigns of Alexander and the Anabasis of Xenophon* (London, 1829), 249.

19. Customs: Kinneir, *Journey*, 487; the same trope (customs unchanged but no liquor) in R. Wilbraham, *Travels in the Trans-Caucasian Provinces of Russia, and Along the Southern Shore of the Lakes of Van and Urumiah, in the Autumn and Winter of 1837* (London, 1839), 333-4. Moslem: I. Bird, *Journeys in Persia and Kurdistan* (2 vols; London, 1988-9; orig. pub. 1891), ii. 352.

20. Rolling rocks: 4.7.13. Britons: Anon., review of *Xenophon* (*Valpy's Classical Library* 111), *Gentleman's Magazine* 100 (1830), 615-17, at 616.

21. Bronze: Hughes, *Doniphan's Expedition*, 478 n. Sculpture: e.g. Honour, *New Golden Land*, 56, 75-7, 125, 233-4; W.L. Vance, *America's Rome* (2 vols; New Haven and London, 1989), i. 182, 302-12, 335, 345; Sundquist, 'Literature of Expansion', 232; H. Liebersohn, *Aristocratic Encounters: European Travelers and North American Indians* (Cambridge, 1998), 14-15, 152-3; S. Conn, *History's Shadow: Native Americans and Historical Consciousness in the Nineteenth Century* (Chicago and London, 2004), 59 (and 41-2 for an inversion: Benjamin West comparing Roman statues with Indians). Roman: F.A. Wislizenus, *A Journey to the Rocky Mountains in the Year 1839* (St Louis, 1912; Ger. orig. 1840), 150; cf. W. Irving, *A Tour of the Prairies*, in *Three Western Narratives* (Library of America; New York, 2004), 20, 27 (and cf. also 894); Richard, *Golden Age*, 32 (chief named 'Roman Nose'); Truettner, *West*, 153 n. 12. Catlin: quoted by Honour, *New Golden Land*, 236; cf. Truettner, *West*, 323. Crest: F.H. Ludlow, *The Heart of the Continent: A Record of Travel across the Plains and in Oregon* (New York, 1870), 458; cf. G. Catlin, *Life among the Indians* (London, 1874), 71. Cavalry: Catlin, *Life among the Indians*, 73. Councils: Liebersohn, *Aristocratic Encounters*, 86; B.W. Sheehan, *Seeds of Extinction: Jeffersonian Philanthropy and the American Indian* (Chapel Hill, 1973), 111. Philosophy: C. Sumner, *Fame and Glory: An Address before the Literary Societies of Amherst College, at their Anniversary, August 11, 1847* (Boston, 1847), 9. Eloquence: Sheehan, *Seeds of Extinction*, 107; R.H. Pearce, *The Savages of America: A Study of the Indian and the Idea of Civilization* (Baltimore, 1953), 180 ('a savage Cicero', from a 1772 poem).

22. Imagined: F. Millingen, *Wild Life among the Koords* (London, 1870), 133-4.

23. Parkman: quoted by Sundquist, 'Literature of Expansion', 178. Kurds: Porter, *Travels*, ii. 457, 639. For such geological metaphors, cf. Spurr, *Rhetoric of Empire*, 99-100.

24. Defiles: Porter, *Travels*, ii. 674. Doniphan: Hughes, *Doniphan's Expedition*, 288, 299-300 (curiously ignoring Hannibal's more famous Alps crossing).

25. Energy: Hughes, *Doniphan's Expedition*, 289.

26. Indians: Edwards, *Campaign*, 9, 39. Kurdistan: Porter, *Travels*, ii. p. v (from the transcriber's preface). For the American picturesque, see e.g. B.L. Lueck, *American Writers and the Picturesque Tour: The Search for National Identity, 1790-1860* (New York, 1997); J. Conron, *American Picturesque* (University Park, PA, 2000).

27. Code: M.F. Jacobson, *Barbarian Virtues: The United States Encounters Foreign Peoples at Home and Abroad* (New York, 2000), 124. Subjugated: A.E. Silliman, *A Gallop among American Scenery* (Philadelphia, 1843), 141-2 (quoted in Cunliffe, *Soldiers and Civilians*, 407).

28. Desert: Ch. 4 n. 22. Pictures: Anon., review of *Xenophon*, 616. Scott: review of 'Tales of a Grandfather', *Westminster Review* 10 (April 1829), 258-83, at 258.

29. Thrace: Rev. N.S. Smith (trans.), *Anabasis Kurou, or the Expedition of Cyrus into Persia, and the Retreat of the Ten Thousand Greeks* (London, 1824), 483 n. 1, referring to 7.3.15-33. For Xenophon and Scott, cf. also J.A.K. Thomson, *Greeks and Barbarians* (London and New York, 1921), 61 (same natural tastes but Scott 'an incomparably greater man').

30. Guignet: *Paris Salon de 1843* (New York and London, 1977; reprint of *Explication des ouvrages de peinture, sculpture, architecture, gravure et lithographie des artistes vivants exposés au Museé Royal le 15 Mars 1843*), 73 (no. 564); see further J.G. Bulliot, *Le Peintre Adrien Guignet, sa vie et son oeuvre* (Autun, 1878); S. Laveissière (ed.), *Adrien Guignet, peintre: 1816-1854* (Autun, 1978).

31. Cooper in France: Liebersohn, *Aristocratic Encounters*, 75 (with n. 29 for further refs).

32. Bows: 4.2.28.

33. Parthians: Strabo 16.1.24.

34. Indians/Parthians/Scythians: R.G. Thwaites (ed.), *Jesuit Relations and Allied Documents: Travels and Explorations of the Jesuit Missionaries in New France, 1610-1791* (73 vols; Cleveland, 1896-1901), xxii. 35; O.P. Dickason, *The Myth of the Savage and the Beginnings of French Colonialism in the Americas* (Edmonton, 1997), 34 and 290 n. 43; Cooke, *Conquest*, 5, 8, 153. Tactics: M.W. Mather and J.W. Hewitt (eds), *Xenophon's Anabasis: Books I-IV* (New York, Cincinnati and Chicago, 1910), 358 (n. on 3.3.10).

35. Critics: W. Tenint, *L'Album du Salon de 1843* (Paris, 1843), 46; F. Pillet, *Le Moniteur universel*, 3 April 1843, p. 665.

36. Rosa: F. Haskell, 'The Old Masters in Nineteenth Century French Painting', *Art Quarterly* 34 (1971), 55-85, fig. 19; J.S. Patty, *Salvator Rosa in French Literature: From the Bizarre to the Sublime* (Lexington, KY, 2005), 124. Baudelaire: cited by M. Butor, *Histoire Extraordinaire: Essay on a Dream of Baudelaire's*, trans. R.J. Howard (London, 1969; Fr. orig. 1961), 160 (cf. 130-1 on the dandyism of North American savages).

37. Taochians: 4.7.1, 2, 13; H.W. Herbert, *The Captains of the Old World* (New York, 1852), 217 (Herbert was British-born but based in the US throughout his writing career); cf. also T.S. Hughes, *Travels in Greece and Albania* (2 vols; 2nd edn; London, 1830; orig. pub. 1820), ii. 184 n. (from where the phrase 'a wild people' is taken). Suliotes: W. Haygarth, *Greece: A Poem* (London, 1814), 9; C. Wordsworth, *Greece: Pictorial, Descriptive, and Historical* (London, 1844; orig. pub. 1839), 260; cf. D. Roessel, *In Byron's Shadow: Modern Greece in the English and American Imagination* (Oxford and New York, 2002), 39-40, 87. Darwin: quoted by Winterer, *Mirror of Antiquity*, 186 – but while she attributes the racism to Darwin, I take it that 'is' means 'is [regarded as]'.

38. Mossynoecians: 5.4.32-4 (cf. Herodotus 2.35-6 on Egypt).

39. Scattered: 4.1.7, 10; Thucydides 1.10.2. Location of settlements: 4.4.1; E.C. Semple, *Influences of Geographic Environment on the Basis of Ratzel's System of Anthropo-geography* (New York and London, 1911), 216-17; Thucydides 1.7.

40. Animals: 4.5.25; cf. in general S. Blundell, *The Origins of Civilization in Greek and Roman Thought* (London, 1986).

41. Ethnography as encouraging conquest: see P. Briant (ed.), *Dans les Pas des dix-mille: peuples et pays du Proche-Orient vus par un Grec* (*Pallas* 43; Toulouse, 1995), with the important review by C.J. Tuplin, 'On the Track of the Ten Thousand', *Revue des études anciennes* 101 (1999), 331-66. Wine: 4.5.27, 32; cf. F. Calderón de la Barca, *Life in Mexico, During a Residence of Two Years in that Country* (London, 1843), 35, on Mexican *pulque* ('when one gets over the first shock, it is very agreeable').

42. Fox-skins: 7.4.3-4. Blubber: 5.4.28.

43. Ravine: 6.5.18.

44. Wolfe: Rev. W. Jones, *Letters from a Tutor to his Pupils* (London, 1780), 68 (the earliest source I have found). Indian-style: cf. e.g. J.F. Cooper, *The Last of the Mohicans* (Oxford, 1994; orig. pub. 1826), 48.

45. Mutilation: 3.4.5; Thomson, *Greeks and Barbarians*, 68. Eat: 4.8.14 – a sentence that was admired by Emerson (*Journals*, v. 246); cf. also Conclusion, n. 11. Wrestle: 4.8.26.

46. Pisidians: 2.5.13; cf. S. Mitchell, *Anatolia: Land, Men, and Gods in Asia Minor* (2 vols; Oxford, 1993), i. 71-2.

47. Abandoning, guide: 4.1.8 (*eklipontes*: cf. e.g. Herodotus 7.37.3, 8.41.3), 23. This effective use of murder is cited in a recent American book on interrogation methods: C. Mackey and G. Miller, *The Interrogators: Inside the Secret War against Al Qaeda* (New York, 2004), 282; for similar US techniques in Vietnam, see Gibson, *Perfect War*, 185-6.

48. Eagles: Hughes, *Doniphan's Expedition*, 154; Edwards, *Campaign*, 76.

49. March: Hughes, *Doniphan's Expedition*, 393. Futurity: O'Sullivan, 'The Great Nation of Futurity', re-printed e.g. in N.A. Graebner (ed.), *Manifest Destiny* (New York, 1968), 15-21, at 20, 17 (originally *Democratic Review* 6 (November 1839), 426-30); cf. e.g. *Oration of Hon. O.P. Morton*, 21, 24, 26; Pearce, *Savages*, 112; Graebner, *Manifest Destiny*, p. xix, 141; Horsman, *Race and Manifest Destiny*, 25, 35, 96, 228, 236, 273, 287; A. Stephanson, *Manifest Destiny: American Expansionism and the Empire of Right* (New York, 1995), 58, 89, 99, 118.

50. Jefferson: quoted in Dekker, *American Historical Romance*, 81-2.

51. Colonies: 5.6.15, 25. Longing: 6.4.8. 'Acquire extra' (*prosktasthai*): cf. Herodotus 1.73.1, 3.34.4, 134.1, 7.8.a.1, a.2, 9.2; Thucydides 6.18.2, 24.3. Animals: 5.7.32.

52. Mediterranean: Turner, *Frontier*, 38.

53. Hercules: Arrian, *Anabasis* 4.30.4. Alexander and *aporia*: see e.g. C. Jacob, 'Alexandre et la maîtrise de l'espace. L'art du voyage dans l'*Anabase* d'Arrien', *Quaderni di Storia* 34 (1991), 5-40. Longing (*pothos*): see e.g. P.A. Brunt, *Arrian* (2 vols; Cambridge, MA, 1976), i. 469-70. Omen: Arrian, *Anabasis* 1.18.6-9; Plutarch, *Alexander* 33.2-3.

54. Alexander: Elliott, *Notes*, 221 (cited by Dawson, *Doniphan's Epic March*, 29); Dawson, *Doniphan's Epic March*, 195. Corwin: Strohm, *Speeches*, 375; Doniphan alluded to Corwin in his speech at the St Louis reception (Ch. 6 n. 40).

Intermezzo: Xenophon and Frémont

1. Ruffians: *Boston Daily Atlas*, 21 December 1855; reprinted in the *Bangor Daily Whig & Courier* (Bangor, ME), 24 December 1855.

2. Ratification: *Boston Daily Atlas*, 12 July 1856.

3. Laugh: letter to Rev. Dr. J. Hill, 18 November 1856 (Harvard University Archives). Felton's speech itself does not survive in his papers in the Harvard archives.

4. Entrenching: quoted e.g. in the *Daily National Intelligencer*, 11 November 1846; also by Z.S. Eldredge, *The Beginnings of San Francisco from the Expedition of Anza, 1774 to the City Charter of April 15, 1850* (San Francisco, 1912), 383-4.

5. Pen: *The Californian*, 12 June 1847.

6. 'Whoops', 'sun-burnt': W.B. Hesseltine and R.G. Fisher (eds), *Trimmers, Trucklers & Temporizers: Notes of Murat Halstead from the Political Conventions of 1856* (Madison, 1961), 96, 84. Arrows, mountains: J.W. Stout et al., *The Nation's Great Crisis: The Question Fairly Stated* (New Brunswick, 1856), 13. Poetry: G.S. Burleigh, *Signal-Fires on the Trail of the Pathfinder* (New York, 1856), 66, 138.

7. Conqueror: J.W. Gordon, *An Argument Designed to Show the Origin of the Troubles in Kansas, and the Remedy Therefor* (Indianapolis, 1856), 55. Indomitable: *Platforms and Candidates of 1856: Speech of Hon. John J. Perry, of Maine, Delivered in the House of Representatives, August 7, 1856* (Washington, DC, 1856), 8. Pathfinder: quoted by T. Chaffin, *Pathfinder: John Charles Frémont and the Course of American Empire* (New York, 2002), p. vii, as from the *U.S. Magazine* *and Democratic Review*; though it was originally from the biography of Frémont in M.B. Brady, *The Gallery of Illustrious Americans* (New York, 1850), widely reprinted elsewhere. Columbus: e.g. J. Bigelow, *Memoir of the Life and Public Services of John Charles Frémont* (New York and Cincinnati, 1856), 214. Washington: e.g. H. Greeley, *Life of Col. Fremont* (New York, 1856), 32; also 'Washington and Fremont' in e.g. *Boston Daily Atlas*, 10 July 1856, and *Milwaukee Daily Sentinel*, 14 July 1856.

8. Illustrious: Felton, *Greek Reader*, 229; cf. Ch. 3 n. 5.

9. School edition: J. Robertson, *The First and Second Books of Xenophon's Anabasis* (Philadelphia, 1850), 3-5. Biographies: e.g. by C.W. Upham, *Life, Explorations and Public Services of John Charles Fremont* (Boston, 1856), 11-15; Bigelow, *Memoir*, 24-7. Newspapers and journals: e.g. *New York Times,* 27 June 1856; *The Ripley Bee* (Ohio), 5 July 1856; *The Massachusetts Teacher and Journal of Home and School Education* 9 (1856), 369. Often articles citing the passage were reprinted: the article 'Fremont the Schoolboy' was published in Ohio (*Daily Cleveland Herald*, 15 July 1856) and Maine (*Bangor Daily Whig & Courier*, 15 July 1856); 'Washington and Fremont' in Massachusetts (*Boston Daily Atlas*, 10 July 1856) and Wisconsin (*Milwaukee Daily Sentinel*, 14 July 1856). The passage had already appeared in newspapers five years earlier (*St Louis Union*, 3 May 1851; *Daily National Intelligencer* (Washington, DC), 17 May 1851).

10. Washington: see the article 'Washington and Fremont', cited n. 9 above.

11. Exploring: J.F. Macmichael (ed.), *The Anabasis of Xenophon* (London, 1872), p. xxi.

12. Space book: Turner, *Frontier*, 11; Benton, *Thirty Years' View*, 580; E.G. and E.K. Gudde (trans. and ed.), *Exploring with Frémont: The Private Diaries of Charles Preuss, Cartographer for John C. Frémont on His First, Second, and Fourth Expeditions to the Far West* (Norman, OK, 1958), 5; cf. W.E. Smythe, *The Conquest of Arid America* (New York and London, 1900), p. xvi (the West as 'a clean, blank page, awaiting the makers of history').

13. Balboa: Jackson and Spence, *Expeditions*, i. 501.

14. Golden: Frémont, *Oregon and California*, 4 (cf. Ch. 4 n. 13 for the attribution of these words).

15. Scholar-soldier: 'Scenes in the Far West', *The United States Catholic Magazine and Monthly Review* 5 (1846), 14-22, at 22.

16. Next time: unpublished letter to Hill (n. 3).

8. Advance and Retreat: Sherman in Georgia

1. Century: A. Badiou, *The Century*, trans. A. Toscano (Cambridge and Malden, MA, 2007; Fr. orig. 2005), 81. Sherman: D.P. Conyngham, *Sherman's March through the South: With Sketches and Incidents of the Campaign* (New York, 1865), 427 (the occasion of the speech is not given: it was probably the banquet in Sherman's honour on 25 July).

2. 'Brush up': G.M. Dodge, 'Introductory Address', in De B.R. Keim (ed.), *Sherman: A Memorial in Art, Oratory, and Literature by the Society of the Army of Tennessee with the Aid of the Congress of the United States of America* (Washington, DC, 1904), 53. Pageant: W.T. Sherman, *Memoirs of General W. T. Sherman* (New York, 1990; orig. pub. 1875), 865-6.

3. Machine: Sherman, *Memoirs*, 495. President: R.S. Thorndike (ed.), *The Sherman Letters: Correspondence between General and Senator Sherman from 1837 to 1891* (New York, 1894), 246.

4. Bronzed: S.J. Niccolls, *A Tribute to General William Tecumseh Sherman, Delivered at the Public Memorial Service of Ransom Post No. 131, Department of Missouri, G.A.R., May 30th, 1891* (St Louis, 1891), 12. 'Ragged', 'chatted', 'stiff': quoted by S. McConnell, *Glorious Contentment: The Grand Army of the Republic, 1865-1900* (Chapel Hill, 1992), 7, part of an excellent account of the ideology of the grand review (1-17); see also T. Fleming, 'The Big Parade', *American Heritage* 41 (March 1990), 98-104 (stressing East/West union); W.M. McClay, *The Masterless: Self and Society in Modern America* (Chapel Hill, 1994), 9-39 (stressing centralization).

5. Caesar: G.W. Pepper, *Personal Recollections of Sherman's Campaigns in Georgia and the Carolinas* (Zanesville, OH, 1866), 121; S.H.M. Byers, *The March to the Sea: A Poem* (Boston, 1896), 83; for the row, see M. Fellman, *Citizen Sherman: A Life of William Tecumseh Sherman* (New York, 1995), 247-54.

6. Rebel papers: M.A. Andersen (ed.), *The Civil War Diary of Allen Morgan Geer* (Denver, 1977), 180.

7. Atlanta: Sherman, *Memoirs*, 655-6. Lyrical: cf. E. Wilson, *Patriotic Gore: Studies in the Literature of the American Civil War* (New York, 1962), 196; D.W. Blight, *Race and Reunion: The Civil War in American Memory* (Cambridge, MA, 2001), 163.

8. Disappeared: G.R. Agassiz (ed.), *Meade's Headquarters, 1863-1865: Letters of Colonel Theodore Lyman from the Wilderness to Appomattox* (Boston, 1922), 296. Romantic: P.M. Angle (ed.), *Three Years in the Army of the Cumberland: The Letters and Diary of Major James A. Connolly* (Bloomington, 1996), 292-3.

9. Modern Anabasis: *Augusta Constitutionalist*, 19 November 1864; partly quoted in *New York Times*, 26 November 1864, and F. Senour, *Major General William T. Sherman and his Campaigns* (Chicago, 1865), 304-5; J.B. McMaster, *A History of the People of the United States during Lincoln's Administration* (New York and London, 1927), 488.

10. Packing: *Daily Whig & Courier* (Bangor), 3 December 1864. Chuckle: *Daily News*, 17 December 1864.

11. Xenophon/Xerxes: quoted by *Milwaukee Daily Sentinel*, 28 December 1864; *Wisconsin State Register*, 31 December 1864; P.T. Sherman, *General Sherman in the Last Year of the Civil War: An Address Delivered at the Thirty-eighth Reunion of the Society of the Army of the Tennessee at St. Louis, Missouri* (New York, 1908), 10; L. Lloyd, *Sherman: Fighting Prophet* (New York, 1932), 457.

12. Moscow: D. Rowland (ed.), *Jefferson Davis, Constitutionalist: His Letters, Papers and Speeches* (10 vols; Jackson, MO, 1923), vi. 341.

13. *Times*: 20 June 1864, p. 8; 8 August 1864, p. 8; 5 December 1864, p. 8; 20 December 1864, p. 6. The Xenophon editorial was cited by 'Owls-Glass', *Rebel Brag and British Bluster: A Record of Unfulfilled Prophecies, Baffled Schemes, and Disappointed Hopes, with Echoes of Very Insignificant Thunder* (New York, 1865), 65; C.E. Lester, *The Glory and Shame of England* (New York, 1866), 537; cf. also A. Grant, *The American Civil War and the British Press* (Jefferson, NC, 2000), 133. Besieged: Thucydides 7.11.4; for Roman examples, cf. A.J. Woodman (ed.), *Velleius Paterculus: The Caesarian and Augustan Narrative (2.41-93)* (Cambridge, 1983), 92.

14. Arduous: *Belfast News-Letter*, 26 December 1864.

15. Christmas: Sherman, *Memoirs*, 711 (letter to Lincoln dated 22 December 1864). Anabasis: *Chicago Tribune*, 28 December 1864; quoted by J.F. Marszalek, *Sherman's Other War: The General and the Civil War Press* (Kent, OH, and London, 1999; orig. pub. 1981), 189, and alluded to by E. Caudill and P. Ashdown,

Sherman's March in Myth and Memory (Lanham, MD, 2008), 47 – where 'Anabasis' is assumed to be the name of a general.

16. Anabasis: *The Spectator* 1905, 31 December 1864, p. 1491. Retreat: *The Times* (London), 4 January 1865, p. 9.

17. Xenophon allusions: e.g. *The New England Historical and Genealogical Register* 19 (1865), 109 (a speech delivered on 4 January 1865). Reversed: *United States Service Magazine* 3 (1865), 76; the same magazine the following year spoke of Sherman 'rehears[ing] offensively, thirty centuries after it occurred, the Anabasis' (*United States Service Magazine* 5 (1866), 494). Cf. Ch. 3 n. 31.

18. Hager: Anon., *The Great Rebellion: Grand National Allegory and Tableaux* (Buffalo, NY, 1865), 24. The Xenophon allusion was omitted when the piece was renamed *The Great Republic* and the focus changed from Union triumph to reconciliation.

19. Melancholy: *North American and United States Gazette*, 23 February 1865. Memoirs: *Sentinel* (Indianapolis), 17 May 1875.

20. Business: C.V. Woodward (ed.), *Mary Chesnut's Civil War* (New Haven, 1981), 701.

21. Thermopylae: J.B. Hood, *Advance and Retreat: Personal Experiences in the United States and Confederate Armies* (Lincoln, NE, and London, 1996; orig. pub. 1880), 150-1. The analogy has been immortalized (as Tom Phillips pointed out to me) in M. Mitchell, *Gone with the Wind* (New York, 1975; orig. pub. 1936), 270, and in the 1939 film; cf. also W.G. Simms, *A City Laid Waste: The Capture, Sack, and Destruction of the City of Columbia*, ed. D. Aiken (Columbia, SC, 2005; orig. pub. 1865), 49.

22. Richmond: Woodward, *Mary Chesnut's Civil War*, 607.

23. Moscow: Woodward, *Mary Chesnut's Civil War*, 240.

24. English interest: G.W. Nichols, *The Story of the Great March: From the Diary of a Staff-Officer* (London, 1865), p. v. Sherman's letter: quoted by H.S. Commager, *The Blue and the Gray: The Story of the Civil War as Told by Participants* (2 vols; Indianapolis, 1950), 967. Name of Sherman: H. Adams, *The Letters of Henry Adams*, ed. J.C. Levenson (6 vols; Cambridge, MA, and London, 1982-8), i. 466. For the interest taken by English newspapers, see E.D. Adams, *Great Britain and the American Civil War* (2 vols; London, 1925); cf. e.g. Adams, *Letters*, i. 445, 461. *Blitzkrieg*: B.H. Liddell Hart, 'Introduction', in W.T. Sherman, *From Atlanta to the Sea* (London, 1961). 60,000: B.H. Liddell Hart, *Sherman: The Genius of the Civil War* (London, 1930), 391.

25. Vainglorious: Rowland, *Jefferson Davis*, viii. 244 (letter from Lewis Cruger). Letter to wife: quoted by Commager, *The Blue and the Gray*, 967. West Point: W.T. Sherman, *Address to the Graduating Class of the U.S. Military Academy, West Point, June 15th, 1869* (New York, 1869), 11. E.D. Samet, *Willing Obedience: Citizens, Soldiers, and the Progress of Consent in America, 1787-1898* (Stanford, 2004), 106-7, citing L.B. Kennett, *Sherman: A Soldier's Life* (New York, 2001), 349, states that Sherman in private acknowledged the *Anabasis* as a parallel; but this comment seems to be based on Kennett's gloss rather than a direct citation of Sherman himself.

26. Ornaments: *Wisconsin State Register*, 31 December 1864. American: A.H. Guernsey and H.M. Alden (eds), *Harper's Pictorial History of the Great Rebellion* (New York, 1866-8), 684; quoted by V.D. Hanson, *The Soul of Battle: From Ancient Times to the Present Day, How Three Great Liberators Vanquished Tyranny* (New York, 1999), 227; *New York Times*, 20 July 1866, p. 2.

27. Patent: J.D. Cox, *The March to the Sea: Franklin and Nashville* (New York,

1882), 2-3. Attack and defence: H. Van Boynton, *Sherman's Historical Raid: The Memoirs in the Light of the Record* (Cincinnati, 1875), 129-61 (chapter headed: 'The March to the Sea – Did Grant or Sherman Plan it?'); C.W. Moulton, *The Review of General Sherman's Memoirs Examined, Chiefly in the Light of its Own Evidence* (Cincinnati, 1875), 48-50.

28. Howl: Sherman, *Memoirs*, 627; see further e.g. 466-7, 492, 494 for supplies; 604, 620, for Hood; 641 for the overall question of responsibility.

29. Exaggerated: Thorndike, *The Sherman Letters*, 242. Napoleon: W.S. Sherman, 'The Grand Strategy of the Last Year of the War', in R.U. Johnson and C.C. Buel (eds), *Battles and Leaders of the Civil War* (4 vols; New York, 1884-8), iv. 247-59, at 255.

30. Ruin: B.D. Simpson and J.V. Berlin (eds), *Sherman's Civil War: Selected Correspondence of William T. Sherman, 1860-1865* (Chapel Hill, 1999), 730. Offensive: Sherman, *Memoirs*, 524, cf. 617, 628-9.

31. Century: Badiou, *The Century*, 81. Thanks to Paul Cartledge for introducing me to Badiou's 'Anabasis' chapter.

32. Foundered: Badiou, *The Century*, 94, 89-90.

33. *Anabano*: Badiou, *The Century*, 83 (the mistaken form is also used in the French original).

34. Oracular: *North American and United States Gazette*, 23 February 1865.

35. Nichols: *Peterson's Magazine* 48 (October 1865), 291; *The Examiner*, 23 September 1865; *North American Review* 102 (January 1866), 312.

36. Smashing: Sherman, *Memoirs*, 629.

9. The Brutal Romance of War: Reconstruction and Beyond

1. War: M.A. De W. Howe (ed.), *Home Letters of General Sherman* (New York, 1909), 298.

2. Statue: K.A. Jacob, *Testament to Union: Civil War Monuments in Washington, D.C.* (Baltimore, 1998), 91-9. Speeches: Keim, *Sherman*, 64 (triumphal), 53-4 (happiest); cf. also 70 (Gen. Henderson), 122 (Mrs Logan) for references to the scene.

3. Tom Sherman: T.J. Durkin, *General Sherman's Son* (New York, 1959), 190-2 (from where the newspaper quotes are taken); Wilson, *Patriotic Gore*, 209-18; Caudill and Ashdown, *Sherman's March*, 154-63. These writers all ignore a chronological problem: the Sherman statue was unveiled in October 1903; Father Sherman's trip to Georgia took place in May 1906. It seems that the causal link between the two events is a convenient fiction.

4. Anabasis: Montgomery (Alabama) *Advertiser*, 5 May 1906. Retreat: Atlanta *Constitution*, 2 May 1906 (quoted by Caudill and Ashdown, *Sherman's March*, 158).

5. Suffering: D.G. Faust, *This Republic of Suffering: Death and the American Civil War* (New York, 2008), p. xiii, cf. 188-90, 268-71.

6. Industrial: E.L. Doctorow, *The March* (London, 2006; orig. pub. 2005), 218-19.

7. Vance: C. Dowd, *Life of Zebulon B. Vance* (Charlotte, NC, 1897), 470, 478, 475, 479 (the speech is reproduced on pp. 463-93; it was also issued as a pamphlet). Reunions: see e.g. K.S. Bohannon, '"These Few Gray-Haired, Battle-Scarred Veterans": Confederate Army Reunions in Georgia, 1885-95', in G.W. Gallagher and A.T. Nolan (eds), *The Myth of the Lost Cause and Civil War History* (Bloomington, 2000), 89-110.

8. Restraining: *The Old Guard* 4 (1866), 408. Spencer and Vance: see S.E. Gardner, *Blood and Irony: Southern White Women's Narratives of the Civil War, 1861-1937* (Chapel Hill, 2006), 49-52.

9. Foraging: C.P. Spencer, *The Last Ninety Days of the War in North-Carolina* (New York, 1866), 54-5 (originally published in the New York *Watchman*); citing J. Kent, *Commentaries on American Law* (2nd edn; 4 vols; New York, 1832; orig. pub. 1826), i. 91, which itself alludes to *Cyropaedia* 5.4.24-7.

10. Soldiers/farmers: cf. P. Hunt, *Slaves, Warfare and Ideology in the Greek Historians* (Cambridge, 1998), 196. Plunder: *Cyropaedia* 5.4.28. Hand-mills: *Cyropaedia* 6.2.31; cf. W.K. Pritchett, *The Greek State at War* (5 vols; Berkeley, 1971-91), v. 456.

11. Critique: Isocrates 4.146 (written 380 BC). Infamous: Sherman, *Memoirs*, 716.

12. Fire: 5.2.24-5, 27.

13. Volcanoes: Simms, *City Laid Waste*, 66. Defence: Sherman, *Memoirs*, 659, 662, 667; cf. J.T. Glatthaar, *The March to the Sea and Beyond: Sherman's Troops in the Savannah and Carolinas Campaigns* (New York, 1985), 119-55, for evidence on foraging, destruction, and pillaging from soldiers' journals and letters. Enquiry: Sherman, *Memoirs*, 980-7, cf. 967, 988. Carthago: F.Y. Hedley, *Marching through Georgia: Pen-Pictures of Every-day Life in General Sherman's Army, from the Beginning of the Atlanta Campaign until the Close of the War* (Chicago, 1884), 375.

14. Damage: 2.4.27 (Parysatis), 3.5.1-3 (scorching), 4.1.8-9 (utensils). Defence: 5.5.14-16. Mill: Wilkinson, *Memoirs*, iii. 455 (cf. Ch. 3 n. 10), also citing the attack on Asidates (see below).

15. Cerasus: 5.3.3-4; see Pritchett, *Greek State at War*, v. 223-45, for the enslavement of (esp. non-Greek) captives.

16. Foraging: Sherman, *Memoirs*, 697, 659. On counting in Sherman's *Memoirs*, see J. Dawes, *The Language of War: Literature and Culture in the U.S. from the Civil War through World War II* (Cambridge, MA, 2002), 29-35; for the racial aspect, see M.E. Neely, *The Civil War and the Limits of Destruction* (Cambridge, MA, 2007).

17. Asidates: 7.8.8-23.

18. Aeneas: 4.7.13. Eagle: 6.1.23 (cf. M.A. Flower, *The Seer in Ancient Greece* (Berkeley, 2008), 200).

19. Longing: Doctorow, *The March*, 362-3.

20. Modern Anabasis: 'Oration of General Cruft', in *The Army Reunion: With Reports of the Meetings of the Societies of the Army of the Cumberland; the Army of the Tennessee; the Army of the Ohio; and the Army of Georgia* (Chicago, 1869), 37-70, at 52; R.S. Rantoul (ed.), *Report of the Harvard Class of 1853: 1849-1913* (Cambridge, MA, 1913), p. vii (Xenophon quote). Tedious: *Report of the Proceedings of the Society of the Army of the Tennessee at the Twenty-Sixth Meeting* (Cincinnati, 1895), 96. Schoolboy: *Proceedings of the Senate and Assembly of the State of New York: On the Life and Services of Gen. William T. Sherman, held at Harmanus Bleecker Hall, Albany, March 29, 1892* (Albany, NY, 1892), 35. Replaced: C.M. Depew, 'Speech at the Dinner to Celebrate the Anniversary of the Birthday of General Grant' (delivered 27 April 1888), in *Orations and After-Dinner Speeches of Chauncey M. Depew* (New York, 1896), 170. Indiana: *Report of the Proceedings of the Society of the Army of the Tennessee: Eleventh, Twelfth, and Thirteenth Annual Meetings* (Cincinnati, 1885), 263 (speech by Gov. T.A. Hendricks, Indianapolis, 1878, responding to toast 'Indiana'). Cf. *Report of the Proceedings of the*

Society of the Army of the Tennessee: Sixth, Seventh, Eight, Ninth, and Tenth Annual Meetings (Cincinnati, 1877), 414 (telling of the achievements of Sherman's army as 'a task worthy of a Homer, a Virgil or a Xenophon').

21. Paper: Sherman, *Memoirs*, 761; cf. Simpson and Berlin, *Sherman's Civil War*, 824 (paper sent to his wife with letter of 12 March 1865). Romance: G.C. Eggleston (ed.), *American War Ballads and Lyrics: A Collection of the Songs and Ballads of the Colonial Wars, the Revolution, the War of 1812-15, the War with Mexico, and the Civil War* (New York and London, 1889), 195.

22. Song: Sherman, *Memoirs*, 762-4. Sales: M.P. Holsinger (ed.), *War and American Popular Culture: A Historical Encyclopedia* (Westport, CT, 1999), 135. Reunions: *Report of the Proceedings of the Society of the Army of the Tennessee at the First Annual Meeting* (Cincinnati, 1867), 27, 113; S.H.M. Byers, *Twenty Years in Europe: A Consul-General's Memories of Noted People, with Letters from General W. T. Sherman* (Chicago, 1900), 297; the lyrics were also often reprinted (without attribution to Byers) in the published proceedings of reunions of Sherman's army. Name: e.g. Eggleston, *American War Ballads*, 195 (quoting Sherman); *The Arena* 47 (1896-7), 173; it had occasionally been termed a 'march to the sea' before Byers' song became known, e.g. *New York Times*, 19 November 1864 (without initial capitals); one campaign diary has as entry for 22 December 1864: 'Thus ends our great "march to the sea". A wonderful and successful campaign it has been' (W.C. Johnson, 'The March to the Sea', in *G.A.R. War Papers: Papers Read Before Fred. C. Jones Post, No. 401, Department of Ohio* (Cincinnati, 1891), 303-36, at 335) – but this may well be a later re-writing.

23. Composition: S.H.M. Byers, *With Fire and Sword* (New York, 1911), 154-61. Picture: Byers, *Twenty Years*, 59.

24. Reminiscent: Hanson, *Soul of Battle*, 234. March vs retreat: *New York Times*, 20 July 1866, p. 2; *Third Reunion of the Society of the Army of the Cumberland* (Cincinnati, 1869), 59. Sea-coast: T. Keightley, *An Elementary History of Greece* (London, 1841), 120.

25. Tramp: S.H.M. Byers, *The Happy Isles and Other Poems* (New York, 1891), 72-6. Spirit: *The Congregationalist* (Boston), 19 November 1896, p. 768. Genius: *The Arena* 47 (1896-7), 173.

26. Xenophon's March to the Sea: e.g. J.D. Steele, E.B. Steele, and J.H. Vincent, *Brief History of Greece: With Readings from Prominent Greek Historians* (New York, 1883), 152 (title given to an extract from G.W. Cox's 1876 *General History of Greece*, which does not use the phrase); *The Theatre* (1887), 289, on 'Anabasis' as a 'misnomer' for the 'march to the sea'. Shout: Byers, *March to the Sea*, 124-5; for Sherman as Columbus, cf. J. Tillson, *The March to the Sea: Delivered before the Army of the Tennessee on their Eighth Annual Reunion at Springfield, Illinois, October 14th, 1874* (Quincy, 1874), 5; and for the Xenophon/Columbus parallel, cf. *The Sea! The Sea!*, 26. Peal: Chelifer, 'A Poet of the Civil War', *Godey's Magazine* 135 (1897), 496-9, at 499. Paraphrase: *The Arena* 47 (1896-7), 173.

27. Ecstatic: S. Merrill, *The Seventieth Indiana Volunteer Infantry in the War of Rebellion* (Indianapolis, 1900), 240 (from a chapter entitled 'Then they marched five parasangs': Merrill unusually stresses the hardships beyond the sea for both the Ten Thousand and Sherman's troops, cf. n. 40). Sea: Keim, *Sherman*, 318.

28. Romantic interest: 'Owen's *Anabasis of Xenophon*', *North American Review* 57 (1843), 505-7, at 505. Romantic: Byers, *March to the Sea*, 145; Tillson, *March to the Sea*, 7; Cox, *The March to the Sea*, 42; A. Badeau, *Military History of Ulysses S. Grant* (3 vols; New York, 1885; orig. pub. 1868-81), iii. 300; J. Kilpatrick, 'Gen. Sherman's Memoirs', *New York Times*, 20 January 1876, p. 5.

29. Knights: G. Murray, *A History of Ancient Greek Literature* (New York, 1897), 318 (with some irony – the knight ends as 'filibuster'; but cf. *The Sea! The Sea!*, 17, for another example); Byers, *March to the Sea*, 18, 81. Sherman: quoted in G.F. Linderman, *Embattled Courage: The Experience of Combat in the American Civil War* (New York and London, 1987), 284.

30. Byers: *The Congregationalist* (Boston),19 November 1896, p. 768; cf. *Examiner*, 23 September 1865, on Nichols' *Story of the Great March*. Bierce: quoted by Linderman, *Embattled Courage*, 282. Classic: J.H. Kennaway, *On Sherman's Tracks, or, The South after the War* (London, 1867), p. vi . Herculaneum: Pepper, *Personal Recollections*, 309. Athens: S. Andrews, *The South since the War, as Shown by Fourteen Weeks of Travel and Observation in Georgia and the Carolinas* (Boston, 1866), 2. Integrating: L. Murray, 'A Newly Discovered Country: The Post-Bellum South and the Picturesque Ruin', *Nineteenth-Century Prose* 29 (2002), 94-119, at 95; cf. also N. Silber, *The Romance of Reunion: Northerners and the South, 1865-1900* (Chapel Hill, 1993); N.M. Knight, 'A Lovely Ruin: Sherman's March in the Literary Imagination' (PhD thesis, Harvard, 2007); and more broadly Rainey, *Creating Picturesque America*.

31. Name: Byers, *Twenty Years*, 69 (cf. Sherman on the 'captivating label', quoted in Eggleston, *American War Ballads*, 195). Campaign: S.H.M. Byers, 'The March to the Sea', *North American Review* 143 (September 1887), 235-45, at 245. Sherman: M.F. Force, *General Sherman* (New York, 1899), p. v. Distinctive: G.W. Curtis, 'Editor's Easy Chair', *Harper's Magazine* 82 (1891), 959-64, at 963. Reports: A.H. Guernsey, 'Sherman's Great March', *Harper's Magazine* 31 (1865), 571-89, at 571-2.

32. Holiday: Byers, *March to the Sea*, 101. Teacher: see *The Sea! The Sea!*, 17. Frolic: Cox, *March to the Sea*, 42. Picnic: Conyngham, *Sherman's March*, 266; cf. e.g. *Report of the Proceedings of the Society of the Army of the Tennessee: First, Second, Third, Fourth, and Fifth Meetings* (Cincinnati, 1877), 24, 359. Gala: Pepper, *Personal Recollections*, 517. Holiday: C.C. Jones, *The Siege of Savannah in December, 1864, and the Confederate Operations in Georgia and the Third Military District of South Carolina during General Sherman's March from Atlanta to the Sea* (Albany, 1874), p. vi. Pleasant: Rowland, *Jefferson Davis*, viii. 244 (letter from Lewis Cruger); see Ch. 7 n. 25 for the false Xenophon allusion. Cf. Ch. 4 n. 2 for Doniphan's march as holiday.

33. Quotations from Byers, *March to the Sea*, 139 (parade), 147 (Israel), 142-3 (epilogue).

34. Sectional: 'Sherman's March to the Sea', *Current Literature* 21 (1897), 402-3, at 403. War of giants: Niccolls, *Tribute*, 16. Cf. in general Linderman, *Embattled Courage*, 266-97; Kammen, *Mystic Chords*, 101-31; Blight, *Race and Reunion*; and, on reunions, McConnell, *Glorious Contentment*, 190-1.

35. Heroism: R.S. Bevier, *History of the First and Second Missouri Confederate Brigades: 1861-1865; And, From Wakarusa to Appomattox, a Military Anagraph* (St Louis, 1879), 13. Masterly: 'Discourse of Rev. B.M. Palmer, D.D.', *Southern Historical Society Papers* 18 (1890), 210-17, at 211. Chesnut: Ch. 8 n. 22.

36. Nez Percés: for a recent account, see E. West, *The Last Indian War: The Nez Perce Story* (Oxford, 2009); for Sherman's role, see R.G. Athearn, *William Tecumseh Sherman and the Settlement of the West* (Norman, OK, 1956), 315-22.

37. Congress: E. Ellis, *Henry Moore Teller, Defender of the West* (Caldwell, ID, 1941), 102. Anabasis: G.W. Baird, 'The Capture of Chief Joseph and the Nez Perces', *The International Review* 7 (1879), 209-15, at 209; reprinted in P. Cozzens (ed.), *Eyewitnesses to the Indian Wars, 1865-1890* (5 vols; Mechanicsburg, PA,

2001-5), ii. 584-9, at 584. 'Modern Xenophon': N.B. Wood, *Lives of Famous Indian Chiefs* (Aurora, IL, 1906), p. viii, 497. 'Indian Xenophon': J.F. Finerty, *War-path and Bivouack, or, The Conquest of the Sioux* (Chicago, 1890), 303; Wood, *Lives*, 500, 501, 658. 'Nez Perces': E.T. Seton, *The Book of Woodcraft and Indian Lore* (Garden City, NY, 1912), 55 (juxtaposed with 'Dull Knife, the Leonidas of the Cheyennes', and in chapter entitled 'The Spartans of the West'; cf. p. vi). Swarthy: S.G. Drake, *The Aboriginal Races of North America* (15th edn, rev. H.L. Williams; New York, 1880), 715. 'Did no more': E.S. Meany, *Chief Joseph, the Nez Perce* (Madison, 1901), 1 (C.A. Coolidge: no source given). Famous: W.E. Yager, *The Onéota: The Red Man as Soldier* (Oneonta, NY, 1913), 144. Further examples: F.W. Hodge, *Handbook of American Indians North of Mexico* (2 vols; Washington, 1907), i. 634; W.T. Dovell, *'A Scrap of Paper'* (Seattle, 1924), 10 ('pen of a Xenophon'); cf. P.A. Armstrong, *The Sauks and the Black Hawk War* (Springfield, IL, 1887), 207, 475, for a retrospective use of similar language about Black Hawk (linked with Hannibal too).

38. Runaways: see Ch. 3 n. 9. Exceptional: cf. Sundquist, 'Literature of Expansion', 184-5, on the heroization of individual Indians. US troops: *St. Louis Globe-Democrat*, 27 April 1882. Custer: *Inter Ocean* (Chicago), 8 September 1874; cf. 30 July 1874; *Daily Rocky Mountain News*, 10 July 1874 (misspelt 'Custar's'); H. Krause and G.D. Olson, *Prelude to Glory: A Newspaper Accounting of Custer's 1874 Expedition to the Black Hills* (Sioux Falls, SD, 1974), 222-3, also cite *New York Tribune*, 29 August 1874: Custer's soldiers asking '"How many miles to-day?" just as Xenophon was asked'. Cf. also 'anabasis' allusions to expeditions abroad: the American journalist Stanley in Africa (*North American*, 18 September 1878), the British general Roberts in Afghanistan (*St-Louis Globe Democrat*, 19 December 1880, explicitly invoking Xenophon).

39. Carolinas: P.T. Sherman, *General Sherman*, 11; cf. e.g. J. B. Foraker, 'Sherman Memorial Address', in *G.A.R. War Papers: Papers Read Before Fred. C. Jones Post, No. 401, Department of Ohio* (Cincinnati, 1891), 372-90, at 383-4.

40. Books 1-4: e.g. *Harvard University Catalog* (1837), 28 (requirement for Divinity School entrance); (1884-5), 67 (basis for sight test for Freshmen admission); the tradition continued with the popular 1910 school edition by Mather and Hewitt; see also Ch. 3 n. 5. Merrill, *Seventieth Indiana Volunteer Infantry*, 240, is unusual in stressing the toils that lay ahead for both armies: see n. 27.

41. Persian Wars: 3.2.11-13 (cf. Rood, 'Panhellenism and Self-Presentation', 310-17, for further implicit hints of the Persian Wars). Sparta: 6.1.27, 7.1.27. I discuss the ideological significance of the false closure often given to the *Anabasis* more fully in the final chapter of *The Sea! The Sea!*.

Conclusion: Anabasis Investments

1. Quotations from St.-J. Perse, *Letters*, 130 (to Paul Claudel, 10 June 1911); M. Straight, *Carrington* (London, 1961; orig. pub. 1960), 170; *New York Magazine*, 6 April 1987, 52.

2. Stack: Swofford, *Jarhead*, 53-4.

3. Reviews: M. Kakutani, *New York Times*, 19 February 2003; F.J. West, *Wall Street Journal*, 30 May 2003.

4. Mesopotamia: K. Roosevelt, *War in the Garden of Eden* (London, 1920; orig. pub. 1919), 57, 72; W. Irwin (ed.), *Letters to Kermit from Theodore Roosevelt, 1902-1908* (New York and London, 1946), 3, wrongly states that it was the *Anabasis* that was dropped by plane. Advertising: e.g. *Scribner's Magazine* 66.6 (December 1919), p. 52 of opening advertising section.

5. Train journey: T. Roosevelt, *Cowboys and Kings: Three Great Letters*, ed. E.E. Morison (Cambridge, MA, 1954), p. ix (information attributed to David Goodrich, Harvard rower and former Rough Rider); see 1-23 for Roosevelt's own account of the journey. Benton: Ch. 3 n. 13. 'Roosevelt's Anabasis' was the heading of an article on Roosevelt's 1910 hunting trip to Africa – where he was pictured shouting 'Thalassa!' as he returned from the jungle to the sea: *The Independent*, 31 March 1910. For Roosevelt and adventure, cf. M. Green, *The Great American Adventure* (Boston, 1984), 151-63.

6. Hannibal, Napoleon: see Index s.vv.; the trio of Xenophon, Hannibal, and Napoleon is also found in a report on the march of a US detachment in *Fayetteville Observer*, 10 January 1861, and *Milwaukee Daily Sentinel*, 11 January 1861 ('Yet another unprecedented march …'); note also 'Hannibal and Bonaparte', *Southern Literary Messenger* 14 (1848), 421-35, for a favourable comparison of the two generals. Smaller distances: e.g. direct citation of 'The Sea! The Sea!' for sight of a river in the Seven Days' Retreat in the 1862 Peninsular Campaign (H. Greeley, *The American Conflict: A History of the Great Rebellion in the United States of America, 1860-'64* (2 vols; New York, 1866), ii. 164 n. 40, citing *New York Tribune*; also W. Swinton, *Campaigns of the Army of the Potomac* (New York, 1866), 157); and cf. the Confederate officer's diary cited in *The Sea! The Sea!*, 29 ('Thalatta! Thalatta!' for sight of mountains). Cumberland: G.J. Prokopowicz, *All for the Regiment: The Army of the Ohio, 1861-1862* (Chapel Hill, 2001), 149 (John Easton, 17 October 1862).

7. Czech: Ch. 1 n 27. German: Ch. 2 n. 10. Tolstoy: R. Lane Fox, 'Introduction', in id. (ed.), *The Long March: Xenophon and the Ten Thousand* (New Haven, 2004), 1-46, at 3. Town names: W. Zelinsky, 'Classical Town Names in the United States: The Historical Geography of an American Idea', *Geographical Review* 57 (1967), 463-95. Personal names: e.g. Senator Xenophon P. Wilfley (1871-1931); Judge Xenophon Hicks (1872-1952). Seal: e.g. R.T. Hughes, *Myths America Lives By* (Urbana, IL, 2003), 100-1; for a survey of American attitudes to the past and future, see D. Lowenthal, *The Past is a Foreign County* (Cambridge, 1985), 105-23. Ordo: Virgil, *Eclogues* 4.5.

8. Romantic: C.E. Bishop, 'Sam Houston of Texas', *The Chatauquan* 10 (1890). Class: see e.g. Greenberg, *Manifest Manhood*, 45-6. Middle ground: see esp. R. White, *The Middle Ground: Indians, Empires, and Republics in the Great Lakes Region, 1650-1815* (Cambridge, 1991). Odyssey: F. Fernández-Armesto, *Millennium* (London, 1995), 649.

9. Joseph: Ch. 9 n. 37. 'Marched to the sea': G.B. Grinnell, *The Fighting Cheyennes* (New York, 1915), 384 (contrasting the greater fame of Chief Joseph). 'Nothing compared': S. Burt, *Powder River: Let 'er Buck* (New York, 1938), 190; cited e.g. in advertisements in *Montana: The Magazine of Western History* 4 (1954), 62, and *New York Times*, 22 November 1953 – in both cases with reviews in the same issue also applying the Xenophon label; cf. also D. Mason, 'Varieties of Poetic Experience', *Hudson Review* 52 (1999), 141-9, at 142. The comparison also appears in two nineteenth-century journals that were not published at the time: W.R. Kime (ed.), *Indian Territory Journals of Colonel Richard Dodge* (Norman, OK, 2000), 444 ('a feat more marvellous than the "Retreat of the Ten Thousand"' – though this was written in the erroneous expectation that the march would succeed); C.M. Robinson III (ed.), *The Diaries of John Gregory Bourke*, iii: *June 1, 1878-June 22, 1880* (Denton, TX, 2007), 176 ('I little imagined that this Exodus from the land of American Pharaohs, should assume such an importance that it would one day rank with the Retreat of the Ten

Thousand or put to blush the desperation and valor of the Greeks at Thermopylae'
– it is not clear when exactly this was written).

10. Katabasis: C. McCarthy, *Blood Meridian* (London, 1989; orig. pub. 1985),
122; cf. B. Sørensen, 'Katabasis in Cormac McCarthy's *Blood Meridian*', *Orbis
Litterarum* 60 (2005), 16-25.

11. Legacy: Lane Fox, 'Introduction', 4. Commemorated: P. French, 'Anabasis
in Manhattan', *The Observer*, 13 May 1979. For the film as western, cf. D. Desser,
'"When We See the Ocean, We Figure We're Home": From Ritual to Romance in
The Warriors', in M. Pomerance, *City that Never Sleeps: New York in the Filmic
Imagination* (New Brunswick and London, 2007), 123-37, at 132-3. Epigraph: S.
Yurick, *The Warriors* (London, 1966; orig. pub. 1965), 6; cf. Ch. 7 n. 45.

12. Home: cf. *The Sea! The Sea!*, 187-8, on the ending of *The Warriors*, film and
novel; for Xenophon, cf. J. Ma, '"You Can't Go Home Again": Displacement and
Identity in Xenophon's *Anabasis*', in R. Lane Fox (ed.), *The Long March: Xenophon
and the Ten Thousand* (New Haven, 2004), 330-45 (evoking T. Wolfe, for whom see
Ch. 2 n. 44).

13. Comic: Yurick, *The Warriors*, 135, 117; cf. *The Sea! The Sea!*, 186-7.

14. New life: J.E. Bowman, 'Anabasis', *The Youth's Companion* 95 (January
1921), 42.

15. Nelson: Ch. 1 n. 34. *Gates of Fire*: Ch. 1 n. 8. Children's books: Ch. 1 n. 3.
Swofford: n. 2 above.

16. Carrington: Straight, *Carrington*, 58, 170-2. Proxenus: 2.6.19. Cf. M. Lubet-
kin, *Jay Cooke's Gamble: The Northern Pacific Railroad, the Sioux, and the Panic
of 1873* (Norman, OK, 2006), 121, for a similar imaginative recreation ('Most
officers knew of Xenophon's *Anabasis* and probably felt like the 10,000 Greeks ...
surrounded by native tribes who hated their presence').

17. Scull: L. McMurtry, *Comanche Moon* (London, 1997), 129 (history), 128-30
(Alps), 133-4 (Xenophon), 329-30 (Homer).

18. This technological transformation receives especial stress in D.W. Howe,
What Hath God Wrought: The Transformation of America, 1815-1848 (Oxford and
New York, 2007); see Index s.vv. 'communications', 'postal system', 'railroads',
'telegraphy', 'transportation'.

19. Zenophon: J.M. Favill, *The Diary of a Young Officer Serving with the Armies
of the United States during the War of the Rebellion* (Chicago, 1909), 141 (3 June
1862).

20. Nostalgic: W.C. Williams, *Paterson* (New York, 1963; orig. pub. 1946-58),
201; cf. *The Sea! The Sea!*, 189-91; also 73 (Sturgis, Longfellow), 78-9 (Chambers),
80-1 (Brown), 195-7 (Funaroff), 197 (Neugass), for other American writers.

21. Quotation from St.-J. Perse, *Letters*, 56-7 (to Jacques Rivière, 21 October
1910); I have altered the translation slightly ('singularity' for 'uniqueness').

22. Sculpture: N. Del Roscio (ed.), *Cy Twombly: Catalogue Raisonné of Sculpture* (Munich, 1997), no. 53; description from H. Cooper, 'Cy Twombly: The
Sculpture', *Artforum International* 39 (2000), 147; see also K. Schmidt, *Cy Twombly: Die Skulptur / The Sculpture* (Ostfildern-Ruit, 2000), 67. For the works on
paper, see *Cy Twombly: Katalog IV* (Cologne, 1984); also *Cy Twombly: Paintings,
Works on Paper, Sculpture* (Munich and New York, 1987), nos 93-6; K. Varnedoe
(ed.), *Cy Twombly: A Restrospective* (New York, 1994), no. 85; *Cy Twombly: Fifty
Years of Works on Paper* (Munich and New York, 2004), no. 49.

23. Name-dropping: P.C. Johnson, 'The Scrawl Guy', *The Houston Chronicle*, 29
May 2005. Condensing: R. Leeman, *Cy Twombly: A Monograph* (London, 2005),
97. Barthes: R. Barthes, *'Non Multa Sed Multum'*, in N. Del Roscio (ed.), *Writings*

on Cy Twombly (Munich, 2002), 88-113, at 89, 88, 93. Imitating: J. Bird, 'Indeterminacy and (Dis)order in the Work of Cy Twombly', *Oxford Art Journal* 30 (2007), 484-504, at 499-501. Essence: S. Schama, 'Cy Twombly', in *Cy Twombly: Fifty Years of Works on Paper* (Munich and New York, 2004), 15-22, at 16; contrast e.g. J.L. Schefer, 'Cy Twombly: Uncertainty Principle', in id., *The Enigmatic Body: Essays on the Arts*, trans. P. Smith (Cambridge, 1995), 146-55 (orig. pub. *ArtStudio* 1 (1986)).

24. Cy(rus): cf. S. Bann, 'The Mythical Conception in the Name: Titles and Names in Modern and Post-modern Painting', *Word and Image* 1 (1985), 176-90, at 186-9; id., '"Wilder Shores of Love": Cy Twombly's Straying Signs', in H.U. Gumbrecht and K.L. Pfeiffer (eds), *Materialities of Communication* (Stanford, 1994), 198-213, at 206; id., *The True Vine: On Visual Representation and the Western Tradition* (Cambridge, 1989), 198-200; Leeman, *Cy Twombly*, 292-4 (quotation from 294); Bird, 'Indeterminacy', 501-2.

25. Transfer: cf. Bann, '"Wilder Shores of Love"', 200. Dryden: K. Schmidt, 'The Way to Arcadia: Thoughts on Myth and Image in Cy Twombly's Painting' in N. Del Roscio (ed.), *Writings on Cy Twombly* (Munich, 2002), 143-73, at 163; note that the focus on translation is reinforced by the common later misspelling of 'silvae' as 'sylvae'; cf. also 'Proem' in two of the later drawings in the 'Anabasis' series, identified by the catalogue as alluding to a poem by the New England writer J.G. Whittier, which alludes to 'The songs of Spenser's golden days, / Arcadian Sidney's silvery phrase' (*The Poetical Works of John Greenleaf Whittier* (2 vols; Boston, 1861), i. p. iv); and also Twombly's two 'SYLVAE' drawings paired with a 'NIKE' (J. Brodie and A. Robison, *A Century of Drawing: Works on Paper from Degas to LeWitt* (Washington, DC, 2001), 276-9). Rush: D. Sylvester, *Interviews with American Artists* (London, 2001), 176. East/West conflict: cf. K. Varnedoe, 'Cy Twombly's Lepanto', in *Cy Twombly: Lepanto* (New York, 2002), 45-62, at 53; Schama, 'Cy Twombly', 21-2; note also that the ninth drawing in the series is entitled 'Lycian' (after Lycia in Asia Minor) and that the Cologne catalogue starts with a picture of Twombly perched on a sand-dune in Yemen, looking at a series of pillars inscribed with some arabic script (perhaps encouraging us to read the misspelling 'anabasias' as an allusion to Ozymandias).

26. Chariot: P. Weitmann, 'Giacometti, Twombly und die Antike: Die Realität als Frage versus fragwürdige Idealitäten', *Antike und Abendland* 50 (2004), 161-203, at 168, comparing the chariot in *Fifty Days at Iliam*; so too Bird, 'Indeterminacy', 500. Red: N. Cullinan, 'Abject Expressionism: The *Ferragosto* Paintings', in N. Serota (ed.), *Cy Twombly: Cycles and Seasons* (London, 2008), 98-109, at 99. A: Sylvester, *Interviews*, 177-8. Sexual: Vance, *America's Rome*, 439 (seemingly based on an exhibition where the *Nike* drawings came last, rather than seventh and eighth, as in the Cologne catalogue).

27. Perse: see n. 1. Capitals: *Honneur à Saint-John Perse: hommages et témoignages littéraires suivis d'une documentation sur Alexis Léger* (Paris, 1965), 419 (letter to Perse dated 15 January 1927). Korea: L. Montross, *Washington Post*, 26 June 1953; cf. Ch. 1 n. 11.

28. Twombly and violence: cf. R.E. Krauss, *The Optical Unconscious* (Cambridge, MA, 1994), 256-66. Unceasing anabasis: my formulation owes something to Leeman, *Cy Twombly*, 294: 'Twombly's oeuvre repeats, in a neverending anabasis, the law of language incarnate in the father's name.' Cy! Cy! ...

Select Bibliography

Ainsworth, W.F., *Travels in the Track of the Ten Thousand Greeks: Being a Geographical and Descriptive Account of the Expedition of Cyrus and of the Retreat of the Ten Thousand Greeks, as Related by Xenophon* (London, 1844).

Anderson, J.K., *Xenophon* (London, 1974).

Anon., review of *Xenophon* (*Valpy's Classical Library* 111), *Gentleman's Magazine* 100 (1830), 615-17.

Badiou, A., *The Century*, trans. A. Toscano (Cambridge and Malden, MA, 2007; Fr. orig. 2005).

Bann, S., "'Wilder Shores of Love": Cy Twombly's Straying Signs', in H.U. Gumbrecht and K.L. Pfeiffer (eds), *Materialities of Communication* (Stanford, 1994), 198-213.

Baylies, F., *A Narrative of Major General Wool's Campaign in Mexico, in the Years 1846, 1847, and 1848* (Albany, NY, 1851).

Benton, T.H., *Thirty Years' View: Or, A History of the Working of the American Government for Thirty Years, from 1820 To 1850* (2 vols; New York, 1858).

Bigelow, J., *Memoir of the Life and Public Services of John Charles Frémont* (New York and Cincinnati, 1856).

Bird, J., 'Indeterminacy and (Dis)order in the Work of Cy Twombly', *Oxford Art Journal* 30 (2007), 484-504.

Bishop, J.P., 'The Sorrows of Thomas Wolfe', in *Collected Essays*, ed. E. Wilson (New York, 1948), 131-2 (orig. *Kenyan Review* 1 (1939), 7-17).

Blight, D.W., *Race and Reunion: The Civil War in American Memory* (Cambridge, MA, 2001).

Byers, S.H.M., *The March to the Sea: A Poem* (Boston, 1896).

────── *Twenty Years in Europe: A Consul-General's Memories of Noted People, with Letters from General W.T. Sherman* (Chicago, 1900).

Cabañas, A., *The Cultural 'Other' in Nineteenth-Century Travel Narratives: How the United States and Latin America Described Each Other* (Lewiston, NY, 2008).

Carroll, A., *Medicine Bags and Dog Tags: American Indian Veterans from Colonial Times to the Second Iraq War* (Lincoln, NE, 2008).

Cartledge, P., *Thermopylae: The Battle that Changed the World* (London, 2006).

Caudill, E., and Ashdown, P., *Sherman's March in Myth and Memory* (Lanham, MD, 2008).

Coffin, C.C., *Our New Way Round the World* (Boston, 1869).

Commager, H.S. (ed.), *The Blue and the Gray: The Story of the Civil War as Told by Participants* (Indianapolis, 1950).

Conyngham, D.P., *Sherman's March through the South: With Sketches and Incidents of the Campaign* (New York, 1865).

Cooke, P. St. G., *The Conquest of New Mexico and California: An Historical and Personal Narrative* (New York, 1878).

Cotten, A.R. (ed.), *'Always Yours, Max': Maxwell Perkins Responds to Questions about Thomas Wolfe* (Thomas Wolfe Society, 1997).

269

Select Bibliography

Covington, H.A., *The March Up Country* (Reedy, WV, 1987).

Cox, J.D., *The March to the Sea: Franklin and Nashville* (New York, 1882).

Cox, S.S., *Diversions of a Diplomat in Turkey* (New York, 1893).

Cunliffe, M., *Soldiers and Civilians: The Martial Spirit in America, 1775-1865* (Boston, MA, 1968).

Cutts, J.M., *The Conquest of California and New Mexico by the Forces of the United States, in the Years 1846 & 1847* (Philadelphia, 1847).

Danelo, D.J., *Blood Stripes: The Grunt's View of the War in Iraq* (Mechanicsburg, PA, 2006).

Dawson, J.G. III, *Doniphan's Epic March: The 1st Missouri Volunteers in the Mexican War* (Lawrence, KS, 1999).

Dekker, G., *The American Historical Romance* (Cambridge, 1987).

DeLay, B., *War of a Thousand Deserts: Indian Raids and the U.S.-Mexican War* (New Haven and London, 2008).

Dillery, J., *Xenophon and the History of his Times* (London, 1995).

Doctorow, E.L., *The March* (London, 2006; orig. pub. 2005).

Edwards, F., *A Campaign in New Mexico with Colonel Doniphan* (Albuquerque, 1996; orig. pub. 1847).

Edwards, M.B., Johnston, A.S., and Ferguson, P.G., *Marching with the Army of the West*, ed. R.P. Bieber (Glendale, CA, 1936).

Eggleston, G.C. (ed.), *American War Ballads and Lyrics: A Collection of the Songs and Ballads of the Colonial Wars, the Revolution, the War of 1812-15, the War with Mexico, and the Civil War* (New York and London, 1889).

Elliott, R.S., *Notes Taken in Sixty Years* (St Louis, 1883).

Elson, R.M., *Guardians of Tradition: American Schoolbooks of the Nineteenth Century* (Lincoln, NE, 1964).

Emerson, R.W., *The Early Lectures of Ralph Waldo Emerson*, ed. S.E. Whicher and R.E. Spiller (3 vols; Cambridge, MA, 1959-72).

—— *The Journals and Miscellaneous Notebooks of Ralph Waldo Emerson*, ed. W.H. Gilman et al. (16 vols; Cambridge, MA, 1960-82).

Felton, C.C. (ed.), *A Greek Reader for the Use of Schools* (Hartford, CT, 1840).

Fick, N.C., *One Bullet Away: The Making of a Marine Officer* (Boston, 2005).

Foos, P.W., *A Short, Offhand, Killing Affair: Soldiers and Social Conflict during the Mexican-American War* (Chapel Hill, 2002).

Fox-Genovese, E., and Genovese, E.D., *The Mind of the Master Class: History and Faith in the Southern Slaveholders' Worldview* (Cambridge, 1995).

Frémont, J.C., *Oregon and California: The Exploring Expedition to the Rocky Mountains* (Buffalo, NY, 1851).

Frost, J., *Life of Major General Zachary Taylor* (New York and Philadelphia, 1847).

Gardner, M.L. (ed.), *Brothers on the Santa Fe and Chihuahua Trails: Edward James Glasgow and William Henry Glasgow, 1846-1848* (Niwot, CO, 1993).

—— and Simmons, M. (eds), *The Mexican War Correspondence of Richard Smith Elliott* (Norman, OK, 1997).

George, I., *Heroes and Incidents of the Mexican War* (Greensburg, PA, 1903).

Gibson, G.R., *Journal of a Soldier under Kearny and Doniphan*, ed. R.P. Bieber (Glendale, CA, 1935).

Gibson, J.W., *The Perfect War: TechnoWar in Vietnam* (Boston, 1986).

Giddings, L., *Sketches of the Campaign in Northern Mexico in Eighteen Hundred Forty-Six and Seven* (New York, 1853).

Gilpin, W., *Mission of the North American People, Geographical, Social, and Political* (2nd edn; Philadelphia, 1874; orig. pub. 1873).

Greenberg, A.S., *Manifest Manhood and the American Empire* (Cambridge and New York, 2005).

Gregg, J., *Commerce of the Prairies* (Norman, OK, 1954; orig. pub. 1844).

Grote, G., *A History of Greece from the Earliest Period to the Death of the Generation Contemporary with Alexander the Great* (10 vols; London, 1904; orig. pub. 1846-56).

Hanson, V.D., *The Soul of Battle: From Ancient Times to the Present Day, How Three Great Liberators Vanquished Tyranny* (New York, 1999).

—— *The Western Way of War: Infantry Battle in Classical Greece* (2nd edn; Berkeley, Los Angeles and London, 2000; orig. pub. 1989).

—— *Carnage and Culture: Landmark Battles in the Rise of Western Power* (2nd edn; New York, 2002; orig. pub. 2001).

Harper, M.M., *The Aristocracy of Art in Joyce and Wolfe* (Baton Rouge and London, 1990).

Hartley, J.C., *Just Another Soldier: A Year on the Ground in Iraq* (New York, 2005).

Higgins, W.E., *Xenophon the Athenian: The Problem of the Individual and the Society of the Polis* (Albany, NY, 1977).

Honour, H., *The New Golden Land: European Images of America from the Discoveries to the Present Time* (New York, 1975).

Horsman, R., *Race and Manifest Destiny: The Origins of American Racial Anglo-Saxonism* (Cambridge, MA, 1981).

Hughes, J., *Doniphan's Expedition and the Conquest of New Mexico and California*, ed. W.E. Connelley (Kansas City, 1907; orig. pub. 1847).

Jackson, D., and Spence, M.L. (eds), *The Expeditions of John Charles Frémont* (3 vols in 4; Urbana, IL, 1970-80).

Johannsen, R.W., *To the Halls of the Montezumas: The Mexican War in the American Imagination* (New York, 1985).

Kammen, M., *Mystic Chords of Memory: The Transformation of Tradition in American Culture* (New York, 1991).

Karnes, T.L., *William Gilpin, Western Nationalist* (Austin, TX, 1970).

Keim, De B.R. (ed.), *Sherman: A Memorial in Art, Oratory, and Literature by the Society of the Army of Tennessee with the Aid of the Congress of the United States of America* (Washington, DC, 1904).

Kellogg, L.P., 'Wisconsin Anabasis', *Wisconsin Magazine of History* 7 (1924), 322-39.

Kennedy, R.S., *The Window of Memory: The Literary Career of Thomas Wolfe* (Chapel Hill, 1962).

Kennerly, W.C., *Persimmon Hill: A Narrative of Old St Louis and the Far West* (Norman, OK, 1948).

Kinneir, J.M., *Journey through Asia Minor, Armenia, and Koordistan, in the Years 1813 and 1814, with Remarks on the Marches of Alexander and Retreat of the Ten Thousand* (London, 1818).

Lane Fox, R., 'Introduction', in id. (ed.), *The Long March: Xenophon and the Ten Thousand* (New Haven, 2004), 1-46.

Larrabee, S.A., *Hellas Observed: The American Experience of Greece, 1775-1865* (New York, 1957).

Launius, R.D., *Alexander William Doniphan: Portrait of a Missouri Moderate* (Columbia, MO, 1997).

Lee, J.W.I., *A Greek Army on the March: Soldiers and Survival in Xenophon's Anabasis* (Cambridge, 2007).

Leeman, R., *Cy Twombly: A Monograph* (London, 2005).

271

Select Bibliography

Liebersohn, H., *Aristocratic Encounters: European Travelers and North American Indians* (Cambridge, 1998).

Linderman, G.F., *Embattled Courage: The Experience of Combat in the American Civil War* (New York and London, 1987).

Lippard, G., *Legends of Mexico* (Philadelphia, 1847).

McCaffrey, J.M., *Army of Manifest Destiny: The American Soldier in the Mexican War, 1846-1848* (New York, 1992).

McConnell, S., *Glorious Contentment: The Grand Army of the Republic, 1865-1900* (Chapel Hill, 1992).

McGroarty, W.M. (ed.), 'William H. Richardson's Journal of Doniphan's Expedition', *Missouri Historical Review* 22 (1928), 193-236, 331-60, 511-42 (orig. pub. 1847).

Mansfield, E.D., *The Mexican War: A History of its Origin, and A Detailed Account of the Victories Which Terminated in the Surrender of the Capital* (New York, 1848).

Mather, M.W., and Hewitt, J.W. (eds), *Xenophon's Anabasis: Books I-IV* (New York, 1910).

Merk, F., *Manifest Destiny and Mission in American History* (New York, 1963).

Merrill, S., *The Seventieth Indiana Volunteer Infantry in the War of Rebellion* (Indianapolis, 1900).

Merwin, W.S., *A Mask for Janus* (New Haven, 1952).

Morier, J.J., *A Second Journey through Persia, Armenia, and Asia Minor, to Constantinople, between the Years 1810 and 1816* (London, 1818).

Morton, O.P. et al., *Oration of O. P. Morton, Address of Major General G. G. Meade, and Poem of Bayard Taylor, with the Other Exercises at the Dedication of the Monument in the Soldiers' National Cemetery at Gettysburg, July 1, 1869* (Gettysburg, 1870).

Niccolls, S.J., *A Tribute to General William Tecumseh Sherman, Delivered at the Public Memorial Service of Ransom Post No. 131, Department of Missouri, G.A.R., May 30th, 1891* (St Louis, 1891).

Parkman, F., *The Oregon Trail* (Oxford, 2000; orig. pub. 1849).

Pearce, R.H., *The Savages of America: A Study of the Indian and the Idea of Civilization* (Baltimore, 1953).

Pepper, G.W., *Personal Recollections of Sherman's Campaigns in Georgia and the Carolinas* (Zanesville, OH, 1866).

Perse, St.-J., *Anabasis*, trans. T.S. Eliot (London, 1959; orig. edn 1930; Fr. orig. *Anabase* published 1924).

—— *Letters*, trans. and ed. A.J. Knodel (Princeton, 1979).

Porter, R.K., *Travels in Georgia, Persia, Armenia, Ancient Babylonia, &c. &c., during the Years 1817, 1818, 1819, and 1820* (2 vols; London, 1821-2).

Prescott, W.H., *History of the Conquest of Mexico* (3 vols; London, 1850; orig. pub. 1843).

Pritchett, W.K., *The Greek State at War* (5 vols; Berkeley, 1971-91).

Rainey, S., *Creating Picturesque America: Monument to the Natural and Cultural Landscape* (Nashville, 1994).

Rennell, J., *Illustrations, (Chiefly Geographical,) of the History of the Expedition of Cyrus, from Sardis to Babylonia, and the Retreat of the Ten Thousand Greeks, from thence to Trebisonde and Lydia* (London, 1816).

Richard, C.J., *The Founders and the Classics: Greece, Rome, and the American Enlightenment* (Cambridge, MA, 1994).

—— *The Golden Age of the Classics in America: Greece, Rome, and the Antebellum United States* (Cambridge, MA, 2009).

Ridpath, J.C., *Cyclopaedia of Universal History: Being an Account of the Principal Events in the Career of the Human Race, from the Beginning of Civilization to the Present Time* (3 vols; Cincinnati, 1885).

───── *The Citizen Soldier: His Part in War and Peace* (Cincinnati, 1891).

Robinson, J.S., *A Journal of the Santa Fe Expedition under Colonel Doniphan* (Princeton 1932; orig. pub. 1848).

Rood, T., *The Sea! The Sea! The Shout of the Ten Thousand in the Modern Imagination* (London and New York, 2004).

───── 'Panhellenism and Self-Presentation: Xenophon's Speeches', in R. Lane Fox (ed.), *The Long March: Xenophon and the Ten Thousand* (New Haven, 2004), 305-29.

Rowland, D. (ed.), *Jefferson Davis, Constitutionalist: His Letters, Papers and Speeches* (10 vols; Jackson, MO, 1923).

Ruxton, G.F., *Adventures in Mexico and the Rocky Mountains* (New York, 1848).

Schama, S., 'Cy Twombly', in *Cy Twombly: Fifty Years of Works on Paper* (Munich and New York, 2004), 15-22.

Sherman, P.T., *General Sherman in the Last Year of the Civil War: An Address Delivered at the Thirty-Eighth Reunion of the Society of the Army of the Tennessee at St. Louis, Missouri* (New York, 1908).

Sherman, W.T., *Memoirs of General W. T. Sherman* (New York, 1990; orig. pub. 1875).

Simms, W.G., *A City Laid Waste: The Capture, Sack, and Destruction of the City of Columbia*, ed. D. Aiken (Columbia, SC, 2005; orig. pub. 1865).

Simpson, B.D., and Berlin, J.V. (eds), *Sherman's Civil War: Selected Correspondence of William T. Sherman, 1860-1865* (Chapel Hill, 1999).

Slotkin, R., *Regeneration through Violence: The Mythology of the American Frontier, 1600-1860* (Middletown, CT, 1973).

───── *The Fatal Environment: The Myth of the Frontier in the Age of Industrialization, 1800-1890* (New York, 1985).

Smith, H.N., *Virgin Land: The American West as Symbol and Myth* (2nd edn; Cambridge, MA, 1970; orig. pub. 1950).

Spaulding, O.L., and Wright, J.W., *The Second Division American Expeditionary Force in France, 1917-1919* (New York, 1937).

Spurr, D., *The Rhetoric of Empire: Colonial Discourse in Journalism, Travel Writing, and Imperial Administration* (Durham, NC, 1993).

Straight, M., *Carrington* (London, 1961; orig. pub. 1960).

Streeby, S., *American Sensations: Class, Empire, and the Production of Popular Culture* (Berkeley, 2002).

Strohm, I. (ed.), *Speeches of Thomas Corwin, with a Sketch of his Life* (Dayton, OH, 1859).

Sundquist, E.J., 'The Literature of Expansion and Race', in S. Bercovitch (ed.), *The Cambridge History of American Literature*, ii: *1825-1865* (Cambridge, 1995), 125-328.

Swofford, A., *Jarhead: A Marine's Chronicle of the Gulf War* (London, 2003).

Sylvester, D., *Interviews with American Artists* (London, 2001).

Taine, H., 'Xénophon: *L'Anabase*', in *Essais de critique et d'histoire* (5th edn; Paris, 1887; orig. publ. 1858), 49-95.

Thorndike, R.S. (ed.), *The Sherman Letters: Correspondence between General and Senator Sherman from 1837 to 1891* (New York, 1894).

Tillson, J., *The March to the Sea: Delivered before the Army of the Tennessee on their Eighth Annual Reunion at Springfield, Illinois, October 14th, 1874* (Quincy, 1874).

Select Bibliography

Truettner, W.H. (ed.), *The West as America: Reinterpreting Images of the Frontier, 1820-1920* (Washington and London, 1991).

Turner, F.J., *The Frontier in American History* (Tucson, 1986; orig. pub. 1920).

Vance, W.L., *America's Rome* (2 vols; New Haven, and London, 1989).

Walker, D.L., *Pacific Destiny: The Three-Century Journey to the Oregon Country* (New York, 2000).

Warren, J.A., *American Spartans: The U.S. Marines: A Combat History from Iwo Jima to Iraq* (New York, 2005).

West, F.J., and Smith, R.L., *The March Up: Taking Baghdad with the 1st Marine Division* (New York, 2003).

Wilkinson, J., *Memoirs of My Own Times* (3 vols; Philadelphia, 1816).

Wilson, E., *Patriotic Gore: Studies in the Literature of the American Civil War* (New York, 1962).

Winterer, C., *The Culture of Classicism: Ancient Greece and Rome in American Intellectual Life, 1780-1910* (Baltimore, 2002).

—— *The Mirror of Antiquity: American Women and the Classical Tradition, 1750-1900* (Ithaca, NY, 2007).

Wislizenus, F.A., *Memoir of a Tour to Northern Mexico* (Washington, DC, 1848).

Wolfe, T., *You Can't Go Home Again* (New York, 1940).

—— *The Letters of Thomas Wolfe*, ed. E. Nowell (New York, 1956).

—— *The Notebooks of Thomas Wolfe*, ed. R.S. Kennedy and P. Reeves (Chapel Hill, 1970).

—— *The Autobiography of an American Novelist*, ed. L. Field (Cambridge, MA, and London, 1983).

—— *O Lost: A Story of Buried Life*, ed. A. and M.J. Bruccoli (Columbia, SC, 2000).

—— *The Autobiographical Outline for Look Homeward, Angel*, ed. L. Conniff and R.S. Kennedy (Baton Rouge, 2004; orig. pub. 1991).

Woodward, C.V. (ed.), *Mary Chesnut's Civil War* (New Haven, 1981).

Yurick, S., *The Warriors* (London, 1966; orig. pub. 1965).

Index

29, 68, 204, 205, 206, 214, 238n.3, 239n.4; surpassed by US marches 80, 102, 205, 216, 234n.3, 239n.3, 243n.31, *see also* anabasis, Doniphan's march, Sherman's march; far-famed 28, 53, 59, 176, 179, 197, 203; continuing memory of 56, 58, 65-6, 164, 197-8, 199; immortalized 63, 185, 242n.28; *see also* Black Sea, sight of; Ten Thousand, the
Xerxes: 84, 96, 176; at Thermopylae 100, 102, 104, 155; or Xenophon 176-7, 181; and Xenophon 185; *see also* Persian Wars

Yale Review: 44
Yale University: 219, 220
Yemen: 267n.25
Yorktown: 54
Yosemite: 77
Young, B.: 28
Young, Cyclone: 223
Youth's Companion, The: 218
Yurick, S.: *The Warriors* 217-18, 219

Zab (River): 205
Zeugma: 74
Zeus: 84, 88; Soter 44, 133
Žižek, S.: 13
Zulus: 44, 107